A *Thousand Plateaus* and Philosophy

A Thousand Plateaus and Philosophy

Edited by HENRY SOMERS-HALL,
JEFFREY A. BELL and
JAMES WILLIAMS

EDINBURGH
University Press

Edinburgh University Press is one of the leading university presses in the UK. We publish academic books and journals in our selected subject areas across the humanities and social sciences, combining cutting-edge scholarship with high editorial and production values to produce academic works of lasting importance. For more information visit our website: edinburghuniversitypress.com

© editorial matter and organisation Henry Somers-Hall, Jeffrey A. Bell and James Williams, 2018
© the chapters their several authors, 2018

Edinburgh University Press Ltd
The Tun – Holyrood Road
12(2f) Jackson's Entry
Edinburgh EH8 8PJ

Typeset in 11/13 Adobe Garamond by
Servis Filmsetting Ltd, Stockport, Cheshire

A CIP record for this book is available from the British Library

ISBN 978 0 7486 9726 7 (hardback)
ISBN 978 0 7486 9727 4 (webready PDF)
ISBN 978 0 7486 9728 1 (paperback)
ISBN 978 0 7486 9729 8 (epub)

The right of Henry Somers-Hall, Jeffrey A. Bell and James Williams to be identified as the editors of this work has been asserted in accordance with the Copyright, Designs and Patents Act 1988, and the Copyright and Related Rights Regulations 2003 (SI No. 2498).

Contents

Notes on Contributors   vii

    Introduction   1
    Henry Somers-Hall, Jeffrey A. Bell and James Williams

1   'A book? What book?' Or Deleuze and Guattari on the Rhizome   9
    Miguel de Beistegui

2   One or Several Wolves: The Wolf-Man's Pass-Words   28
    Brent Adkins

3   Who the Earth Thinks It Is   46
    Ronald Bogue

4   Postulates of Linguistics   64
    Jeffrey A. Bell

5   587 BC–AD 70: On Several Regimes of Signs   83
    Audrey Wasser

6   November 28, 1947: How Do You Make Yourself a Body without Organs?   99
    John Protevi

7   Year Zero: Faciality   115
    Nathan Widder

8   'What Happened Next?': Hjelmslev's Net, Arachne's Web and the Figure of the Line   134
    Helen Palmer

9 Micropolitics and Segmentarity   152
   Eugene W. Holland

10 Memories of a Deleuzian: To Think is Always to Follow the
   Witches' Flight   172
   Simon O'Sullivan

11 Of the Refrain (The Ritornello)   190
   Emma Ingala

12 1227: Treatise on Nomadology – The War Machine   206
   Paul Patton

13 7000 BC: Apparatus of Capture   223
   Daniel W. Smith

14 The Smooth and the Striated   242
   Henry Somers-Hall

15 Concrete Rules and Abstract Machines: Form and Function in
   A Thousand Plateaus   260
   Ray Brassier

Bibliography   280
Index   291

Contributors

Miguel de Beistegui is Professor of Philosophy at the University of Warwick. His most recent book, *The Government of Desire: A Genealogy of the Liberal Subject* (Chicago University Press) will be out in late 2017. He is also the author of articles and books on Deleuze, including *Truth and Genesis: Philosophy as Differential Ontology* (2005) and *Immanence and Philosophy: Deleuze* (2010), the aesthetics of metaphor (*Proust as Philosopher* and *Aesthetics After Metaphysics: From Mimesis to Metaphor*, 2012), and Heidegger (*Heidegger and the Political, Thinking with Heidegger, The New Heidegger*).

Jeffrey A. Bell is Professor of Philosophy at Southeastern Louisiana University. He is the author of *The Problem of Difference: Phenomenology and Poststructuralism* (1996), *Philosophy at the Edge of Chaos: Deleuze and the Philosophy of Difference* (2006), *Deleuze's Hume: Philosophy, Culture and the Scottish Enlightenment* (2009) and *Deleuze and Guattari's What is Philosophy?: A Critical Introduction and Guide* (2016). He edited *Deleuze and History* (2009) with Claire Colebrook, and *Beyond the Analytic-Continental Divide: Pluralist Philosophy in the Twenty-First Century* (2015) with Andrew Cutrofello and Paul Livingston.

Ronald Bogue is Distinguished Research Professor Emeritus of Comparative Literature at the University of Georgia. He is the author of *Deleuze and Guattari* (1989), *Deleuze on Music, Painting and the Arts* (2003), *Deleuze's Wake* (2004), *Deleuze's Way* (2007) and *Deleuzian Fabulation and the Scars of History* (2010).

Ray Brassier is Professor of Philosophy at the American University of Beirut. He is the author of *Nihil Unbound: Enlightenment and Extinction*

(Palgrave, 2007) and the English translator of works by Alain Badiou and Quentin Meillassoux. He is currently working on a book entitled *Reasons, Patterns, and Processes: Sellars's Transcendental Naturalism*.

Eugene W. Holland is Professor of Comparative Studies at Ohio State University. He is the author of *Baudelaire and Schizoanalysis* (1993) and *Nomad Citizenship* (2011), as well as readers' guides to *Anti-Oedipus* (Routledge, 1999) and *A Thousand Plateaus* (Bloomsbury, 2013). He is currently completing a book on *Perversions of the Market*.

Emma Ingala is Senior Lecturer at the Universidad Complutense de Madrid. She is the co-editor, with Gavin Rae, of *Subjectivity and the Political: Contemporary Perspectives* (Routledge, forthcoming), and has published various articles on Deleuze, Lacan and twentieth-century French philosophy.

Simon O'Sullivan, Professor of Art Theory and Practice in the Department of Visual Cultures at Goldsmiths, University of London, is the author of *Art Encounters Deleuze and Guattari: Thought Beyond Representation* (Palgrave, 2005) and *On the Production of Subjectivity: Five Diagrams of the Finite-Infinite Relation* (Palgrave, 2012). He is currently working on a collaborative volume of writings, with David Burrows, *Mythopoesis, Myth-Science, Mythotechnesis* (forthcoming with Edinburgh University Press).

Helen Palmer is Lecturer in English Literature at Kingston University, London. She is THE author of *Deleuze and Futurism: A Manifesto for Nonsense* (2014). She has recently published articles on new materialism and gender, and is working on a book called *Queer Defamiliarisation: A Reassessment of Estrangement*.

Paul Patton is Scientia Professor of Philosophy at the University of New South Wales in Sydney, Australia. He is the author of *Deleuze and the Political* (2000) and *Deleuzian Concepts: Philosophy, Colonization, Politics* (2010). He edited *Deleuze: A Critical Reader* (1996). He co-edited (with Duncan Ivison and Will Sanders) *Political Theory and the Rights of Indigenous Peoples* (2000), (with John Protevi) *Between Deleuze and Derrida* (2003), (with Simone Bignall) *Deleuze and the Postcolonial* (2010) and (with Sean Bowden and Simone Bignall) *Deleuze and Pragmatism* (2015). His current research deals with the political philosophy of Deleuze, Derrida and Foucault, as well as issues in contemporary liberal political philosophy.

John Protevi is Phyllis M. Taylor Professor of French Studies and Professor of Philosophy at Louisiana State University, Baton Rouge. He is the author of *Political Affect* (Minnesota, 2009) and *Life, War, Earth* (Minnesota, 2013), as well as editor of the *Edinburgh Dictionary of Continental Philosophy* (Edinburgh, 2004).

Daniel W. Smith, Professor in the Department of Philosophy at Purdue University, is the author of *Essays on Deleuze* (2012) and has published widely on topics in contemporary philosophy. He is the translator of Gilles Deleuze's *Francis Bacon: The Logic of Sensation* and *Essays Critical and Clinical* (with Michael A. Greco), as well as Pierre Klossowski's *Nietzsche and the Vicious Circle* and Isabelle Stengers's *The Invention of Modern Science*.

Henry Somers-Hall is a Reader in Philosophy at Royal Holloway, University of London. He is the author of *Hegel, Deleuze, and the Critique of Representation* (2012) and *Deleuze's Difference and Repetition* (2013), and co-editor of the *Cambridge Companion to Deleuze* (2012). He is currently completing a monograph on judgement in modern French philosophy.

Audrey Wasser is Assistant Professor of French at Miami University, Ohio. She is the author of *The Work of Difference: Modernism, Romanticism, and The Production of Literary Form* (2016) as well as articles on Deleuze, Beckett and Spinoza. She is currently at work on a book on literary judgement.

Nathan Widder is Professor of Political Theory at Royal Holloway, University of London. He is the author of *Genealogies of Difference* (2002), *Reflections on Time and Politics* (2008) and *Political Theory after Deleuze* (2012). He is currently working on a book on the role of the concept of sense in Deleuze's philosophy.

James Williams is Honorary Professor of Philosophy at Deakin University. He is the author of *Gilles Deleuze's Philosophy of Time: A Critical Introduction and Guide* (2011), *Gilles Deleuze's Logic of Sense: A Critical Introduction and Guide* (2008), *Gilles Deleuze's Difference and Repetition: A Critical Introduction and Guide* (2005, 2nd edn, 2013) and *The Transversal Thought of Gilles Deleuze* (2005). He is currently working on signs in process philosophy, following his book *A Process Philosophy of Signs* (2016) and a book project on the egalitarian sublime.

Introduction

Henry Somers-Hall, Jeffrey A. Bell and James Williams

Despite *A Thousand Plateaus* being one of the first texts by Deleuze or Guattari to be translated into English, its reception as a *philosophical* text has largely been secondary to the uses it can be put to in other domains, and to the reception of Deleuze's own sole-authored works, such as *Difference and Repetition*, with their more traditional structures and frequent connections with the history of philosophy. The aim of this volume is to explore the specifically philosophical vision of Deleuze and Guattari's project. Despite the frequent assertions that the kernel of Deleuze and Guattari's thought is to be found in Deleuze's earlier project, even in their final collaboration they are insistent that the notion of the overcoming of philosophy is merely 'tiresome, idle chatter' (Deleuze and Guattari 1994: 9). This book brings together fifteen leading scholars on the work of Deleuze and Guattari, each addressing one of the plateaus, focusing on an aspect of that plateau that connects to their own research interests. The result of this process is a volume that both serves as a guide to *A Thousand Plateaus*, but also provides detailed analysis of specific questions, concepts and relations throughout the different plateaus. In this introduction, I want to set out some of the reasons for taking *A Thousand Plateaus* as a *philosophical* text, beginning with how it seeks to fulfil a promise made in *Difference and Repetition*, before moving on to look at why this project requires a substantial revision of our ideas about the style and structure of a philosophical text.

A Thousand Plateaus and philosophy

There has been a tendency to dismiss the philosophical import of *A Thousand Plateaus*. Alain Badiou's *Deleuze: The Clamour of Being*, for instance, contains hardly any references to Deleuze's collaborations with Guattari, which are dismissed by Badiou as 'the superficial doxa of an anarcho-desiring Deleuzianism'.[1] The orthodox response to this dismissal has been to focus on Deleuze's early single-authored works as the kernel of his philosophy, and to see the later work as moving away from traditional philosophical concerns. In 1968, twelve years before the publication of *A Thousand Plateaus*, Gilles Deleuze claimed in his first major work of independent philosophy, *Difference and Repetition*, that we needed not simply a new approach to philosophy, but also a new mode of philosophical expression. 'The time is coming when it will hardly be possible to write a book of philosophy as it has been done for so long: "Ah! The old style . . ."' (Deleuze 1994: xxi). *Difference and Repetition* sets out many of the philosophical themes that are at the heart of *A Thousand Plateaus*: a metaphysics of intensity, a critique of *urdoxae* and the concomitant move to a philosophy of the creation of concepts, and a thoroughgoing critique of representation. This earlier work presents these ideas in a style where the words resonate with each other on the page, at points seemingly departing the philosophical for the poetic.[2] Despite the vibrant rhetorical style running throughout the work, digging a little deeper into *Difference and Repetition* reveals a structure very much like that of a traditional philosophical work, developing a sustained argument from initial claims about how we understand the concept of difference across a number of chapters into a novel account of how we must recognise and think the intensive nature of the world. It is because of this classical structure that *Difference and Repetition* is favoured for philosophical analysis. Despite a rejection of truth as the primary axis of evaluation of claims, it is nonetheless replete with arguments open to evaluation precisely along those lines.

In a later series of interviews, however, Deleuze claims that this early work describes an exercise of thought, but notes that 'describing it was not yet exercising thought in that way' (Deleuze and Parnet 1987: 16). As such, while *Difference and Repetition* recognises the need to move away from traditional approaches to philosophising, it does not itself institute this movement. In an interview with *Libération*, Deleuze makes clear that *A Thousand Plateaus* is very much a philosophy project, and a philosophical system. In this interview, he answers the question, 'what is philosophy?' by claiming, 'Everyone knows that philosophy deals with concepts. A system's a set of concepts' (Deleuze 1995a: 32). As Deleuze and Guattari note, there are two related aspects to this. There are several ways of conceiving both of a system and of a concept. We can develop a system of essences, which is the traditional model of philosophy. This is a closed system, and defines the traditional model of how philosophy operates. Alternatively, we can develop a notion of a philosophical system that is open. 'It's an open system when the concepts relate to circumstances rather than essences' (Deleuze 1995a: 32). I will return to this point when I come to the notion of a root-book in *A Thousand Plateaus* itself, but we can note that this distinction runs throughout Deleuze's work, and is at the heart of *Difference and Repetition*, where Deleuze explicitly opposes Aristotle's account of definition, which attempts to rigorously determine the essential nature of a thing ('Socrates is rational'), excluding those features which are purely accidental ('Socrates is sitting'), with his own account of determination through the Idea, which attempts to capture all of the dynamics at play in a system without distinguishing between the essential and inessential. 'No doubt, if one insists, the word "essence" might be preserved, but only on condition of saying that the essence is precisely the accident, the event, the sense; not simply the contrary of what is ordinarily called the essence but the contrary of the contrary' (Deleuze 1994: 191). This distinction is also at the heart of *A Thousand Plateaus*. In the rhizomatic structure of *A Thousand Plateaus*, 'the concepts relate to circumstances rather than essences'. Similarly here, we find a move originally made in *Difference and Repetition*, where the question of essence, 'What is x?' is replaced with the questions, 'How many?', 'How?', 'In which cases?' (Deleuze 1994: 182).

If a system is a set of concepts, then what is a concept? The key point to note is that philosophical concepts 'don't, first of all, turn up ready-made' (Deleuze 1995a: 32). As Deleuze and Guattari note in *What is Philosophy?*, the project of philosophy has traditionally been misconceived as involving 'contemplation, reflection, or communication' (Deleuze and Guattari 1994: 6). That is, philosophy has traditionally presupposed the concepts we use to engage with the world, whereas it is the constitution of these concepts that is the task and object of inquiry of philosophy itself. As they put it, 'The first principle of philosophy is that Universals explain nothing but must themselves be explained' (Deleuze and Guattari 1994: 7). As such, Deleuze and Guattari do not abandon the role of concepts, but argue for a renewed focus on their genesis, attempting to develop a rigorous account of philosophical concept creation that would avoid replacing 'critique with sales promotion'[3] (Deleuze and Guattari 1994: 10).

In *Difference and Repetition*, the attempt to think how concepts are constituted revolves around an attempt to develop an account of how thinking operates before it is represented. Thus concepts are seen as constituted by the reflection of thinking on itself, which generates concepts while covering over their origin. Deleuze attempts to develop an account of a 'thought without image' (Deleuze 1994: 276) that would be the constitutive force behind our representation. Thus, the project of *Difference and Repetition* owes much to the Bergsonian project of reversing the natural direction of thought that leads from the process of thinking to its fixed forms. *Difference and Repetition* therefore takes up both the notion of an open system and that of a constituted character of concepts. Nonetheless, we can see why Deleuze later believes that it is only with Guattari that he moves from describing the activity of philosophy to actually doing philosophy. We can note that while Deleuze argues that the question, 'What is *x*?' is an illegitimate question deriving from a philosophy of essence, this form of question is at the heart of *Difference and Repetition*. As he concludes his introduction:

> We therefore find ourselves confronted by two questions: what is the concept of difference – one which is not reducible to simple conceptual difference but demands its own Idea, its own singularity at the level of Ideas? On the other hand, what is the essence of repetition – one which is not reducible to difference without concept, and cannot be confused with the apparent character of objects represented by the same concept, but bears witness to singularity as a power of Ideas? (Deleuze 1994: 27)

As Deleuze was later to write of this text, 'for my part, when I was no longer content with the history of philosophy, my book *Difference and Repetition* still aspired nonetheless toward a sort of classical height and even toward an archaic depth. The theory of intensity which I was drafting was marked by depth, false or true; intensity was presented as stemming from the depths' (Deleuze 2006: 65). This reliance on traditional categories comes through in Deleuze's characterisation of the project as attempting to think 'difference-in-itself', which, mirroring Kant's transcendental idealism, is itself characterised as 'the closest noumenon'.

In *A Thousand Plateaus*, this methodological reliance on traditional categories of philosophy such as essence is left behind. Deleuze writes of his first collaboration with Guattari that 'no longer has height or depth, nor surface. In this book everything happens, is done, the intensities, the events, upon a sort of spherical body or scroll painting: The Organless Body' (Deleuze 2006: 66), and the same claim could be made of *A Thousand Plateaus* itself. The central question of *A Thousand Plateaus* is not 'What is?', but 'How does one make?' This move to a loose pragmatism involves a different conception of what philosophy entails. Rather than the attempt to distinguish true and false depths – the project of distinguishing lineages of images that still holds to Plato's model of philosophy just as a photographic negative maintains the detail of the image it inverts – Deleuze and Guattari joyously take up one of the central concepts of *Difference and Repetition*: the image of thought. In *Difference and Repetition*, the image of thought is the surface effect of the subrepresentational nature of thinking – a paralogism created by the reflection of thinking on itself that is at the heart of philosophy's inability to think depth appropriately. In *A Thousand*

Plateaus, by contrast, the philosophical project does not involve the search for a moment prior to an image of thought, but the construction of a new image of thought – the 'vegetal image of thought' (Deleuze 1994: xvii). As such, it eschews the effort to seek the essence of the world in favour of a more pragmatic concern of developing a rigorous but different systematic way of relating elements together.

Deleuze and Guattari met in 1969, when Deleuze was convalescing after the removal of a lung and Guattari was searching for a creative outlet that would allow him to give structure to his militant left-wing activities, work on psychoanalysis at the La Borde clinic and ideas around machines, political and social structures, capitalism and schizophrenia (Dosse 2010: 3). These latter themes bring new directions and different concepts to the philosophy developed in *Difference and Repetition* and *The Logic of Sense*. With Guattari, philosophy becomes machinic and political, a multiple practice, and an intervention on psychoanalysis and modern psychoses.

Thinkers such as Badiou, therefore, who argue that the philosophical content of Deleuze's thought is contained purely within the early works show a fundamental misunderstanding of the project of Deleuze and Guattari. They invert the natural order of Deleuze and Guattari's own account of their work. *Difference and Repetition* sets out the criteria which a new style of philosophy must adopt, but it is *A Thousand Plateaus* which takes seriously the need to move away from a philosophy of essence, and hence a thinking in terms of depth, a form of thought itself criticised in *The Logic of Sense*. It is in his collaborations with Guattari that Deleuze claims that the actual practice of the new philosophy heralded in *Difference and Repetition* became possible. *A Thousand Plateaus*, for Deleuze, did not represent simply a new philosophical position, but rather a whole new way of doing philosophy.

The root-book

So if *A Thousand Plateaus* takes up Deleuze's critique of classical philosophy, how does this critique manifest itself in the structure of *A Thousand Plateaus* itself? At the heart of *A Thousand Plateaus* is the vegetal image of thought. It is this that leads Deleuze's major collaboration with Guattari, *A Thousand Plateaus*, to manifest a new philosophical style. We can begin to see how it achieves this by turning to the contents page of the book itself. Here, rather a set of chapters, we find a list of fifteen plateaus, each on idiosyncratic topics such as how one makes a body without organs, war machines, and the possibility of a geology of morals. Superficially, these appear to be chapters in all but name, but as Deleuze and Guattari note, 'it's like a set of split rings. You can fit anyone of them into any other. Each ring, or each plateau, ought to have its own climate, its own tone or timbre' (Deleuze 1995a: 25). We can understand the move Deleuze and Guattari are making by comparing it to their characterisation of the alternative – the root-book:

> A first type of book is the root-book. The tree is already the image of the world, or the root the image of the world-tree. This is the classical book, as noble, signifying, and subjective organic interiority (the strata of the book). The book imitates the world, as art imitates nature: by procedures specific to it that accomplish what nature cannot or can no longer do. (ATP 5)

We can work through some implications of this account now. First, this definition of a philosophical work dates back to Plato, who makes a similar claim that a work must have an organic structure:

> Every discourse (logos) must be put together like a living creature, with a body of its own; it must be neither without head nor without legs; and it must have a middle and extremities that are fitting both to one another and to the whole work.[4]

At the heart of the concept of the organism is that it is teleological – it functions for some purpose. It is this purpose that gives meaning to the parts of the organism by allowing them to be defined by their relations to the whole. Secondly, as Kant writes in the *Critique of Judgement*, the nature of the whole is defined by the reciprocal relations of the parts. Thus, Kant writes that 'just as each part exists only *as a result* of all the rest, so we think of each part as existing *for the sake* of the others and of the whole, i.e. as an instrument (organ)' (Kant 1987: §373). As Kant makes clear, the reason for the introduction of the categories of the organic is that an understanding of the world purely in terms of physics is unable to explain why certain objects have an inside and an outside rather than simply being heaps of matter. Seeing the organism as unified according to a purpose gives us a way of making a sharp distinction between the inside and the outside, and understanding a philosophical text on the model of an organism similarly allows us to see it as closed and complete. Once we do so, we develop the other characteristics of the root-book. As the book is complete in itself, its reference to the world is as a model for what it discusses. The root-book introduces an ontological rift between the world and our representation of it. Further, this structure of imitation operates in a manner that differs from what it is discussing. The book accomplishes 'what nature cannot or can no longer do'. A traditional text does not simply imitate nature as it is, but rather determines those features of it that are essential.

The classic model of an organic system would be Hegel's philosophy, which develops a sophisticated web of concepts where the meaning of each is determined by the meaning of all of the others, as in a form of life, and while the system extends to infinity, it remains closed or totalised. Here, the determination of concepts takes place immanently, purely in terms of the unfolding of internal principles. We can see a precursor to this in the immanent development of Descartes' metaphysics from the single Archimedean point of the *cogito*. Here we have here a sequence of linear descent, which Deleuze and Guattari align with an arborescent image of thought.[5]

The rhizome

So here we can return to the notion of a plateau. In a classical philosophical text, the chapters follow one another in a sequence, with each building on the results of the previous chapter. The structure is much like Descartes' hierarchy of the sciences, where we progressively move from a set of presuppositions to a conclusion through a series of arguments. However, the plateaus of *A Thousand Plateaus* are not determined by an overarching unity that closes the text in on itself. While Deleuze and Guattari still take up the model of life, rather than the closed model of the organism, they favour an open model that encompasses symbiotic relationships between organisms, and the transversal communication of DNA between species.[6] As such, in *A Thousand Plateaus*, Deleuze and Guattari try to put into practice the implications of their critique of the philosophical question, 'What is it?' In moving to the questions, 'Which one?' 'Where?' 'When?' 'How?' 'How many?' 'In which case?' and 'Who?', they call for a new form of writing. For this reason, *A Thousand Plateaus* is rhizomatic rather than taking the tree as its model. It presents itself as a series of interconnected moments, where one can begin anywhere, and read the plateaus in any order. As such, rather than seeing plateaus as layers that one must move through, they are better seen as the dimensions of a space, where one can move from one plateau to another simply by a reorientation and change in direction, and each intersects all of the others. Deleuze and Guattari describe it as follows:

> The rhizome is altogether different, a map and not a tracing. Make a map, not a tracing. The orchid does not reproduce the tracing of the wasp; it forms a map with the wasp, in a rhizome. What distinguishes the map from the tracing is that it is entirely oriented toward an experimentation in contact with the real. The map does not reproduce an unconscious closed in upon itself; it constructs the unconscious. It fosters connections between fields,

the removal of blockages on bodies without organs, the maximum opening of bodies without organs onto a plane of consistency. It is itself a part of the rhizome. The map is open and connectable in all of its dimensions; it is detachable, reversible, susceptible to constant modification. It can be torn, reversed, adapted to any kind of mounting, reworked by an individual, group, or social formation. It can be drawn on a wall, conceived of as a work of art, constructed as a political action or as a meditation. Perhaps one of the most important characteristics of the rhizome is that it always has multiple entryways; in this sense, the burrow is an animal rhizome, and sometimes maintains a clear distinction between the line of flight as passageway and storage or living strata (cf. the muskrat). A map has multiple entryways, as opposed to the tracing, which always comes back 'to the same'. (ATP 12)

Whether this project is successful (and Deleuze would later suggest that *A Thousand Plateaus* may indeed be a productive failure) (Deleuze and Parnet 1987: 17), it at the least opens up new possibilities for doing philosophy, and shows that any re-evaluation of the philosophical enterprise cannot simply be restricted to a change in argument, but calls also for a reappraisal of the whole style of philosophical enquiry.

Notes

1. Badiou 2000. Quotation taken from translator's introduction, xii.
2. This more creative approach to the practice of philosophy, as a forerunner of the innovations of *A Thousand Plateaus*, can be found in the serial structure, textual openness, conceptual ambiguity and multiple voices of *The Logic of Sense*, a text contemporary to *Difference and Repetition*. See Williams 2008: ch. 1.
3. For a detailed account of Deleuze and Guattari on the creation of concepts, see Bell 2016: ch. 1.
4. Plato 1997a: 264c. Cf. Jacques Derrida's essay, 'Plato's Pharmacy', in Derrida 1982 for a discussion of organic metaphors in Plato. Derrida is close to Deleuze and Guattari in this essay, both in his analysis of the impossibility of the organicist conception of the text actually providing closure, and in his own recognition that the implications of this are a new style of philosophising.
5. See Miguel Beistegui's contribution to this volume for the relationship between Descartes and arborescence.
6. As Simon O'Sullivan notes in his contribution to this volume, the very openness of Deleuze and Guattari's system means that any attempt to delimit a purely philosophical content to the project risks construing it as a closed system. Nonetheless, we follow Deleuze and Guattari here, when they note in the analysis of smooth and striated space that 'de facto mixes do not preclude a de jure, or abstract, distinction' (ATP 475). In this volume, we recognise that any purely philosophical content must be seen as growing rhizomatically with the 'non-philosophical'.

Chapter 1

'A book? What book?' Or Deleuze and Guattari on the Rhizome

Miguel de Beistegui

In an upland area in the Limousin region of France stretches the vast and sparsely populated Plateau de Millevaches. Nearby lies the village of Saint-Léonard-de-Noblat, where Deleuze and his wife shared a house, which Fanny had inherited from her father. From the house, when the weather permits it, one can see the plateau. Deleuze wrote most of his books while on holiday in that part of the country, which he described as 'very soft and powerful' (Maggiori 2000). It is apt, therefore, that one of his books, if only by way of something resembling a humorous homage, include a reference to the plateau that harbours a thousand *vaches* (the etymology of which is entirely disputed). But, as we know, it is in fact more than a reference: 'plateau' is a key deleuzo-guattarian concept. To name a book of philosophy after a place, or, better said perhaps, to turn a geographical entity into a philosophical concept is not an innocent gesture. It is a very deliberate one, which treats its 'chapters' as if they were geological formations, and the book as a whole as if it were a map that could be read in a variety of ways, and infinitely redrawn. Yet even this 'as if' is insufficient: the book is indeed a map or mapping of a land (let us say, the land of philosophical problems) that does not exist 'out there', already made, and this in such a way that an acute vision equipped with the necessary tools would be able to trace its contours; it exists even less in the authors' minds, as a testimony to the richness of their imagination. Rather, it is itself part of the reality it describes: it is not a copy, a representation, or even an interpretation of the world, but a conceptual construction (with concepts such as 'stratification', 'assemblage', 'rhizome', 'body without organs', 'deterritorialisation', 'abstract machine', 'multiplicity', 'becoming', 'major and minor', 'molar and molecular'), a small machine that connects with other machines, a concept-thing plugged into a variety of things (the unconscious, language, the earth, literature, power, capitalism, space, history), an assemblage that produces innumerable effects. It is not *about* those things, or about anything: 'a book has neither object nor subject; it is made of variously formed matters' (ATP 3). We desperately want books to mean something (preferably something important), to signify. Of a book, a painting, or an event, we ask: 'What does it mean?' To which Deleuze and Guattari answer: 'We will never ask what a book means, as signifier and signified; we will not look for anything to understand in it; but we will ask what it functions with . . .' This functionalist conception of thought, of writing, and of the book, replaces its classical hermeneutic and essentialist ('What is it about?') conception.

A Thousand Plateaus is a breath of fresh air for philosophy: a new climate, a new landscape. A biting, sweeping wind blows on these plateaus, one that also stirs the blood, carrying you away. *Mille plateaux* is a new way of understanding philosophy, not through its great authors or texts, not as a succession of endlessly redefined periods, and even less as a history whose development would be driven by a Meaning or by the promise of an End. It is not even a series of responses to its 'fundamental problems'. Philosophy, and more generally, thought, now consists of wild, nomadic lines inscribed on a system grid-locked by power apparatuses, on rigid and fixed frames of thought, or patterns of territorialisation. *A Thousand Plateaus* turns everything outwards: it is a book that tears thought away from inwardness, from the hearth, from domesticity, and sends it outside; in other words, into that with which it can combine and assemble itself, and *become* something else. Its concepts are now gusts in a landscape: gusts of wind, visceral cries, a hammer's blow. They are formed in proximity to strange creatures and objects that populate these plateaus: beasts (rats, wolves, tics, ants, cockroaches, lobsters); familiar tunes (*ritournelles*), songs and groans; conceptual characters (Professor Challenger, the 'Indian', 'a' woman, 'a' child); waves; eggs; tubers; faces; fabrics . . . the list goes on. There are even dates (1914, 1000 BC, 20 November 1923, etc.) and illustrations (a blueprint, a photograph, a drawing, a score) corresponding to the different plateaus. And yet there is no chronology, no history for this philosophy that departs from Meaning in order to engage with Experimentation. It is no longer a question of interpretation, nor is it even one of understanding; rather, it is a question of learning – in other words, of daring: daring to experiment, to create, to make one's own machines (social, amorous, literary, scientific, etc.). If we write, it is to become something else, to fall into another state, to live differently. That is what is called 'to rhizome' ('faire rhizome').

As a result, *Mille plateaux* is not a book on or about which one should write. It doesn't lend itself to exegetical readings, interpretations or critiques. It is there to be written or experimented with, to be picked up and used – or not. In fact, Deleuze and Guattari argue that other than the conclusion, which they claim should be saved for the end, the plateaus can be read in any order. Still, very much aware of the novelty of their approach, of the new demands that they put on the genre of the philosophical book, Deleuze and Guattari write an Introduction in which they raise the question of the book. What is a book? What is it for? What sort of book is *A Thousand Plateaus*?

The question of the book

It is a question that Deleuze had already raised towards the very beginning of *Difference and Repetition*, a book in which he spoke in his own name for the first time: 'The time is coming when it will hardly be possible to write a book of philosophy as it has been done for so long: "Ah! The old style ..."' (Deleuze 1994: xxi).[1] In the same preface, and much to our surprise, Deleuze presents his book as a kind of detective novel, as well as a work of science fiction (Deleuze 1994: xx). A detective novel, insofar as the characters that populate it, namely, concepts, should be seen as detectives who intervene to resolve local and changing problems, or 'dramas', imbedded in a 'here-and-now'. Concepts, then, insofar as they are local and respond to a logic of the 'encounter', rather than of 'recognition', are forced into existence by a power that is not their own doing, and which Deleuze defines as Ideas, or 'problems'. As such, they are created, like fictitious characters whose existence is mapped not after general ideas and eternal essences, but specific – yet not straightforwardly empirical – situations.

As for the reference to science fiction, it stems from the fact that the 'here-and-now' in question is also 'nowhere': at once impersonal, in that it does not find its source in a self or a cogito, and pre-individual, in that it envelops the conditions of all individuality, it is best understood as *Erewhon*. This reference to Samuel Butler's novel and fictitious country evokes a space and time – an intensive *spatium* – of thought that is no more our own, that of mankind, than that of God.[2] Elsewhere, Deleuze claims that 'what is neither individual nor personal are ... emissions of singularity' that 'occur on an unconscious surface'. They are characterised by a '*nomadic distribution*', which contrasts with the 'sedentary' or fixed distribution that characterise the syntheses of consciousness (Deleuze 1990b: 102). With its concepts of 'virtuality' and 'actuality', of pure, intensive 'multiplicities', on the one hand, and intensities that are already developed in 'extensions' and covered over in 'qualities', on the other, *Difference and Repetition* had only begun to map those impersonal surfaces and spaces, insisting all along that this transcendental 'ground' was nothing like – that is, did not resemble, or was not modelled after – the empirical world. Recognition (*récognition*) and resemblance are two of the key 'postulates' or 'illusions' of the 'dogmatic image of thought', which *Difference and Repetition* identifies, and sees as limiting the essentially creative power of thought.[3]

But the reference to science fiction in *Difference and Repetition* should also be understood in another sense: to write a book of philosophy is to write at the very limit of one's knowledge (*savoir*), that is, at the point at which the process of learning becomes more important than that of actual cognition (*connaissance*) and recognition. It is not, therefore, a matter of epistemology: 'I am well aware,' Deleuze writes in *Difference and Repetition*, 'that I have spoken about science in a way that was not scientific' (Deleuze 1994: xxi). Echoing this early statement, *A Thousand Plateaus* says: 'At no point do we claim the title of science' (ATP 22). But to write at the limit is also to write at the limit of *oneself*, that is, at the point at which one is finally able to become someone or something else:

> Why have we kept our own names? Out of habit, purely out of habit. To make ourselves unrecognisable in turn . . . To reach, not the point when one longer says I, but the point where it is no longer of any importance whether one says I. We are no longer ourselves. (ATP 3)

In many ways, Deleuze's prophetic statement regarding 'the old style' doesn't quite apply to *Difference and Repetition*, which, because of its doctoral and academic nature, continued to conform to the classical model of the book. *Logic of Sense*, published only a year after *Difference and Repetition*, introduced a significant stylistic break and a series of formal (as well as conceptual) innovations, such as the 'series', which replace the traditional chapters. But it is not until Deleuze began to write with Guattari that this new image of the book, and this new style, which was to match the new, non-dogmatic image of thought already introduced in *Difference and Repetition*, became a reality. *Anti-Oedipus* demonstrates the critical, satirical and utterly irreverent side of their collaboration. It is philosophising with a hammer at its freest. *A Thousand Plateaus* introduces a dose of sobriety and reflexivity, visible throughout the book, but articulated as such in the Introduction. 'Rhizome' is a presentation of the book as a whole, and a reflection on the manner in which it operates – not according to a linear, arche-teleological structure, with chapters written in succession, and marking its progress, but as a juxtaposition of 'plateaus', which communicate with one another simultaneously and in a potentially infinite number of ways: 'We are writing this book as a rhizome. It is composed of plateaus' (ATP 22). The book does not have a beginning, a middle and an end: 'a rhizome has no beginning or end; it is always in the middle, between things, interbeing, *intermezzo*' (ATP 25). Like grass, or like the sentence of Proust and the *Recherche* as a whole, *A Thousand Plateaus* grows from the middle. It happens in the middle, between fixed points, where things gather speed and initiate transversal movements, through which they communicate with other in-betweens. Speaking of Kleist, Lenz and Büchner in relation to the German language, but also Henry Miller, the beatniks, Patti Smith or native Americans, Deleuze and Guattari write: 'they know how to move between things, establish a logic of the AND, overthrow ontology, do away with foundations, nullify endings and beginnings' (ATP 25). If – and that is a big 'if' – ontology is necessarily archaeological and teleological, foundational and destinal, then 'nomadology' is the suspension of ontology: it cuts across it, passes through its mesh, deterritorialises it.

The classical image of the book: the tree

In their Introduction (a final concession, perhaps, to the classical genre of the book), Deleuze and Guattari contrast the image of the rhizome, to which we will return, with that of the tree, which Western thought, if not Western culture as a whole (and that includes its agriculture), has privileged systematically. There is, to begin with, the tree of knowledge and the tree of original sin, the genealogical tree and its archetype, the tree of Jesse. We use the image of the tree, with its roots, branches and fruits, to define our sense of provenance, personal identity and future. We want things and people to have an origin and a goal, or a purpose. This is what Deleuze and Guattari have to say about this kind of interest: 'Where are you going? Where are you coming from? What are you heading for? These are totally useless questions' (ATP 25). We should be asking instead: 'How do you (or they) work, what do you (or they) work with? And what effects do those connections produce?'

The tree is also, and primarily, as Bachelard has argued, the image of the image itself, or the primordial symbol: it contains and even gathers the fundamental images – water, air, fire, earth – from which the life of the imagination springs, the elemental stuff that sustains our *rêveries*, fantasies and metaphors. In *La terre et les rêveries du repos*, for example, Bachelard goes as far as to claim that 'imagination is a tree'.[4] If that's the case, we shouldn't be surprised to see trees proliferate not only in myths and narratives, but in philosophy and science as well. We need only think of the 'family tree' of Porphyry, which classifies things under genera and species, the bishop of Orléans Théodulphe's tree of knowledge and wisdom (*sophia*), or the tree of natural historians (Pallas, Buffon, Lamarck), which was itself followed by the phylogenetic tree of evolution (Darwin, Haeckel). It is important to emphasise the taxonomic as well as symbolic value of the image of the tree: we use it to define how we think, know and make sense of the world, and ourselves; but we also use it to distinguish, classify, order. It is a model that we find at work in more recent sciences, such as computer science (the 'data tree'), neurophysiology (in connection with the brain, and memory especially), and linguistics. Until Saussure, who, tongue in cheek, illustrates his theory of the arbitrariness of the sign, and thus of the operation of signification, with the example of the word 'tree', the genesis and evolution of idioms was – and still is – thought through the image of the tree, and of roots. But it is the production of sense that is itself thought of through the paradigm of arborescence. Even Chomsky, who breaks with the idea of linguistics as a kind of verbal botany, aims to classify the elements of human languages and, in the process, operates through dichotomies. His 'generative grammar' is a theory regarding the deep structures of sentences that underlie their surface structures. On their own, the latter cannot account for a wide range of syntactical facts, such as ambiguous sentences, or the potentially infinite number of sentences contained in any language.[5] As a result, structuralist linguists tended to avoid them. In his grammar, Chomsky organised the structure of the sentence according to an arborescent plan, which, from the sentence, led to its different branches and sub-branches (the noun phrase, which can itself be divided into article and noun; the verb phrase, which can itself be divided into verb and noun phrase, etc.). In addition, and in order to account for the fact that phrase structure rules tend to overlook certain ambiguities of language and conceal differences, Chomsky also included 'transformational rules', which also correspond to a tree-like structure.

Should we be surprised, in the end, to see the tree elevated to the level of the image of thought and knowledge itself? Deleuze and Guattari mention the relatively late example of Julien Pacotte, author of *Le réseau arborescent, schème primordial de la pensée*, in which he defines that structure as 'the real foundation of formal thought'.[6] But all philosophers have in mind Descartes. To be sure, in his philosophical dialogue, *The Search for Truth by Means of Natural Light*, Epistemon, who incarnates the figure of the scholar, registers his discontent before the manner in which Eudoxus (Descartes' spokesperson) treats Porphyry's tree, and the knowledge for which its stands: 'I am sorry you despise the tree of Porphyry, which the learned have always admired, and . . .' (Descartes 1984: 410). And yet, if he criticises it, it is to replace it with a more adequate image of the tree of knowledge, expressed in the following famous passage from the *Principles of Philosophy*:

> Thus the whole of philosophy is like a tree. The roots are metaphysics, the trunk is physics, and the branches emerging from the trunk are all the other sciences, which may be reduced to three principal ones, namely medicine, mechanics and morals. (Descartes 1985a: 186)

Such would be the destiny of Western thought: to find the ground, to uncover the roots; to go ever deeper and discover the unshakable foundation, the undisputable origin.

The critique of arborescent thought

It is that image that Deleuze and Guattari want to uproot from our mind, that tree – of life, knowledge and thought – that they want to cut down: 'We have grown tired of the tree . . .' (ATP 15) But why? What exactly is the problem with arborescent thinking?

To begin with, it is mimetic: it functions according to principles of imitation and resemblance. This, in turn, should be understood in two ways. First of all, it claims to represent the word, or to be an image of it. But in the end, it is just that, namely, an image, a representation, and one that is necessarily disconnected from the world. In fact, it introduces a dualism between it and the world. It is not *of* the world, it does not interact with it, or transform it. It is only a copy (*calque*) of the world. But – and this is the second aspect – it is a false copy, in that the tracing paper it uses to reproduce the world only selects some of its features, those that agree in advance with the image of the world it has already generated. The tracing paper of the tree has been drawn up in advance, and is superimposed on to the world, thus giving us the same image. In truth, it is the world itself that is modelled after the tree. Thus, language, the unconscious, the brain, power, etc. are all illustrations of the arch-image of the tree. The logic of the tree 'consists of copying and tracing [*décalquer*], on the basis of an overcoding structure of supporting axis, something that we assume is ready-made [*quelque chose qu'on se donne tout fait*]' (ATP 12, translation modified). The principle of imitation – especially in the form of the Idea and its copies – is one that Deleuze had already criticised and deconstructed in 'Plato and the Simulacrum' and *Difference and Repetition*: it is, he claims, at the heart of the system of representation that Plato introduces, and Aristotle systematises.[7] The ontological sameness (*auto kath'auto*) of the Platonic Idea gives way to the identity of the Aristotelian concept, which divides itself into specific differences, and those differences into further differences. The principle of imitation is carried over into transcendental philosophy, which tends to model the transcendental after the empirical, and thus identify conditions that are only conditions of *possibility*. This is how, in *Difference and Repetition*, Deleuze sees Kant's transcendental deduction of the pure concepts of the understanding, and of the exposition of the *a priori* upon which the possibility of experience rests, as a betrayal of the 'prodigious domain of the transcendental', which, 'like a great explorer', Kant had nonetheless discovered. The betrayal in question, Deleuze argues, is precisely due to the fact that, in his attempt to locate the conditions of experience in the threefold synthesis of 'apprehension in intuition', of 'reproduction in imagination' and of 'recognition in a concept', Kant ultimately subordinates them to the latter, and to the figure of the 'I think', to which all the faculties are related:

> It is clear that, in this manner, Kant traces [*décalque*] the so-called transcendental structures from the empirical acts of a psychological consciousness: the transcendental synthesis of apprehension is directly induced from an empirical apprehension, and so on. In order to hide this all too obvious procedure, Kant suppressed this text in the second edition. Although it is better hidden, the tracing method [*la méthode du décalque*], with all its 'psychologism', nevertheless subsists. (Deleuze 1994: 134)

A second problem with the image of the tree, as we have just begun to see, is that it is irreducibly binary, or dichotomous: first, we are told, there is the One, then the One becomes two, and the two four, etc. But this is not the way nature works. In nature 'roots are taproots with a more multiple, lateral, and circular system of ramification, rather than a dichotomous one' (ATP 5). Dichotomies are the very structure of reproduction, and can be reproduced *ad infinitum*: $n+1$. Thirdly, and as an immediate consequence of its binary structure, the tree is hierarchical and vertical. As such, it perpetuates a model of thought and reality that is essentially a model of centralised and authoritative power. It presupposes a point of origin, a source, from which all follows, through a process of derivation, division, reproduction and copying. Consider the example of psychoanalysis. To be sure, it discovers this great new continent, the unconscious, with its wealth of productive potential, but only to subject it to arborescent structures and to an entire centralised system, a command centre, the Father, or the Phallus, from which everything else derives. We should not be surprised, therefore, to see psychoanalysis also generate its own generals, and quarrel over who is the true leader (General Freud or General Lacan?). In the end, the tree or the root 'inspire a sad image of thought', which nomadic thought is to replace with a more joyous one, that of the rhizome. It is sad because it severs thought from its noetic, experimental power, because it brings it back into the fixed, vertical and hierarchical structure of the tree, when all it wants is to grow horizontally and in different directions at the same time, connect with other stems, in short, *faire rhizome*. Any attempt to introduce a moment of transcendence in the immanence of thought generates a blockage, a sedentary or fixed structure, which inhibits thought.

The new image of the book: the rhizome

The image of the rhizome makes its first appearance in *Kafka: Toward a Minor Literature*, published in 1974 (Deleuze and Guattari 1986). It is introduced at the very outset, and with a view to explaining the sort of books that Kafka writes: 'How can we enter into Kafka's work? This work is a rhizome, a burrow' (Deleuze and Guattari 1986: 3). Like the hotel in *America*, which has many main and side doors, Kafka's works – his longer novels especially – have many points of entrance, each equally valid, each denying from the start the possibility of a centre, a single sensitive point or signifier, from which the work as a whole would radiate, and from which it would be interpreted:

> We will enter, then, by any point whatsoever; none matters more than another ... We will be trying only to discover what other points our entrance connects to, what crossroads and galleries one passes through to link two points, what the map of the rhizome and how the map is modified if one enters by another point. (Deleuze and Guattari 1986: 3)

In other words, the manner in which the points connect with one another is not set in advance, and is susceptible to endless variations, each producing a different map, and a different experience. Connect this point (or door) with that one, rather than with that other point, and the reality in question reveals a new assemblage, new horizons, and a new map (of life, the social body, the heart, history or the unconscious). This new distribution of singular points, this new and changing cartography, is indistinguishable from experimentation, which now replaces interpretation or cognition as the main task of thinking. Yet we need to be careful, as not all points, and not all assemblages, are equal: some points criss-cross an area, coordinate, striate, delimit, enclose, territorialise, sedentarise; others are free, floating, oceanic points, which escape the grid-like assemblages of the former, drift and head off for the open sea, deterritorialise, like a submarine beneath the striated surface of the ocean. Some points trace (*décalquent*) and stratify, while others map. Some points draw dichotomies, while others construct rhizomes. For example, there is the triangle of desire that is generated by singling out the points 'daddy', 'mummy', 'me'. This triangulation of desire is its strangulation. And then there is the multiplicity of animals that populate Kafka's world. There is the becoming-cockroach of Gregor, which is entirely constituted by vibrations, intensities, thresholds that, taken together, amount to lines of flight that escape the family triangle, but also the bureaucratic and commercial triangle. Equally, we could say that the academic philosopher's desire to teach and write is (increasingly) triangulated, and territorialised, through the construction of the bureaucratic machine (and its 'Research Excellence Framework', 'Teaching Excellence Framework', 'National Student Survey', etc.), the commercial machine (with its paradigm of productivity as defined by external powers), and the technological machine (with the platforms on and through which that desire is oriented and framed). But there are also lines of flight and resistance, encounters and surprises, generated by books (such as *A Thousand Plateaus*), students, demonstrations, etc.

Two years after the publication of *Kafka*, Deleuze and Guattari published a short book entitled *The Rhizome*, in which they turned that image into a philosophical concept, and around which they eventually organised their philosophy and new 'image' of thought.[8] It is the content of that short text that was inserted as the Introduction to *A Thousand Plateaus*, a book which Deleuze and Guattari wanted to construct like *The Castle*. Why the rhizome? Because, like the tree and the root, it signals a process of growth, or the manner in which something unfolds, or happens. However,

> A rhizome as subterranean stem is absolutely different from roots and radicles. Bulbs and tubers are rhizomes. Plants with roots or radicles may be rhizomorphic in other respects altogether: we can wonder whether botany, in its specificity, is not entirely rhizomatic. Even some animals are, in their pack form. Rats are rhizomes. Burrows are too, in all of their functions of shelter, supply, movement, evasion, and breakout. (ATP 7–8, translation modified)

Yet even in the rhizome, there is something to leave out: 'the best and the worst: potato and couchgrass, or weeds'. It is not a panacea or a universal remedy. Besides, no lateral movement, no process of deterritorialisation, no line of flight will ever guarantee a final and definitive protection against processes of reterritorialisation, micro-fascisms, reactionary organisations of power. In fact, the latter are almost inevitable, which means that the lines of flight need to be reactivated, reinvented or replaced by entirely new ones.

But a slightly more systematic approach is required. The rhizome can be said to have the following advantages over the tree. To begin with, and where the image of the tree privileges a logic of imitation, resemblance and identity, the rhizome privileges one of connection and heterogeneity. A book does not try to imitate the world, or be like it, but to 'form a rhizome with the world [*faire rhizome avec le monde*]' (ATP 11). In a rhizome, and as we have already seen in connection with Kafka's novels and stories, a point can and must be connected with any other point. This is unlike the tree, which fixes points along a vertical axis. This, in turn, means that the rhizome corresponds to a changing or nomadic distribution of points, one that leads to a manifold of configurations and connections. By the same token, the rhizome does not correspond to a dialectical logic of division, to a One that becomes two, or a command centre that distributes itself all the way down (or up) the tree. Earlier, I suggested that the reason why arborescent thought was problematic was because of its binary approach, which reduces a system (linguistic, unconscious, physical, or economic) with many singular points that changes its nature as it expands its connections, to the repetitive and dull play of the One and the two, four, etc. A rhizome, Deleuze explains in *Negotiations*, is a kind of *open* system, and an open system is precisely one whose concepts correspond to events and circumstances, rather than essences (Deleuze 1995a: 32). An open system is defined by its 'thresholds' and 'points of bifurcation', which force it into a different state. It is defined by differences that are qualitative. Let me return to the example of Chomsky. The charge, in essence, is that his grammar remains too hierarchical and abstract, too syntactical, too authoritarian, too closed up on itself to understand the manner in which language is always and from the start connected with linguistic contents that are semantic and pragmatic, with statements that are collective, in short, with a 'micropolitics of the social field' (ATP 7). Naturally, Chomsky's radical politics aren't what is at stake here. What matters, rather, is the fact that his generative grammar remains caught up in the diktat of the Sentence, in the same way that Lacanian psychoanalysis remains hung up on that of the Signifier: 'Chomsky's grammaticality, the categorical S symbol that dominates every sentence, is first and foremost a marker of power, and then a syntactic marker: you will construct grammatically correct sentences, you will divide each sentence into a noun phrase and a verb phrase (first dichotomy . . .)' (ATP 7, translation modified). The problem with trees – no matter how formal and scientific – is that they introduce structures of power, and turn a phenomenon – an 'assemblage' – that is essentially fluid and collective into a fixed order and a sedentary hierarchy.

What, instead, does the rhizomatic approach to language offer? It identifies 'semiotic chains [*chaînons*]' that are connected not internally, according to formal rules, but externally, through other connections: 'A rhizome ceaselessly establishes connections between semiotic chains, organisations of power, and circumstances relative to the arts, sciences, and social struggles' (ATP 7). A semiotic chain is not a discrete linguistic unity, but a linguistic segment or 'tuber' that connects with, and is traversed by, all those heterogeneous elements (social struggles, power structures, cultural circumstances). In that respect, it is 'closer' to those elements, without being 'like' them. This principle is crucial, as it can apply to a variety of phenomena and fields: in the end, there is more in common between a motorcycle and a race horse than between a race horse and plough horse; or there is more in common between a fin and a hand than between a hand and a glove. This is because rhizomatic thought connects segments of bodies with other segments by referring them back to a logic not of resemblance, division and categorical consistency, but of problems. Of course, it will always be possible to break language down into internal structural elements, and go down the path of dichotomies. But that operation is a taming and police operation, one that closes language on itself. The rhizomatic approach, on the other hand, treats language like 'a patch of oil' that spreads outwards and laterally, and joins other segments, to reveal a 'machinic assemblage' or a 'multiplicity' (ATP 7).

Deleuze never tired of repeating the distinction between the dialectical play of the One and the many, and the substantive 'multiplicity'.[9] *Difference and Repetition* already defined philosophy as the science of pure multiplicities, or virtual singularities, and saw the latter as the conditions of emergence of actual phenomena, or as the real (but not actual) horizon from which they arise. A multiplicity is defined not by a fixed distribution of points within a given dimension, but by the fact that its nature changes as its connections and dimensions increase. In other words, it does not have a core nature, a centre or an essence, which tolerates variations, modifications or additions. Rather, it is entirely exhausted by its connections or lines, and its (rhizomatic) unity does not require a higher unity: 'There are no points or positions in a rhizome, such as those found in a structure, tree, or root. There are only lines' (ATP 8). Unlike *Difference and Repetition*, which did not quite manage to be or function like a multiplicity, and remained caught within the traditional structure of the book, *A Thousand Plateaus*, through the connections it establishes with the world outside it, and between its various plateaus, does. Or at least it does its very best to function like one: 'The ideal for a book would be to lay everything out on a plane of exteriority of this kind, on a single page, the same sheet: lived events, historical determinations, concepts, individuals, groups, social formations' (ATP 9). This flattening of concepts and discursive practices, of social groups and political circumstances, of lived experiences and economic flows, amounts to a systematic dismantling of the order and hierarchies that root-thought tries to introduce. The world of multiplicities is entirely flat and exogenous. Together, they constitute a 'plane of consistency':

> All multiplicities are flat, in the sense that they fill or occupy all of their dimensions: we will therefore speak of a *plane of consistency* of multiplicities, even though the dimensions of this 'plane' increase with the number of con-

nections that are made on it. Multiplicities are defined by the outside: by the abstract line, the line of flight or deterritorialisation according to which they change in nature and connect with other multiplicities. (ATP 9)

By plane of consistency, then, Deleuze and Guattari mean the flat plane on which all multiplicities occur and grow (*flat multiplicities of n dimensions*), and which renders them consistent with one another, without locating them on a vertical axis or ascribing them a direction or goal.

To write, then, is to form a rhizome with the world, and not produce an image of it. It is to mix one's own destiny and heterogeneity with that of the world, to evolve with it, but in a way that is 'aparallel'. To illustrate their view, Deleuze and Guattari refer to the example of the wasp and the orchid, and to the phenomenon known as 'sexual deception'. On the face of it, the relation between the orchid and the wasp is one of imitation and signification, of resemblance and deception: doesn't the orchid masquerade as a wasp, and simulate in its core the presence of the sexual organ of the wasp female? This is how one biologist puts it:

> Ophys flowers mimic virgin females of their pollinators, and male insects are lured to the orchid by volatile semiochemicals and visual cues. At close range, chemical signals from the flowers elicit sexual behaviour in males, which try to copulate with the flower labellum and respond as if in the presence of female sex pheromones. Thereby the male touches the gynostemium, and the pollinia may become attached to his head or, in some species, to the tip of his abdomen. His copulatory attempts with another flower ensure that the pollinia are transferred to the flower's stigmatic surface and pollination is ensured. (Ayasse et al. 2003: 517)

The point, here, is that orchids have evolved with the capacity to produce the sexual pheromones of a wasp that serves as its pollinator, and to present the appearance of the female wasp herself. What, if anything, is wrong with that picture? It perpetuates the Platonic idea (and ideal) of an original and a copy, of a model and a (more or less authentic) imitation. Instead, Deleuze and Guattari want to see the relation between the wasp and the orchid as a single material process, a vital and evolutionary assemblage that defies the representational logic of fixed, already individuated substances, as well as the purely arborescent image of evolution, which would proceed only and inevitably from the least to the more differentiated. Deleuze and Guattari replace that image (the image of the image itself) with a rhizomatic model that operates from the start within the domain of heterogeneity, with one already differentiated line jumping to another.[10] In the case of the orchid and the wasp, there is no deception or lure; there is only a 'becoming' bringing together two sets of dispositions and capacities. In the wasp–orchid assemblage, it becomes impossible to say where one begins, and the other ends: the boundaries between them become blurred. In fact, the reality takes place not between two previously individuated substances, but as the process of individuation itself. The reality is the in-between itself, the *intermezzo*. What we have is a complex process of territorialisation and deterritorialisation, in which the stratum of a plant line intersects unexpectedly with the stratum of an animal line:

> The orchid deterritorialises by forming an image, a tracing of a wasp; but the wasp reterritorialises on that image. The wasp is nevertheless deterritorialised, becoming a piece in the orchid's reproductive apparatus. But it reterritorialises the orchid by transporting its pollen. Wasp and orchid, as heterogeneous elements, form a rhizome. It could be said that the orchid imitates the wasp, reproducing the image in a signifying fashion (mimesis, mimicry, lure, etc.). But this is true only on the level of the strata – a parallelism between two strata such that a plant organisation on one imitates an animal organisation on the other. At the same time, something else entirely is going on: not imitation at all but a capture of code, surplus value of code, an increase in valence, a veritable becoming, a becoming-wasp of the orchid and a becoming-orchid of the wasp. (ATP 10)

To the fixed reality of the strata, and of the relations of resemblance to which they lend themselves, Deleuze and Guattari oppose the reality of a complex process of rerritorialisation and deterritorialisation between heterogeneous (and thus not similar) elements. The reality in question is that of a becoming. Only becoming is true being. If there is an ontology here, it is, once again, that of transversal and heterogeneous connectivity, of the in-between or the 'and', and not that of substance, ground and roots. Similarly, and to turn now to a literary example borrowed from Proust's *Recherche*, it would seem that, in her sleep and before the eyes of her lover, Albertine resembles a plant and then a landscape. In fact, though, she is revealing lines and codes that emanate from the materiality of her sleeping body, which intersect and compose with those of a plant, and then, at a different, deeper state of sleep, with those of a certain landscape. We could go on: Daphne does not imitate a laurel tree, the crocodile does not imitate the trunk, and the chameleon does not imitate its surroundings. Rather, the two elements are caught in a reciprocal belonging, through which they become something else.

Another way of understanding the relation between the wasp and the orchid, and another way of asserting the rhizome as a new image of thought, is through the distinction between the map (*carte*) and the tracing (*calque*). Earlier on, and especially in relation to Kant's treatment of the *a priori* conditions of experience, we saw Deleuze criticise the method that consists in discovering the extraordinary domain of the transcendental, but only to trace it from the empirical form of the 'I think'. *A Thousand Plateaus* takes this critique one step further by opposing to the image of the map that of tracing, and, in the process, doing away with the very distinction between the transcendental and the empirical, between structure and genesis, or depth and surface. There is only one continent, which thoughts map not by applying a tracing paper on to its pre-defined contours, but by connecting with it, generating new assemblages, and revealing the thousand ways in which it can be read, drawn and redrawn:

> The map is open and connectable in all of its dimensions; it is detachable, reversible, susceptible to constant modification. It can be torn, reversed, adapted to any kind of mounting, reworked by any individual, group, or social formation. (ATP 12)

Thought draws a map of and with the world, or an aspect of it, in the same way that 'the orchid does not reproduce the tracing of the wasp, but forms a map of and with [*fait carte*] the wasp, in a rhizome' (ATP 12). Thought does not translate the world into an image; it connects with it. It is not a matter of interpretation and expertise, but of experimentation. Consider the example of little Hans, and its interpretation by Freud the Expert (Freud 1962b). Written in 1909, four years after *Three Essays on Sexuality*, it consists of a close analysis of Hans's phobia of horses, the genesis and unfolding of which his father, himself a great admirer of Freud, had meticulously recorded. In addition to the horse, there are other large animals mentioned, such as giraffes. Hans speaks not of a dream, but of a thought – immediately interpreted as a phantasy – regarding a large giraffe calling out for a smaller, 'crumpled' giraffe, on which Hans claims to have sat in his room. The father asks his son: 'What can it mean, a crumpled giraffe?' But he already knows the answer: the big giraffe is the father himself, or rather his 'big penis', and the crumpled giraffe his wife, or rather her 'genital organ' (Freud 1962b: 39). It is a phantasy of incest, doubled by a castration complex caused by guilt: Hans is afraid of horses because they might bite his finger, by which he means, of course, his own 'widdler' or *wiwimachen*. When he speaks of his fear of seeing the carts pulled by bus-horses fall down as a result of having to negotiate a sharp turn in front of the family house, his father asks him: 'Now, who is it that's the bus-horse? Me, you or Mummy?' (Freud 1962b: 58). What is the child to say, when his desire has been triangulated in that way? How can one ever escape this triangulation and surveillance of the unconscious? How can one extract desire from the grip of those coordinates? Like Kant, Freud discovers a new continent and a 'prodigious domain', that of the unconscious, but only to territorialise it, that is, to impose a fixed tracing on it, and thus force every assemblage of desire, every becoming, into its grid of intelligibility. Once the grid (or the triangle) is in place, the operation of interpretation must begin and never end. For in the face of any thought, any desire, the question will always be: who or what stands for me, Daddy or Mummy? As such, this grid is an instrument of power and control, and psychoanalysis a policing of the unconscious. This is how, extending their sustained critique of psychoanalysis in *Anti-Oedipus*, Deleuze and Guattari describe the fate of little Hans:

> They kept on BREAKING HIS RHIZOME and BLOTCHING HIS MAP, setting it straight for him, blocking his every way out, until he began to desire his own shame and guilt, until they had rooted shame and guilt in him, PHOBIA (they barred him from the rhizome of the building, then from the rhizome of the street, they rooted him in his parents' bed, they radicled him to his own body, they fixated him on Professor Freud). (ATP 14)

With his drawing and stories, Deleuze and Guattari suggest, Hans is attempting to produce his own lines of flight, to draw his own map, that is, to connect with the world outside – the animal world, the natural world, the urban world. In vain: 'once a rhizome has been obstructed, arborified, it's all over, no desire stirs; for it is always by rhizome that desire moves and produces' (ATP 14).

To the tracing of psychoanalysis, Deleuze and Guattari oppose the cartography of schizo-analysis, as represented, for example, by the educator and social worker Fernand Deligny, who joined the clinic of La Borde in the 1960s and worked closely with autistic children.[11] In the words of one commentator: 'He provided a space for severely autistic, mostly mute children to work through their difficulties by teaching them to make and spin wandering lines with no emphasis on reasons or meaning as such and to perform various open ended daily wanderings of "acting" and "doing"' (Burk 2013). The rhizomatic nature of those maps is striking.[12] The Deligny method, Deleuze and Guattari claim, consists in 'mapping the gestures and movements of an autistic child, combining several maps for the same child, for several different children' (ATP 14). No two maps are the same, not even for the same child. They are indeed wandering lines, lines of flight without origin and destination. As such, they are perhaps unliveable, or the unliveable within the liveable, namely, that which arborescent life cannot conceive or sustain.

Conclusion

Oedipus is a tracing, Chomsky's tree is a tracing, Kant's threefold synthesis is a tracing. They coordinate, triangulate and strangle the unconscious, language or thought. Later on in the book, Deleuze and Guattari oppose Cuvier's tracing and Geoffroy's mapping in the domain of biology,

Euclid's metric space and Riemann's topology in the domain of geometry, or the nomadic war machine (Genghis Khan) and the sedentary state apparatus (Odysseus). But does this not amount to another dualism, or a series of dualisms? It is true that, thus far, the series of distinctions we have come across, beginning with that of the tree and the rhizome, under which all the others are subsumed, seem to amount to something like an opposition. Yet taproots and rhizomes, tracings and maps, strata and lines of flight, processes of territorialisation and deterritorialisation (as we saw in relation to the wasp and the orchid) do not designate two separate worlds, or two parallel dimensions, but 'assemblages' in which two different structures are intertwined:

> Thus, there are very diverse map-tracing, rhizome-root assemblages, with variable coefficients of deterritorialisation. There exist tree or root-structures in rhizomes; conversely, a tree branch or root division may begin to burgeon into a rhizome ... A new rhizome may form in the heart of a tree, the hollow of a root, the crook of a branch. Or else it is a microscopic element of the root-tree, a radicle, that gets rhizome production going. (ATP 15)

This, in turn, means that the operation of thought consists not in applying universal concepts to a given situation, but in a pragmatics that will identify and exploit its rhizomatic resources. Pragmatic rhizomes can burgeon from within Chomsky's syntagmatic trees,[13] from the bureaucratic and commercial tree of the Austro-Hungarian empire (Kafka), or even from within an oedipalised or paranoid subject (President Schreber). Conversely, though, every rhizomatic *élan* carries its own risks of solidification, encrustation and impasse, whether in nature, art or politics. Each political or artistic group or enterprise, each rebellion or revolution will face the risk of its own collapse – its own bureaucratisation, massification, fascisation:

> Every undertaking of destratification (for example, going beyond the organism, plunging into a becoming) must therefore observe concrete rules of extreme caution: a too-sudden destratification may be suicidal, or turn cancerous. In other words, it will sometimes end in chaos, the void and destruction, and sometimes locks us back into the strata, which become more rigid still, losing their degrees of diversity, differentiation, and mobility. (ATP 503)

The plane of arborescence is always introducing depth, hierarchies, strata and roots. The rhizome, on the other hand, implies a generalised destratification of all of nature. It does away with depth, roots and strata by introducing lines (lines of flight) and diagonals. But one plane does not replace the other, whichever way we look at it. There never is just one plane. The two planes coexist, and are always engaged in undoing one another. The first has always and already begun to give way to the second. The plane of arborescence – or, as Deleuze and Guattari call it, of organisation – is constantly working away at the plane of consistency, always trying to stop or interrupt the movements of deterritorialisation, to restratify them, reconstitute roots and radicles in a dimension of depth. At the same time, however, rhizomes are constantly growing in the root systems, breaking down hierarchies and generating assemblages. *Faire rhizome, faire carte* is an ongoing task, and one about which we can never say that it has ended or reached its goal. To the thousand plateaus of the eponymous book, many more need to be added. To the extraordinary range of connections it establishes, and the vertiginous creation of concepts it displays, philosophy needs to respond by making and creating many more.

Notes

1. See also Deleuze 2004b: ch. 4.
2. See Butler 1872. For the Deleuze of *Difference and Repetition*, 'erewhon' indicates less a fictitious country and more the nomadic, impersonal and pre-individual Ideas that underpin and generate the world of phenomena. Ideas differ from the categories or concepts of representation, which are universal, and correspond to a sedentary distribution. But they also differ from the *hic et nunc* or *now here* of the diversity to which categories apply in representation. As such, 'they are complexes of space and time, no doubt transportable but on condition that they impose their own scenery' and thus become 'the objects of an essential encounter rather than of recognition' (Deleuze 1994: 285).
3. The epistemological concept of *récognition* translates the Kantian concept of *Rekognition* in the first edition of the Transcendental Deduction of the *Critique of Pure Reason* (Kant 1929: A103–110), and should be distinguished from the social and political concept of *Anerkennung*, also translated as recognition in English, but as *reconnaissance* in French.
4. Bachelard 1948: 300. Chapter 9 is devoted to 'The Root'. See also Bachelard 1943: ch. 10.
5. See Chomsky 1957. This book was followed by another and more ambitious work, *Aspects of the Theory of Syntax* (Chomsky 1965), in which Chomsky, in addition to syntax, recognised a phonological and a semantic component of grammar.
6. Pacotte 1936. See ATP 519.
7. See 'Plato and the Simulacrum' in Deleuze 1990b, and Deleuze 1994: 265.
8. Deleuze and Guattari 1976. In an article entitled 'The Fascism of the Potato', and under the pseudonym of Georges Peyrol, Badiou attacked and condemned the book as 'protofascist'. See Dosse 2010: 365–6.
9. From his early work on Bergson to *Difference and Repetition*, his 1970 lecture on the 'Theory of Multiplicities in Bergson' (http://www.webdeleuze.com) and *A Thousand Plateaus*, Deleuze's thought unfolds under the banner of a theory of multiplicities. For accounts of Deleuze's use of the concept of multiplicity, and its mathematical and physical roots, see Ansell Pearson 1999: 155–9; DeLanda 2002: 10–28; Smith 2012: 287–311; Somers-Hall 2012: 93–111.
10. This model, they claim, drawing on the works of R. E. Benveniste and G. J. Todaro on a type C virus that is known to have migrated from one species (the baboon) to another (certain domestic cats), and, in the process, carried over genetic information, allows one to think of 'aparallel' evolution as an example of rhizomatic processes.

11. Deligny 1975. The journal *Recherches* was created by Guattari in 1965. Deligny contributed to it on a regular basis between 1966 and 1976.
12. See Deligny 2013 for examples of his maps.
13. Drawing on Wunderlich 1972: 50ff., Deleuze and Guattari mention the attempts by Mac Cawley, Sadock and Wunderlich to introduce 'pragmatic properties' in Chomskyan trees.

Chapter 2

One or Several Wolves: The Wolf-Man's Pass-Words

Brent Adkins

In *Anti-Oedipus* Deleuze and Guattari settle accounts with psychoanalysis. Their critique is both subtle and devastating. On the one hand, they credit Freud with discovering the unrestrained productive capacity of the unconscious. On the other hand, they excoriate him (and psychoanalysis in general) for restricting the productive capacity of the unconscious to the theatre of Oedipal representation. At the same time, their argument is not that Oedipus is illusory. On the contrary, Oedipus has very real effects. 'We are not saying that Oedipus and castration do not amount to anything. We are oedipalised, we are castrated; psychoanalysis didn't invent these operations, to which it merely lends the new resources and methods of its genius' (Deleuze and Guattari 1983: 67).

Rather than simply being an invention of psychoanalysis, Deleuze and Guattari argue that Oedipus names a particular way that the productive capacity of the unconscious gets captured. On this point, they differ from psychoanalysis in two important respects: 1) Oedipus is not the seal of psychological health and well-being. It is precisely at this point that we can locate Deleuze and Guattari's opposition between schizophrenia and neurosis which subtends both *Anti-Oedipus* and *A Thousand Plateaus*. Neurosis is the tendency to capture the productive unconscious in the straitjacket of Oedipus. Schizophrenia is the tendency of the productive unconscious to escape that straitjacket. 2) Like all restrictions on the productive unconscious, Oedipus is a contingent, historical restriction and thus subject to genealogical analysis. Far from being the universal structure of the unconscious, Oedipus is the result of the particular confluence of capitalism and the privatisation of the family that occurs under capitalism (Deleuze and Guattari 1983: 51–271).

Given the thoroughness of their critique and the delimitation of psychoanalysis in *Anti-Oedipus*, it is somewhat surprising that they would return to the same ground (albeit briefly) in *A Thousand Plateaus*' 'One or Several Wolves'. Indeed in the 'Preface to the Italian Edition of *A Thousand Plateaus*', Deleuze claims that while *Anti-Oedipus* was intended to be ground-clearing work of critique, *A Thousand Plateaus* seeks to use that cleared ground in order to build something new (Deleuze 2006: 308–11). What, then, do Deleuze and Guattari gain by returning to psychoanalysis in this plateau? Or, perhaps better, what do they create on this cleared ground? A multiplicity. The turn to multiplicities is signalled in the very title of the plateau, which echoes a question that Deleuze poses in his 1966 study of Bergson: 'in what sense can one get beyond the ontological alternative of one/several?' (Deleuze 1991a: 49). A multiplicity is what lies beyond the ontological alternative of one or several.

How to avoid dialectics

In what sense, though, is multiplicity beyond the alternative of one or several? It is a testament to how deeply embedded this alternative is that it is natural to assume that 'multiplicity' is simply a synonym for 'several'. This is a tempting way to read this plateau. Freud was foolish to work so hard to reduce the several wolves of the Wolf-Man's dream to one, when it is clear that there are, *in fact*, several wolves. Six or seven, if one believes the initial account of the dream. Five, if one believes the Wolf-Man's drawing. To be sure, there is a criticism here of Freud's mania to reduce several wolves to one wolf. It is only by means of this reduction that the Wolf-Man's neurosis can be organised in accordance with Oedipal representation. 'There aren't several wolves. There is only one wolf, and it's your father.' However, the force of Deleuze and Guattari's criticism here is not simply to insist on the obvious several-ness of the wolves in the dream in opposition to Freud's reduction. The reason for this is that 'one' and 'several' are just two sides of the same coin.

If we return to Deleuze's *Bergsonism*, we can see why this is the case. For Bergson, one/several is a false choice constructed out of concepts that are too vague to be helpful, 'like baggy clothes' or 'a net so slack that everything slips through' (Deleuze 1991a: 49). It makes no difference whether one begins with 'one' or 'several'. Each is equally vacuous and generates its equally vacuous opposite. This vacuity is precisely why Freud is able to perform his reduction from several wolves to one. At this level of vagueness one can easily be shown to be several, and several can easily be shown to be one. Bergson's solution to the lack of precision generated by a dialectic of one/several is to eliminate it altogether in favour of 'multiplicities'.

Multiplicities are not generated through negation; they do not generate a higher unity through sublation; they do not have opposites. Deleuze and Guattari write,

> In *A Thousand Plateaus*, our commentary on the Wolf-Man ('one or several wolves') waves good-bye to psychoanalysis and tries to show how multiplicities cannot be reduced to the distinction between the conscious and the unconscious, nature and history, body and soul. Multiplicities are reality itself. They do not presuppose a unity of any kind, do not add up to a totality, and do not refer to a subject. Subjectivations, totalisations, and unifications are in fact processes which are produced and appear in multiplicities. (Deleuze 2006: 310)

There are two important things to note about this passage. The first is that all of the opposing pairs (conscious/unconscious, nature/history, body/soul) listed here are simply versions of the one/several dialectic. Depending on the philosopher, either side of the opposition can be 'one' to the other side's 'several'. The second thing to note is the way in which Deleuze and Guattari's 'problematic' view of philosophy comes to the fore here (Smith 2012: 290–9; Duffy 2013: 1–2).

In *A Thousand Plateaus* this comes up in numerous ways, but here we can illustrate it using the history of mathematics. In the history of mathematics Archimedes champions the problematic view of geometry, which is distinguished from the axiomatic view of geometry championed by Euclid (ATP 364–9). The distinction between the two can be summarised in the question, Which comes first, roundness or the circle? Is the rounded line a deficient circle, or is the circle a special instance of roundness? Euclidean geometry argues that the circle comes first. All other curvilinear shapes are deviations from the circle. Or, in the terms we have already used, rounded lines are the several to the circle's one. For Archimedes, there is only roundness. Roundness does not add up to anything, nor is it a fragment of some lost whole. There are only rounded lines interacting with other rounded lines. Sometimes these interacting rounded lines temporarily form into circles or other unities, but any unity (in the language of *Anti-Oedipus*) is a *residuum* of a process, not its goal or ground (Deleuze and Guattari 1983: 20).

The replacement of the one/several dialectic with a problematic rather than axiomatic methodology gets to the heart of Deleuze and Guattari's project in *A Thousand Plateaus* and the trajectory of Deleuze's career as a whole. The project is fundamentally creative, designed to create new concepts. The project is fundamentally experimental, testing and expanding on minority hypotheses abandoned and scattered throughout history. In *A Thousand Plateaus*, Deleuze and Guattari refer to this methodology as a 'perceptual semiotics' (ATP 23; Adkins 2015: 1–20). What they are trying to avoid here is an ontological dualism in which the world is divided up into two distinct kinds of things, rounded lines and circles, things subject to a dialectic and multiplicities, for example. Instead they acknowledge that since everything can be *seen as* rounded lines or *seen as* circles, *seen as* multiplicities or *seen as* subject to a dialectic, the fundamental question is, Which kind of seeing is more likely to result in the creation of something new? Deleuze and Guattari's contention is that seeing problematically, seeing roundness, seeing multiplicities is more likely to produce something new. In the case of the Wolf-Man, as we will see below, producing the new entails seeing the 'pass-words' underneath his 'order-words', which Deleuze and Guattari discuss in 'Postulates of Linguistics' (ATP 110).

Multiplicities

The tempting question to ask at this point is, What is a multiplicity? The problem with this question is that it supposes that we could define a set of essential characteristics that would allow us to distinguish multiplicities from non-multiplicities. But, as we have seen, Deleuze and Guattari's entire project is predicated on the perceptual semiotics of seeing everything as a multiplicity, so the kind of ontological dualism generated by questions of essence is eliminated from the outset. If everything is seen as a multiplicity, doesn't everything become 'the night in which all cows are black'? Aren't Deleuze and Guattari guilty of the charge that Alain Badiou levels against Deleuze that his philosophy produces a monotonous sameness (Badiou 2000: 14–18)? This charge, however, confuses ontology and epistemology. The ontology of all of Deleuze's work (with or without Guattari) is univocal. That is, regardless of the object one is talking about, it *exists* in exactly the same way as any other object. All multiplicities *are* in the same way. However, it does not follow from the univocity of being that everything is indifferently the same. In fact, the univocity of being is precisely that which makes possible the distinction among different multiplicities. Only insofar as multiplicities exist in the same way can they also be said to actually differ from one another. In contrast to this, an equivocal view of being can never affirm real difference. It can only produce analogical difference. That is, everything will both resemble and fail to resemble everything else to a certain degree, but whether things *actually* differ becomes unknowable (Deleuze 1990b: 179–80; Adkins and Hinlicky 2013: 68–72; Widder 2001).

Supposing, then, for the sake of experiment that there are only multiplicities and that they all exist in the same way, how can we distinguish among them without denying the univocity of being? Deleuze answers this question by noting that since the invention of the term 'multiplicity' by the mathematician Bernhard Riemann, various thinkers (including Bergson and Russell) have posited two kinds of multiplicities. Riemann posited discrete and continuous multiplicities, Bergson posited extended and durational multiplicities, and Russell posited qualitative and quantitative multiplicities (ATP 32–3, 484; Deleuze 1991a: 38–43; Duffy 2013: 89–115). In this context, Deleuze and Guattari write,

> We are doing approximately the same thing when we distinguish between arborescent multiplicities and rhizomatic multiplicities . . . On the one hand, multiplicities that are extensive, divisible, and molar; unifiable, totalisable, organisable; conscious or preconscious – and on the other hand, libidinal, unconscious, molecular, intensive multiplicities composed of particles that do not divide without changing in nature . . . The elements of this second kind of multiplicity are particles . . . their quantities are intensities, differences in intensity. (ATP 33)

The obvious problem here is that dividing multiplicities into two types seems to reinstall the ontological dualism that multiplicity was designed to overcome in the first place. Deleuze and Guattari are aware of this difficulty and say as much: 'There is no question, however, of establishing a dualist opposition between the two types of multiplicities . . . that would be no better than the dualism between the One and the [several]' (ATP 34). Even if they are explicit about wanting to avoid a dualism of multiplicities, how do they actually avoid it? As we saw above in our discussion of perceptual semiotics, the key here is to avoid assuming an exclusive disjunction between intensive and extensive multiplicities. The goal is not to group everything into one category or the other. Rather, I think it is much more helpful to think about the distinction between multiplicities as opposed tendencies on an ontologically univocal continuum. That is, any given assemblage will be some heterogeneous ratio of multiplicities with tendencies towards both the intensive and the extensive, towards stasis and change, the rhizomatic and the arborescent. There are no pure rhizomes any more than there are pure trees. There are only mixtures and tendencies. 'There are only multiplicities of multiplicities forming a single *assemblage*, operating in the same *assemblage* . . . Trees have rhizome lines, and the rhizome points of arborescence' (ATP 34). That is, even in assemblages where the tendency towards arborescence dominates, rhizomatic tendencies will remain.

How to avoid masses

If we suppose, then, that *A Thousand Plateaus* is a metaphysics of multiplicities, how does that inform Deleuze and Guattari's analysis in 'One or

Several Wolves'? Ultimately, their critique of Freud hinges on a distinction between two possible tendencies of a multiplicity: mass and pack. These tendencies in turn compose assemblages. The distinction between mass and pack is drawn from Elias Canetti's *Crowds and Power*, but as with most of their sources Deleuze and Guattari transform Canetti here, as well. For Canetti, the pack is the more primordial kind of group and the mass (or crowd) is a later development (Canetti 1978: 93). For Deleuze and Guattari, though, both are equiprimordial. There are no masses without packs and no packs without masses. Or, better, for any given assemblage there will be tendencies towards mass and tendencies towards pack. Freud's problem is not that he sees tendencies towards mass (Oedipus, the father, extensive, representational, arborescent, etc.) but that he sees *only* masses. Even when he is presented with a pack tendency (dreams, intensive, rhizomatic, etc.), he is determined to turn it into a mass. Once Freud converts the pack into a mass he declares the Wolf-Man cured. Deleuze and Guattari argue that one can only see what is new in the Wolf-Man insofar as one sees both tendencies. 'In the case of the Wolf-Man, it is impossible to separate the becoming-wolf of his dream from the military and religious organisation of his obsessions . . . There are not two multiplicities or two machines; one and the same machinic assemblage produces and distributes the whole . . .' (ATP 34; Holland 2013: 93–6).

The complexity of the Wolf-Man's assemblage becomes clear in 1926, twelve years after he is declared 'cured' by Freud. After becoming increasingly obsessed with a bump on his nose, he returns to analysis with one of Freud's students, Ruth Mack Brunswick. The Wolf-Man still dreams of wolves, but the dream has changed. This time the Wolf-Man stands in the street next to a wall with a closed door, but 'behind the wall is a pack of grey wolves, crowding toward the door and rushing up and down' (Gardiner 1971: 289). For Brunswick, this new dream is clearly connected to the Bolshevik revolution in the Wolf-Man's native country. What she cannot resist doing, however, is reducing the expression of this social-political assemblage to an individual Oedipal drama, castration anxiety. Abraham and Torok do much the same thing in their extended analysis of the Wolf-Man (Abraham and Torok 1986: 12). Behind everything psychoanalysis always finds the Wolf-Man's father. It is deaf to all statements except Oedipal statements.

What is the alternative, though? Should we see the Wolf-Man's dreams as purely social rather than libidinal? Is the solution to subsume Freud into Marx? No, the social/libidinal opposition is simply another version of the dialectic of the one/several. The only difference between Freud and Marx on this score is that Freud takes the libidinal to be one and the social to be the diffuse expression of it, while Marx takes the social to be one and the libidinal to be the diffuse expression of it. Thus, in Deleuze and Guattari's terms Marx and Freud are still only dealing in molar masses, while ignoring or reducing molecular packs. They offer three things to keep in mind at all times:

1. that a social machine or an organised mass has a molecular unconscious that marks not only its tendency to decompose but also the current components of its very operation and organisation;
2. that any individual caught up in a mass has his/her own pack unconscious, which does not necessarily resemble the packs of the mass to which that individual belongs;
3. that an individual or mass will live out in its unconscious the masses and packs of another mass or another individual. (ATP 35)

Again, Deleuze and Guattari emphasise that within a metaphysics of multiplicities every assemblage will have tendencies towards both the intensive and the extensive, towards both packs and masses. The multiplicities enter into relations of continuous variability. Crucially, even though the multiplicities are in relation to one another, the relation is not one of resemblance or representation. Thinking that the pack resembles or represents the mass with which it is related is the first step in reducing the pack to the mass, and a multiplicity to the dialectic of the one/several.

How to avoid selecting Oedipal statements

If the logic of resemblance and representation does not account for the relation among multiplicities, what do Deleuze and Guattari propose to take its place? As we will see, the short answer is a distinction between 'content' and 'expression'. Importantly, however, the content/expression distinction does not correspond to the mass/pack distinction. In order to fully explicate this, I would like to look briefly at some material from 'The Geology of Morals' and 'Postulates of Linguistics' plateaus, in particular, as well as a few others. I am interested in the content/expression distinction from 'The Geology of Morals' plateau, and the elaboration of that distinction in terms of a 'machinic assemblage' and a 'collective assemblage of enunciation' from 'Postulates of Linguistics'. Ultimately, this material will give us a better handle on the concluding claim of 'One or Several Wolves':

> We are not just criticising psychoanalysis for having selected Oedipal statements exclusively. For such statements are to a certain extent part of a

> machinic assemblage, for which they could serve as correctional indexes, as in a calculation of errors. We are criticising psychoanalysis for having used Oedipal enunciation to make patients believe they would produce individual, personal statements, and would finally speak in their own name. The trap was set from the start: never will the Wolf-Man speak . . . He could have spoken in his own name only if the machinic assemblage that was producing particular statements in him had been brought to light. (ATP 38)

In brief, the criticism centres on the fact that under psychoanalysis the Wolf-Man was never allowed to speak in his own name. What exactly, though, does speaking in one's own name entail? For Deleuze and Guattari, it entails bringing to light 'the machinic assemblage that was producing particular statements'. In order to understand how machinic assemblages produce statements we need to look briefly at the problem of stratification in 'The Geology of Morals'. Stratification is one of the ways that Deleuze and Guattari talk about the tendency of assemblages towards the extensive, the arborescent, the molar, organisation. Of course, things are stratified in multiple ways. Deleuze and Guattari discuss physical, organic and linguistic strata. Furthermore, every stratum articulates itself into two irreducible components, content and expression. What distinguishes one type of stratum from another is the nature of the distinction between content and expression.

Deleuze and Guattari borrow the content/expression distinction from the Danish linguist Louis Hjelmslev, whose express purpose in positing it was to replace the form/content distinction, though they reject his thoroughgoing structuralism (Genosko 1994: 58). Deleuze and Guattari are sympathetic to this move since the form/content distinction typically reproduces the dialectic of the one/several. How does the content/expression distinction avoid this same problem? If it were a matter of simply replacing the terms, nothing would be gained. However, content and expression are themselves complex. Every content has both a substance and a form, and every expression has both a substance and a form. We can schematise the relation as shown in Diagram 1.

In order to illustrate this relation, let's take sandstone as an example. A

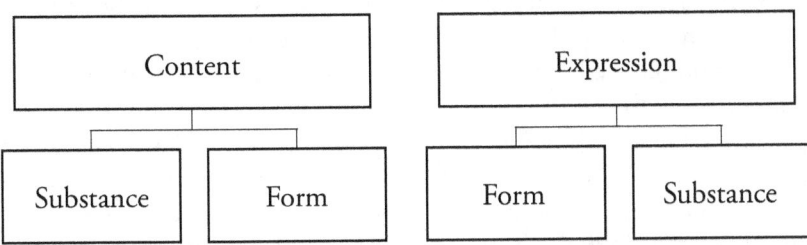

Diagram 1 The content–expression distinction

river flows swiftly enough to 'select' and carry material. The movement of the water also 'sorts' the material into bands of roughly the same size. The 'selection' process is the substance of content, and the 'sorting' process is the form of content. The movement from sediment to sedimentary rock fixes these sorted materials into an assemblage with extensive relations among its parts. The hardening of sediment into sedimentary rock is the form of expression, while the relation of the layers to one another and the size of the deposit are the substance of expression. Deleuze and Guattari are adamant that while the distinction between substance and form is a merely modal difference, the distinction between content and expression is a real difference, albeit a relative one. Thus, for example, a mason could use this same sandstone to build a wall. In this case the sandstone becomes the content and the wall the expression. Below we will flesh out these terms in relation to the Wolf-Man's assemblage, what I will call the '*fin-de-siècle* European assemblage'.

Since Deleuze and Guattari's concern in 'One or Several Wolves' is to let the Wolf-Man speak in his own name, we will restrict ourselves to the linguistic stratum. While much could be said (and will be said in later chapters), for our purposes here we can note several points. First, it would be a mistake to assume that the linguistic stratum concerns language in isolation. Secondly, it would be a mistake to assume that language is composed of signifiers related to signifieds, or of words related to things. Thirdly, Deleuze and Guattari replace talk of signifiers with an analysis of signs. What sets signs apart from signifiers is that 'signs cannot be equated with language in general but are defined by regimes of statements that are so many real usages or functions of language . . . Signs are not signs of a thing; they are signs of deterritorialisation and reterritorialisation . . .' (ATP 67). At this point it is important to recall how important the word/thing relation is for Freud in his distinction between neurotics and psychotics. It is taking words for things that marks the psychotic as such. The Wolf-Man, although Freud considers him neurotic, cannot speak in his own name until the word/thing distinction is overcome. Thus, for Deleuze and Guattari, the question is not how the word 'wolf' relates to the Wolf-Man's father, or how a 'pack of wolves' signifies the Bolsheviks, but the interrelation of 'two constantly intersecting multiplicities, "discursive multiplicities" of expression and "non-discursive multiplicities" of content' (ATP 67).

On the linguistic stratum, assemblages of content and assemblages of expression interact with one another but are independent of one another. They do not relate to one another as molecular and molar (though this is the case on the physical stratum). They do not relate to one another as signified and signifier. They do not relate to one another as content and form.

They do not relate to one another as base and superstructure. Nor do they relate to one another as matter and mind (ATP 67–9). How exactly, then, can we think the relation between content and expression on the linguistic stratum, and how does this help us to allow the Wolf-Man to speak?

Deleuze and Guattari are explicit that the distinction between content and expression on the linguistic stratum is essential, or categorical, or attributional, which is the same as saying that one is not the cause of the other and that each can be thought independently, even though they reciprocally interact with one another 'in a state of unstable equilibrium or reciprocal presupposition' (ATP 67). They expand on the complex nature of assemblages, especially with regard to the linguistic stratum, in 'Postulates of Linguistics':

> We may draw some general conclusions on the nature of Assemblages from this. On a first, horizontal, axis, an assemblage comprises two segments, one of content, the other of expression. On the one hand it is a *machinic assemblage* of bodies, of actions and passions, an intermingling of bodies reacting to one another; on the other hand it is a *collective assemblage of enunciation*, of acts and statements, of incorporeal transformations attributed to bodies. (ATP 88)

The content of an assemblage is a machinic assemblage of bodies, and the expression of an assemblage is a collective assemblage of enunciation, at least for assemblages that intersect with the linguistic stratum. The distinction between content and expression, however, only gives us part of the picture. As we have seen, both content and expression have a form and a substance. In order to illustrate how this works for assemblages of this type, Deleuze and Guattari turn to what they call the 'feudal assemblage'. The content of this assemblage, its machinic assemblage of bodies, would include a whole host of 'interminglings of bodies defining feudalism' (ATP 89). This would include, but obviously not be limited to, the ways in which the bodies of the king, knight and serf differ and overlap. This would include issues such as food production and distribution. What can be grown? What can be eaten? How does warfare change when the stirrup is added to the knight-horse assemblage? All of these questions concern the *form of content* for the feudal assemblage. The *form of expression* for the feudal assemblage concerns not the intermingling of bodies but the way in which regimes of signs can effect 'incorporeal transformations' in the bodies of the feudal assemblage. To take a very simple example, when the king 'knights' a subject through a series of highly prescribed motions and statements (not just words, not just language), the body of the subject is transformed incorporeally. That is, the body remains the same as body, but by means of this transformation ('translation') it begins to intermingle with new bodies and intermingles differently with old bodies.

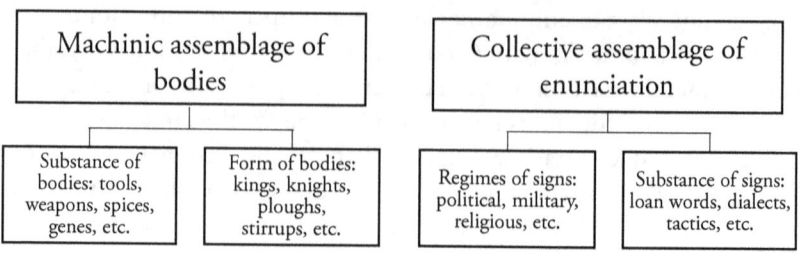

Diagram 2 The feudal assemblage

The substance of both content and expression, as we saw above, concerns the selection of material or variables. This selection constitutes the 'vertical axis' of an assemblage and concerns the process of deterritorialisation and reterritorialisation. We can see this very clearly if we think about the ways in which the feudal machine interacted with Islam in the Crusades. On the side of content, new materials were encountered, such as Damascus steel, that was reterritorialised into the feudal assemblage and changed it. On the side of expression, encounters with Islamic theology and battle tactics, for example, deterritorialised expression, which was then reterritorialised around new theological arguments and loan words such as 'kismet'. We can now use this example to give some content to our schematic representation, as in Diagram 2.

While the model proposed by Deleuze and Guattari has the great advantage of highlighting the relational complexity among multiplicities, let us return to the relation between words and things to see where that now stands. 'There is a primacy of the machinic assemblages of bodies over tools and goods, a primacy of the collective assemblage of enunciation over language and words' (ATP 90). A whole critique of linguistics is contained in this rich quote, but for our purposes we need to examine the impact it has on psychoanalysis.

Deleuze and Guattari's model would require that psychoanalysis change in two ways with regard to the word/thing relation. First, the model short-circuits the reduction of the word/thing relation to a causal signifier/signified relation. There are, in fact, two reductions here. The first reduction is the extraction of words from the collective assemblage of enunciation and things from the machinic assemblage of bodies. The second reduction is the articulation of a system of representation in which words signify things. Thus, psychoanalysis functions by asking the patient to speak and then looking for the things that those words signify. The second change that Deleuze and Guattari's model would require of psychoanalysis with regard to language is that the unifying function of the word in psychoanalysis would have to be replaced with intensive multiplicities.

Eliminating the causal relation between word and thing and the unifying function of the word causes two insurmountable difficulties for psychoanalysis, though. The first is that psychoanalysis has already decided what the words signify – Oedipus, always Oedipus. The second, and Freud clearly recognises and is disturbed by this possibility, is that psychoanalysis only functions when words refer to things. This is the case with neurotics whose words betray libidinal investments in things. In the case of psychotics, however, they do not hold the word/thing relation as sacrosanct. They are just as likely to connect words with other words. At this point analysis breaks down because the analyst has no way to uncover the libidinal investments at play. In his essay 'The Unconscious', written shortly after declaring the Wolf-Man 'cured', Freud notes with some consternation that the psychotic's tendency to connect words with other words (rather than things) bears an uncomfortable similarity to the psychoanalytic practice of free association (Freud 1962c: 204).

We are now in a position to begin making sense of Deleuze and Guattari's summary remarks about the problem with psychoanalysis. The problem is not simply that psychoanalysis only selects Oedipal statements. Oedipal statements are undoubtedly a real and powerful part of the collective assemblage of enunciation. They can unquestionably produce incorporeal transformations on the bodies of a machinic assemblage. This is not only the case for patients, but for culture. 'Of course there are Oedipal statements ... you can always do it, you can't lose, it works every time, even if you understand nothing' (ATP 37). Oedipal statements work precisely because they function according to a dialectic of one/several, 'like baggy clothes' or 'a net so slack that everything slips through' (Deleuze 1991a: 44–5). Deleuze and Guattari are much more interested in what escapes than what fits, though.

How to avoid individual statements

Beyond selecting only Oedipal statements, the further difficulty with psychoanalysis is making 'patients believe they would produce individual, personal statements, and would finally speak in their own name' (ATP 38). There are, in fact, two difficulties here. The first is the production of individual, personal statements. The second is the ability to speak in one's own name. The production of individual, personal statements is one way to think about the ultimate goal of psychoanalysis. On the first point, Deleuze and Guattari are explicit. 'There are no individual statements, only statement-producing machinic assemblages' (ATP 36). One could easily draw affinities here with Wittgenstein's arguments against private languages or even Heidegger's claim, that 'Language is the house of Being' (Wittgenstein 1986: 92–3; Heidegger 1993: 217).

For our purposes here, though, we can simply return to the metaphysics of multiplicities. What this precludes at the outset is a self-defining subject that might serve as a ground and produce its own statements. Deleuze and Guattari are not claiming that there are no subjects, only that subjects are produced by the interaction of multiplicities in an assemblage (ATP 119–34). In precisely the same way statements are not the product of subjects or even language (both of which are typically terms in a dialectic of one/several) but are themselves products of interacting multiplicities. 'We can no longer even speak of distinct machines, only of types of interpenetrating multiplicities that at any given moment form a single machinic assemblage . . . Each of us is caught up in an assemblage, and we reproduce its statements . . .' (ATP 36). A moment's reflection shows the vast array of factors that affect what we say. I am obviously writing in a determinate language, English, but I am also writing in an American variant of English (though this variation may be obscured by my UK editors and press). This variant is affected by a whole host of social, economic, educational and regional factors. These variants reciprocally affect one another, as well. The fact that I'm writing on a computer for publication instead of speaking to a class or using social media is at play here. The very existence of social media is part of this assemblage. The assemblage produces statements, which I reproduce. These statements are neither individual nor personal.

The second difficulty with psychoanalysis concerns the possibility of speaking in one's own name. Not surprisingly Deleuze and Guattari think quite differently about names compared to linguistics in general and psychoanalysis in particular. On their reading, psychoanalysis treats the name as a noun that unifies the set of things that it refers to.

> It will be noted that names are taken in their *extensive* usage, in other words, function as common nouns ensuring the unification of an aggregate they subsume. The proper name can be nothing more than an extreme case of the common noun, containing its already domesticated multiplicity within itself and linking it to a being or object posited as unique. This jeopardises, on the side of words and things both, the relation of the proper name as an *intensity* to the multiplicity it instantaneously apprehends. (ATP 27–8)

In this instance the name becomes the 'one' to its referents' 'several'. In order to articulate the relation in this way, both the name and its referents must be treated as discrete, as molar, as extensive. This psychoanalytic understanding of the name leads directly to the false promise that through analysis one might speak in one's own name. Freud's reasoning here is straightforward. The Wolf-Man cannot speak in his own name because he doesn't understand all the objects that his name contains, especially the primal scene. These misunderstood objects manifest themselves in neurotic symptoms, such as obsessional attachment to religious objects during a bedtime ritual (Freud 1962a: 61–71; Gardiner 1971: 204). Notice how Freud talks about the Wolf-Man's dream early in his analysis:

> We also concluded from the first incomplete analysis of the dream that the wolf may have been a father-surrogate; so that, in that case, this first anxiety-dream would have brought to light the fear of his father which from that time forward was to dominate his life. This conclusion, indeed, was in itself not yet binding. But if we put together as the result of the provisional analysis what can be derived from the material produced by the dreamer, we then find before us for reconstruction some such fragments as these:
> A real occurrence – dating from a very early period – looking – immobility – sexual problems – castration – his father – something terrible. (Freud 1962a: XVII, 34; Gardiner 1971: 179)

The first thing to note is how casually Freud converts the Wolf-Man's dream about a pack of wolves to a dream about 'the' wolf. Thus, we see the move from the molecular, intensive pack to the molar, extensive wolf. This movement is not in itself sufficient. An explanation is required for why the Wolf-Man is dreaming about wolves in the first place. The answer is that he is not really dreaming about wolves; he is dreaming about his father and his fear of castration. Now the proper name can unify all the objects that belong to it. The dream refers to a 'real occurrence'. Once the Wolf-Man sees this, he can be cured.

For Deleuze and Guattari, though, names don't function this way at all. Names are intensive, not extensive. In order to understand what this means, let's look at a discussion of names from the 'Becoming-Intense . . .' plateau.

> The proper name does not indicate a subject; nor does a noun take on the value of a proper name as a function of a form or a species. The proper name fundamentally designates something that is of the order of the event, of becoming or of the haecceity. It is the military men and meteorologists who hold the secret of proper names, when they give them to a strategic operation or a hurricane. (ATP 264)

Deleuze and Guattari reiterate here that proper names are not species under which particulars can be organised and subsumed. Rather, proper names designate events, haecceities or becomings. Without unpacking all of these terms, suffice it to say that all of these are intensive phenomena. This becomes clear when we look at the examples provided, the military penchant for naming operations and the meteorological custom of naming hurricanes. Why is it helpful to think about a hurricane as an intensive event rather than a discrete object, though? To begin with, a hurricane marks the confluence of numerous intensive gradients, air temperature, pressure and humidity, combined with water temperature and wind speed. It is only when all of these cross a certain threshold that the storm achieves the consistency of a hurricane. Of course, a hurricane-event doesn't happen in a vacuum. Its approach results in the marshalling of a wide array of resources, military, government, media, personal, etc., in preparation. Furthermore, when and where the hurricane makes landfall produces effects indefinitely into the future. The hurricane is not a thing but an event. Nevertheless, the full panoply of these radiating effects can be 'instantaneously apprehended' in the hurricane's proper name. Andrew, Hugo and Katrina are not subjects, nor are they nouns that unify discrete objects. They are the proper names of unique events (Protevi 2009: 163–83).

Deleuze and Guattari's contention is that 'Wolf-Man' is a proper name in precisely the same sense that Andrew, Hugo and Katrina are proper names. They are all intensive rather than extensive. 'The Wolf-Man, a true proper name, an intimate first name linked to becomings, infinitives, and intensities of a multiplied and depersonalised individual' (ATP 37–8). For Freud, proper names function extensively, by reducing multiplicities, which are always seen as a 'several' to the proper name's 'one'. Thinking the proper name in this way, though, actually precluded the Wolf-Man from speaking in his own name. 'He could have spoken in his own name only if the machinic assemblage that was producing particular statements in him had been brought to light' (ATP 38).

The *fin-de-siècle* European assemblage

Let us take some time to unpack the assemblage that was producing particular statements in the Wolf-Man. Let's call it the '*fin-de-siècle* European assemblage'. On the content side of the assemblage there are a whole host of intermingling bodies, both human and non-human. These interminglings are not random, however. They are given form, regulated. The regulation of bodies has political dimensions – the Austro-Hungarian Empire and its relation to Russia. The First World War is only a few years away. There is also a medical regulation of bodies. In his memoirs the Wolf-Man recounts an encounter with a psychiatrist in Odessa. The Wolf-Man had already undergone various treatments for bouts of depression, including hypnosis and an extended stay at a sanatorium in Munich to no effect.

> After Dr. D. had listened patiently to my complaints, he told me I had no reason to despair, for until now I had been going about treatment in the wrong way. He told me that emotional conflicts and suffering are cured neither by a long stay in a sanatorium nor by the physical therapy practiced

there, such as baths, massages, and so forth. This was the first time I had ever heard such a thing from the mouth of a medical specialist, and it made a great impression on me because I, myself, through my own experience, had come to the same conclusion. (Gardiner 1971: 79)

Here we see the collision between two ways of medically regulating bodies that ultimately leads to the Wolf-Man meeting Freud. By this time the Wolf-Man has also fallen in love with the woman he will eventually marry, Therese. Love and marriage are two quite distinct ways of regulating bodies. The Wolf-Man must overcome his mother's disapproval as well as political turmoil in order to bring Therese to Russia during the First World War. Class, money and property also regulate bodies. The Wolf-Man has been raised as an upper-class Russian but loses everything in the Bolshevik revolution. What about wolves? From the Middle Ages through the Early Modern period, wolves were systematically eliminated in most of Europe. The major exception is Russia, which never eliminated or even isolated its wolf populations (Graves 2007). The *New York Times* even reported on 29 July 1917 that wolf attacks became so bad at one point on the Russian front that a temporary truce was negotiated so that the wolves could be dealt with first. The intermingling of wolves, people and livestock would necessarily have been regulated in Russia in a way that it could not have been regulated in the rest of Europe.

Not surprisingly, the collective assemblage of enunciation is equally complex. Here, though, we have sets of statements rather than intermingling bodies, or discursive multiplicities rather than non-discursive multiplicities (ATP 69). Discursive multiplicities have a form, or are regulated, in the same way that non-discursive multiplicities are regulated. Some of the regulated sets of statements that compose the expression of the *fin-de-siècle* European assemblage include competing psychiatric discourses, the discourse of the sanatorium and the new psychoanalytic discourse. A new political discourse that refigures the relations between 'the state', 'the worker', 'the means of production' and 'revolution' is on the rise. At the same time a discourse about 'the nation', 'blood' and 'purity' is taking hold in other quarters. Other sets of statements are on the verge of disappearing. 'I am a citizen of the Austro-Hungarian Empire' and all of the statements commensurate with it will no longer make sense after the First World War. Of course, there are Oedipal statements. Freud does not invent Oedipal statements. He simply arranges analytic discourse such that all other statements, whether literary, political, social or oneiric, are ultimately revealed to be simply Oedipal statements.

The interminglings of bodies and sets of statements are the *form* of content and the *form* of expression, respectively. The *substance* of content and the *substance* of expression, as we have seen, are the variables that are selected by a given assemblage. These variables always exist somewhere on a continuum between deterritorialisation and reterritorialisation, and the degree of deterritorialisation among these variables makes the reciprocal interaction between content and expression possible. 'In short, the way an expression relates to content is not by uncovering or representing it. Rather, forms of expression and forms of content communicate through a conjunction of their quanta of relative deterritorialisation, each intervening, operating on the other' (ATP 88).

In order to illustrate this idea, let us look at the body of a labourer and the sign 'worker'. The rise of capitalism requires deterritorialised bodies, bodies that can leave ancestral homelands – regulated by family relations and connection to the land – for factories in urban centres. Prior to leaving for the big city, discourse about the labourer would not be organised around a set of statements about 'workers', 'owners', 'wages' or 'factories'. Rather, it would be organised around a set of statements that included words such as 'vocation', 'obligation' and 'market day'. When the body of the labourer becomes deterritorialised from its autochthonic origins and reterritorialised in a capitalist economy, the body is regulated in a new way. Foucault's *Discipline and Punish* is a compendium of these new corporeal regulations, as Deleuze and Guattari make explicit (ATP 66–7). At the same time, two discourses began to resonate with one another, physics and sociology. Both took up the concept of 'work' in seemingly different registers, but the result was that the 'wage regime had as its correlate a mechanics of force. Physics had never been more social, for in both cases it was a question of defining the constant mean value of a force of lift and pull exerted in the most uniform way possible by a standard-man' (ATP 490). Thus, through deterritorialisation and reterritorialisation the regulation of the body of the labourer is mutually implicated in sets of statements concerning 'work' and 'value'. With this rough sketch in place we can schematise the assemblage 'producing particular statements' in the Wolf-Man, as in Diagram 3.

Psychoanalysis works by using Oedipal statements to 'overcode' or 'translate' the interminglings of bodies. This is precisely what Freud does

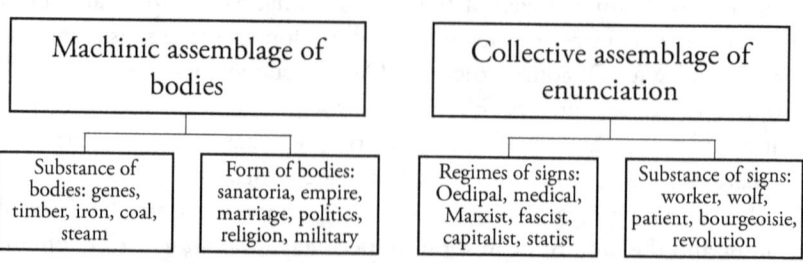

Diagram 3 The *fin-de-siècle* European assemblage

with the Wolf-Man's dream and the Wolf-Man himself. As a result, the Wolf-Man does not speak in his own name; he only reproduces the Oedipal translation. In contrast to this, Deleuze and Guattari are proposing that the Wolf-Man can only speak in his own name under two conditions: 1) his name is understood intensively; 2) the intensities apprehended by his name traverse one or more assemblages.

Conclusion – the Wolf-Man's pass-words

What we might create, and what we might give space for the Wolf-Man to create will lie on the deterritorialising edge between the content and expression of the *fin-de-siècle* European assemblage. Along this edge we find not 'the' wolf but a wolf pack, which is a selection of bodies tending towards deterritorialisation. We find a pack that moves in and constitutes smooth spaces, a pack that is a selection of intensities. At the edge of expression, we find a series of words, 'wolf', 'hole', 'wasp', that Freud is determined to understand as 'order-words'. He understands these words as indicative of Oedipal stratification and all his questions serve to lead the Wolf-Man back here so that his words might be reterritorialised and overcoded. This is the same impetus that drives Freud to see the pack as an instance of the dialectic of one/several instead of a multiplicity. Order-words mark the tendency towards the extensive, the arborescent, the molar, organisation. As we have seen, though, there is another way of seeing these words, a perceptual semiotics that recasts these order-words. Deleuze and Guattari call these recast order-words 'pass-words'.

> There are pass-words beneath order-words. Words that pass, words that are components of passage, whereas order-words mark stoppages or organised, stratified compositions. A single thing or word undoubtedly has this twofold nature: it is necessary to extract one from the other – to transform the compositions of order into components of passage. (ATP 110)

The words the Wolf-Man selects are not indications of castration anxiety or even the abuse of his sister by the father (Abraham and Torok 1986). Rather, the words he selects are intensive lines of flight, becomings that escape the organisations and stratifications of his assemblage. These words show the possibility of creating something new. These intensities are apprehended by the name Wolf-Man. These words, understood as pass-words, are what the Wolf-Man says in his own name.

Chapter 3

Who the Earth Thinks It Is

Ronald Bogue

The title of the third plateau is not just a joke. If Nietzsche's *Genealogy of Morals* traces the lineage of forces that have transformed an active, affirmative evaluation of good and bad into a reactive, negative judgement of good and evil, Deleuze and Guattari's 'Geology of Morals' offers a terrestrial account of the processes of stratification that eventuate in the human strictures that enforce the judgment of God. The 'Geology of Morals', in this sense, is an extension of the Nietzschean critique of conventional morality. Nor is the plateau's subtitle insignificant. 'Who Does the Earth Think It Is?' (*pour qui elle se prend, la terre?*) has as its counterpart a parenthetical remark later in the plateau: 'Who does man think he is?' (*pour qui il se prend, l'homme?*) (ATP 63). The idiom *se prendre pour* is used to accuse someone of pretentious self-importance, such that *pour qui tu te prend?*, 'Who do you think you are?', might also be rendered as 'What makes you so special?' *Pour qui elle se prend* is comic when addressed to the geological earth, at least if one regards the planet as the third, inert rock from the sun. But the phrase is very serious when addressed to human beings, especially as we move further into the anthropocene epoch and suffer the consequences of our species' arrogance. A central purpose of Plateau Three, then, is to put humans in their place, in the sense of both countering our collective pride and positioning us in relation to other earthly entities. Once so positioned, humans may take seriously the question posed to the earth and perhaps discern in its response the hints of what Manuel DeLanda calls 'the wisdom of the rocks' (DeLanda 1992: 160); not a geology of morals, but a geology of ethics, or terrestrial ethology. My focus in examining the geology of morals and terrestrial ethology will be on the role of language in the plateau, first as terminological point of departure, and eventually as object of analysis. In between, I will identify the problem addressed in the plateau, sketch the complex workings of the model of stratification, and then consider the position of the domain of the human in relation to those of the inorganic and the organic.[1]

The problem

In both volumes of *Capitalism and Schizophrenia*, Deleuze and Guattari advocate a materialism of a special sort. In *Anti-Oedipus* they review at length the traditional opposition of mechanism and vitalism, arguing that their concept of machinic desiring production escapes the limitations of that opposition (Deleuze and Guattari 1983: 283–90). In *A Thousand Plateaus*, they make essentially the same point, saying that their approach to bodies in terms of differential speeds and affective intensities 'is not animism, any more than it is mechanism; rather it is universal machinism' (ATP 256). Yet they also state that there 'is a life proper to matter, a vital state of matter as such, a material vitalism' (ATP 411). That life is 'inorganic, germinal and intensive' (ATP 499), 'anorganic' (ATP 503), 'nonorganic' (ATP 507).[2] Matter is not inert stuff, but 'matter-movement . . . matter-energy . . . matter-flow . . . matter in variation' (ATP 407), matter that has both dynamic properties of self-differentiation and self-organisation and capacities of mutation, transformation and creativity. The life immanent to all matter, whether inorganic, organic, natural or artificial, is that of the machinic processes of self-differentiation, self-organisation, de-differentiation, de-organisation, reconfiguration and creation at work in the morphogenesis and metamorphosis of everything in the world.

Deleuze and Guattari open Plateau Three by saying that 'the Earth . . . is permeated by unformed, unstable matters, by flows in all directions, by free intensities or nomadic singularities, by mad or transitory particles' (ATP 40). This is the earth as matter-movement, matter-energy and matter-flow, imbued with an anorganic life, but 'unformed' and 'unstable'. The problem Deleuze and Guattari address in this plateau is how such unformed matter becomes organised and stabilised in the relatively fixed forms of inorganic and organic entities, as well as the homeostatic configurations of their relations. Deleuze and Guattari identify the process of such stabilisation and organisation as stratification. The choice of this term is significant, given that 'stratification' has among its principal meanings that of a geological arrangement of sedimentary rocks in distinct layers, and that of a sociological organisation of people in hierarchies of class and status. What Deleuze and Guattari will show is that rocks and humans, the extremes of the traditional Great Chain of Being, are equally subject to the process of stratification, as are all formed entities in between.

From semiology to ontology

Deleuze and Guattari take the primary terms of their description of stratification from linguistics – André Martinet's concept of double articulation and Louis Hjelmslev's notions of matter, form, substance, content and expression. In the heyday of French structuralism in the 1960s, Martinet's double articulation figured prominently in efforts to extend linguistic concepts to construct a general semiology, such as Saussure had envisioned earlier in the century. Martinet's distinction between two fundamental levels in linguistic expression – a first articulation of morphemes (monemes, in Martinet's parlance), or the smallest units possessed of form and meaning; and a second articulation of phonemes, the smallest units that distinguish or contrast meaning, without themselves having any meaning but solely form – was seen by many semiologists as a guide to the analysis of non-linguistic sign systems, leading them to ask how the fundamental elements of a given sign system – art, architecture, music, genetics – might be construed in terms of a double articulation of meaning-bearing units and purely formal units of differentiation.

This line of reasoning is evident, for example, throughout Roland Barthes's influential *Elements of Semiology* (1964). In *Elements*, Barthes also recognises the potential of Hjelmslev's linguistics for a general semiology. After defining the sign in Saussurean terms as signifier and signified, Barthes states that 'the plane of the signifiers constitutes the *plane of expression* and that of the signifieds *the plane of content*', adding that Hjelmslev specifies that 'each plane comprises two *strata: form* and *substance*' (Barthes 1967: 39–40). Attention to the form and substance of both expression and content, he argues, provides an important tool for analysing the language-like regularities of non-linguistic semiological systems.

It is against this background that Deleuze and Guattari's use of Hjelmslev and Martinet may be seen as a playful appropriation of linguistics' schemas and redeployment of those terms to counter linguistics' imperialistic semiological ambitions. Decisive in their reconfiguration of Hjelmslev is their attention to 'matter', the one element involved in Hjelmslev's form/substance opposition that Barthes ignores. Hjelmslev entertains the possibility of extracting from the world's languages something 'common to all languages' (Hjelmslev 1961: 50), which he calls *mening* ('meaning' in Danish), an 'amorphous 'thought-mass'' like a 'handful of sand' (Hjelmslev 1961: 52). This amorphous *mening*, translated as 'purport' in English, but serendipitously as *matière* in French, is the universal 'thought-mass' of meanings carved up in different ways by different languages. *Mening* is 'unformed', and hence 'in itself inaccessible to knowledge' (Hjelmslev 1961: 76). It can only be approached through the forms of a given language, which turn the amorphous thought-mass into formed substances – 'just as an open net casts its shadows down on an undivided surface' (Hjelmslev 1961: 57), the outline of each square of the net constituting a form, and the surface so delineated a substance.

By taking Hjelmslev's *matière* not as 'thought-mass' but as matter per se, Deleuze and Guattari convert the schema of a general semiology into a component of a general ontology. This matter, however, is not inert, brute matter, but 'the plane of consistency or body without organs, in other words, the unformed, unorganised, nonstratified or destratified body and all its flows; subatomic and submolecular particles, pure intensities, pre-vital and preindividual free singularities' (ATP 48). It is from this matter that the process of double articulation produces the forms and substances of the strata of content and expression. This double articulation is so varied that 'we cannot begin with a general model, only a relatively simple case' (ATP 40) – that of the processes of sedimentation and cementation that form sedimentary rock.[3] In the first articulation of sedimentation (content), pebbles (substance) are extracted from a silt flow and then sorted into uniform layers (form). In the second articulation of cementation (expression), the statistically ordered layers are further organised through inter-pebble structuration (form), this structuration producing sedimentary rock (substance). Framed more abstractly, 'the first articulation chooses or deducts, from unstable particle-flows, metastable molecular or quasi-molecular units (*substances*) upon which it imposes a statistical order of connections and successions (*forms*)', whereas the second articulation 'establishes functional, compact stable structures (*forms*), and constructs the molar compounds in which these structures are simultaneously actualised (*substances*)' (ATP 40–1). Forms organise, or 'code', substances and thereby fix, or 'territorialise', substances. Hence, the substance of content is territorialised matter that is coded by the form of content; and the form of expression further codes, or 'overcodes', the stratum of content and thereby increases territorialisation in the substance of expression.

In Deleuze and Guattari's initial formulation of double articulation, then, a linguistic concept is once again transformed. The double articulation of morphemes and phonemes yields a meaning-bearing content and a meaningless vehicle for the expression of that content. In Deleuze and Guattari's double articulation, there is no vehicle for the conveyance of meaning, but two constituents in a relational process. Content is a coded territorialisation that is overcoded and further territorialised in expression, which produces 'phenomena of centring, unification, totalisation, integration, hierarchisation, and finalisation' (ATP 41). Unlike the relation between morphemes and phonemes, this formulation of the content/expression relation 'is never correspondence or conformity between content and expression, only isomorphism with reciprocal presupposition' (ATP 44). And as we shall see, the isomorphisms of content and expression are subject to multiple variations at different levels of scale and organisation.

Strata, epistrata and parastrata

By analysing the formation of sedimentary rock in terms of double articulation, Deleuze and Guattari take what must seem the most mechanistic of phenomena – the mere aggregation and solidification of inert particles via brute forces – and transform them into an instance of a process of selection/coding and overcoding/integration that occurs throughout all natural systems. Double articulation is evident, for example, in the determination of the three-dimensional structure of certain globular proteins. As Jacques Monod observes, this process involves a '"primary" structure . . . constituted by a topologically linear sequence of amino acid residues linked by covalent bonds' (first articulation), which is then stabilised via non-covalent interactions such that 'the polypeptide fibre folds in a very complex way into a compact, pseudo-globular bundle' (second articulation) (Monod 1971: 90–2). The cellular chemistry of the bacterium *Escherichia coli* also involves a two-stage process, the first in which elements are combined to form a limited number of compounds, and a second in which these unstable small molecules are assembled to produce chains of macro-molecules (Jacob 1973: 217). On a much higher scale, the functioning of an animal's organ systems (circulatory, respiratory, digestive and so on) may be analysed in terms of double articulation (though not as a temporal sequence of articulations). The animal's organs constitute the substance of content, and their regulation the form of content; the homeostatic regulation of those flows is the overcoding form of expression, and the organism as emergent process is the substance of expression.[4]

Each double articulation constitutes a stratum, and the unity of composition of the stratum involves three components: 'molecular materials, substantial elements, and formal relations or traits' (ATP 49). The molecular materials are selected from unformed matter to constitute a substratum, or exterior milieu, for the stratum; further organisation of those materials creates substantial elements, which emerge as an interior milieu; and formal relations both separate and connect the exterior and interior milieus. A supersaturated solution of sulphur, for example, begins to crystallise with the introduction of a seed crystal. As crystallisation commences, the molecular materials of the metastable solution (external milieu) are organised as substantial elements within each new crystal (interior milieu), the crystal surface delineating outside and inside (formal relation). Similarly, catalysts in a prebiotic soup may be seen as seed crystals in a metastable medium, an emergent organism forming an interior milieu, its membrane constituting the formal relation that divides and connects interior and exterior milieus.

Deleuze and Guattari insist that the exterior milieu, interior milieu and surface/membrane are all components within the stratum. But no stratum comes alone or undivided. Intermediary states fragment each stratum, dividing it into *epistrata*. In the formation of a crystal, for example, the crystallisation of the metastable solution does not proceed in a single, continuous process, but by distinct and discontinuous intermediary metastable states, each state constituting an epistratum. In a complex organism, intermediaries are evident in the organism's interior milieu, which consists of topologically complex milieus of relative interiority and exteriority, such that one interior milieu may serve as the exterior milieu of another. In the process of digestion, for example, the digestive cavity is the exterior milieu for the blood that irrigates the intestinal wall, while the blood is the exterior milieu for the digestive glands that discharge the products of their activity into the blood. The diverse interiorities and exteriorities within the organism constitute so many epistrata, and together 'they regulate the degree of complexity or differentiation of an organism' (ATP 50). A stratum, then, 'exists only in its substantial epistrata, which shatter its continuity, fragment its ring, and break it down into gradations' (ATP 50–1).

Besides fragmenting into epistrata, strata divide into *parastrata*. Epistrata mark intermediate states within internal milieus, 'piled one atop the other', whereas parastrata fragment the strata 'into sides and "besides"' (ATP 52). On the inorganic level, parastrata are intermediary states within exterior milieus. In crystal formation, for example, parastrata are varying opportunities for expansion afforded by the surrounding supersaturated solution. On the organic level, however, the nature of parastrata changes, for there they are associated with a third kind of milieu, neither exterior nor interior, but an *'annexed or associated milieu'* (ATP 51). In physico-chemical systems the interior milieu's substantial elements are formed from its exterior milieu's molecular materials – a crystal's substantial elements from the molecular materials of a supersaturated solution, or a primitive anaerobic organism's substantial elements from the molecular materials of a prebiotic soup. Both processes of replication via a conversion of external materials into internal elements constitute a fundamental 'alimentation', but one that exhausts itself with the eventual internal assimilation of all of the exterior milieu's materials. With the evolution of aerobic bacteria, however, organisms emerge that are capable of appropriating 'sources of energy different from alimentary materials' (ATP 51), sources available outside the organism's immediate exterior milieu in an annexed, or associated milieu. Such primitive aerobic respiration, then, may be taken as representative of the basic process of energy annexation beyond alimentation common to all organic life forms. Deleuze and Guattari also argue that associated milieus entail perception and reaction as well as alimentation (and hence a certain degree of cognition). Thus, the associated milieu is 'defined by the capture of energy sources (respiration in the most general sense), by the discernment of materials, the sensing of their presence or absence (perception), and by the fabrication or nonfabrication of the corresponding compounds (response, reaction)' (ATP 51). In organic systems, then, parastrata are the fragmentations of strata via associated milieus.

Epistrata involve substances and processes of territorialisation and deterritorialisation, whereas parastrata involve forms and processes of coding and decoding. An interior milieu is a territorialisation (a crystal or a cell, for example, constituting a territory within an exterior milieu), and epistrata consist of varying numbers of interior milieus. In no way is an interior milieu absolutely territorialised, however. To some degree, it is always relatively territorialised and relatively deterritorialised, and the same is true of the relations among interior milieus within epistrata, where 'variations that are tolerated below a certain threshold of identity' (ATP 50) mark the fluctuations between territorialisation and deterritorialisation among interior milieus that may be maintained within a given system of epistrata without the system collapsing. Likewise, in parastrata there is no coding without decoding. In genetic codes, for example, there is 'an essential margin of decoding: not only does every code have supplements capable of free variation, but a single segment may be copied twice, the second copy left free for variation' (ATP 53). Viruses may also transfer fragments of codes from one species to another. And on a population level, there is always 'genetic drift', variations in a species gene pool regulated by population sizes and degrees of habitat isolation.

The plane of consistency and the abstract machine

Stratification creates formed substances from unformed matter. The unformed matter of this global stratification is the earth, 'the Deterritorialised, the Glacial, the giant Molecule ... a body without organs' (ATP 40). It is the '*Omnitudo*' as 'potential totality of all BwOs' (ATP 157), 'the plane of consistency of Nature' (ATP 254). The strata are relative de/territorialisations and de/codings, whereas the earth is the plane of consistency of absolute deterritorialisation and absolute decoding. The earth's matter is 'unformed, unstable' (ATP 40), but it is not 'a chaotic white night or an undifferentiated black night' (ATP 70). It is a virtual domain, real without being actual, with characteristics that are immanent within the actual domain of formed substances. It is matter before individuation has taken place, 'prevital and prephysical' (ATP 43). It is a body without organs in that it is not an organism, or organised, individuated and regulated entity; it is, 'in other words, the unformed, unorganised, nonstratified or destratified body and all its flows' (ATP 43). It is the source of forces and processes of morphogenesis and self-organisation immanent within matter, which are made manifest in the actualisations of those forces and processes. Though its matter is unformed, the plane of consistency is permeated 'by flows in all directions, by free intensities or nomadic singularities, by mad or transitory particles' (ATP 40) and filled with 'subatomic and submolecular particles, pure intensities, prevital and prephysical free singularities' (ATP 43).

The primary elements that occupy the plane of consistency, then, are singularities, intensities, particles and flows. Singularities mark thresholds between stable dynamical systems, points of bifurcation from one system to another. A given distribution of singularities determines a multiplicity's virtual space of potentialities or capacities, which then may be actualised in an unspecified number of ways. When considered on the plane of consistency, however, singularities are absolutely deterritorialised, unassigned to any particular distribution, free and nomadic. Intensities are nonmetric aspects of multiplicities, a given degree of heat being an intensity that changes quality with any increase or decrease in temperature and that cannot be attained through simple metric addition (a substance at 40 degrees added to another at 40 degrees does not generate a substance at 80 degrees). More generally, intensities are like Kant's 'intensive magnitudes', which may be 'apprehended only as unity, and in which multiplicity can be represented only through approximation to negation = 0' (Kant 1929: A168/B210). In Deleuze and Guattari's appropriation of Kant, intensity = 0 is not negative, but positive, various intensities being measured by their relative distance from zero, and zero itself functioning as the matrix of relatively deterritorialised intensities, the zero degree being pure deterritorialised intensity. The plane of consistency, or body without organs (BwO), 'causes intensities to pass', but the BwO itself 'is nonstratified, unformed, intense matter, the matrix of intensity, intensity = 0' (ATP 153). (Hence the characterisation of the earth as 'the Glacial' – intensity at absolute zero.) Particles, or particles-signs, are 'elements of molecular multiplicities' (ATP 32) undifferentiated by distinctions between the semiotic and non-semiotic. The concept of particles-signs is derived from the science of subatomic particles, but like its antithesis, the concept of black holes, it is used in a broad sense, in this case to designate deterritorialised elements that have escaped the domination of any formed entity and become 'mad or transitory' (ATP 40) on the plane of consistency. Flows, finally, are passages of matter-energy of all sorts – fluids, money, people, ideas – continuities that strata separate, control and regulate, but that inherently resist organisation, becoming pure currents of matter-movement on the plane of consistency.

That which connects the singularities, intensities, point-signs and flows of the plane of consistency is the abstract machine. It composes itself and composes the plane of consistency (ATP 511). It 'develops alone and in its own right on the plane of consistency whose diagram it constitutes, the same machine at work in astrophysics and in microphysics, in the natural and in the artificial, piloting flows of absolute deterritorialisation' (ATP 56). One might say, then, that it is 1) the active dimension of the plane of consistency's self-constitution; 2) the open system of connections that define the capacities of the plane of consistency for the distribution of singularities and disposition of intensities, particles-signs and flows; and 3) the agency that outlines or 'diagrams' the relations among singularities, intensities, particles-signs and flows.

But the abstract machine is also immanent within the strata, where machinic assemblages '*effectuate* the abstract machine' (ATP 71). Machinic assemblages co-adapt content and expression, establish bi-univocal relations between them, guide the formation of epistrata and parastrata, and relate strata to other strata. In the strata, singularities are actualised in discrete distributions, and intensities, particles-signs and flows are territorialised and coded: 'The only intensities known to the strata are discontinuous, bound up in forms and substances; the only particles are divided into particles of content and articles of expression; the only deterritorialised flows are disjointed and reterritorialised' (ATP 70). In short, the virtual potentialities of the plane of consistency are actualised in the specific, and hence necessarily limiting and restricting, forms and substances of the strata, and the abstract machine serves a piloting role in that actualisation, which the machinic assemblages effectuate. The abstract machine is enveloped in the strata, and it constitutes the unity of the strata. The enveloped abstract machine is 'the Ecumenon' (ATP 50), and its enveloped manifestation is the abstract machine of double articulation.

The abstract machine on the plane of consistency, by contrast, is 'the Planomenon' (ATP 50). This is the same abstract machine, no longer enveloped, but now developed on the plane of consistency (and, one might add, de-enveloped through interventions in the strata). The developed abstract machine '*constructs continuums of intensity*', '*emits and combines particles-signs*' and '*performs conjunctions of flows of deterritorialisation*'. 'Continuum of intensities, combined emission of particles or signs-particles, conjunction of deterritorialised flows: these are the three factors proper to the plane of consistency; they are brought about by the abstract machine and are constitutive of destratification' (ATP 70). It is important to note that although the developed and enveloped abstract machines are the same machine, the developed has priority over the enveloped:

> In fact, what is primary is an absolute deterritorialisation, an absolute line of flight, however complex or multiple – that of the plane of consistency or body without organs (the Earth, the absolutely deterritorialised). This absolute deterritorialisation becomes relative only after stratification occurs on that plane or body: It is the strata that are always residue, not the opposite. (ATP 56)

The inorganic, organic and alloplastic strata

'The organisation of epistrata moves in the direction of increasing deterritorialisation' (ATP 53). The same may be said of the strata of the inorganic, the organic and the human. Decisive in Deleuze and Guattari's differentiation of these three strata is François Jacob's 1974 article 'Le modèle linguistique en biologie'. In this essay, Jacob notes the widespread adoption of a linguistic model for understanding the genetic code (a model he himself uses frequently in *The Logic of Life*), but argues that DNA sequences and languages differ in important ways. He sees two principles underlying the analogy between the genetic code and language: a 'combinatory of elements, phonemes or chemical radicals, which, in themselves, are devoid of meaning but which, grouped in certain ways, acquire a signification' and 'a strict linearity of the message'. He observes, however, that a combinatory of elements need not entail linearity. Atoms constitute a combinatory of limited elements, and in inorganic systems they combine to form countless complex molecules and compounds. 'But in this case, it's a matter of complex structures in three dimensions. By contrast, what is limited to heredity and language is the linearity of the structures they engender.' The sole question is whether 'in the two systems, this linearity resides in the same logic, if it is founded on the same constraints' (Jacob 1974: 201). His conclusion is that it is not. Linguistics studies messages transmitted from a sender to a receiver, but 'there is none of that in biology: neither sender nor receiver' (Jacob 1974: 200). The transfer of information in the gene sequence is unidirectional, from nucleic acids to proteins. The linearity of the gene sequence is fixed to a single temporal unfolding, one that is constrained by the needs of guiding the morphogenesis of the individual organism and passing the genetic information on to the next generation of organisms. The linearity of language, by contrast, is constrained by 'an apparatus, vocal and auditory, which preexists it' (Jacob 1974: 201). The nature of the vocal–auditory medium necessitates a sequential enunciation and reception of information, but communication proceeds in two directions in an open succession of messages, and the relation between messages is unconstrained by any predetermined, fixed temporality.

Jacob's differentiation of the three-dimensional, nonlinear structuration of inorganic compounds, the fixed, unidirectional linearity of the genetic code, and the flexible, bidirectional linearity of language provides Deleuze and Guattari with the basic framework for their analysis of the inorganic, organic and human strata – with the proviso, of course, that their conception of the double articulation of content and expression dramatically reconfigures Jacob's schema.

On the inorganic stratum, the relationship between content and expression is that of the molecular to the molar. The crystal, for example, is the molar expression of the molecular content of the supersaturated solution within which it arises. The propagation of additional crystals takes place along the surfaces of the incipient crystals, and it proceeds in all directions. Hence, expression in crystallisation may be said to be 'voluminous or superficial' (ATP 59). Expression on the inorganic stratum in general, like that of crystallisation, is a process of 'induction', like the induction of an electrical current or magnetic field, 'from layer to layer and state to state, or at the limit' (ATP 60). The passage from molecular to molar is also one of a unidirectional territorialisation. Hence, one may say of the crystal that its 'subjugation to three-dimensionality, in other words its index of territoriality', makes 'the structure incapable of formally reproducing and expressing itself; only the accessible surface can reproduce itself, since it is the only deterritorialisable part' (ATP 60).

Genuine reproduction, that exhibited by organic life forms, requires a qualitative increase in deterritorialisation, and that increase is provided by the linear genetic sequence. In the organic stratum, the relationship between expression and content is not solely that of the molar to the molecular, although the molar–molecular relation does pervade the process of morphogenesis, in that development proceeds via the formation of increasingly large-scale structures. In the genetic sequence, expression becomes molecular and *'independent in its own right, in other words, autonomous'*. Genetic expression involves 'nucleic acids of expression and proteins of content' (ATP 59). The nucleic acids and proteins are independent formed substances, their only specified connection being that each protein corresponds to a given sequence of three nucleotides. This deterritorialisation of expression in the linear genetic sequence makes possible multiple deterritorialisations of the organism as a whole. Unlike a crystal, which merely induces further replication within its exterior milieu, the organism reproduces itself independently of its immediate exterior milieu. In morphogenesis, the linear genetic sequence allows a further deterritorialisation, in that the multiple interior and exterior milieus within the organism are put in mutual topological contact with one another through the genetic sequence. On the inorganic stratum, epistrata and parastrata are mere inductions. On the organic stratum, by contrast, epistrata and parastrata are transductions, fragmentations of the strata that are both molecular and molar 'independently of order of magnitude' (ATP 60). The epistrata of substances within the organism are relatively deterritorialised through the topological mutual presence of systems to one another without regard to distance. And the parastrata of forms afford the establishment of associated milieus through mutative decodings, recodings and intercodings of the organism with other organisms.

What I have referred to as the human stratum to this point is actually named the alloplastic stratum by Deleuze and Guattari, and the difference between the two designations is significant. The human is not an essence, but a product of a distribution of content and expression that differs from those of the inorganic and organic strata. The human is a mere result of the universal process of double articulation, which in this stratum has attained a new level of deterritorialisation. The stratum is alloplastic (Greek *allo* = other) in that 'it brings about modifications in the external world' (ATP 60). Of course, all systems, inorganic and organic, mutually modify one another, but the modifications of the alloplastic stratum are brought about by tools and language, *tekhnē* and *logos*, which are components specific to the alloplastic stratum that intervene in the inorganic and organic strata as forces external to those strata.

The alloplastic stratum has a single exterior milieu, not a pre-physicochemical soup (the inorganic stratum), nor a prebiotic soup (the organic stratum), but a pre-human soup: 'the cerebral-nervous system' (ATP 64). This brain-soup substratum tends towards two poles of differentiation – the hand and the face – and double articulation performs a 'manual articulation of content' and a 'facial articulation of expression' (ATP 64) that eventuates in the distinction between gestures-tools and speech-language. Although central to the unity of composition of the alloplastic stratum, the brain-soup does not have priority as a causal force in human evolution. Deleuze and Guattari follow André Leroi-Gourhan in arguing that cerebral development is not the motor of human evolution but instead a secondary phenomenon made possible by antecedent muscular-skeletal adaptations related to locomotion and an increased mastery of space and time. Leroi-Gourhan sees the emergence of an erect posture as the decisive event in the evolution of the hominins that led to *Homo sapiens*. Through major modifications of the feet and spine, hominins gained the ability to stand, walk and run, and as a result their hands were freed from the function of locomotion, and their mouths from the function of grasping. Hands could then invent and manipulate tools, and mouths could invent and articulate language. And concomitant with the development of the new capacities of the hands and mouth was an expansion of the cerebral cavity and increase in the size of the brain, only made possible by the structural modifications necessary for an upright posture and a reconfiguration of the face (the projecting mouth-snout suitable for grasping giving way to a flattened face, which provided more room for the cerebral cavity in the skull).

In Deleuze and Guattari's terms, these evolutionary developments are so many deterritorialisations and reterritorialisations, which eventuate in a general increase in the deterritorialisation of humans. The deterritorialising reconfiguration of feet and spine deterritorialises the locomotive hands and grasping mouth, allowing the reterritorialisation of hands as gestural agents of tool-making and the mouth as an apparatus for producing speech. Deleuze and Guattari elaborate further on Leroi-Gourhan's analysis, linking the evolution of an erect posture to a deterritorialisation of primates from the forest to the steppe.[5] Locomotion within the trees of the forest was facilitated by four grasping limbs, but when hominids ventured to the steppe, the absence of trees favoured the development of an erect posture, locomotive feet, and hands capable of fine-motor manipulation. Through such an erect posture, hominids gained an increased freedom of movement, and hence a higher degree of deterritorialisation. The steppe also made possible modifications of the vocal apparatus. The noise of the forest favoured the development of large lungs and a larynx capable of producing loud cries and screams; the relative quiet of the steppe, by contrast, allowed the development of a suppler sound instrument, with lips, tongue and descended larynx capable of producing finer sonic distinctions. The arboreal voice, in short, was deterritorialised on the steppe and reterritorialised in a freer, more deterritorialised vocal apparatus.

The formation of the alloplastic stratum proceeds via deterritorialisations of the hands and mouth, eventuating in a double articulation of hand-tool content and mouth-language expression. But it is the linearity peculiar to language that separates the organic and alloplastic strata. Language is not linear, but superlinear, more deterritorialised than the genetic sequence, since the temporal succession of its phonation does not limit its ability to represent various time relations. Further, such superlinearity 'engenders a phenomenon unknown on the other strata: *translation* [*traduction*], translatability, as opposed to the previous inductions and transductions' (ATP 62). Such translation is to be conceived in the broadest terms as 'the ability of language ... to represent all the other strata and thus achieve a scientific conception of the world' (ATP 62). It is this power of translation that fosters the semiological imperialism of using linguistic models to explain all systems. (Witness Jacob's presupposition that physico-chemical, genetic and linguistic phenomena should be seen fundamentally as a Martinetian 'combinatory of elements ... which, in themselves, are devoid of meaning but which, grouped in certain ways, acquire a signification' [Jacob 1974: 201].)

Language, power and the geology of morals

Content and expression on the alloplastic stratum, then, may be parsed into a 'technological content' and a 'semiotic or symbolic expression' (ATP 61). But Deleuze and Guattari make a crucial addition to this formulation:

> Content should be understood not simply as the hand and tools but as a technical social machine that preexists them and constitutes states of force or formations of power [*puissance*]. Expression should be understood not simply as the face and language, or individual languages, but as a semiotic collective machine that preexists them and constitutes regimes of signs. A formation of power [*puissance*] is much more than a tool; a regime of signs is much more than a language. (ATP 61)

Despite the assignment of power solely to the machine of content, both these machines – technical social and semiotic collective – are assemblages of power, or *pouvoir*, as Plateaus Four and Five's analyses of order-words and regimes of signs make clear. It is telling in this regard that Deleuze and Guattari's explanatory model of the alloplastic relations between content and expression comes from Foucault's *Discipline and Punish* (ATP 66–7). Besides providing a clear example of the autonomy of content and expression (the prison-form of content versus expression's discourse of delinquency), their relation respectively to technical social and semiotic collective machines, and their relation to the abstract machine, the panopticon makes evident that alloplastic stratification not only codes, territorialises, controls, restricts and rigidifies, but also effectuates asymmetrical power relations, which, in a word Deleuze will use later in characterising Foucault's project, constitute the 'intolerable' (Deleuze 1995a: 103).

Plateau Three's trajectory is from geological stratification to the asymmetrical power relations of social stratification. The process of double articulation pervades the earth, at every level of organisation. Humans are produced on the alloplastic stratum as emergent but contingent manifestations of powers of relative deterritorialisation. Through primate and hominin corporeal deterritorialisations, the hands and mouth gain new capacities. Out of unformed matter a substratum of molecular materials takes shape, a pre-human soup, which gives a unity of composition to the alloplastic stratum. This pre-human brain-soup 'is a population, a set of tribes tending toward two poles' (ATP 64), those of the hand and mouth, which undergo double articulation as content and expression, *tekhnē* and *logos*, hand-gesture-tool and mouth-speech-language. In this co-emergence of content and expression, the form of expression attains the autonomy of superlinearity, which makes possible the translation of all strata into linguistic representations. Subtending this articulation of content and expression are pre-existing relations of force: technical social machines, or formations of power; and semiotic collective machines, or regimes of signs. The emergence of the alloplastic stratum marks a qualitative increase in deterritorialisation, but by no means is this a sign of progress, no ascent from the biosphere to the noosphere, à la Teilhard de Chardin (ATP 69). Such notions of human superiority, in fact, are illusory products of the alloplastic stratum. Technological and semiotic machines emerge on this stratum and increasingly transform the world. Such machines are part of the stratum, 'but at the same time rear up and stretch their pincers out in all directions at all the other strata' (ATP 63). Techno-semiotic machines seem to constitute an intermediary state between the enveloped and developed states of the abstract machine, fully a part of the alloplastic stratum, yet sufficiently autonomous and pervasive in the other strata to engender the belief that they constitute the abstract machine of all strata. 'This is the illusion constitutive of man', however, and 'this illusion derives from the overcoding immanent to language itself' (ATP 63).

In an allusion to Antonin Artaud's 1947 radio play, *To Have Done with the Judgment of God*, Deleuze and Guattari say that 'the strata are the judgments of God', and that 'the earth, or the body without organs, constantly eludes that judgment, flees and becomes destratified, decoded, deterritorialised' (ATP 40). The God of stratification is the immanent abstract machine of double articulation ('God is a lobster' [ATP 40]), and conventional human moral codes are but a few of the multiple epistrata and parastrata that proliferate on the alloplastic stratum. In this narrow sense, Plateau Three provides a geology of morals, but in the broadest sense the geology of morals is a geology of language, the superlinear element that differentiates the alloplastic from the organic and inorganic strata. What the geology of morals reveals is the constitutive illusion of man, the belief that *tekhnē* and *logos* have dominance over all strata, and the pernicious tendencies of the relations of forces that have arisen, and continue to arise, in the technical social machines of content and the semiotic collective machines of expression.

Beyond the strata

As John Protevi aptly observes, the Lobster-God of double articulation is unlike Spinoza's God, in that the Lobster-God is not all of nature, *Deus sive natura*, but only a part of it (Protevi 2001: 39). The other part is the absolute deterritorialisation of the plane of consistency, the body without organs whose singularities, intensities, points-signs and flows compose the anorganic life of the earth. Deterritorialisation is primary, whereas stratification is a secondary residue, yet neither appears without the other. There is no virtual without the actual. Hence, in the real of nature, absolute deterritorialisation and absolute stratification are tendencies, limits never fully reached, and we, like everything else, are always relatively stratified and relatively deterritorialised. The question posed by the geology of morals is which tendency we promote: that of a morality of stratification, or that of an alternative ethics of the earth, a terrestrial ethology that valorises a deterritorialising mode of existence. Plateau Three does not articulate such an ethology; that task is reserved for the other plateaus. But it does provide an ontology of terrestrial systems that makes the valorisation of deterritorialisation more than a human choice.

Paul Patton has argued that Deleuze and Guattari's ontology 'is not ontology in the strong philosophical sense of the term but a pragmatic and relativized ontology . . . normative in a specific and formal sense' (Patton 2010: 142) in that it grants systematic priority to movements of deterritorialisation in all its various guises. Hence, Deleuze and Guattari's ontology 'is also an ethics or an ethology', which Patton calls 'an ethics of becoming' (Patton 2012: 142). Patton rightly stresses the ethico-political priorities that guide Deleuze and Guattari's thought and that are evident in all the plateaus of *A Thousand Plateaus*. But the Third Plateau suggests that their ontological commitments are more than pragmatic, that the primacy of deterritorialisation is fundamental to their view of all terrestrial systems. Given that associated milieus are defined by energy capture and the cognitive functions of perception and response/reaction, the emergence of associated milieus on the organic stratum suggests that Deleuze and Guattari do make room for normativity, but a normativity that reaches beyond the human to all organic life forms. In this sense, their thought follows lines delineated by Georges Canguilhem, who sees all life forms as normative, the health of a given life form being determined by its normativity – that is, by the norms and the domain of normality it produces for itself.

> Any normality open to possible future correction is authentic normativity, or health. Any normality limited to maintaining itself, hostile to any variation

in the themes that express it, and incapable of adapting to new situations is a normality devoid of normative intention. When confronted with any apparently normal situation, it is therefore important to ask whether the norms that it embodies are creative norms, norms with a forward thrust, or, on the contrary, conservative norms, norms whose thrust is toward the past. (Canguilhem 1994: 352)

This opposition of the authentic normativity of a creative, flexible, future-oriented health and the inauthentic normality of a conservative, rigid, past-oriented pathology is clearly consonant with the opposition of a deterritorialising ethology of becoming and a territorialising geo-morality of stratification.

But the primacy of deterritorialisation extends beyond the organic to the inorganic stratum as well, and whether such primacy retains a normative dimension on that stratum is doubtful. In crystallisation, for example, individuation proceeds from a deterritorialised supersaturated solution, the incipient crystal's surface being its 'only deterritorialisable part'. The crystal's structure is 'incapable of formally reproducing and expressing itself' (ATP 60) because it is insufficiently deterritorialised. Only on the organic stratum do entities arise with sufficient deterritorialisation to allow them to annex associated milieus and thereby make normative evaluations of health or pathology. The primacy of deterritorialisation in crystallisation resides solely in the supersaturated solution, which is pre-individual and hence devoid of discrete agents capable of valorising deterritorialisation.

The absence of normative agents is even more striking in stratification, and this is one of the reasons that the organisation of unformed matter is framed in terms of stratification rather than crystallisation. Whereas crystallisation involves the individuation of a discrete entity, sedimentation-cementation involves the production of a cohesive plurality. A geological stratum is an aggregate of materials, a geological formation rather than an individuated form. There is no clear agent internal to the system of sedimentation-cementation, for which reason it lends itself so well to a mechanistic analysis. But if there are no agents, there are 'agencings', *agencements machiniques*, machinic assemblage-forming processes. Such machinic agencings are 'interstrata', relations-forces between content and expression, between strata and across strata, but also 'metastrata', between the strata and the developed abstract machine. They '*effectuate* the abstract machine insofar as it is developed on the plane of consistency or enveloped in a stratum' (ATP 71). They are the agencings of deterritorialisation and reterritorialisation that play through all cohesive formations, individuated entities and agents, without belonging to any of them. They are the anonymous agencings of a universal machinism, a vital materialism of anorganic life. Thus, the primacy of deterritorialisation is ontological in a strong sense; it is the primacy of creation, metamorphosis and becoming in all terrestrial systems. And normative valorisations of deterritorialisation are emergent properties of the organic stratum, effectuations of machinic agencings specific to that stratum and, by extension, to the alloplastic stratum.

What Plateau Three offers us, I believe, is a means of understanding Deleuze and Guattari's geophilosophy as a chaosmopolitanism, a contemporary counterpart to the cosmopolitanism of the Cynics and early Stoics.[6] The Cynics and early Stoics viewed philosophy as a way of living, and their cosmopolitanism entailed living in accordance with nature – for the Cynics, in harmony with plant and animal life, for the early Stoics, in harmony with law and reason (which they saw as at once both *physical* and *ethical* principles). The ethics of chaosmopolitanism, by contrast, calls for living in immanent resonance with the chaosmos of nature, affirming and participating in the creative, mutagenic and metamorphic powers of anorganic life, working to transform the stratifications that constrict that life and to invent new modes of existence. The Planomenon, the abstract machine on the plane of consistency, constructs continuums of intensity, emits and combines particles-signs, and forms conjunctions of flows of deterritorialisation. Thus, a chaosmopolitan ethics calls for engagement with the Planomenon, for the construction of intensive continuums, the emission of particles-signs, and the conjunction of flows of deterritorialisation.

Notes

1. Adkins 2015 and Holland 2013 offer outstanding introductions to *A Thousand Plateaus* and to the complexities of Plateau Three. I find Holland's remarks on Plateau Three especially helpful – indeed, this essay is largely an elaboration of his reading (p. 62) of the 'constitutive illusion of man' (ATP 63). Invaluable as well is the glossary of Bonta and Protevi 2004.
2. On non-organic life, see DeLanda 1992; Protevi 2012.
3. Deleuze and Guattari call the second articulation 'folding', but as DeLanda points out (DeLanda 1997: 290), they are actually describing cementation, folding being a subsequent process following cementation.
4. I take this last example from Bonta and Protevi 2004: 152.
5. Deleuze and Guattari draw on Devaux 1933 for the idiosyncratic association of homonisation with the steppe. The more widely accepted savanna theory of homonisation, however, establishes a forest-savanna opposition that is roughly correlative to the forest-steppe opposition of Devaux.
6. For an extended exposition of Deleuze and Guattari's chaosmopolitanism, see Bogue 2012.

Chapter 4

Postulates of Linguistics

Jeffrey A. Bell

If one turns to the table of contents of *A Thousand Plateaus*, one might be puzzled to find that each of the chapters, or what readers will soon discover are more appropriately titled plateaus, has a date to go along with the title. 'One or Several Wolves' has the date 1914, 'Geology of Morals' 10,000 BC, and the title of the plateau that will be the concern of this essay, 'Postulates of Linguistics', has the date 20 November 1923. For reasons that will be discussed in this essay, Deleuze and Guattari argue that dates will always be important – 'History will never be rid of dates' (ATP 81). The importance and significance of dates, however, presupposes, as will be argued below, a plateau or plane of consistency that is the condition of possibility for the significance of the event itself, for the fact that things changed. The date henceforth marks the transformation brought about as a result of the event. A couple will celebrate their anniversary, the event of their marriage, or the day they were transformed (incorporeally, as we will see) from being single into being married. In the case of 20 November 1923, this is the date that is often marked as the beginning of the end of the hyperinflation that had ravaged Weimar Germany. For Deleuze and Guattari, however, this event provides an opportunity for exploring a more wide-ranging phenomenon – namely, the conditions for the possibility of language itself. This chapter will retrace the steps of Deleuze and Guattari's arguments. In the first section, the importance of 20 November 1923 will be explored both for its historical relevance and for the set of incorporeal transformations that attend and make possible such historically significant events. In the next section, Hume's arguments will be brought in to clarify the *incorporeal* nature of incorporeal transformations, and the relationship of these transformations to the order-words they effectuate. It is with the concept of order-words that Deleuze and Guattari move forward their radical views regarding linguistics. Turning to the influence of Hume's thought on the work of Deleuze will help us to clarify these important notions. Hume's influence on Deleuze and Guattari is at its most profound, as we will see, as they come to develop the notion of an incorporeal transformation.[1] This discussion will lead us to the importance of learning for both Deleuze and Guattari, and to why the 'Postulates of Linguistics' plateau begins with the case of a schoolmistress who is instructing her students on the rules of grammar. The significance of the schoolmistress example is that it begins to show how it is a process of learning that is both the condition of possibility of language itself, and more precisely for the rules and grammar of language. With these arguments in place, the final two sections will examine Deleuze and Guattari's critical approach to the postulates of traditional linguistics – most notably the linguistics found in the work of Noam Chomsky – and they will offer instead some suggestions for how linguistics ought to proceed and the implications of such a linguistics for the lives of those who speak a language.

I

Prior to the outbreak of the First World War, it cost a German 4.2 marks to buy a single US dollar. During the war the German currency began to weaken against the dollar. By the end of the war, the rate was nearly double the pre-war level. After the war, the costs of reparations were now piled on top of the debt that had already been amassed to fund the war, and in an effort to pay these debts the Reichsbank abandoned the gold standard and began to print an increased supply of marks (often referred to as papiermarks to highlight the move away from the gold standard) in order to buy currencies they could then use to pay their debts. These efforts backfired and the eventual result was the devastating hyperinflation of the early 1920s. The collapse of the mark is stunning. In April 1919 the exchange rate was 12 marks to the dollar; by the end of 1919 it was 47; in November 1921 it was 263; and by July 1922 it was 493. As if this were not bad enough (and most were able to adjust to the ever-changing prices), as 1922 came to a close the inflation became hyperbolic. The exchange rate of 7,000 in December 1922 quickly exploded, becoming 24,000 by April, 353,000 by July, and at its official peak 4.2 trillion marks to the dollar on 20 November 1923.

As has been discussed in numerous historical accounts of the hyperinflation in Weimar Germany, the effects on everyday citizens were extreme. At its worst, prices changed by the hour. In one of many similar cases, a gramophone that cost 5 million marks at 10 a.m. cost 12 million at 3 p.m.[2]

Workers would receive their pay, often in wheelbarrows or large sacks given the number of notes needed, and then spend the entire sum immediately since they could not wait and watch the value of their earnings depreciate. As public transport and other essential services began to shut down given the extreme inflation, the German authorities launched a series of measures to break the fever of hyperinflation. Among several factors that came together was the ascension to the Chancellorship of Gustav Stresemann on 13 August and the establishment of the Rentenbank on 17 October, which was soon followed by the approval of legislation by the Reichstag giving the Rentenbank the power to issue a new currency. The Rentenbank began issuing new currency, the rentenmark, on 15 November, but in strictly limited quantities to counter the mark (papiermark) and the unlimited printing of notes that had been the Reichsbank's approach since the war. On 20 November 1923 the exchange rate for the rentenmark was established by lopping off 12 places from the then current exchange rate of 4.2 trillion marks to the dollar. With this move, the Rentenbank was able to re-establish the long-standing pre-war exchange rate of 4.2 marks to the dollar, and thus 20 November 1923 marked the beginning of the end of the hyperinflation that had been plaguing Germany.

What interests Deleuze and Guattari in the events that led to the declaration of the exchange rate for the rentenmark on 20 November 1923, and the reason their 'Postulates of Linguistics' plateau has this date associated with it, is not the fact that this date is important in the economic history of Weimar Germany. Although this is certainly true, what interests Deleuze and Guattari is the act that fixed the exchange rate of the rentenmark, and the incorporeal transformation this act presupposes. For Deleuze and Guattari, there is the 'real history' of the economy of Weimar Germany, the history that leads to and accounts for the significance of 20 November 1923, and then there are the 'pure acts intercalated into that development' (ATP 81). The declaration that established the rentenmark's exchange rate is an example of a 'pure act', as is the judge's reading of the verdict in a courtroom, which is the well-known example Deleuze and Guattari offer of such a 'pure act'.[3] For Deleuze and Guattari, the judge's act of reading the verdict 'is a pure instantaneous act' and it involves an 'incorporeal transformation [that] is recognizable by its instantaneousness, its immediacy, by the simultaneity of the statement expressing the transformation and the effect the transformation produces' (ATP 81). When the judge reads the verdict 'guilty', this act simultaneously and instantaneously transforms the accused into a convict; when someone declares 'I love you' to a person they have recently begun to date, this declaration suddenly and instantly transforms the status of the relationship; and when the Rentenbank declared the fixed exchange rate for the rentenmark it instantly created a new currency to replace the mark (papiermark) and effectively brought the hyperinflation to an end. In each of these instances we have examples of what Deleuze and Guattari call the order-word, where an order-word is not an act of communication or information transfer but rather a 'pure act', an act that transforms through the very immediacy and redundancy of the statement and the act itself. More precisely, Deleuze and Guattari claim that 'order-words . . . [are] not a particular category of explicit statements . . . but the relation of every word or every statement to implicit presuppositions, in other words, to speech acts that are, and can only be, accomplished in the statement' (ATP 79).

The transformation of the accused into a convict, the rentenmark into the fixed currency of Germany, and so on, is a transformation that presupposes both the statement that expresses and enacts the transformation but also the incorporeal transformation that is inseparable from or redundant to the statement. Not everyone, however, can go about declaring an accused guilty and thereby transform them into a convict; the rentenmark could not have been declared legal currency without other factors already being in place; and not anyone can declare their love to another and thereby transform the relationship. What is needed in each of these cases, Deleuze and Guattari argue, is an 'effectuated variable', for 'in the absence of an effectuated variable, giving that person the right to make such a statement is an act of puerility or insanity, *not an act of enunciation*' (ATP 82, emphasis added). It is by virtue of the fact that the judge has the institutional authority to read the verdict and that he or she belongs to an institution with the power to imprison persons who are convicted that the judge is able to declare the accused guilty and transform them into a convict. The shouts of 'guilty' from angry bystanders outside the courtroom will not produce the same effect. An effectuated variable, in other words, presupposes a set of variables and conditions that allow for the possibility that a statement can become an act of enunciation. This set of variables, what Deleuze and Guattari call the 'collective assemblage of enunciation', is not to be confused, however, with the set of external conditions that render a statement meaningful. Deleuze and Guattari are not arguing for a Wittgensteinian theory of meaning whereby the social forms of life associated with various language-games are what are presupposed by meaningful utterances. In his reaction to the conception of a private, mental life, most evident in his private-language arguments, Wittgenstein argued that the meaning of a word is not to be understood in terms of some mental phenomenon, or even a rule one follows that is somehow in the head. For Wittgenstein, by contrast, the meaning of a word is simply its use, and a stated rule is simply an expression of the fact that a given way of doing things is accepted by a community of speakers. Wittgenstein argues, for example, that I cannot simply go about and say 'bububu', and mean that 'If it doesn't rain I shall go for a walk' (Wittgenstein 1986: 18). This utterance is not, given the current external circumstances of those to whom I might make such an utterance, an accepted move in current language-games, and thus it would be seen as meaningless. I can, however, announce that I have taken a selfie today and others would know what I mean, for the term 'selfie' has reached a threshold point of use within a community such that it has become an accepted move within current language-games, a move that would not have been accepted ten years ago when people would have had no idea what 'selfie' meant. Wittgenstein's theory thus understands the meaningfulness of utterances in terms of their actual use given a current state of affairs, and more precisely whether a community of speakers recognises a particular behaviour and utterance as one that constitutes an acceptable move within an already established language-game.[4]

Deleuze and Guattari, by contrast, are quite forthright in arguing that the circumstances that constitute the effectuated variable 'should not leave the impression that it is a question *only* of external circumstances', for while it is true, as Deleuze and Guattari continue, that '"I swear" is not the same when said in the family, at school, in a love affair, in a secret society, or in court: it is not the same thing, and neither is it the same statement; it is not the same bodily situation, and neither is it the same incorporeal transformation' (ATP 82, emphasis added). In other words, the circumstances that account for the effectuated variables are not only those circumstances that account for the diversity of ways in which 'I swear', for instance, may be meant, but there are also the incorporeal transformations that are redundant to and inseparable from the circumstances and statements. The collective assemblage of enunciation, therefore, is not, as a Wittgensteinian might argue, the set of social behaviours and external conditions that account for an act's being an 'act of enunciation'; rather, Deleuze and Guattari argue that 'if the collective assemblage is in each instance coextensive with the linguistic system considered, and to language as a whole, it is because it expresses *the set of incorporeal transformations that effectuate the condition of possibility of language* and utilise the elements of the linguistic system' (ATP 85, emphasis added). The collective assemblage of enunciation is indeed 'coextensive' with the statements, utterances and behaviours that constitute the language-games Wittgenstein discusses, but it is the 'set of incorporeal transformations' these statements express that is 'the condition of possibility of language'. And this set of incorporeal transformations, moreover, is precisely what allows for the relationship of language to a world outside language, or it is what allows for the signifying function of language as that which refers to something else. Deleuze and Guattari are quite clear in arguing that incorporeal transformations, although they apply to bodies, are nonetheless 'incorporeal, internal to enunciation', and are, they add, 'variables of expression *that establish a relation between language and the outside, but precisely because they are immanent to language*' (ATP 82, emphasis in original). The collective assemblage of enunciation is precisely the set of incorporeal transformations that is immanent to language. It is the condition of possibility of language itself.

To clarify this point further and show how 'variables of expression' may allow, by being immanent to language, for a relationship to an external world, and hence a signifying relationship between word and world, we can turn to the significance of David Hume for both the work of Deleuze alone and Deleuze and Guattari together.

II

The significance of David Hume's work for the 'Postulates of Linguistics' plateau arises, perhaps surprisingly, in relationship to the *incorporeal* nature of the incorporeal transformations order-words express, and which are the condition of possibility of language itself. The theme of incorporeal transformation as it relates to Hume emerges in response to a particular problem concerning the genesis of a subjective self – namely, how can a subject which is irreducible to the given (to wit, impressions and ideas for Hume) arise from nothing other than that which is given? 'The problem,' as Deleuze states it in his early book on Hume, *Empiricism and Subjectivity*, 'is as follows: how can a subject transcending the given be constituted in the given?' (Deleuze 1991b: 86). This problem is intimately connected to Hume's related problem of accounting for the emergence of the idea of causation or 'power and connexion', for this idea is an idea that cannot be accounted for by that which is given, for what is given, Hume argues, is simply the 'repetition of perfectly similar instances', and these 'can never alone give rise to an original idea' (Hume 1978: 163). Moreover, Hume goes even further in stressing the significance of this original idea when he argues that

> we ought not to receive as reasoning any observations we make concerning *identity*, and the *relations* of *time* and *place*; since in none of them can the mind go beyond what is immediately present to the senses, either to discover the real existence or the relations of objects. 'Tis only *causation*, which produces such a connexion. (Hume 1978: 73)

What then is the source of this original idea of causation as a necessary 'power and connexion', an idea that allows us to 'go beyond what is immediately present to the senses' and yet draws from nothing other than what is immediately given to the senses? It is at this point that Hume turns to an incorporeal transformation, to use Deleuze and Guattari's phrase. More precisely, Hume turns to a transformation or change that occurs in the mind in an act of contemplation. Since the repetition of perfectly similar instances 'can never alone give rise to an original idea', and especially to the idea of causation, for Hume what happens is that 'the observation of this resemblance produces a new impression in the mind, which is its [the original idea's] real model' (Hume 1978: 165). What happens then is that the observation of resemblance between previous incidents and the current incident leads to an easy transition and expectation of that which has followed in the past. If a current instance of being given A resembles previous instances where A was immediately followed by B, then we feel a natural easy transition to the thought of B following A. It is this feeling that becomes the model of the new idea. As Hume puts it, we 'draw the idea of it [the idea of 'a power or necessary connexion'] from what we feel internally in contemplating them', with 'them' referring to the objects that are now thought of as being necessarily connected through the power of causation.

It is at this point that we can begin to see how Hume's philosophy influenced Deleuze and Guattari's concept of the incorporeal transformation. In particular, the transformation that occurs for Hume is that a series of repetitions of 'A . . . B' becomes 'A *AND* B', with *AND* being a necessary connexion between A and B. The importance of this AND did not go unnoticed by Deleuze. In an essay published in *Dialogues*, Deleuze argues that 'Thinking *with* AND, instead of thinking IS, instead of thinking *for* IS: empiricism has never had another secret. Try it, it is a quite extraordinary thought, and yet it is life' (Deleuze and Parnet 1987: 57). In other words, what is important for Deleuze is not the identity of that which IS, whether A or B, but rather it is the power of AND, the incorporeal transformations that allow for the identity of a new, determinate entity, and hence for the connection between this and other entities. It is for this reason that Deleuze and Guattari argue that habit is creative, and we see this already with Hume.[5] Upon being presented with a series of repeating instances that are similar, a habit contracts these instances into the expectation or feeling that A will be followed by B, and it is this feeling, when contemplated, that gives rise to a new or original idea. The identity of something new such as the idea of necessary connexion thus arises as a result of contemplating the habit, a contemplation or incorporeal transformation that transforms the habit into something new.[6] Deleuze and Guattari, however, take this even further. In *What is Philosophy?* when arguing that 'Habit is creative', they immediately add, extending the Humean arguments we have sketched to this point, that 'The plant contemplates water, earth, nitrogen, carbon, chlorides, and sulphates, and it contracts them in order to acquire its own concept . . . The concept is a habit acquired by contemplating the elements from which we come' (Deleuze and Guattari 1994: 105). In other words, for Deleuze and Guattari an incorporeal transformation is the process whereby a series becomes contracted into a habit, or into what they call a plane of consistency, and it is this plane of consistency (or plateau) that becomes, through the incorporeal transformation of contemplation (or what Deleuze will also simply call an event), an identifiable entity, a plant, a new idea, etc. Deleuze and Guattari are thus quite serious when they echo Plotinus' claim from the third *Ennead* that 'all is contemplation'.[7]

To flesh out these points, let us return to the events surrounding the fixing of the rentenmark's exchange rate on 20 November 1923, and to the collective assemblage of enunciation this event presupposes as well as the set of incorporeal transformations this assemblage expresses. As discussed earlier, there is what Deleuze and Guattari refer to as the 'real history' of the events that led to the declaration of the exchange rate for the rentenmark on 20 November 1923. What interests Deleuze and Guattari, however, in the explicit command issued on 20 November are the order-words and pure acts these order-words express. The order-words are redundant to the pure acts and incorporeal transformations that allow for the possibility of an 'act of enunciation', and these incorporeal transformations are in turn the variables of collective assemblages of enunciation, assemblages that are the condition of possibility of language itself, or that effectuating condition that allows for the transformative effects order-words bring about. Deleuze and Guattari summarise this thread of their argument as follows:

> We have gone from explicit commands to order-words as implicit presuppositions; from order-words to the immanent acts or incorporeal transformations they express; and from there to the assemblages of enunciation whose variables they are. (ATP 83)

These assemblages of enunciations, moreover, are not to be confused with the external conditions and circumstances that can be used in a causal-historical account of the processes that led to the emergence of the rentenmark. Assemblages of enunciation are sets of incorporeal transformations or contemplations, to develop the Humean line of argument. In the case of the order-word of 20 November 1923, the incorporeal transformation it expresses is a variable of an assemblage of enunciation, or this variable of an assemblage that involves other incorporeal transformations (recall Deleuze and Guattari's claim that 'collective assemblage . . .

expresses the set of incorporeal transformations that effectuate the condition of possibility of language' [ATP 85]). Among the variables that constitute the set of incorporeal transformations that the decree of 20 November 1923 expresses, there was the legislation passed by the Reichstag on 27 October 1923 that established the Rentenbank, then the legislation that gave the Rentenbank the authority to issue new currency; there was the issuance of the rentenmark on 15 November; and there was the appointment of Hjalmar Schacht as currency commissioner by Chancellor Gustav Stresemann (whose own position expresses yet another set of incorporeal transformations). We could go on and list more, of course, but the point for Deleuze and Guattari is that there is a set of conditions (variables of an assemblage) that need to be brought together in such a way that they effectuate the possibility for the incorporeal transformations the order-words express, the order-words one finds in the explicit commands and dates that fill the pages of real history.

To clarify how this process works, we can turn to the very beginning of the 'Postulates of Linguistics' plateau where Deleuze and Guattari begin by looking into the process that unfolds 'When the schoolmistress instructs her students on a rule of grammar . . .' (ATP 75). It is not by chance that Deleuze and Guattari begin with the case of a schoolmistress instructing students, for by understanding the processes associated with learning we can clarify how a set of incorporeal transformations effectuates the possibility of language. In learning, it shall be argued, a similar process of drawing together a set of incorporeal transformations is essential if learning is to become transformed into knowledge; that is, into something that can be stated in the form of a rule, such as a rule of grammar. It is to this that we now turn.

III

As Deleuze and Guattari continue with their discussion of 'the schoolmistress who instructs her students on a rule of grammar or arithmetic', they add that the schoolmistress 'is not informing' her students and 'She does not so much instruct as "insign" (*ensigne*), give orders or commands' (ATP 75). These orders and commands, moreover and more importantly, 'are not external or additional to what he or she teaches . . . an order always and already concerns prior orders, which is why ordering is redundancy' (ATP 75). The information an order and command may convey is only necessary, Deleuze and Guattari claim, for the successful 'emission, transmission, and observation of orders as commands. One must be just informed enough not to confuse "Fire!" with "Fore!"' (ATP 76). The information these commands convey, however, and as was shown earlier, already presuppose order-words and the assemblages of enunciation that are the condition of possibility of language and hence for the possibility of transmitting information regarding external circumstances. So how is it that an order or command is not external to what is being taught but is rather something already caught up within a web of prior orders? It is at this point that the importance of learning as Deleuze understands this comes to the fore.

Deleuze raises the subject of learning in *Difference and Repetition*, where 'learning', he claims, 'is the appropriate name for the subjective acts carried out when one is confronted with the objectivity of a problem', whereas knowledge, by contrast, 'designates only the generality of concepts or the calm possession of a rule enabling solutions' (Deleuze 1994: 164). Deleuze offers the example of learning to swim. For Deleuze, we 'learn nothing from those who say: "Do as I do"', for learning is much more than following an external command or example. On the contrary, as Deleuze continues, learning involves working with teachers 'who tell us to "do with me", and [who] are able to emit signs to be developed in heterogeneity' (Deleuze 1994: 23). In particular, learning entails drawing together the 'distinctive points' or signs of one's body (the motion of one's arms, legs, etc.), the waves, currents, and so on, such that one is able to constitute a 'space of an encounter with signs' (1994: 23), a problem space whereby the distinctive points are drawn into a plane of consistency where there is a systematic order that then allows for the possibility of a solution. In learning to drive a car with a manual gearbox, to use another example, one has to draw together the distinctive points with respect to clutch, hand, foot, accelerator, the gear stick, the slope of the road, etc. When one encounters these distinctive points and signs as a problem space and is able to draw them into a plane of consistency (or plateau), then it becomes possible to acquire the skilled knowledge of driving a manual car, a skill one can then state in the form of a rule (e.g. depress the clutch, shift gears, release clutch and press accelerator to engage the new gear). In yet another example, Deleuze discusses the experiment where a monkey is tasked with finding food that is always under a box of a particular colour. Once the monkey comes to an awareness of the fact that there is food under some of the boxes, the monkey is then 'confronted with the objectivity of a problem', that is, with the problem of drawing together the actions involved with the searching and lifting of boxes, identifying colours, selecting some colours and passing over others, etc. Initially the monkey will pick up boxes at random, but then, Deleuze notes, 'there comes a paradoxical period during which the number of "errors" diminishes even though the monkey does not yet possess the "knowledge" or "truth" of a solution in each case'

(Deleuze 1994: 164). This paradoxical period is precisely the plane of consistency that comes to be drawn within the problem space, and learning is the name Deleuze gives to the process of transforming the problem space into the plane of consistency.

We can now better understand Deleuze and Guattari's claim that the commands of the schoolmistress are not 'external or additional to what he or she teaches', or why she 'does not so much instruct as "insign"'. In short, rather than giving her commands and orders as an external 'do as I do' example of a rule, the commands become one of many signs and distinctive points to be *in*-corporated into the problem space students must then draw into a plane of consistency, and it is only then that it becomes possible to grasp the solutions that come to be known as the rules of grammar. We can again contrast this understanding of language with Wittgenstein's, and for similar reasons to the contrast that was highlighted earlier; namely, in the same way that Deleuze and Guattari challenge the exclusive emphasis on the external circumstances that effectuate the condition of possibility of language, so too they would challenge Wittgenstein's model of learning language. Wittgenstein's model appears early in his *Philosophical Investigations*. In his example of sending someone to the shops with a piece of paper 'marked "five red apples"', Wittgenstein discusses a simplified process whereby the shopkeeper 'opens the drawer marked "apples"; then he looks up the word "red" in a table and finds a colour sample opposite it . . . It is in this and similar ways that one operates with words' (Wittgenstein 1986: 3). When the question arises as to how the shopkeeper knows 'where and how he is to look up the word "red" and what he is to do with the word "five"', Wittgenstein simply notes that 'I assume that he acts as I have described. Explanations come to an end somewhere' (1986: 3). In short, rather than understanding learning as the incorporation of signs that involve incorporeal transformations, Wittgenstein understands learning and speaking a language as being nothing less than coming to act in a certain corporeal, bodily way, with this way being what the members of a community recognise as meaningful. No reasons for why we behave in the ways we do are necessary. At some point 'explanations come to an end' and we are simply left saying that this is what we do, or it is our 'form of life', as Wittgenstein puts it.

Where Deleuze and Guattari break most sharply with Wittgenstein is precisely with his resigned acceptance of brute facts, with forms of life that simply manifest what one does, and this, Wittgenstein adds, is the point where one's spade is turned, where explanations come to an end.[8] Wittgenstein thus rejects the principle of sufficient reason, as his mentor Bertrand Russell did, and therefore he rejects the idea one finds in Spinoza, Leibniz and Bradley, among others, that for every thing there is a reason that explains why it is the way it is rather than another way.[9] Although Deleuze will not accept the notion that there is an explicable reason that accounts for each and every thing, he will not accept brute facts either and he argues instead that difference is the condition for the possibility of identity, and thus for the possibility of an explicable reason or brute fact. In the context of the themes addressed in the 'Postulates of Linguistics' plateau, it is not the extensive relationship between, and identity of, the terms of a language, or between a language and the world, that is crucial to Deleuze and Guattari's understanding of language; it is, rather, and as we have seen, the collective assemblage of enunciation, the set of incorporeal transformations, that 'effectuate the condition of possibility of language' (ATP 85). This set of incorporeal transformations, however, is a heterogeneous set, and thus the set of transformations and distinctive points one brings together in learning to swim, for example, is a set with no commonly shared property or quality. 'The movement of the swimmer', Deleuze points out, 'does not resemble that of the wave', and learning to swim as a result is therefore not a matter of finding a commonality between the swimmer and the wave but rather involves generating a habit and skill out of the differences between these distinctive points. The distinctive points themselves, however, or the incorporeal transformations that order-words express, are not brute facts but presuppose their own (heterogeneous) assemblage that effectuates the condition of possibility of this incorporeal transformation. The declaration issued on 20 November 1923 that set the exchange rate for the rentenmark did indeed entail an incorporeal transformation regarding a particular type of paper. The rentenmark became, suddenly and redundant to the declaration itself, a currency with a fixed rate of exchange. This incorporeal transformation presupposed the appointment of Schacht by Stresemann, the passage of legislation by the Reichstag, and a host of other factors, each of which entail their own heterogeneous assemblage of incorporeal transformations, and so on. For Deleuze and Guattari, therefore, rather than accepting brute facts and forms of life as Wittgenstein does, they argue that it is difference all the way down, or more precisely collective, heterogeneous assemblages all the way down.[10]

IV

The importance of assemblages becomes especially evident in the latter half of the 'Postulates of Linguistics' plateau. After returning to the example of the events surrounding 20 November 1923 in Germany, Deleuze and Guattari argue that they can now 'draw some general conclusions about the nature of Assemblages from this' (ATP 88). In fact, they argue that we can now understand the 'tetravalence of the assemblage' (ATP 89). First we can distinguish between a horizontal and a vertical axis of the assemblage. The horizontal axis, they argue,

> comprises two segments, one of content, the other of expression. On the one hand it is a machinic assemblage of bodies, of actions and passions, an intermingling of bodies reacting to one another; on the other hand it is a collective assemblage of enunciation, of acts and statements, of incorporeal transformations attributed to bodies. (ATP 88)

With respect to the rentenmark, on the one side of the horizontal axis it is indeed a physical thing, a body, and a body in relationship to other bodies – the papiermark, the dollar, purchasers, sellers, things offered for sale, and so on. On the other side of the horizontal axis, it was the collective assemblage of enunciation that allowed for the possibility of declaring the exchange rate for the rentenmark, and thus the incorporeal transformation this declaration brings about. As for the vertical axis, Deleuze and Guattari argue that 'the assemblage has both territorial sides, or reterritorialised sides, which stabilise it, and cutting edges of deterritorialisation, which carry it away' (ATP 88). For the German economic assemblage of the early 1920s, the reichsmark became 'the deterritorialising inflation of the monetary body', and the creation of the Rentenbank and the eventual declaration of the rentenmark's exchange rate made possible a reterritorialisation of the monetary body on the rentenmark.

With the two segments of the horizontal axis and the two segments of the vertical axis of the assemblage, we have what Deleuze and Guattari call 'The tetravalence of the assemblage'. The 'feudal assemblage', to highlight Deleuze and Guattari's example, entails

> the interminglings of bodies . . . the body of the earth and the social body; the body of the overlord, vassal, and serf; the body of the knight and the horse and their new relation to the stirrup; the weapons and tools assuring a symbiosis of bodies – a whole machinic assemblages. (ATP 89)

We then have the other segment of the horizontal axis, the 'statements, expressions, the juridical regime of heraldry, all of the incorporeal transformations, in particular oaths and their variables (the oath of obedience, but also the oath of love' (ATP 89). Along the vertical axis of the feudal assemblage we have the 'feudal territorialities and reterritorialisations' – the village, the land, the castle, etc. – 'and at the same time the line of deterritorialisation that carries away both the knight and his mount, statements and acts' (ATP 89) – on a Crusade, for example, to fulfil the word and will of God.

With the tetravalence of the assemblage understood in this way, we can now turn more directly to the claims Deleuze and Guattari make regarding linguistics. Of particular significance in the 'Postulates of Linguistics' plateau are the linguistic theories Deleuze and Guattari are critical of, and the reasons for their criticisms. One of the key mistakes to be found among those working in linguistics, Deleuze and Guattari claim, is to assume that the forms of expression are adequate for understanding a linguistic system, whether this system be 'conceived as a signifying philological structure, or as a deep syntactical structure. In either case', they add, these structures are 'credited with engendering semantics, therefore of fulfilling expression, whereas contents are relegated to the arbitrariness of a simple "reference" and pragmatics to the exteriority of nonlinguistic factors' (ATP 90). Understood as an assemblage, however, one cannot separate out the formal structures of expression from the material contents, whether these contents be understood as the arbitrary reference of an expression or as external non-linguistic factors. An assemblage has both its segment of expression, the collective assemblage of enunciation as the set of incorporeal transformations, and it has the segment of material content where bodies intermingle and interact with one another. What linguists who assume that the formal structures of expression alone are sufficient for engendering a semantics do is to offer an abstraction from language, but an abstraction of the wrong kind, for in the end they set up an 'abstract machine of language but as a synchronic set of constants'. Pragmatics is thus not to be relegated to being among the class of external, non-linguistic factors, but rather, due to the tetravalent nature of the assemblage, 'linguistics itself is inseparable from an internal pragmatics involving its own factors' (ATP 91).

With these criticisms in place, Deleuze and Guattari set their sights on Chomsky's linguistics. In abstracting formal, syntactical structures of deep grammar from language and by assuming that these are sufficient for engendering an understanding of the semantics of language, Deleuze and Guattari accuse Chomsky of succumbing to the wrong form of abstraction. Chomsky thus adopts, they argue, 'an arborescent model and a linear ordering of linguistic elements in sentences and sentence combinations' (ATP 91), and in particular Chomsky establishes an arborescent model of linguistic constants, or 'pseudoconstants' as Deleuze and Guattari put it, that remain unchanged throughout the processes that lead to meaningful expressions. If one recognises the tetravalent nature of the linguistic assemblage, however, and thereby brings into play the pragmatic, bodily components of the assemblage, then one has taken abstraction further and 'one necessarily reaches a level where the pseudoconstants of language are superseded by variables of expression internal to enunciation itself; [and]

these variables of expression are then no longer separable from the variables of content with which they are in perpetual interaction' (ATP 91). We no longer have a fixed, arborescent model of abstract constants but we have instead a rhizomatic model of variables of expression – incorporeal transformations – in continual reciprocal variation with variables of content, and the emergence of rule-like constants is to be understood as being made possible by a process of learning (recall our earlier discussion) rather than as the invariant structure of predetermining constants that guide the processes of learning.

From this critique of Chomsky we can turn to the postulates of linguistics themselves and see which of the postulates one finds prevalent within the field of linguistics Deleuze and Guattari will be most at odds with – namely, the postulate that proposes that 'signification and reference are bound up with a supposedly autonomous and constant structure' (ATP 91). In other words, the semantic relationship between a meaningful expression and the reference or content which accounts for the meaningfulness of this expression is supposedly accounted for, according to much of traditional linguistics, in terms of 'structural invariants' (ATP 92), whether these be 'conceived as a signifying philological structure, or as a deep syntactical structure' (ATP 90). The 'very idea of structure' within traditional linguistics is, Deleuze and Guattari argue, 'inseparable from invariants, whether atomic or relational – [and it] is essential to linguistics' (ATP 92). Deleuze and Guattari, by contrast, do not account for the semantics of language by way of structural invariants; on the contrary, these invariants are themselves accounted for by a linguistic assemblage that involves both a pragmatics and assemblage of material bodies, an intermingling and politics of bodily relations, as well as a collective assemblage of enunciation, a regime of signs. For this reason, Deleuze and Guattari reject the notion that signification is bound up with autonomous structural invariants, and argue instead that 'Content is not a signified nor expression a signifier; rather, both are variables of the assemblage' (ATP 91). Instead of engendering semantics from syntactic and philological structures, these structures, they claim, 'need to be linked to assemblages of enunciation'. Or, as with learning, a set of structured relations between constants is the result of processes of habituation (recall Hume) that engender the possibility of incorporeal transformations that come to be expressed in the determinate terms and commands that become, after the fact, mistaken for structural invariants. The variables of an assemblage are precisely these incorporeal transformations, and they need to be brought into an order – a plane of consistency – that is sufficient to effectuate the possibility of language itself. Without being drawn into a plane of consistency, without an assemblage, language itself would not be possible. It is at this point that we again see the significance of learning for Deleuze and Guattari, for the person who learns to swim also needs to draw the distinctive points of their body, the waves, etc., into that 'paradoxical point' (i.e. plane of consistency) that can then become actualised as a known skill or rule, just as the assemblage of incorporeal transformations that effectuate language makes possible the rules of grammar (structural invariants).

From here we come to a second and related critique of Chomsky. As we have seen, an assemblage is heterogeneous, and thus the collective assemblage of enunciation that is the condition of possibility of language involves a diversity that cannot be reduced to a homogeneous set of elements. In the case of learning to swim, for instance, the distinctive points of one's body and the distinctive points of the waves do not share a common reality, but rather it is the dynamic, intensive difference of the assemblage that is drawn into a plane of consistency. The same is the case for 'assemblages of enunciation', for they too entail a heterogeneous array of 'variables of content' and 'variables of expression' (ATP 88). For Deleuze and Guattari, as a result, 'Every language is an essentially heterogeneous reality' (ATP 93), for it is precisely the heterogeneity of variables of expression and content that are brought into a set and assemblage that 'effectuate the condition of possibility of language' (ATP 85). Instead of recognising and working with the heterogeneous reality of language, however, Chomsky calls for carving from this reality 'a homogeneous or standard system as a basis for abstraction or idealisation, making possible a scientific study of principles' (ATP 93). For Chomsky, Deleuze and Guattari claim, 'even a minor, dialectical, or ghetto language cannot be studied unless invariants are extracted from it and "extrinsic or mixed" variables are eliminated ...' (ATP 103). For the linguist William Labov, by contrast, who Deleuze and Guattari praise and put forward as a contrast to the traditional assumptions regarding the postulates of linguistics, '*You will never find a homogeneous system that is not still or already affected by a regulated, continuous, immanent process of variation*' (ATP 103, emphasis in original). Language is thus always already in process, and in a process of heterogenesis whereby the variables of expression and variables of content, the intermingling of bodies and the set of incorporeal transformations, come to be drawn into a plane of consistency (habituation) that allows for the contemplation and transformation that gives rise to something new, to a determinate expression or rule that then comes to be identified as an established way of speaking, a structural invariant. None of this is to say that it is completely mistaken to point to constants or invariants; rather, for Deleuze and Guattari, the structural invariants of a language are to be understood relative to processes of continuous variation. In short, these invariants 'function as a centre, if only relative' (ATP 95), or they are to be understood in terms of the vertical axis of the tetravalent assemblage, and in particular the territorial/reterritorialised segment of this axis.

V

With this last point concerning the territorial segment of the vertical axis of the linguistic assemblage, we come to an important distinction that will run throughout much of Deleuze and Guattari's collaborative work – the major/minor distinction.[11] A major language involves the territorialised forms of the linguistic assemblage, the set standard and norms whereby other languages are judged and compared. The rules and invariant structures of major languages, however, are made possible by the collective assemblage of enunciation and hence presuppose the deterritorialising segment of the assemblage, the processes of continuous variation as Labov recognised. It is for this reason that Deleuze and Guattari claim that 'majority is never becoming' (ATP 106); it is simply the stasis made possibly by the territorialising tendency of an assemblage, and yet this stasis is only relative, for it is merely a stable centre amid the minor language it presupposes, the minor involving the deterritorialising tendency that entails the becoming-other and continuous variation of the stable centres. A minor language is thus the foreign language within the major language, a stuttering variation and trembling of the established, routine ways of speaking – the everyday language within which Wittgenstein takes refuge.

In *Difference and Repetition*, Deleuze offers linguistic multiplicity as an example to clarify arguments he is making regarding the relationship between faculties (of speech for instance) and Ideas, with Ideas understood in this context as multiplicities. The Idea corresponds to what we have discussed here as the plane of consistency, the paradoxical point that is neither the structured rule one may come to identify and know, nor simply white noise and the absence of order. This Idea or multiplicity, Deleuze argues, 'cannot be spoken in the empirical usage of a given language, but must be spoken and can be spoken only in the poetic usage of speech . . .' (Deleuze 1994: 193). In the 'Postulates of Linguistics' plateau, poetry is offered as an example of a minor language, of the continuous variation and becoming that is masked, hidden and remains unspoken within 'the empirical usage of a given language'. When e. e. cummings writes '"he danced his did" or "they went their came"', he is reconstituting 'the variations through which the grammatical variables pass in virtuality', and in this way the everyday, grammatically correct expressions come to be deterritorialised – expressions such as '"he did his dance", "he danced his dance", "he danced what he did" . . . "they went as they came", "they went their way'" (ATP 99). Cummings's poetic lines are examples of what Deleuze and Guattari call 'atypical expression[s]', and such expressions constitute 'a cutting edge of deterritorialisation of language . . . the role of tensor' (ATP 99). Yet one need not necessarily turn to poetry, Deleuze and Guattari claim, for even 'an expression as simple as AND . . . can play the role of tensor for all of language. In this sense, AND is less a conjunction than the atypical expression of all of the possible conjunctions it places in continuous variation' (ATP 99). In other words, we return to our earlier arguments concerning Hume, and in particular to what Deleuze sees as the secret of empiricism with its stress upon 'Thinking *with* AND, instead of thinking IS' (Deleuze and Parnet 1987: 57). The AND is the cutting edge of any and every assemblage for the very reason that it is the process of drawing together the heterogeneous variables into a plane of consistency that allows for the creativity of habit, and hence for the genesis of something that IS, including the everyday usage of a given language.

We are now in a better position to understand both why Deleuze and Guattari begin the 'Postulates of Linguistics' plateau as they do, and why they conclude it as they do. In the very first paragraph, after introducing the concept of an order-word, they argue that 'Language is not life; it gives life orders. Life does not speak; it listens and waits' (ATP 76). Language, as everyday language, presupposes the creativity of habit, the process whereby a plane of consistency comes to be actualised into something determinate and new, and these actualised forms are then draped over life as the order and structure of our lives as lived (our speaking lives, for instance). Life itself, however, 'does not speak; it listens and waits'. In other words, life is the power of AND, the power of connections and the dynamic creativity of habit that renders effective the 'condition of possibility of language'. As one pushes language towards the deterritorialising pole of the assemblage and away from the everyday, territorialised usage of language, language itself becomes increasingly dynamic and creative, and 'the closer a language gets to this state', Deleuze and Guattari argue, 'the closer it comes not only to a system of musical notation, but also to music itself' (ATP 104). As Deleuze and Guattari draw this plateau to a close, this theme becomes more pronounced, and here we find them calling upon life to answer the tendency of language to give life orders. 'In the order-word,' Deleuze and Guattari say, 'life must answer the answer of death, not by fleeing, but by making flight act and create' (ATP 110). Rather than turning away from the order-words' commands and structuring of life, the death of life as it becomes rigidified stasis, life must push the order-words themselves to the point of deterritorialisation, to the point of becoming musical. This is made possible, as we have seen, because order-words presuppose the collective assemblage of enunciation, and hence the tetravalence of the assemblage and the deterritorialising pole this entails. As a result, Deleuze and Guattari note that there 'are pass-words beneath order-words. Words that pass, words that are components of passage, whereas order-words mark stoppages or organised, stratified compositions' (ATP 110). The point of studying language, therefore, or the point of linguistics as Deleuze and Guattari understand it, is not to reduce language to a composition of structural invariants but rather to 'transform the compositions of order into components of passage' (ATP 110). The task of linguistics is thus to make language stutter, to make it tremble, and in this way allow for the life of language to sing and transform our everyday relationships to one another and to language.

Notes

1. For more on the influence of Hume's philosophy on Deleuze's thought, see my *Deleuze's Hume* (Bell 2009).
2. For more on the history of the German hyperinflation, see Taylor 2013. See also Schacht 1967. Schacht was President of the Reichsbank and currency commissioner for the Weimar Republic on 20 November 1923, and hence he was a key player in these events. His discussion also highlights the importance of the role private banks played in generating the hyperinflation crisis by the manner in which they generated loans and thereby increased the circulation of money.
3. Deleuze and Guattari refer to Ducrot's work in this context, though they equally well could have turned to Austin's discussion of performatives (and they refer to Austin elsewhere in this plateau). Foucault (1989a: 83–4) also draws from the example of such pure acts in speech, or 'performatives' and 'speech acts' as they are more generally known.
4. There are numerous readings of Wittgenstein, and not all agree on the significance of the standard summation of his theory of meaning by the phrase 'meaning is use'. My reading of Wittgenstein is indebted to Saul Kripke's influential *Wittgenstein on Rules and Private Language* (1982).
5. See Deleuze and Guattari 1994: 105.
6. The sense of self, for example, also arises from the incorporeal transformation of the habit of saying 'I'. See Deleuze 1991b: x.
7. See Deleuze and Guattari 1994: 212, but also Deleuze 1994: 75
8. Referring here to *Philosophical Investigations*, section 217, where Wittgenstein famously says, 'If I have exhausted the justifications, I have reached bedrock and my spade is turned. Then I am inclined to say; "This is simply what I do."'
9. For more on this, see the Introduction in Bell 2016.
10. If we keep in mind Deleuze and Guattari's claim that assemblages are the 'working parts' of an abstract machine (1994: 36), and if we understand the abstract machine as the poles an assemblage must stave off if it is to continue to be a functioning assemblage, which will be discussed when we turn next to the tetravalence of the assemblage, then one can see how the claim that it is assemblages all the way down is echoed in the final two sentences of *A Thousand Plateaus*: 'Every abstract machine is linked to other abstract machines, not only because they are inseparably political, economic, scientific, artistic, ecological, cosmic – perceptive, affective, active, thinking, physical, and semiotic – but because their various types are as intertwined as their operations are convergent. Mechanosphere' (ATP 514).
11. See especially Deleuze and Guattari's *Kafka: Toward a Minor Literature* (1986).

Chapter 5

587 BC–AD 70: On Several Regimes of Signs

Audrey Wasser

The familiar narrative regarding French thought in the twentieth century follows, to a great extent, the fortunes of the concept of the sign. From Saussure and his inauguration of structuralist linguistics, to Lévi-Strauss, Barthes, Lacan and other post-war figures who set to work linguistic insights in the fields of anthropology, literary criticism, cultural studies and psychoanalysis – these thinkers revolutionised their disciplines by asserting the primacy of a study of interconnected signs. And they freed signs from immediate reference to things in the world by grasping them primarily as elements of a structure – as manifestations of an underlying system. In literary studies, my own field, structuralism made possible a shift away from the goal of interpreting individual texts towards the broader study of poetics, of systems of convention that subtend multiple texts and yield the conditions of possibility of meaning (Culler 2002: vii; Culler 2001: xi, 12). In Deleuze and Guattari's terms, we might say that in literary criticism, structuralism made possible a shift away from the question 'What does this particular text mean?' to the more pragmatic question 'How does it work?' (cf. Deleuze and Guattari 1983: 108; Deleuze 1995a: 8).

We know that Deleuze and Guattari depart from structuralism in significant ways; indeed, their *Capitalism and Schizophrenia* project has been described as a 'veritable war-machine against structuralism'.[1] Nonetheless, it may be fruitful to continue to consider their work in relation to structuralism in order to bring out finer points of difference. They clearly participate, after all, in their generation's enthusiasm for the study of signs. Yet the term 'regimes of signs' is unique to Deleuze and Guattari's work; and in the plateau 'On Several Regimes of Signs', one of the first things we learn about these regimes is that there is more than one. Asserting this plurality may, in fact, be the most important thing Deleuze and Guattari do in this plateau, and it sets them apart from one of structuralism's most characteristic features: its reliance on the unity of a structure or of a structural plane of analysis.

Jean-Claude Milner (2013), for example, in a recent issue of *Les temps modernes*, has described the distinguishing feature of structuralist analysis as the positing of a unique and unitary set of relations. Consider the unity of what Saussure calls 'la langue', or the system of a language, over and above the diversity of individual speech acts. Terms within a language are defined entirely by their place within a set of relations, in a way that would preclude the possibility of transposing terms from one language to another. Since a term in any given structure has no intrinsic value, in other words, but receives its value from its place in a structure, it cannot travel from structure to structure and retain the same value. The closure of a structure is what produces the value of its terms, and also what would seem to exclude the possibility of thinking a relation that lay outside that structure. In this way, structuralism is unable to think the relation *between* structures, or at least to think them in structuralist terms. Following this thread, we might say that Deleuze and Guattari's attempt to describe the plurality, transformation and mixture *between* what they call regimes of signs diverges significantly from the aims of structuralism.

If we focus on the characteristics of two regimes in particular – namely, what Deleuze and Guattari call the 'signifying regime' and the 'post-signifying regime' – we can arrive at a consideration of what allows us to think the relation between them. Along the way, we will further distinguish Deleuze and Guattari's approach from structuralism by addressing some key questions: most basically, what is a sign, for Deleuze and Guattari? How do signs work, and what does a confrontation with signs look like? Secondly, what is a regime, and how does it differ from a structure? What is involved in the assertion that a given set of signs constitutes a 'regime'?

Prior to *A Thousand Plateaus*, Deleuze's most extensive study of signs appeared in *Proust and Signs*, first published in 1966 and revised significantly in 1972 and 1973, at the height of his collaboration with Guattari. In what follows, I will also extend the reading of Proust through the lens of 'Several Regimes of Signs' as a way of developing the claims of this plateau.

Formalisation in the social field

'We call any specific formalisation of expression a regime of signs', Deleuze and Guattari begin (ATP 111). This formalisation does not take place in a vacuum, though, for, following the work of the Danish linguist Louis Hjelmslev, our authors link every form of expression to a substance of expression, as well as to a form and a substance of content. Even from the point of view of form, 'there is always a form of content that is simultaneously inseparable from and independent of the form of expression' (ATP 111). In this way they expand Hjelmslev's model to non-linguistic organisations, linking sense and meaning to bodies and relations of force. Form and substance of expression; form and substance of content: here we have the four fundamental components of what Deleuze and Guattari call an *assemblage*. This key concept runs throughout *A Thousand Plateaus*, and it can be grasped most basically as Deleuze and Guattari's minimum unit of analysis of the real.[2] An assemblage is a multiplicity, which means that the minimum unit is not simple in itself, but complex and relational. It also means that every assemblage has smaller assemblages within it, reality being assemblages all the way down. 'What is an assemblage?' Deleuze asks in *Dialogues*. 'It is a multiplicity which is made up of many heterogeneous terms and which establishes liaisons, relations between them . . . Thus, the assemblage's only unity is that of co-functioning' (Deleuze and Parnet 1987: 69). An assemblage entails the co-functioning of a form and a substance of expression along with a form and a substance of content.

'Under what circumstances may we speak of signs? Should we say . . . that there is a sign whenever there is a form of expression?' (ATP 64). There are forms of expression proper to the organic realm and the mineral realm – a cellular protein, for example, can be said to express a certain nucleic sequence (ATP 59), or a crystal can be said to express a certain set of molecular interactions (ATP 57). Yet these expressions remain bound to the particular substances in which they appear. Likewise, signs may remain bound to particular territories or bodies, where they serve as 'indexes' (ATP 65) or 'habitudes' (Deleuze 1994: 77).[3] We may properly speak of 'regimes of signs' only when forms of expression become independent from particular substances, and when signs become sufficiently deterritorialised to be able to refer to one another – in other words, when, like languages, they are translatable (Deleuze 1994: 62). Regimes of signs, then, are limited to the human realm of language and culture. In *A la recherche du temps perdu*, when a friendly gesture from the Duc de Guermantes is interpreted as a warning to keep one's distance (Proust 1981: vol. II, 687), we know we are in the presence of a regime of signs of social belonging and exclusion, and we know these signs can be expressed in a myriad of ways – as words, gestures, clothing, ways of speaking, ways of listening to music or behaving towards women.

Forms of expression proper to the human realm are 'set[s] of statements arising in the social field' (ATP 66). With this assertion, Deleuze and Guattari make it clear that they approach the study of regimes of signs, not through a set of postulates about language's abstract and universal nature, but through an affirmation of language's embeddedness in the social. If societies are multiple and exist in states of mixture, the same must be true of languages. Deleuze and Guattari place a primacy on the physical, political and contextual dimensions of regimes of signs, treating these dimensions not as extrinsic factors but as a pragmatics that yields the very conditions of possibility of human signs (ATP 85). 'Pragmatics' here assumes a quasi-transcendental status.

The signifying regime

Under what circumstances, then, may we speak of signifiers and signifieds? Rather than reject the structuralist analysis, Deleuze and Guattari situate it as one regime of signs among many – what they call the 'signifying regime'. And it is through the study of this regime that we grasp the limitations of a strictly linguistic approach and the necessity of introducing social, political and pragmatic considerations.

The signifying regime is characterised by a certain distribution of signs and a certain comportment of people caught up in this distribution. Formally, signs radiate outward from a central point. Every sign refers to another sign, so that signs become signs of signs rather than signs of things, producing a signifying chain that glides over an amorphous continuum of signifieds (ATP 112). What is signified remains indeterminate, a kind of blank wall on which signifiers can be projected. Character types inhabit this regime, crowding it with affects and activities: a paranoid despot with a spreading body sits at the centre, controlling the radiance of signs; priests surround the despot, proliferating interpretations; hysterical and paranoid subjects jump from sign to sign, evading the despot's decrees or else gathering up clues, trying to attain some truth that lies at the centre.[4] As in any centralised and hierarchical organisation, certain elements invariably clash with or escape from the pull of the centre, and these elements are assigned purely a negative or excremental value: they become the goat cast into the wilderness bearing the sins of the people, or the goat offered in blood sacrifice to the despot-god (ATP 112–16).

In this way Deleuze and Guattari create a kind of fantastic fable about the signifying regime, populating it with an outsized tyrant, his interpretive minions, his terrorised and hyper-vigilant subjects, and a combinatory of possible actions. Their fable makes it sound as if the signifying regime belonged to a specific form of pre-modern society, but in fact it can appear in any age, under any official governmental form. It appears whenever there are 'subjected, arborescent, hierarchical, centred groups: political parties, literary movements, psychoanalytic associations, families, conjugal units' (ATP 116). We see, then, that the notion of 'regime' describes at one and the same time a certain relationship to knowledge and a certain distribution of power.

The paranoid method

The signifying regime is structured like a secret and a spiralling series of deceptions. Because the signified is indeterminate, we know we are in the presence of signifiers before we know (if we ever know) *what* is being signified. Considering a subject caught up in this regime, we might say the regime describes the subject's affective response to the fact that signs are not bound to particular substances (to the fact they exhibit a high degree of 'deterritorialisation' [ATP 112]). Because *any* substance can potentially express a sign, *every* substance is suspected of expressing a sign – of containing secret messages that only you can interpret.

> Your wife looked at you with a funny expression. And this morning the mailman handed you a letter from the IRS and crossed his fingers. Then you stepped in a pile of dog shit. You saw two sticks on the sidewalk positioned like the hands of a watch. They were whispering behind your back when you arrived at the office. (ATP 112)

The affect in question is paranoia; and paranoia structures acts of interpretation even as it corrodes them, turning them into so many symptoms of madness. 'Signs and Symbols', a short story by Vladimir Nabokov first published in 1948, imagines just such a madness and names it 'referential mania'. This incurable derangement is coolly defined by Nabokov's narrator as follows:

> In these very rare cases the patient imagines that everything happening around him is a veiled reference to his personality and existence . . . Phenomenal nature shadows him wherever he goes. Clouds in the staring sky transmit to each other, by means of slow signs, incredibly detailed information regarding him. His in-most thoughts are discussed at nightfall, in manual alphabet, by darkly gesticulating trees. (Nabokov 1997: 599)

The fantastic thing about this story is the way it works to infect its readers with the same madness as the referential maniac. It creates a series of spirals, radiating outward from the patient in the sanatorium to his ageing parents who, during the brief span of events of the story, are unable to visit their son but who think of nothing but the mental and physical state he may be in, drawing on various signs in their environment to help them ascertain this state. The reader, in turn, is drawn in to a kind of mimetic interpretosis, invited to make sense of various details in the story that seem to have no determinate meaning: a basket of ten fruit jellies, three mishaps on the way to the sanatorium, three wrong-number phone calls at midnight. In their attempts to find meaning in the story, Nabokov's critics have gone so far as to search for acrostics or hidden numerical codes in the text, though with as-yet unconvincing results.[5]

In the real world, reading every phenomenal encounter as a veiled message or reference to oneself would indeed be a form of madness, but in a short story, readings like this not only can be undertaken, but arguably must be. It is the task of the critic to draw connections, to leave no sign unturned, to suspect design in every element of the literary world, including her own sleuthing participation in this world. Nabokov's story is so uncanny because it suggests that, at its limit, all literary interpretation may be a form of madness.

Have another look at the passage quoted above. In it, clouds 'transmit' in a sky described as 'staring'; the trees 'gesticulate'. The rhetorical device employed here is personification, the projection of human qualities or a human face on to non-human entities. The face is a device, a mask or *persona*, but 'the mask does not hide the face, it *is* the face', in Deleuze and Guattari's words (ATP 115).[6] Meaning makes a face, and it makes the face as a condition of meaning. The face, in turn, organises what would otherwise be free-floating signifiers, giving them a home-base, a substance of expression, and a means of reproducing themselves, fuelling further interpretation. The despot brandishes his face as his most powerful weapon: 'He looked at me queerly, he knitted his brow, what did I do to make him change expression?' (ATP 115). 'Paranoia', from the Greek, literally means being 'outside' or 'beside' one's own mind. It entails the projection of mind on to the external world, attempting to draw, on so many incomprehensible fragments of phenomena, sensible coordinates – two eyes, a nose, a speaking mouth. In this way, in Leo Bersani's words, paranoia does not so much uncover secrets as openly repeat the phenomenal world as design. It entails discovering that 'the orders behind the visible are not necessarily . . . different from the visible; rather they are the visible *repeated as structure*' (Bersani 1990: 183). When structure begins to speak, it looks like a face.

In *Remembrance of Things Past*, consider the Baron de Charlus, prodigious emitter and interpreter of signs (Deleuze 2004b: 5). His face betrays him, for when he first appears in the narrative he gives one the feeling that he might be a crook, a madman or a spy; while he feigns a lack of interest, his eyes remain 'dilated with extreme attentiveness', 'straying in all directions like those of certain frightened animals', firing off glances 'like a last shot which one fires at an enemy as one turns to flee' (Proust 1981: vol. I, 807, 815). The contortions of his face both conceal and reveal a secret. This turns out to be a real secret – his amorous encounters with other men, which he attempts to keep hidden from the oppressive social circles in which he turns – as well as a kind of secret-as-spectacle, a mode of paranoid behaviour fully on display to Proust's narrator, and in turn to the reader.[7] In this way, Charlus is both subject and object of a paranoid regime of interpretation. Deleuze's reading locates him as one of several focal points of madness in *Remembrance of Things Past*, so that through him, we discover to what extent paranoia is a shared structure of interpreter and interpretee. 'There is no way,' Deleuze writes, 'of distinguishing the labour of Charlus's interpretive delirium from the narrator's long labour of interpretive delirium concerning Charlus' (Deleuze 2004b: 116).

In fact, the narrator's interpretive delirium concerning Charlus is echoed in the interpretive delirium concerning his own involuntary memories. Involuntary memory, in *Remembrance of Things Past*, takes the form of a formidable encounter with signs. Periodically the narrator is struck by a sense impression – the taste of a little cake dunked in tea, the clinking of a fork, the loss of balance from stepping on an uneven paving stone – joined by a powerful affect, which together transform him into a relentless detective, putting him on the track of strange signs or hieroglyphs, as he calls them (Proust 1981: vol. III, 912). The content of these signs turns out to be the matter of his own life; and the conversion of this matter into a network of signs to be deciphered promises the spiritual redemption of the years he had previously considered to be so much wasted time.

The narrator's confrontation with the signs of involuntary memory seems to me to be paranoid, above all, because what is conveyed by these phenomenal encounters is ultimately pattern for the sake of pattern alone. Granted, the narrator claims to discover 'essences' or 'truths' hidden behind the signs, or encased within them like so many lost souls trapped in sealed vessels (Proust 1981: vol. I, 47). But these 'souls' turn out to be those of the narrator himself, fragments of his former self; and the 'truth' he discovers lies, not in any particular content of the past, but in the resonance of the past with the present, in the signals flashing between past and present like beacons in the night.

What does the signifying regime signify? Ultimately, it signifies itself: it asserts its own structure as meaningful, and it patches over holes in meaning with the projection of a face.[8] In *Remembrance of Things Past*, this projection is that of the narrator's own being, the construction of a continuity of self, and ultimately of a coherent work of art that can localise resonances between past and present and render legible 'the vast structure of recollection' (Proust 1981: vol. I, 47). The paranoid method belonging to this regime seems, then, to discover no independent truths. Every time it sets to work it really just discovers one thing, and one thing only:

that everything is connected. Again, the paranoid regime repeats the phenomenal world as design; and the will of the despot is a metaphor for the legibility of this design. The despot's face may seem malignant, but much more malignant is the prospect of being assaulted by fragments of sense data without any possibility of organising them at all. The face 'sets the limit of [the] deterritorialisation' of signs (ATP 115).

Infernal signifying machines

When Deleuze writes that Proust's narrator as well as the enigmatic Charlus are caught up in the same interpretive delirium, he draws our attention to the machinic dimension of signs. Proust's work is a 'machine . . . producing signs of different orders' (Deleuze 2004b: viii); and 'there is less a narrator than a machine of the Search, and less a hero than the arrangements by which the machine functions under one or another configuration' (Deleuze 2004b: 117). Like all regimes of signs, the signifying regime is a machine because it defines the mechanism of its own functioning, and it sets the parameters for its own transformation. Its action is not the result of an intentional subject but the product of the political and epistemological demands of signs themselves, signs that set in motion imperatives that are proper to them, transforming the subjectivities and collectivities that get caught up with them.

The imperative dimension of signs appears in Deleuze's work as early as his writing on Nietzsche. In *Nietzsche and Philosophy* (first published in 1962), Deleuze draws out the extent to which signs in Nietzsche's writings are bound up with a philosophy of force and will. For Nietzsche, every existing phenomenon can be grasped as a sign whose meaning is found in a certain relation of forces. This means that when we encounter something in the world, the right question to ask is not *what is the idea behind this phenomenon?* or even *what is the cause of this phenomenon?* but *what are the forces that exploit it, take possession of it, or are expressed in it?* (Deleuze 1983: 3). Interpreting the sense of a phenomenon entails elaborating the agonistic forces at work on it and determining their relative degrees of domination and subordination, action and reaction. So from one perspective, to interpret is to elaborate a structure of forces. From another perspective, however, the phenomenon is already itself an interpretation – already a sign – because its very existence indicates a selection and affirmation of the more dominant forces acting on it. To exist as a sign is to interpret the forces acting on oneself; what is more, to exist is to *evaluate* these forces, because every existing entity entails a judgement passed on what is good or bad for its continued existence.

Nietzsche seeks the sense and value of phenomena, not by posing the classical philosophical question *what is . . .?* but by posing the ethical question *which one?* The question treats 'any given concept, feeling or belief' as the sign of a way of life, of an ethos, a 'symptom of a will that wills something' (Deleuze 1983: 78). Nietzsche's method yields priests and slaves, noble souls and base souls, because it interprets by determining character types, 'the type of the one that speaks, of the one that thinks, that acts, that does not act, that reacts etc.' (Deleuze 1983: 79).[9] These types dramatize a multiplicity of forces that remain virtual, or sub-representational. Likewise, in 'On Several Regimes of Signs' Deleuze and Guattari seek the forms of life that are expressive of sub-representational multiplicities of forces. What I referred to earlier as a 'fable' of the despot and his minions might be better understood, in a Nietzschean vein, as a kind of tragic drama: a dramatisation of force and a theatrical method of interpretation, where characters make manifest the roles accorded to them by the infernal signifying machine. Every regime of signs, in fact, can be understood to submit the formal insights of structuralism to the ethical questions *who?*, *which one?* and *what kind of life?*

In *Difference and Repetition*, Deleuze speaks of structuralism as a kind of theatre:

> It is not surprising that, among many of the authors who promote it, *structuralism* is so often accompanied by calls for a new theatre ... a theatre of multiplicities opposed in every respect to the theatre of representation, which leaves intact neither the identity of the thing represented, nor author, nor spectator, nor character ... Instead, a theatre of problems and always open questions which draws spectator, setting and characters into the real movement of an apprenticeship. (Deleuze 1994: 192)

A theatre of problems and an apprenticeship: this latter term recalls *Proust and Signs*, where Proust's narrator is described as undergoing an apprenticeship in his encounter with signs. 'Apprenticeship', or more simply 'learning', names the cumulative, transformative and machinic process that takes place in response to one's repeated exposure to signs. The process does not yield a representation but a transformed organism, an evolved cognition, or a mutated subjectivity. We call it machinic because it is governed by imperatives that are not themselves organic but that traverse the organism. Both the method of dramatisation and the theory of learning, in sum, reveal the essentially heterogeneous destiny of signs. For signs do not reproduce themselves in an image, or in an imitative action, but initiate a drama of metamorphosis. Signs compel us to learn.[10]

The metamorphosis triggered by a set of signs is not necessarily controlled by a despotic, centripetal force, as it is in the signifying regime. Deleuze and Guattari identify several other regimes of signs, two of which are directly anti-despotic: one is the 'presignifying' regime, which proliferates, along with vocal forms, other expressive forms of content such as gesturality, rhythm, dance and rite (ATP 117). Another is the 'countersignifying' regime, which works through the activity of numbering to create immanent, mobile and plural distributions, distributions that traverse the hierarchy of signification and have the potential to destroy its centralised networks (ATP 118). The metamorphosis of the subject, however, comes to the fore in the regime that Deleuze and Guattari call 'post-signifying'.

The post-signifying regime

The post-signifying regime is triggered by a decisive external occurrence, whether real or imagined, and is characterised by a procedure of subjectification (ATP 120). A sign or a packet of signs breaks away from the centripetal force of the signifying regime and gives rise to a new set of functions, a new machine, one that creates a line of flight away from the centre. A subject is interpellated – Deleuze and Guattari cite Althusser's theory of the social constitution of individuals (ATP 130) – one who will perform his subjectivity by progressing from sign to sign as if carrying out a singular task, undergoing a difficult trial, or bearing out a stay of execution.[11]

There are two major theatres of the post-signifying regime. One is psychiatric in nature: in the late nineteenth and early twentieth century, French psychiatrists identified a distinct kind of delirium, one that was not paranoid but that was still bound by a relation to signs. This was the 'passional delusion', defined by 'querulousness or seeking redress, jealousy, erotomania' as well as monomania, giving rise to actions and passions rather than ideations (ATP 120–1). The erotomaniac is interpellated by the signs of his beloved just as the anorexic (a monomaniac) is interpellated by signs of food; each finds his subjectification in a series of behaviours triggered by a particular signifying object.

The other theatre of this regime is biblical: the ancient Hebrews follow a line of flight out of Egypt – out of a despotic signifying regime – to begin a new trial in the wilderness; a people is born in this exodus, one that maintains its subjectification in a series of rituals that serve less to interpret than to reiterate, by means of signs, the covenant with God. A prophet with a great imagination leads the people, himself led by a sign of the word of God.[12]

What do these two theatres have in common? They show that the function of interpretation changes in this regime, or rather that the mental dimension of interpretation is replaced with a material repetition of signs in concrete practices. The interpretive delirium is replaced by a delirium of action (Deleuze 2004b: 116). Moreover, while the signifying regime produces a redundancy of signifiers – with signifiers referring to other signifiers and so on indefinitely, producing a signifying chain that glides over an amorphous continuum of signifieds – the post-signifying regime bears witness to a redundancy of subjects, to a redoubling of the interpellated subject with his point of subjectification. Recall that Althusser's theory of interpellation stresses the specular structure of subject-formation: 'Hey! You there!' a policeman hails an individual in the street. The individual turns her head because she recognises herself as always-already addressed, as subject to the law, and in a sense as already guilty. There is no need for a repressive apparatus because power is organised immanently in the post-signifying regime and appears in effects of normalisation. Ultimately, the individual recognises herself in the image of an ideal Subject – one that may take the form of God, Christ, the Good Citizen, Human Nature – and her recognition is born out in a series of concrete actions, such as allowing herself to be detained, allowing her bag to be searched, and so forth.

Less easy to spot than the interpellation of a subject, but no less important, is the construction of a point of subjectification. For the monomaniac, this point takes the form of an object commanding a certain set of behaviours (an ingestion-object for the anorexic, a theft-object for the kleptomaniac, an incendiary-object for the pyromaniac), while for the jealous lover, this point takes the form of a mobile object of desire.[13] Albertine, for example, the elusive target of Proust's narrator's tormented affections, presents her lover with a fundamental problem, that of the constitution of her very objecthood. At first she needs to be individuated from a group of girls, for she appears indistinguishable from her friends, all of whose features are scrambled and distributed among one another. Writes the narrator:

> They were known to me only by a pair of hard, obstinate and mocking eyes, for instance, or by cheeks whose pinkness had a coppery tint reminiscent of geraniums; and even these features I had not yet indissolubly attached to any one of these girls rather than to another; and when . . . I saw a pallid oval, black eyes, green eyes, emerge, I did not know if these were the same that had already charmed me a moment ago, I could not relate them to any one girl whom I had set apart from the rest and identified. (Proust 1981: vol. I, 847)

The lesson of Albertine may indeed be, in Deleuze's words, that 'to fall in love is to individualise someone by the signs he bears or emits' (Deleuze 2004b: 5). Once distinguished from her friends, however, Albertine still remains for the narrator a sort of kaleidoscope creature, a changeable performer: 'each of these Albertines was different, as is each appearance of the dancer whose colours, form, character, are transmuted according to the endlessly varied play of a projected limelight' (Proust 1981: vol. I, 1010). And even when she is pinned down for a kiss, she still manages to turn her face away: 'Albertine's round face, lit by an inner flame as by a night light, stood out in such relief that, imitating the rotation of a glowing sphere, it seemed to me to be turning, like those Michelangelo figures which are being swept away in a stationary and vertiginous whirlwind' (Proust 1981: vol. I, 996). This motion of perpetual turning continues even after Albertine's death, for the true nature of her affections remains, for the narrator as for the reader, as elusive as ever. By putting the reader in the same position as the lover, Proust suggests that jealousy may be as much a problem of *reading* as it is of desire, and that like paranoia, jealousy may be generalised to a whole regime of interpretation. The face turning away reveals a new function of faciality in the post-signifying regime. Whereas the despot of the signifying regime controls the network of signs with the frontal image of his face, the beloved turns her face aside. She jealously guards a secret, one that turns out to have no meaning other than her betrayal of the subject that pursues her. If the secret of the paranoid signifying regime is that everything potentially concerns me – including the clouds in the staring sky or the gesticulating trees – we might say that the secret of the passional subjective regime is the lack of concern for me shown by the one I pursue, the one who moves away from me, the one who is perhaps not even thinking about me.[14]

Betrayal arises from the fact that the subject cannot fully absorb his point of subjectification, nor perfectly mirror the speaking subject that interpellates him. Both speaker and the one spoken to turn away from each other. If we return to the ancient Israelites, we find that in Exodus, God shields his face from Moses, showing only his back to the prophet: 'He said, "You shall not be able to see My face, for no human can see Me and live . . . you will see My back, but My face will not be seen"' (Alter 2004: Exodus 33:23). Moses, in turn, hides his own face from the Lord. And when he returns from Mount Sinai, he veils his face from the people. The back or the veil is a material sign that takes the place of a lack of presence – indeed, the biblical Hebrew word for 'face', פנים [*panim*], is the same as the word for 'presence' (Alter 2004: Exodus 33:12 n.14). And this sign that takes the place of a lack, like the secret of the elusive beloved, appears in the empty place of a structure; it does not represent but touches off a series of actions, performs a function of iterability, of repetition with a difference. It speaks only on the condition of a turning aside, literally effecting an apostrophe, Greek for 'turning away'. And in turning aside to address another it produces a subject of the address; or more precisely it produces a split and differentiated subject, a subject of enunciation and a subject of the statement, a lying subject and a subject lied to, or a promising subject and a subject of the promise.

The promise, like the lie, binds its non-identical subjects together. We can see this binding above all in the Jewish notion of the covenant – the notion that a people's relationship to their God is sustained by a contract – which has been described by biblical scholars as unparalleled in the ancient world.[15] What attaches the ancient Israelites to their God, as well as to one another, is not the presence of the deity nor the occupation of a certain territory, but a covenant, a promise and a salvation held in abeyance.

Regime change

I mentioned earlier that what stands out in the title of 'On Several Regimes of Signs' is the assertion of a plurality of regimes. The other thing that stands out are, of course, the dates, for like every chapter or 'plateau' in *A Thousand Plateaus*, the title of this piece is accompanied by a date, or here a set of dates: 587 BC and AD 70. We may recognise these dates as marking two decisive events in the history of the Jewish people: the destruction of the first and second Temples. The dates are associated, then, neither with a despotic regime nor with the subjective regime of the nation of Israel, but with a decisive break – with a regime change, we might say.

Deleuze and Guattari link the destruction of the Temple to a series of renewed proceedings, beginning with the exodus in Egypt and the construction of the ark and tabernacle, a mobile, desert temple (ATP 122), 'a little portable packet of signs'. The Bible describes the ark as veiled, like Moses' face, which suggests that this portable packet of signs took on certain traits of a transformed faciality. In Deleuze and Guattari's words, in the subjective regime the face no longer sets the limits of deterritorialisation, blocking the line of flight from forming or assigning it a purely negative value; rather, the face turned aside creates a line of flight – here, literally a line of march through the desert – and imbues this line with a positive, albeit limited, value. But it does so only on the condition of a betrayal, a promise forsaken. Indeed Moses recites a great canticle of betrayal just before his death, citing Israel's faithlessness as well as his own trespasses, which will result in his exclusion from the promised land (ATP 123; Alter 2004: Deuteronomy 32).

Subjects of broken promises, faces turned aside, enact a betrayal that will forge a new line; they mark a difference from the origin and a deferral of the end that becomes creative of a new way of life. Indeed, we can observe that following the destruction of the first Temple, the nation exiled in Babylon gives birth to a new era of Jewish customs. Ritual sacrifice is replaced by ritual prayer; the physical borders of the kingdom are replaced with dietary customs and the mark of circumcision on the body of the people. The dates Deleuze and Guattari cite mark a moment of rupture, a rupture that becomes a passage to a new mode of being.

As much as Deleuze and Guattari enumerate differences between regimes, then, they elaborate the passages that take place between these regimes. The dates of the destruction of the Temples underscore their focus on rupture; and the line of flight that runs from both regimes, connecting each to what lies beyond it, gives us a way to conceive of an opening, and of a piece of the outside, that exists internally to each regime. For every regime admits a line of flight, whether it codes this line as negative or positive, limited or absolute. These lines reserve the potential to disrupt their regimes and open them to new forms of organisation.

We have seen that a regime of signs differs from a structure insofar as it implicates an organisation of power, along with a number of pragmatic variables that allow meaning to effectuate itself in a lived context, among bodies and states of affairs. Ultimately, then, I think the difference between a regime and a structure lies in the fact that a structure is virtual, a set of a conditions of possibility of a language or of something structured like a language. A regime of signs, on the other hand, is always actual, coinciding 'neither with a structure nor with units of a given order, but rather intersect[ing] them and caus[ing] them to appear in space and time' (ATP 140). The structure intersecting a regime is conceived as a multiplicity (Deleuze and Guattari make this argument in 'Introduction: Rhizome'); a multiplicity is open and in excess of itself by definition, so that a regime is needed – a coup or a capture of forces – to produce any kind of effect of unity.

In other words, it is the unity of a group of signs that needs to be explained in the first place, not the fact of their multiplicity, such that we can even speak of 'a' regime or 'a' structure. Unity, Deleuze and Guattari write, 'appears only when there is a power takeover in the multiplicity by the signifier, or a corresponding subjectification proceeding' (ATP 8). The primary task of any practical analysis of a regime of signs, then, should be to account for the emergence of such a power takeover, a takeover that produces a counting-for-one. While we have not undertaken that particular work here, we have laid the groundwork for it by attempting to show why it is necessary. The erection of a despot has to be accounted for, just as the production of a subject has to be accounted for. Once we trace these lines of construction, once we show how the projection of a face in the signifying regime works to unify and centralise, once we show how the turning aside of the face in the post-signifying regime works to produce a speaking subject and a subject of address, it becomes clear that categories of unity, and ultimately the cohesion of structure as such, is merely a secondary effect. Unity belongs to the actual, to the surface, and is, in the end, an effect of power. But beneath every regime is a rumbling stream of affects, character traits and territorial markers waiting to be harnessed in new organisations.

Notes

1. François Dosse has asserted that 'Anti-Oedipus is conceived as a veritable war machine against structuralism' (Dosse 2012: 126, 135) while Eric Alliez has said the same of the concept of 'rhizome' (Alliez 2011: 38).
2. As Deleuze explains in *Dialogues* with Claire Parnet: 'The minimum real unit is not the word, the idea, the concept or the signifier, but the assemblage' (Deleuze and Parnet 1987: 51). See also Guillaume Sibertin-Blanc's 'L'analyse des agencements et le groupe de lutte comme expérimentateur collectif' (2007) which emphasises the analytic function of the assemblage, describing it as '[l]'unité d'analyse d'une conjoncture objective, de situation d'analyse, et de procès pratique comme agent d'analyse' [the unity of analysis of an objective conjuncture, of an analytic situation, and of a practical process serving as agent of analysis].
3. In this sense, Bonta and Protevi can define as a sign any 'element that triggers a material process in a properly attuned body' (Bonta and Protevi 2004: 141).
4. For a helpful further discussion of the signifying as well as post-signifying regimes, see Adkins 2015: 83–95.
5. See, for example, Leving 2012.
6. See also Rei Terada, who links Deleuze and Guattari's notion of faciality with Paul de Man's analysis of prosopopoeia insofar as, for both, the face is at once 'the cause for and the circumference of interpretive events' (Terada 2001: 122).
7. Eve Sedgwick famously describes the invitation to voyeurism of Charlus's closetedness as a 'spectacle of the closet' (Sedgwick 1990: 223).
8. On this projection of the face over a void, I particularly enjoy Mark Bonta and John Protevi's comparison of the despotic signifier to the Wizard of Oz (Bonta and Protevi 2004: 142).
9. Deleuze takes this Nietzschean insight even further in 'The Method of Dramatization', when he argues that the basic discovery of what an Idea is is inseparable from a certain type of question: *who?, how much?, which one?* allow us to grasp the way Ideas are incarnated or 'dramatised' in space and time (Deleuze 2004a: 94).
10. Deleuze's memorable example of the way signs compel us to learn is of a person learning to swim. In *Difference and Repetition* he writes: 'The movement of the swimmer does not resemble that of the wave, in particular, the movements of the swimming instructor which we reproduce on the sand bear no relation to the movements of the wave, which we learn to deal with only by grasping the former in practice as signs. That is why it is so difficult to say how someone learns: there is an innate or practical familiarity with signs . . . [A] body combines some of its own distinctive points with those of the wave' (Deleuze 1994: 23).
11. Guillaume Sibertin-Blanc (2009) underscores this connection to Althusser's theory of interpellation in his essay 'La malédiction du justicier', in which he argues that regimes of signs are essentially theological and political, in the sense in which Spinoza gives these terms in his *Theological-Political Treatise* (Spinoza 2001).
12. Deleuze and Guattari note that 'it is Spinoza who has elaborated the profoundest theory of prophetism, taking into account the semiotic proper to it' (ATP 123).

13. See Beckett 1965 for a brilliant discussion of the mobility of objects of desire in Proust.
14. In his reading of jealousy in Proust, J. Hillis Miller describes the very annihilation of the self at stake here: 'I find that intolerable, that she can think of something else, and so in a manner of speaking annihilate me, since I have given myself into her keeping' (Miller 1995: 122).
15. See, for example, Christiansen 1995: 8 and n.27.

Chapter 6

November 28, 1947: How Do You Make Yourself a Body without Organs?

John Protevi

The Sixth Plateau of *A Thousand Plateaus* concentrates on the body without organs (hereafter, BwO). Deleuze and Guattari make many distinctions in their treatment of the BwO: 1) procedural: there is a two-step process in fabricating a BwO; 2) structural: a BwO swings between the strata, which organise it, and the plane of consistency, where it connects to other BwOs; 3) generic: there are three kinds of BwOs: full, empty, cancerous; 4) ontological: BwOs are either singular or universal, and within each category they can be either intensive or virtual.

Overall, however, the main distinction is between a political BwO – how humans can break away from the dominant social patterning of their bodies, their 'organism' – and an abstract notion of BwO as any breakdown of order interspersed between moments of organisation. At the end of this chapter, I will illustrate the latter aspect with comments on neuroscience and biology concepts.

Cutting across all these distinctions, the principle that renders the entire plateau consistent is desire. 'The BwO is desire . . . There is desire whenever there is the constitution of a BwO . . . It is a problem not of ideology but of pure matter, a phenomenon of physical, biological, psychic, social, or cosmic matter' (ATP 165). In ranging across the material, biological and social domains, the discussion of the BwO in the Sixth Plateau uses terms developed in the analysis of 'desiring-production' in *Anti-Oedipus*: 'Experimentation . . . biological and political . . . Corpus and Socius' (ATP 150; Deleuze and Guattari 1983: 10, 33, *et passim*).

A reminder is in order before we begin our analysis proper: 'BwO' is something of a misnomer; it would have been better to call it by the more accurate but less elegant term 'a non-organismic body'. Deleuze and Guattari freely admit that 'the BwO is not at all the opposite of the organs.

The organs are not its enemies. The enemy is the organism' (ATP 158). A BwO retains its organs, but they are released from the habitual patterns they assume in its socially produced 'organism' form. Insofar as the organism is a 'stratum', producing a BwO means pushing the body away from stratification and towards a destratified (decentralised, dehabituated) body. As tending to destratification, a BwO is a plateau, a 'piece of immanence', connected to other BwOs/plateaus on the plane of consistency (ATP 158). Hence analysing the BwO, like analysing the 'rhizome', is a way of talking about *A Thousand Plateaus*, the book.

Adding to the potential confusion is a significant change in the term 'full BwO' from *Anti-Oedipus* to *A Thousand Plateaus*. In *Anti-Oedipus*, the BwO is 'full' when the person is catatonic, taken over by a moment of anti-production, so that the body is a mere surface across which desiring-machines are splayed and upon which a nomadic subject moves (Deleuze and Guattari 1983: 8). As such a surface, the full BwO allows for the recording of desiring-production; in the social register it is the socius (Deleuze and Guattari 1983: 10). In *A Thousand Plateaus*, however, the full BwO is positively valued; it is the 'empty' BwO that must be avoided (along with the 'cancerous BwO'). The full BwO allows for connection with other destratified bodies, while the empty BwO is a void in which nothing happens.

A note of caution is prominent in the Sixth Plateau for successfully constructing a productive BwO – one that enhances the power to connect with other body-machines, organic and non-organic. (A 'body-machine' for Deleuze and Guattari is an 'assemblage', which can be comprised of bodies in the biological sense connected with technical apparatus or a 'machine' in the ordinary sense.) A working assemblage will achieve new emergent capacities denied the former non-connected components, but this sense of emergence is still immanent to the assemblage: what emerges are the new powers of the assemblage, not some entity transcendent to the assemblage (although a representational mode of thought might see a new entity by divorcing the product from the production process). Finally, the new assemblage, in exercising its powers, will enhance the joyful affects of those connected elements capable of joy. However, the construction of a productive BwO allowing new assemblages is not assured. It can be botched. Nothing might pass. Or you might fall prey to what Deleuze and Guattari call 'the triple curse' of the priest on desire: lack, pleasure and ideality/phantasy (ATP 154). The immanence of desire is destroyed when it is referred to a lack that it strives for, when it is interrupted by a pleasure that renders it a subjective property, and when it is oriented to an ideal of fulfilment or *jouissance*.

Deleuze and Guattari give three analyses of desiring BwOs, those of the masochist, of courtly love, and of the Tao; all three insist that the 'immanence of desire' is the principle that must be followed. For Deleuze and Guattari, the masochist is not searching for deferred pleasure via relief from endured pain, but 'uses suffering as a way of constituting a BwO and bringing forth a plane of consistency of desire' (ATP 155). In courtly love the analysis of pleasure is nuanced; the key is to keep pleasure immanent to the connections made, that is, to 'desire'. So, while pleasure, normally understood, 'is an affection of a person or a subject' (ATP 156), such attribution breaks the immanence of desire by transforming an intensity of sensation produced by the connection of lover and beloved (physical touch or 'spiritual' connection achieved by glances, speech, writing and so on) into the property of a subject exterior or transcendent to the connections through which intensities circulate. Thus it is the transcendent assignment of pleasure, not its immanent experience, that a properly constructed BwO prevents: 'Everything is allowed: all that counts is for pleasure to be the flow of desire itself' (ATP 156). Finally, the analysis of the Tao shows again how deferred pleasure is not the goal of the BwO process, and adds the danger of orienting the practice to utilitarian ends so that 'the whole circuit can be channelled toward procreative ends (ejaculation when the energies are right)'. Deleuze and Guattari retort 'that is true only for one side of the assemblage of desire, the side facing the strata . . . It is not true for the other side, the Tao side of destratification that draws a plane of consistency proper to desire' (ATP 157).

To allow positive desire to flow on the plane of consistency, we must defeat the organism, that is, echoing Artaud, we must 'be done with the judgment of God' (ATP 150). An 'organism' is a centralised, hierarchical and socially patterned body. It is one of three principal strata composing modern European-American humanity, the other two being 'significance' and 'subjectification'. The strata are the naturalisation of what is known as the 'paralogisms' in the still Kantian psychoanalytic register of *Anti-Oedipus*. The organism is the unification and totalisation of the connective synthesis of production, or the physiological register of *Anti-Oedipus*; organising a body into its organism form means orienting the body's desires and capacities to socially recognised labour (foraging, peasantry, wage labour and, of course, crossing all those, the work of social reproduction [ATP ch. 13]). Significance or 'signifier-ness' is the flattening or 'bi-univocalising' of the disjunctive synthesis of recording, the semiotic register of *Anti-Oedipus* (picked up upon by ATP ch. 5); historically produced by the overcoding performed by empires on the 'presignifying' semiotic of 'primitive' society, significance catches one in the lures of endless interpretation, so that one asks 'What did that mean?' instead of 'Into what flows did that intervene and what affects did it produce?' And finally, subjectification is the reification of the conjunctive synthesis of consummation, the psychological register of *Anti-Oedipus*, producing a passionate egocentricity so that one ends up crying 'It's me, I tell you, it's me: I'm the one to blame / get the credit!' instead of participating in an encounter that surpasses our ability to identify our contribution to it – precisely what Deleuze and Guattari mean by 'the immanence of desire'.

Hence the two-step process – construct the BwO by disrupting organismic patterns, then make intensities pass along novel channels – illustrated in *A Thousand Plateaus* by the masochist programme, the courtly love programme and the Taoist programme, but capable of being produced by other programmes, artistic, athletic and so on (these would all be 'attributes' of the universal BwO as 'substance' according to the Spinozist analysis Deleuze and Guattari provide at ATP 153). Constructing the BwO means destroying the habitual material and affective patterns of the organismically ordered body – what it usually does and feels in accord with the social system in which it was formed– so that something new will pass on the BwO: waves of intensity (the 'modes' according to the Spinozist analysis) according to the form (or 'attribute') that desire takes. These attributes or forms would be pain for the masochist, joy for the courtly lover, creativity for the artist, grace for the dancer, effort for the runner, perhaps even concepts for the philosopher, as when concepts are created on a philosophical plane of consistency, as we are said to do in *What is Philosophy?*

Against the organism

Insofar as Deleuze and Guattari think of 'organisms' in *A Thousand Plateaus* as the political patterning of a biological system, we must first understand the biological sense of organism for them. For them, 'nature' incarnates an 'abstract machine' of stratification and destratification. While stratification reduces complexity in producing a body composed of homogeneous layers, destratification increases complexity by allowing 'consistencies' or 'assemblages', instances of 'transversal emergence' (Protevi 2013: 19). In other words, a consistency or assemblage is a functional whole that preserves the heterogeneity of its component parts and enables further rhizomatic connections, as opposed to a 'stratum', which relies on the homogeneity of components and makes connections pass through a central command structure. The 'abstract' part of the strange term 'abstract machine' simply means that the processes of stratification and destratification occur in many material registers, from the geological through the biological, the social and on to the neuro-endocrinological/subjective; a 'machine' binds parts into a functional whole. An 'abstract machine' is thus the diagram for processes that form functional wholes in different registers. Nature forms strata or systems composed of homogeneous parts layered into a functional whole, but it also breaks down such strata, freeing parts to form connections with heterogeneous others, thereby forming consistencies or assemblages, whose operation preserves the heterogeneity of its components. Nature operates both in, on and between the strata, and also beyond them, on the 'plane of consistency', that is, destratification as the condition for the formation of assemblages (ATP chs 3 and 11 are the major discussions of these points; for comments, see Protevi 2012).

In the 'Geology of Morals' plateau of *A Thousand Plateaus* the abstract process of stratification works by means of a 'double articulation' of content and expression, each of which has both substance and form. The two 'pincers' of content and expression thus explain the figure of the 'lobster'; the reification of the abstract process of stratification results in a 'God' who seemingly performs the operation. (Hence the connection of 'the organism is the judgment of God', and 'God is a lobster.') The abstract machine of stratification has four processes in two articulations. Deleuze and Guattari use the example of sedimentary rock, but the stratifying abstract machine operates in many different registers, social as well as natural. The first process is 'sedimentation', which determines 1) substance of content, that is, the selection of homogeneous materials from a subordinate flow; and 2) a form of content, that is, the deposition of these materials into layers. The second process is 'folding', in which there is 3) a form of expression, that is, the creation of new linkages; and 4) a substance of expression, the creation of new entities with emergent properties (ATP 43).[1]

As a stratum, the organism can be explained using the terminology of form-substance and content-expression developed in chapter 3 of *A Thousand Plateaus* in creative appropriation of Hjelmslev's linguistic schema, though we must remember that on the organic stratum, content and expression must be specified at many different scales: genes and proteins, cells, tissues, organs, systems, organism, reproductive community, species, biosphere. Skipping over several scales (cell, tissue, organ) for simplicity's sake, let us focus on the level of organic systems (e.g. the nervous, endocrine and digestive systems), where the substance of content is composed of organs and the form of content is coding or regulation of flows within the body and between the body and the outside. The form of expression at this level is homeostatic regulation (overcoding of the regulation of flows provided by organs), while the substance of expression, the highest-level emergent unifying effect, is the organism, conceived as a process binding the functions of a body into a whole through coordination of multiple systems of homeostatic regulation.

Organs are points of intensity of matter-energy, a place of activity differentially related to the flows in the environment and in the body's other organs. An organism, then, is a particular socially patterned organisation of organs. The limit of organism-production would be channelling the work of the organs to socially patterned production and reproduction; the organs are thus 'labour' for the organism as emergent pattern of production and reproduction. Though emergent, the pattern is immanent to the production process, so 'the organism' is not a transcendent entity; it is instead the name for the pattern. Through its organisation of the organs, each one biting into and regulating a flow, an organism is a thickening or coagulation of flows of socially desired materials and affects. The organism is thus a stratum with regard to those flows, which are thus the BwO for the organism. An organism is 'a phenomenon of accumulation, coagulation, and sedimentation that, in order to extract useful labour from the BwO, imposes upon it forms, functions, bonds, dominant and hierarchised organisations, organised transcendences' (ATP 159). Like all stratification, however, the organism has a certain value: 'staying stratified – organised, signified, subjected – is not the worst that can happen' (ATP 161), although this utility is primarily as a resting point for further experimentation.

For Deleuze and Guattari, then, organisms occur in at least two registers, the biological and the political, at once. Their treatment of the organism is thus thoroughly naturalising, for the same abstract machine of stratification, the same Lobster-God, operates in any register from geological to social as the way to appropriate matter-energy flows and build a layer that slows down the flow and funnels a surplus to an organised body. The abstract machine of stratification is biological and political at once; we can say that the 'geology of morals' set forth by the Lobster-God in *A Thousand Plateaus* chapter 3 is biopolitical organisation. The political sense of organism means one whose desiring-production, or pattern of organ connection, has been captured and overwritten by a social machine. The organism is a selection of a subset of the possible connections of the body, orienting its organs to docile productive and reproductive labour.

Culture, or the multitude of concrete socialising practices, produces the 'organism'. Cultural production of organisms is a reterritorialisation to make up for a previous deterritorialisation on the organic stratum, the freeing of humans from instinct. Cultural practices – in Deleuze and Guattari's terminology, machinic assemblages operating on the human strata of organism, significance and subjectification – select from a vastly larger pool of potential connections, opened up due to the deterritorialisation of some of our organs (ATP 61). The production of the organism also has a diachronic dimension. *Anti-Oedipus* argues that oedipalisation is not universal but is only the capitalist form of that reterritorialisation. As stratification, that is, selection and consolidation, the social machine selects from the set of potential organ connections and consolidates them, via a series of exclusive disjunctions, into fixed and seemingly irrevocable patterns of allowable organ connections. As such a fixed pattern that provides a centralised and hierarchical organisation of material flows useful to a social machine, the organism is the judgement of God.

Constructing the BwO

Although the organism is a stratum imposed on the BwO, it is equally true that a BwO is an object of construction, a practice; it is 'what remains after you take everything away' (ATP 151), after you take away all the patterns imposed on the BwO: 'The BwO howls: "They've made me an organism! They've wrongfully folded me! They've stolen my body!"' (ATP 159). A BwO has ceased to be content for an expression, that is, it has ceased working as part of a functional structure, and has entered a plane of consistency, a condition in which it is now open to a field of new connections, creative and novel becomings that will give it new patterns and triggers of behaviour. In other words, the BwO is the organism moved from equilibrium or a fixed set of habits to an intensive realm, where it has changeable, 'metastable' habits.

The relation of intensity to virtuality in the BwO is complex; I will use my own terminology here. We should distinguish ontological registers of BwOs, considering both the singular and the universal. First, as singular BwOs, we see 1) an 'intensive singular' BwO: a body whose entry into a non-equilibrium state enables experimentation with patterns that distinguish it from an organism's fixed patterns ('Why not walk on your head, sing with your sinuses . . .? Substitute forgetting for anamnesis, experimentation for interpretation. Find *your* body without organs' [ATP 151, my emphasis]); and 2) a 'virtual singular' BwO: the limit of destratification of any one body ('you never reach the body without organs . . . it is a limit' [ATP 150]). Then, we have the 'universal' BwO as 3) intensive, that is, as the plane of consistency in the process of construction linking assemblages of desire. Here, 'the plane of consistency would be the totality of all BwOs, a pure multiplicity of immanence, one piece of which may be Chinese, another American, another medieval, another petty perverse, but all in a movement of generalised deterritorialisation . . . an intensive continuum of all the BwOs' (ATP 157, 166). Finally, we have 4) the universal virtual BwO, the 'potential totality of all BwOs, the plane of consistency' (ATP 157).

Let us consider the singular BwOs. For contrast, consider that in a 'molarised' population of organisms – what Foucault would call a 'normalised' population – one can determine an 'order-word' that will trigger standardised production; producing such uniform reaction is the goal of disciplinary training, so that, for example, when the officer of a military unit calls out 'attention' the troops will all straighten up into the desired posture (Foucault 1977). On the other hand, with a singular intensive BwO, only experimentation with the cartography of a body, its immanent relations of flows (longitude), will determine the triggers of production (affects or latitude) (ATP 260–1). A singular virtual BwO, for its part, is not reached by regression, for a BwO is not the infantile body of our past, but is the virtual realm of the potentials for different body organisation precluded by the organism form. Thus it is reached by a practice of disturbing the organism's patterns, which are arranged in, to borrow the terms of *Anti-Oedipus*, 'exclusive disjunctions' (specifying which organs can ever meet and outlawing other possible connections). A singular virtual BwO is the result of having disturbed the exclusive disjunctions of the organism to reach the virtual field where multiplicities are series of singularities ordered in 'inclusive disjunctions', that is, series in which any possible connection is equally probable.

Since all actual bodies must make choices, the key ethical move is to construct an intensive body in which patterning is flexible, that is, where a virtual BwO can more easily be reached, so that any one exclusive disjunction can be undone and an alternate patterning be accessed. Constructing an intensive BwO is done by disturbing the organism, that is, by disrupting the homeostatic feedback loops that maintain organismic patterns by a shift in intensity levels or by a change of habitual practices. In this way a body of purely distributed, rather than centralised and hierarchised, organs can be reached, sitting upon its underlying matter-energy flow. In other words, an intensive BwO is purely immanently arranged production; matter-energy flowing without regard to a central point that drains off the extra work, the surplus value of the organs for an emergent organic subject in a 'supplementary dimension' (ATP 265) to those of the organs (ATP 159). As an object of practice reached starting from the organism, a singular intensive BwO needs to be cautiously constructed by experimentation with body practices. It never hurts to come back to this phrase: 'staying stratified – organised, signified, subjected – is not the worst that can happen' (ATP 161). However, the singular intensive BwO is not an individualist achievement: 'For the BwO is necessarily ... a Collectivity (assembling elements, things, plants, animals, tools, people, powers [*puissances*], and fragments of all of these; for it is not "my" body without organs, instead the "me" [*moi*] is on it, or what remains of me, unalterable and changing in form, crossing thresholds)' (ATP 161).

At this point, we can see that the (actual) organism is a limit of a process, just as a (virtual) BwO is limit of a process. The organism and the BwO are limits of the opposed processes of stratification and destratification. There is no such thing as a presently existing organism or a BwO. Both are representations of limits of processes. 'An organism' is only a representation of pure molar fixity, just as 'a BwO' is only a representation of pure molecular flow. The organism versus the BwO is only a de jure distinction, but Deleuze and Guattari insist that such ideal purity never obtains in the world. All we have are de facto mixes, bodies consisting of varying ratios of stratifying and destratifying. After all, a stratum is itself only a ratio of capture versus escape. Neither the organism nor the BwO exists as a transcendent entity; both are the limits of intensive processes, although the organism does achieve emergent effects in channelling the work of the organs to socially desired patterns of production and reproduction.

Why are there only representations of bodies that have reached the limit of the process of stratification (an organism) and destratification (the body without organs)? Because of the relation of actual and virtual: we expand the actual by incorporating more of the virtual, but the two can never fully overlap; the virtual must remain as adjacent, as the road not taken, and the reminder of what might have been. Thus working towards your BwO is not regression, but tapping into previously deselected potentials, a refreshing dip into the pool of the virtual in order to reorganise in a non-organismic fashion, to gain a new non-organism body, an intensive BwO. That not all such bodies are ethically worth selecting is not the point here.

To note the non-actuality of organism and virtual BwO is not to say that bodies cannot move towards either limit. Approaching the virtual BwO by intensifying the flows in a body entails incorporating avenues of access to the virtual into the order of the body with inclusive disjunctions that do not shut off a potential, even when another is temporarily selected. A body must be ordered to some extent: it must have a coordination of organs that negotiate with the external flows. But with inclusive disjunctions, those organs can have roles that shift about, experimentally, over time. Approaching the organism, on the other hand, is ordering a body with exclusive disjunctions, so that, once the organism's pattern of organs is set up, its virtual options are forbidden. The difference between inclusive and exclusive disjunctions in ordering is easy to see in the political sense of organism as oedipalised desire – in this context, inclusive disjunction is nothing more than the ability to make connections that are not reproductive. The incorporation of the virtual via inclusive disjunction is then the criterion of ethical selection for the production of bodies politic.

The three-body problem

Deleuze and Guattari distinguish three types of BwO: full, empty and cancerous. Only the full body is productive. To avoid the others, caution is necessary, for the construction of a BwO is dangerous. The strata must be partially maintained: the body that is not an organism must still be a body, must still have a relative consistency, a difference in intensity of matter-energy flow from the surroundings. Otherwise, we would have death, entropy, no energy differences.

1) A full BwO is what we have called a singular intensive BwO. It is reached by careful experimental destratification, which causes waves of intense matter-energy to flow in immanence. When linked with other selected full BwOs, the plane of consistency or universal intensive BwO is constructed, that is, a Collectivity of freely self-organising bodies, continually producing their own connections. This full BwO is the BwO as 'egg' (ATP 164). In a full BwO one finds 'a distribution of intensive principles of organs, with their positive indefinite articles, within a collectivity or multiplicity, inside an assemblage, and according to machinic connections operating on a BwO' (ATP 165). As we can see from Deleuze and Guattari's insistence on collectivity, multiplicity and assemblage, the full BwO is never a solitary achievement but always a communal project, a political event. To select only full BwOs for the plane of consistency is 'the test of desire' (ATP 165).

2) An empty BwO is reached by too sudden destratification, which empties bodies of its organs. Examples include the hypochondriac body, the paranoid body, the schizo-catatonic body, the drugged body, the masochist body: 'a dreary parade of sucked-dry, catatonised, vitrified, sewn-up bodies . . . Emptied bodies instead of full ones' (ATP 150). These bodies do not connect with others, for they have no energy flowing; no plane of consistency is possible between these mortified bodies.

3) The cancerous BwO is the strangest and most dangerous BwO. It is a BwO that belongs to the organism that resides on a stratum, rather than being the limit of a stratum. It is a runaway self-duplication of stratification. Such a cancer can occur even in social formations, not just in the strata named organism, significance, subjectification (ATP 163). The key to tracking down fascism lies here, in the cancerous BwO, which forms under conditions of runaway stratification, or more precisely, runaway sedimentation, the first 'pincer' of a stratum:

> all a stratum needs is a high sedimentation rate for it to lose its configuration and articulations, and to form its own specific kind of tumour, within itself or in a given formation or apparatus. The strata spawn their own

BwOs, totalitarian and fascist BwOs, terrifying caricatures of the plane of consistency. (ATP 163)

The cancerous BwO breaks down the stratum on which it lodges by endlessly repeating the selection of homogenised individuals in a runaway process of 'conformity'. Social cloning. Assembly-line personalities.

The cancerous BwO occurs with too much sedimentation, that is, too much content or coding and territorialising, with insufficient overcoding. The result is a cancer of the stratum, a proliferation of points of capture, a proliferation of micro-black holes. Thousands of individuals, complete unto themselves. Legislators and subjects all in one. Judge, jury and executioner – and policeman, private eye, home video operator, Neighbourhood Watch organiser . . . Watching over themselves as much as over others in runaway conscience-formation. Deleuze and Guattari call this situation 'micro-fascism': 'What makes fascism dangerous is its molecular or micropolitical power: a cancerous body rather than a totalitarian organism' (ATP 214–15).

Biopolitics of the BwO

Deleuze and Guattari's notion of the organism can be articulated with Antonio Damasio's somatic marker theory of emotion in which a subject of intense emotional experience arises from a singular state of the body. As we have seen, an 'organism' permits itself some connections while forbidding itself others. While Deleuze and Guattari do not provide any details on the psychological mechanisms involved in this patterning, we could further speculate that the positive and negative somatic markers associated with possible futures provide the unconscious emotional valuations that mark off some organ connections as prohibited. Damasio develops the 'somatic marker hypothesis', whereby scenarios of future situations are marked by flashes of 'as if' body images: images that are produced by an imagined scenario of what it would be like to live through the imagined situation.[2] The feeling of what this or that future would be like to live through – as these 'memories of the future' are formed in association with past training as the application of pain or the allowing of pleasure – thus serves to shape the phase space of the body into zones of the permitted and the prohibited, the pleasant and the nauseating. Unconscious emotional premonitions thus assign an emotional weight to the imagined scenarios, and these connections are policed by exclusive disjunctions. In other words, in entertaining the possibility of organ connections marked as 'deviant' a negative emotional weight is unleashed which turns the body away from that possible connection and back to other patterns with more positive emotional weights. Deleuze and Guattari put it like this: 'the points of disjunction on the body without organs form circles that converge on the desiring-machines; then the subject – produced as a residuum alongside the machine . . . passes through all the degrees of the circle, and passes from one circle to another' (Deleuze and Guattari 1983: 27). The subject follows the patterns of organ connection that are set up by inscription by a social machine.

To sum up then, the 'neurobiologico-desiring machines' (Deleuze and Guattari 1983: 63) form an 'organism' when their patterns produce a body that serves its social machine. The organism as oedipalised body is a selection of a subset of the possible connections of the body, orienting it to docile reproductive labour. What is reproduced? Either products at work (connect your organs with those of the technical machines of the capitalist) or species reproduction via heterosexual penile-vaginal intercourse (connect your organs the way they should be connected to make babies). In other words, oedipalisation means the fitting of difference into a pre-existing categorical scheme or 'horizon of identity' whereby recognition of identities, especially those of gendered personal identity, is possible.

We might next entertain a brief discussion of the BwO in relation to the questions of transversal emergence and organic form. In dialogue with Keith Ansell Pearson (1999), Mark Hansen (2000) points to the need to distinguish timescales when discussing the relation of organism and BwO; he claims that Deleuze and Guattari conflate the macro-evolutionary timescale of symbiogenesis (the theory propounded by Lynn Margulis that the eukaryotic cell is the result of a merger of different prokaryotic cells; see Margulis 1998 for an accessible treatment) with the timescale of ontogeny or individual development. At stake is the relation of the universal virtual BwO of 'life' as self-ordering and creative to the portion of the virtual field relevant to an organism (a singular virtual BwO, the BwO of the organism, as what this particular body 'can do'). Hansen claims that Deleuze and Guattari neglect the constraints of the viability of organic form in favour of what he calls their 'cosmic expressionism'. That is, Hansen believes that Deleuze and Guattari postulate a completely open 'molecular' field for any possible combination of organic forms, without regard to the conservation of viable organic form in species-wide norms. Thus even organic form is a haecceity, or arbitrary selection from an open and heterogeneous virtual field. The key complaint is that Deleuze and Guattari consider individuation as (synchronic) haecceity while neglecting diachronic emergence from a morphogenetic field, which needs the constraint of natural kinds channelling development. Hansen pinpoints Deleuze and Guattari's identification of 'life' with the universal virtual

BwO, as plane of immanence and absolute deterritorialisation, neglecting the constraints on the universal intensive BwO as plane of consistency in the process of construction, that is, a condition of bodies formed by relative deterritorialisation always accompanied by reterritorialisation, or in other words, developmental plasticity (West-Eberhard 2003; discussed in Protevi 2013) constrained by the necessity of viability.

Hansen is on to something here. As a fixed habitual pattern locked on to normal functioning as determined by species-wide average values, the organism deadens the creativity of life, the possibilities of diachronic emergence; it is 'that which life sets against itself in order to limit itself' (ATP 503). The organism is a construction, a certain selection from the virtual multiplicity of what life can be, and hence a constraint imposed on the universal virtual BwO as the virtual realm of life, the set of all possible organic forms. Like all stratification, however, the organism has a certain value, as we have had occasion to stress repeatedly: 'staying stratified – organised, signified, subjected – is not the worst that can happen' (ATP 161) – although we should recognise that, for Deleuze and Guattari, this utility is primarily as a resting point for further experimentation, the search for conditions that will trigger diachronic emergence. Hansen is correct here: Deleuze and Guattari's insistence on caution in experimentation only recognises individual organism survival as a negative condition for further experiment without giving any positive role to the organism-level self-organising properties of the morphogenetic field.

The only thing to say on behalf of Deleuze and Guattari is that Hansen's analysis is organic, all too organic. While the statement 'staying stratified is not the worst thing' is negative, we also have to remember that all the strata intermingle (ATP 69), that the body is a politically formed body, that in the context of bio-social-technical transversal emergence, 'organism' is a political term. 'Organism' refers to body patterns being centralised so that 'useful labour is extracted from the BwO' (ATP 159). We see that 'organism' is a term for a particular type of body politic when we realise that, for Deleuze and Guattari, the opposite of the organism is not death, but 'depravity': 'You will be an organism . . . otherwise you're just depraved' (ATP 159). That is, being an organism means that your organs are Oedipally patterned for hetero-marriage and work. Getting outside the organism does not mean getting outside homeostasis guaranteed by a certain organic form so much as getting outside Oedipus into what Oedipal society calls 'depravity'. Furthermore, the thought of politically formed bodies means we have to think the body (*le corps*) as socially embedded, as an example of transversal emergence: we are all a Corps of Engineers. When a body links with others in a bio-social-technical assemblage it is the complex, transversally emergent body that increases its virtual realm, that is, it is the singular intensive BwO of the bio-social-technical body that is at stake, not that of each individual organism or somatic body. So the experimentation Deleuze and Guattari call for is not so much with somatic body limits (although that is part of it) but with bio-social-technical body relations in diachronic transversally emergent assemblages, what Deleuze and Guattari will call a 'consistency'.

Let me spell out the evolutionary biological sense of 'virtual BwO' here. Evelyn Fox Keller (2000) proposes a difference between functional genes as end products of the transcription process and hereditary genes as strings of DNA on the chromosomes. Keller writes that we might

> consider the mature mRNA transcript formed after editing and splicing to be the 'true' gene. But if we take this option (as molecular biologists often do), a different problem arises, for such genes exist in the newly formed zygote only as possibilities, designated only after the fact. A musical analogy might be helpful here: the problem is not only that the music inscribed in the score does not exist until it is played, but that the players rewrite the score (the mRNA transcript) in their very execution of it. (Keller 2000: 63)

The constructed nature of functional genes implies that they are only potentially there in the hereditary genes; with Deleuze's help we can see that such potentiality is virtual, that is to say, using Keller's metaphor, gene expression networks are activated in the musical performance in which epigenetic factors play – and thereby rewrite – the genomic score. In other words, we find distributed and differential systems of dynamic interaction between genomic and epigenetic processes. That is to say, the differential nature of the elements, relations and singularities of these distributed systems make them a multiplicity or BwO in Deleuze's sense.

For a last comparison with scientific work, let us take up the use of dynamical systems methods in neurodynamics as an area in which Deleuze's concepts can help us with the ontology involved. Neurodynamics shows the brain as generating coherent wave patterns out of a chaotic background. During any one living act (perception, imagination, memory, action) the brain functions via the 'collapse of chaos', that is, the formation of a 'resonant cell assembly' or coherent wave pattern (Varela et al. 2001). Here, in the chaotic firing between resonant cell assemblies, we could see a BwO in the widest possible sense of a breakdown of order intervening between instances of organisation.

Walter Freeman offers a dynamic systems account of the neurological basis of intentional behaviour (Freeman 2000a; 2000b), while Alicia Juarrero uses dynamic systems to intervene in philosophical debates about decisions and intentional action (Juarrero 1999). The basic notion in their accounts is that nervous system activity is a dynamic system with massive internal feedback phenomena, thus constituting an 'autonomous' and hence 'sense-making' system in Varela's terminology. That is, sense-making is the direction of action of an organism in its world; in organisms with brains, then, the object of study when it comes to sense-making is the brain–body–environment system (Thompson and Varela 2001; Chemero 2009; Protevi 2009; 2013). Sense-making proceeds along three lines: sensibility as openness to the environment, signification as valuing, and direction as orientation of action. The neurological correlates of sense-making show neural firing patterns, blending sensory input with internal system messages, as emerging from a chaotic background in which subliminal patterns 'compete' with each other for dominance.[3] Once it has emerged victorious from this chaotic competition and established itself, what Varela (1995) calls a 'resonant cell assembly' forms a determinate pattern of brain activity.

Continuing with the perspective of somatically and environmentally supplemented neurodynamics, we make the link with Deleuze by seeing the neuro-somatic-environmental system as a BwO in its most abstract sense as a plane of consistency, or multiplicity, or pre-individual virtual field: 1) a set of differential elements (reciprocally determined functions – in other words, neural functions are networked: i.e., they emerge from global brain activity and hence cannot be understood in isolation – and neither can global brain activity be understood in isolation from its somatic and environmental relations); 2) with differential relations (linked rates of change of neural firing patterns as they mesh with rates of change in body, world and body–world interaction); and 3) marked by singularities (as critical points determining turning points between patterns of relations among brain, body and world).[4] The dynamics of the system as it unrolls in time are intensive processes or impersonal individuations.

That is to say, behaviour patterns emerge at a singularity or threshold in the differential relations. Over time, the repetition of a number of such actualisations provides a temporary structure to the singular virtual BwO, a virtually available response repertoire, a set of capacities for the politically formed body. With regard to any one actualised behaviour pattern – any one 'organismic' behaviour – the repertoire is virtual, and any one decision is an actualisation, a selection from the repertoire. But 'virtually available' cannot mean that the behaviour patterns are individuated before their triggering. To respect Deleuze's ontological difference, we must say that before their triggering, behaviour patterns do not exist, are not actual, which is to say that the BwO is a limit. Furthermore, we cannot say that the repertoire is fixed – you can always construct your BwO by experimentation.

Notes

1. DeLanda corrects the imprecise linking of 'sedimentation' and 'folding' by claiming that it is geologically more correct to have 'cementation' as the second articulation, with 'folding' occurring at a different spatial scale (DeLanda 1997: 290 n.82).
2. See Damasio 1994: 165–201 for an extended discussion of somatic markers, particularly 180–3 for the role of somatic mapping in the pre-frontal cortex. At Damasio 1999: 281, he cites work in mirror neurons located in the cortex as possibly involved in 'as if' loops or 'internal simulation'.
3. 'Neurological correlates' is a loaded term in this context and should be approached in terms that Chemero lays out clearly: 'Experiences do not happen in brains. Even though it is perfectly obvious that *something* has to be happening in neurons every time an animal has an experience, for the radical embodied cognitive scientist, as for the enactivist, this something is neither identical to, nor necessary and sufficient for, the experience' (Chemero 2009: 200, emphasis in original).
4. A fuller treatment of this issue would take us to the distributionist vs. localist dispute in neuroscience. Deleuze is on the side of the distributionists. Thus he would agree that, for example, while the hippocampus may indeed be necessarily involved in long-term memory, the retrieval of a memory involves the integration of distributed neural systems. In many ways, the dispute between distributionists and localists is a dispute between dynamicists and anatomists, and Deleuze, as a process philosopher, will side with the dynamicists.

Chapter 7

Year Zero: Faciality

Nathan Widder

This chapter will explicate the main themes of Deleuze and Guattari's 'Year Zero: Faciality' plateau by putting them into conversation with the ideas and theses of three key thinkers concerned with the constitution of language and subjectivity. After first introducing Deleuze and Guattari's notion of faciality, I relate it to Lacan's analysis of the mirror stage and the role of the face in setting the stage for the construction of Oedipal subjectivity. I then explore Foucault's account of the structure of discursive formations and how it plays a role in the organisation of the disciplinary and normalising power relations that constitute the modern subject, using that discussion as a way to understand how faciality for Deleuze and Guattari similarly underpins contemporary structures of language and the subject. I then address Deleuze and Guattari's reasons for dating the origin of faciality as the year of Christ's birth by examining Nietzsche's thesis concerning the creation of the subject of guilt through the image of the crucifixion. The final section offers some starting points to think about the dismantling of the face, or what Deleuze and Guattari call 'defacialisation'.

Faciality is only mentioned a handful of times outside the plateau bearing its name. Nevertheless, it is an important component of Deleuze and Guattari's broader analysis. Faciality, or the faciality machine, can be considered an infrastructure that undergirds and makes possible certain hegemonic stratifications. Stratifications are hierarchical organisations that impose and operate according to principles of identity and representation. *A Thousand Plateaus* locates three fundamental axes of stratification: the organism, signifiance and subjectification (ATP 159–60). The organism stratifies both individual bodies and collections of bodies by training the body to be a cog in a larger machine, such as a military machine, a machine of economic production, etc.[1] Signifiance moulds language into a representational form by consolidating meaning around a transcendent signifier, and it also stratifies the unconscious to the extent that the unconscious is susceptible to being structured like a language.[2] Finally, subjectification shapes consciousness into an ego or I whose unity is defined by its negative relation to what it is not. Together, these stratifications are 'acts of capture' that 'operate by coding and territorialisation upon the earth; they proceed by code and by territoriality' (ATP 40). What they capture are fugitive differences or 'lines of flight' that would 'deterritorialise' the invariances the strata work to establish.

In truth, the strata are always wrapped up in one another. Were we to try to isolate the stratum of significance by dividing off its expressive regime of linguistic signs, for example, we would find that 'there is always a form of content that is simultaneously inseparable from and independent of the form of expression, and the two forms pertain to assemblages that are not principally linguistic' (ATP 111). Despite this real inseparability, however, 'one can proceed as though the formalisation of expression [the regime of signs] were autonomous and self-sufficient' (ATP 111), and in this way it is possible to analyse strata in relative isolation. This is how Deleuze and Guattari proceed in the 'Faciality' plateau. Their move here is not unlike what Foucault does when he segregates discursive and non-discursive domains in *The Archaeology of Knowledge* (1989) in order to examine the regularities immanent to discourse independently of the institutional structures that undeniably also shape real discourses. Like Foucault, Deleuze and Guattari's move is justified by what it illuminates – namely, the close connections and passages between the strata of significance and subjectification, these connections and passages being especially important, they maintain, in what they call a contemporary 'mixed semiotic' where significance and subjectification fully interpenetrate. Under these conditions, they hold, the third axis of stratification, that of the organism, is determined in accordance with the requirements of this signifying–subjectifying mixture. This last claim also resonates with Foucault, who, long after leaving behind the discursive/non-discursive distinction, argues in *Discipline and Punish* (1977) that the modern organisation and punishment of the body has as its target not the body but the soul – that is, the subject and its interiority. For Deleuze and Guattari, the disciplining of bodies follows from the need of the assemblages of power that impose significance and subjectification to remove the corporeal coordinates through which earlier, polyvocal semiotics had operated (ATP 180–1).

It is by separating signifying and subjectifying stratifications from the stratification of the organism that the structure and function of faciality comes to light. As will be seen as this chapter proceeds, by subtending both the signifier and the subject, faciality enables their coordination in the assemblages of power that require them. These assemblages, in turn, are defined less by the force they may impose on bodies and more by their subtle and sophisticated control of language and consciousness. The lines of flight that can undermine the assemblages similarly emerge from these same mechanisms that control signifiance and subjectivity.

The face and faciality

The face, Deleuze and Guattari declare, is a *'white wall/black hole* system' situated at the intersection of signifiance and subjectification (ATP 167). Signification's semiotic involves both a configuration in which every sign refers to another sign and so on ad infinitum and a supreme signifier presented as both excess and lack (ATP 117), but all this is impossible without a white wall on which signification can inscribe its signs. Conversely, subjectification, which gives birth to a subject in a line of flight from the regime of signification, a subject simultaneously liberated and subjected to authority (ATP 127, 129–30), requires a black hole into which it lodges its hidden power.[3] Even the simplest image of the face – say, the drawing of two dark circles for eyes and a line for a mouth – presents this kind of white wall/black hole system and is enough to give the face a 'substance of expression' (ATP 115) that is essential to signification and subjectification's force of transmission. Concretely, in any real communication, 'the form of the signifier in language, even its units, would remain indeterminate if the potential listener did not use the face of the speaker to guide his or her choices ("Hey, he seems angry ..."; "He couldn't say it ..."; "You see my face when I'm talking to you ..."; "look at me carefully ...")' (ATP 167). The same is true of the transmission of subjectivity, as, for example, the 'Hey you!' hail of Althusser's police officer (ATP 130), which transforms the person on the street into a subject, and depends on the 'facialised' uniform and badge that express the officer's authority – or, rather, that present the officer as a proxy for a hidden authority standing behind and above him. In this way, the face operates as a second-order redundant structure, a backup system for signification's and subjectification's specific redundancies – the supreme signifier and the authority figure on the street – that reinforces these in the event of their failure (ATP 167–8, 180).

Actual faces, Deleuze and Guattari maintain, 'are engendered by an *abstract machine of faciality* [*visagéité*], which produces them at the same time as it gives the signifier its white wall and subjectivity its black hole' (ATP 168). As a machine, faciality names a field of heterogeneous intensive forces that function through their strife and friction to produce the face and related facialised entities. This field neither resembles the regime it engenders nor imposes on this regime a uniform likeness. Deleuze and Guattari offer the example of the bouncing balls that follow the eponymous main character of Kafka's 'Blumfeld, an Elderly Bachelor', which make their presence known by their irritating sound yet swing around to remain behind Blumfeld every time he turns to look at them. This irritating yet invisible presence is enough, Deleuze and Guattari say, to create a signifying and subjectifying regime: 'Nothing in all of this resembles a face, yet throughout the system faces are distributed and faciality traits organised' (ATP 169). The face further facialises the body, clothing, external objects and the whole landscape, not by making these resemble faces but instead by giving them 'new coordinates' and 'an order of reasons' (ATP 170). The facialised world, for example, becomes a milieu of observability, expressing the signifier's 'unlocalised omnipresence' (ATP 115) and operating as a 'point of subjectification': 'you might say that a house, utensil, or object, an article of clothing, etc., is *watching me*, not because it resembles a face, but because it is taken up in the white wall/black hole process, because it connects to the abstract machine of facialisation' (ATP 175).

Significance and subjectification refer to distinct assemblages of power – despotic and authoritarian respectively – with distinct principles and thus different forms of the face. Yet each is also part of 'a de facto *mix*' (ATP 182) with the other, such that 'there is no signifiance that does not harbour the seeds of subjectivity; there is no subjectification that does not drag with it remnants of signifier' (ATP 182). Deleuze and Guattari present the limit form of the despotic face as a forward-facing image, with black holes serving as eyes distributed across the white wall, these eyes signifying the omnipresence of the despot and his representatives (ATP 182–3). Here the subjectifying black hole accommodates itself to the signifying white surface of inscription. Conversely, with the limit form of the authoritarian face, the wall turns sideways to become a line, whose curvatures sketch a profile face that has a single black hole as its eye. There are in fact two faces in this scheme, either facing or turning away from each other, since the subject is always constituted in relation to another, authoritative subject. Signification here accommodates itself to this subjectifying relation (ATP 183–4). Real semiotics, for Deleuze and Guattari, combine these two limit forms in diverse ways, but they always presuppose 'assemblages of power that act through signifiers and act upon souls and subjects' (ATP 180). 'The face is a politics' (ATP 181), they maintain, because of the way it relates on one side to an abstract machine that produces it and on the other side to an assemblage of power that requires it. But it is the capitalist assemblage's semiotic that 'has attained this state of mixture in which significance and subjectification effectively interpenetrate. Thus it is in this semiotic that faciality, or the white wall/black hole system, assumes its full scope' (ATP 182).

The Lacanian moment: the face in the mirror

Lacan remains an important interlocutor for Deleuze and Guattari even as their work becomes increasingly critical and openly hostile to psychoanalysis. The reason is that even though Lacanian thought (if not always Lacan himself) in their view remains complicit with the contemporary capitalist order, it nevertheless elaborates some of this order's necessary conditions, and thus indicates ways in which this order can be left behind. On the one hand, Lacan elucidates both the co-emergence and interpenetration of significance and subjectification by demonstrating how these orders are united by the displacement and subjection that results from the subject assuming its place in language, and he also shows how this assumption of language depends on the imaginary unity and alienation constituted by a prior experience of faciality. On the other hand, he indicates a route towards a non-facialised relation to the face.

The subject, Lacan contends, comes into being on the terrain of the Other when the child takes up the position of an 'I' in discourse and articulates its needs to others. The cost of this articulation is the suppression of need's particularity, since its expression must accord with the generality of common signifiers. Language thus establishes a bar between signifier and signified – the latter here being the particularity the child seeks to communicate – such that the signifier is determined only by its relation to other signifiers and the signified becomes a subordinate, inarticulable support – a white wall upon which the signifiers operate, as Deleuze and Guattari put it.[4] Consequently, 'the subject finds his signifying place in a way that is logically prior to any awakening of the signified' (Lacan 2006: 579). This is the place of a split subject.

Signification's universal nature entails that the articulation of need becomes a universal demand: the child demands love from its mother, who is constituted 'as having the "privilege" of satisfying needs, that is, the power to deprive them of what alone can satisfy them' by way of 'the radical form of the gift of what the Other does not have – namely, what is known as its love' (Lacan 2006: 580). Henceforth, 'demand annuls [*aufhebt*] the particularity of everything that can be granted, by transmuting it into a proof of love' (Lacan 2006: 580), as every response to the child becomes proof or disproof of absolute devotion. But need's cancelled particularity reappears as a desire '*beyond* demand' (Lacan 2006: 580), as no response can meet demand's requirement for unconditional love: even if the child receives everything it needs and demands, it continues to feel lack, but this lack remains unnameable because the child has voiced all it can articulate. For this reason, 'desire is neither the appetite for satisfaction nor the demand for love, but the difference that results from the subtraction of the first from the second, the very phenomenon of their splitting [*Spaltung*]' (Lacan 2006: 580).

The subject constituted in language thus always arises with a sense of loss, which entails its further subjectification. That an unnameable object of desire – an *objet a* – is withheld from the subject implies that it is desired and enjoyed by an Other. This is not the Other of demand who gives or withholds love; rather, it is an Other who exercises a power of prohibition. The ground of the child's subjectivity thus shifts from the mother who provides love to the father who intervenes in the mother–child relationship, thus heralding the inception of the Oedipus complex. The speaking subject's freedom is consequently circumscribed by its Oedipal subjection, as it either searches in vain for a substitute for the prohibited *objet a* – another who would complete it, but no particular other can be adequate to the task – or prostrates itself before this authoritative Other in an equally futile attempt to become the *objet a* of the Other's desire.

The phallus here assumes the status of privileged signifier. It stands first for the power of paternal prohibition, and thus for the subject's repudiated desire. But as such it is also the signifier of the unnameable particularity the speaking subject must exclude, and so marks the point at which this unnameable makes itself felt in language, though felt as the trace of something primordially excluded. The phallus functions through its withdrawal and absence, as the unnameable cannot have a positive representation, and thus it is positioned as both an excess and a lack in relation to the signifying system.[5] As supreme or master signifier, it secures the sense of the entire signifying semiotic – it 'is destined to designate meaning effects as a whole, insofar as the signifier conditions them by its presence as signifier' (Lacan 2006: 579) – because it embodies the force that bars the signified from the semiotic structure: it is 'a sign of the latency with which any signifiable is struck' (Lacan 2006: 581). As this bar also constitutes the subject in its subjection to the Other, the stratifications of significance and subjectification blend completely: 'A condition of complementarity is thus produced in the instating of the subject by the signifier', which involves, on the one hand, 'that the subject designates his being only by barring everything it signifies', and, on the other hand, 'that the part of this being that is alive in the *urverdrängt* [primally repressed] finds its signifier by receiving the mark of the phallus's *Verdrängung* [repression] (owing to which the unconscious is language)' (Lacan 2006: 581).

A subject born from loss is also a subject of trauma. Trauma implies an original unity that has been fractured, but since no real unity ever existed – for that would imply a pre-existing subject – the lost piece that would restore unity is unrecoverable. The required unity is therefore imaginary, but it cannot arise on the signifying or subjectifying registers, which are characterised by splitting. This unity instead emerges for Lacan in the earlier mirror stage, which manifests 'in an exemplary situation the symbolic matrix in which the *I* is precipitated in a primordial form, prior to being objectified in the dialectic of identification with the other, and before language restores to it, in the universal, its function as subject' (Lacan 2006: 76). Here the face becomes the foundation of the mixed semiotic, as the mirror stage develops from 'the child's very early perception of the human form, a form which, as we know, holds the child's interest right from the first months of life and, in the case of the human face, right from the tenth day' (Lacan 2006: 91; see also 148). This interest culminates with 'the phenomenon of recognition, implying subjectivity', in 'the signs of triumphant jubilation and the playful self-discovery that characterise the child's encounter with his mirror image starting in the sixth month' (Lacan 2006: 91). The self's identification with its image is 'the rootstock of secondary identifications', 'symbolises the *I*'s mental permanence' and establishes 'a relationship between an organism and its reality – or, as they say, between the *Innenwelt* [inner life] and the *Umwelt* [environment]' (Lacan 2006: 76, 78). But the identification is also an alienation, since it builds upon the infant's previous encounters with other faces, so that 'it is in the other that the subject first identifies himself and even experiences himself' (Lacan 2006: 148). The mirror experience also highlights the divide between the ideal imaginary unity seen in the reflection and the child's real underdevelopment, revealing 'a certain dehiscence at the very heart of the organism, a primordial Discord betrayed by the signs of malaise and motor uncoordination of the neonatal months' (Lacan 2006: 78; see also 92). The combination of identity and alienation, established in relation to the face, 'dominates the whole dialectic of the child's behaviour in the presence of his semblable between six months and two and a half years of age' (Lacan 2006: 92), including moments of identification with other children, early aggressive competition, and the order of ego defences (Lacan 2006: 78–9, 92, 147, 152). Its influence continues until 'the specular *I* turns into the social *I*' (Lacan 2006: 79) and signification and subjectification take hold by way of oedipalisation. These later developments retroactively give the mirror stage its full meaning.

Deleuze and Guattari criticise Lacan for reducing the face to a human form, 'appealing to a form of subjectivity or humanity reflected in a phenomenological field or split in a structural field' and failing to see that '*the mirror is but secondary in relation to the white wall of faciality*' (ATP 171).⁶ This human form, they insist, misses the field of impersonal and intensive forces that comprises faciality's abstract machine prior to and independent of any resemblance to the human face. But it is Lacan himself who shows that the mirror stage is not really foundational when he turns to the adult who places the infant before the mirror. For the infant does not spontaneously recognise the image as his or her own, but only by way of the adult's signification – an encouraging 'look, that's you!' or comparable act of validation.⁷ The Other's discourse thus

> extends all the way to the purest moment of the specular relation: to the gesture by which the child at the mirror turns toward the person who is carrying him and appeals with a look to this witness; the latter decants the child's recognition of the image, by verifying it, from the jubilant assumption in which *it* [*elle*] certainly *already was*. (Lacan 2006: 568)

The mirror stage is precipitated by and imbued with what Deleuze and Guattari call 'order-words', which link acts – here the infant's recognition – to statements and serve as redundancies for signifiance and subjectivity (ATP 79). Order-words effect 'incorporeal transformations', which change nothing of the physicality of a body but everything about its sense and meaningfulness: 'that's you!' – the order-word that transforms the infant and paves the way for later stratification by the signifier and the subject.⁸ The mirror stage is thus always already imbued with specific signifying and subjectifying assemblages of power.

Nevertheless, is there not another kind of faciality at work prior to the mirror stage, in the infant's initial interest in the human face? While Lacan merely notes its role in preparing for recognition in the mirror, Deleuze and Guattari seem to do little more in the 'Faciality' plateau to explore the matter, suggesting only, in the context of recounting American psychology's interest in the facial relationship between mother and newborn, that it presents a 'Four-eye machine' (ATP 169), and referring to it as part of an abstract machine of 'maternal power operating through the face during nursing' (ATP 175). Yet the face here is not simply a mechanism for incorporeal transformations, as it operates in a relationship combining 'manual, buccal, or cutaneous proprioceptive sensations; and the visual perception of the face seen from the front against the white screen, with the shape of the eyes drawn in for black holes' (ATP 169). Moreover, the connected mouth–breast is Deleuze and Guattari's first example of a desiring-machine, presented in the opening sentences of *Anti-Oedipus*,⁹ and in this respect, its heterogeneous connected components are better interpreted as forming a rhizome, like that of wasp and orchid, but here coordinated by the face. In this context, the face is not part of the productive process (the connective synthesis by which the desiring-machine works), but enters into the corollary recording process (the disjunctive synthesis by which the machine is explained),[10] establishing the desiring-machine's sense and meaningfulness. This sense may or may not be signifying, and thus may or may not pave the way for an Oedipal coding of the parent–child relationship.[11] It is thereby a faciality that, while it may be taken up into a signifying and subjectifying regime, may also connect to other possible stratifications, or to deterritorialisations of strata.

The Foucauldian moment: faciality and the statement; faciality and normalisation

Foucault's presence is discernible at many points throughout *A Thousand Plateaus*, though it is perhaps not often recognised and appreciated. Attention tends to focus on Deleuze and Guattari's stated points of difference with Foucault on the priority of desire versus power and on the nature of Foucauldian resistance versus lines of flight.[12] But there are also clear ways in which the structure of abstract machines and the way they function in concrete assemblages reflect Foucault's account of discursive formations and their role in the organisation of disciplinary and normalising power relations. This is certainly the case with the abstract machine of faciality.

Foucault defines a discursive formation as a system of statements that establishes a regular dispersion of objects, concepts and themes in such a way as to delineate an identifiable field of discourse, such as the discourse of medicine, law, grammar and so forth (Foucault 1989a: 37–8). Both 'dispersion' and 'statement' here have specific technical meanings that will be elaborated shortly. Foucault opposes this idea of a system of dispersion to the standard principles of unity used to define discourse, such as tradition, author, oeuvre, book, science and literature. Each of the latter, he maintains, imposes its organisation onto discourse from the outside, erects bulky abstractions and 'diversifies the theme of continuity' (Foucault 1989a: 21). Foucault says he proceeds this way 'not to deny all value to these unities or to try to forbid their use [but] to show that they required, in order to be defined exactly, a theoretical elaboration' (Foucault 1989a: 71). Removing the priority of these principles of unity allows the dispersion of discursive formations to appear. But this dispersion is not a scattering of elements into open space, as when one says that a crowd disperses or that seeds are dispersed in a flower bed. Rather, dispersion in this context connotes a mixture in which one element remains distinct rather than dissolved into the other – in chemistry, for example, when a liquid is dispersed in another liquid or in a gas, thereby constituting an emulsion or an aerosol.[13] It is the regularity of such mixtures, which engender 'an order in their successive appearance, correlations in their simultaneity, assignable positions in a common space, a reciprocal functioning, linked and hierarchised transformations' (Foucault 1989a: 37), that defines the discursive formation.

The nineteenth-century discourse of psychopathology, for example, mixes heterogeneous discursive regimes, from which emerge the subjects and objects that the discipline of psychopathology subsequently organises. The 'surfaces of emergence' for its objects are found within the family, workplace and religious community, while the expert subjects of this new discipline gain legitimacy as 'authorities of delimitation' through the convergence of the discourses of medicine and law, which maps the clinical distinction of health/sickness onto the legal distinction of citizen/criminal, this link then being brought to bear on the family, workplace and religious environments to establish 'grids of specification' that define and group various forms of madness (Foucault 1989a: 40–9). Each domain, however, is itself the product of dispersion/mixing: the clinic, as the site of production of clinical discourse, forms at the intersection of various medical, political and juridical discourses (Foucault 1989a: 50–4), as does the family, workplace, and so on. Strife and conflict inevitably plague the intersections constituting a discursive formation, as its components do not come together cleanly: the health/sickness binary often operates in contradiction to the citizen/criminal binary, and the hodgepodge of discourses that legitimate authoritative subjects frequently has nothing to do with any actual knowledge and expertise these subjects are supposed to have.[14] The disciplines such as psychopathology that rest upon these formations thus remain uncertain. Discursive formations do not create subjects and objects as such. Instead, they are the conditions of possibility for subjects and objects to appear or become visible. For this reason, discursive relations are neither primary relations of causal dependency among real institutional and social forces nor secondary relations that retroactively organise components of already established discourses (Foucault 1989a: 45–6). They are neither internal nor exterior to discourse, but instead

> are, in a sense, at the limit of discourse: they offer it objects of which it can speak, or rather ... they determine the group of relations that discourse must establish in order to speak of this or that object, in order to deal with them, name them, analyse them, classify them, explain them, etc. These relations characterise not the language [*langue*] used by discourse, nor the circumstances in which it is deployed, but discourse itself as a practice. (Foucault 1989a: 46)

Although a discursive formation's unity is found in the regularity of its dispersion, this stability is not reflected in the visibilities that emerge from it. A discursive formation may persist even when its objects mutate or new objects are found, when knowledge changes and old truths are abandoned, or when new authoritative subjects emerge or old ones return. Instead, Foucault maintains, the coherence and endurance of the formation lies in the regularity of its statements. A statement (*énoncé*) is neither a proposition, sentence nor speech act, which all depend on networks of statements (Foucault 1989a: 80–4). Nor is it a language (*langue*), which, while like statements being a condition for propositions, sentences and speech acts, is both the material from which statements are constructed and dependent on statements for its own existence (Foucault 1989a: 85). Statements are rather what allow propositions, sentences and speech acts to 'make sense' (Foucault 1989a: 86), with sense here being more than a matter of whether these linguistic entities are well formed or grammatically correct, since even incoherent propositions, grammatically incorrect sentences and illegitimate speech acts can still have sense. A statement operates by making the connections across heterogeneities necessary to establish a discursive formation, and for this reason 'it is not in itself a unit, but a function that cuts across a domain of structures and possible unities, and which reveals them, with concrete contents, in time and space' (Foucault 1989a: 87). The already mentioned link between medicine and law enables the propositions and sentences of psychopathology to make sense, just as the link between desire and truth, as Foucault's later works demonstrate, underpins the sense of various discourses of disciplinary society. These links are never articulated in sentences, propositions or speech acts, but are nevertheless *expressed* in them, and in this way the statement operates not on the level of what is said but on the level of the sense of what is said:[15] it is because the actual discourses of psychoanalysis, whatever they say, express and reinforce the sense that one's desires contain the hidden truth about oneself and must be confessed to an authority able to interpret them that these discourses belong to a regime of sexual normalisation. The study of discursive formations, Foucault says, includes study of the rarity of statements, which, in circumscribing the sense of what is said, indicate how, despite discourse's infinitude, it is still not possible to say anything at any time and from any place. This makes the study of discourse also a study of power and politics.[16]

Disciplinary and normalising power relations function off the subjects, objects, forms of knowledge and sense established by modern discursive formations. They embody what Foucault, following Nietzsche, calls a will to truth, which is not a will to 'have truth' but an insistence that the world conform to an ideal of truth that operates by standards of normality and deviance. These standards are indispensable in a modern world that can no longer rely on hierarchical modes of governance that use negative threats of punishment and death, a world that requires instead a form of governmentality premised on promoting the life and efficiency of the body politic. This new governmentality works by constituting individuals who can be subjected to discipline and normalisation, measured against standards of normality and rewarded or corrected on the basis of the degree to which they conform or deviate. Its most important techniques and practices of power – observation, examination, normalising judgement and confession – operate at the microscopic rather than macroscopic level – that is, at the level where authoritative and subordinate subjects, objects of knowledge and grids of specification are made visible and deployed in order to secure the disciplinary and normalising sense that modern society requires. These mechanisms of power appear in diverse institutions and sites, with the unsurprising consequence that 'prisons resemble factories, schools, barracks, hospitals, which all resemble prisons' (Foucault 1977: 228). They create an explosion of discourses in the human sciences and an army of experts in psychology, criminality, sexuality, pedagogy and population management who all seek to establish standards of normality and to identify, isolate and classify whatever deviates from them.

Seen in these terms, the abstract machine of faciality is a discursive formation that, taken up in assemblages of power that require it, determines the assemblages' sense, or their distribution of content and expression. Once installed, Deleuze and Guattari contend, the faciality machine assumes two functions: bi-univocalisation and selection. In the first, 'the machine constitutes a facial unit, an elementary face in biunivocal relation with another: it is a man *or* a woman, a rich person or a poor one, an adult or a child, a leader or a subject, "an x *or* a y"' (ATP 177). These dichotomies determine the concrete types or norms that define individuals, such as teacher and student, father and son, worker and employer, the child with the military calling, and so on, as a result of which 'you don't so much have a face as slide into one' (ATP 177). In the second function, the machine 'assumes a role of selective response, or choice: given a concrete face, the machine judges whether it passes or not, whether it goes or not, on the basis of the elementary facial units. This time, the binary relation is of the "yes-no" type' (ATP 177). The face here becomes a 'deviance detector' (ATP 177–8), subjecting individuals and groups to discipline and normalisation based on how they measure up against the norm. Crucially, the abstract machine does not work by exclusion – those subjected to discipline and normalisation are not expelled – but by inclusion through facialisation: deviations from the norm 'are also inscribed on the wall, distributed by the hole. They must be Christianised, in other words, facialised' (ATP 178). Indeed, the mixed semiotic 'has an exceptional need to be protected from any intrusion from the outside. In fact, there must not be any exterior: no nomad machine, no primitive polyvocality must spring up, with their combinations of heterogeneous substances of expression. Translatability of any kind requires a single substance of expression' (ATP 179). This leads facialisation to expand into all areas of life, just as discipline and normalisation expand for Foucault.

The faciality machine's bi-univocalisations and selections are not the same as the dualisms found in signifying language or the selections made by existing subjects; rather, the latter presuppose that 'the black hole/white wall system must already have gridded all of space and outlined its aborescences or dichotomies for those of signifier and subjectification even to be conceivable' (ATP 179). The machine, then, establishes the grid of specification upon which the differences made by language users are then articulated – 'the faces it produces draw all kinds of aborescences and dichotomies without which the signifying and the subjective would not be able to make the aborescences and dichotomies function that fall within their purview in language' (ATP 179). Just as faciality does not resemble the facialised heads, objects and landscapes that it engenders, 'the binarities and biunivocalities of the face are not the same as those of language, of its elements and subjects. There is no resemblance between them. But the former subtend the latter' (ATP 179). These subjacent binarities and bi-univocalities, for Deleuze and Guattari, are, *pace* Foucault, expressed in statements that make language possible: 'A language is always embedded in the faces that announce its statements and ballast them in relation to the signifiers in progress and the subjects concerned' (ATP 179). Faces, in turn, 'choose their subjects' (ATP 180), determining by way of incorporeal transformations the authoritative or subordinate status of those who speak and those who are subjected.

Statements carry the sense of propositions, but 'the same proposition can be tied to completely different statements' (ATP 147). A proposition can be disconnected from the statements of one discursive regime and mixed with or transported over to those of another regime, or one could even 'try to create new, as yet unknown statements for that proposition, even if the result were a patois of sensual delight, physical and semiotic systems in shreds, asubjective affects, signs without signifiance where syntax, semantics, and logic are in collapse' (ATP 147). This mutability entails a pragmatics of language that can delineate possible translations, transferences and lines of flight within a regime of signs. The face is a politics concerning abstract machines and assemblages of power (ATP 181), while 'pragmatics is a politics of language' (ATP 82). These two politics are connected by the statement. A politics that challenges faciality is necessarily one that generates new statements as lines of flight.

The Nietzschean moment: the face of God on the cross

Deleuze and Guattari declare:

> If it is possible to assign the faciality machine a date – the year zero of Christ and the historical development of the White Man – it is because that is when the mixture ceased to be a splicing or an intertwining, becoming a total interpenetration in which each element suffuses the other like drops of red-black wine in white water. (ATP 182)

The face 'is not a universal', but nor is it the 'white man' (ATP 176). It is rather the 'White Man', a specificity raised to the universal as norm. It operates as 'the third eye' (ATP 177) that establishes facial binaries, the 'deviance detector' that determines what must be normalised – that is to say, Christianised (ATP 177–8) – and it carries out 'the facialisation of the entire body . . . and the landscapification of all milieus' (ATP 178). There is no contradiction in the fact that the faciality machine is dated centuries before the capitalist assemblage that realises it, just as there is no contradiction in the fact that, as Foucault notes, disciplinary techniques are ancient but disciplinary society is recent. It simply means that the Christ-face did not function as a faciality machine expressing the sense of these pre-capitalist societies, even if it was present in them.

The question, however, remains: why Christ's face? The answer lies in the associations Deleuze and Guattari draw in *Anti-Oedipus* between primitive, despotic and capitalist social forms and moments in the second essay of Nietzsche's *Genealogy of Morality*, which trace the transformation of debt (*schulden*) into guilt (*schuld*) or bad conscience. The primitive social machine, whose polyvocity is expressed in a system of corporeal cruelty that marks the body through 'tattooing, excising, incising, carving, scarifying, mutilating, encircling, and initiating' (Deleuze and Guattari 1983: 144), corresponds to the prehistorical system that Nietzsche identifies as the basis for conscience, where memory is 'burned into' men to give them 'the right to make promises' (Nietzsche 1994: 2.1–2.3). In contrast, the despotic machine, which replaces primitive cruelty with terror and primitive polyvocity with signifiance, corresponds to the idea of infinite debt that Nietzsche initially hypothesises can be equated with guilt before declaring that guilt can only be explained by a deeper 'moralisation' of conscience that transfigures it qualitatively into bad conscience.[17] What distinguishes primitive and despotic systems from the capitalist machine is that while the former submit desire to codes, establishing value distinctions that police desire by condemning and excluding its most decoded flows, capitalism replaces codes with an axiomatic of exchange value, affirming free and decoded flows of desire but reterritorialising them by way of market logics and the creation of an Oedipal, capitalist subject. Capitalism thereby represses desire not by exclusion but by manipulating it to desire its own repression: Oedipus becomes 'the baited image with which desire allows itself to be caught' (Deleuze and Guattari 1983: 166), leading desire down 'a path of resignation' (Deleuze and Guattari 1983: 60) and transmuting it into 'resignation-desires' (Deleuze and Guattari 1983: 62). Here too, the resonances are Nietzschean, as Deleuze and Guattari hold that desire's force is 'essentially active, aggressive, artistic, productive, and triumphant' (Deleuze and Guattari 1983: 122), and that repression comes by separating this active force from what it can do.[18] Desire repressed in this way is not arrested, but instead is channelled into circulation around lacks and lost objects, tied to a subject, a desiring 'I', defined by 'collective and personal ends, goals or intentions' (Deleuze and Guattari 1983: 342) rather than any creative impulse, and led to condemn this desiring subject as sinful or guilty.

For Nietzsche, the image that consolidates this self-repression is God on the cross. Infinite debt may be unrepayable because of its size, but the failure to repay does not necessitate self-condemnation. The idea of Christ's sacrifice, however, moves debt onto the register of guilt because its gift of undeserved redemption, which cannot even be formulated as a debt, solidifies the idea that humans are unworthy:

> God sacrificing himself for man's debt, none other than God paying himself back, God as the only one able to redeem man from what, to man himself, has become irredeemable – the creditor sacrificing himself for his debtor, out of love (would you credit it? –), out of love for his debtor! (Nietzsche 1994: 2.21)

All this, Nietzsche maintains, reflects

> that will to torment oneself, that suppressed cruelty of animal man who has been frightened back into himself and given an inner life . . . man's will to find himself guilty and condemned without hope of reprieve, his will to think of himself as punished, without the punishment ever being equivalent to the level of guilt. (Nietzsche 1994: 2.22)

It universalises *ressentiment*, for whereas the *Genealogy*'s first essay describes how the self's *ressentiment* is directed outwards in a limited way – its formula being 'they are evil; we are not like them; therefore we are good' – the second essay describes how this idea of evil is turned back onto the self so that *all* become guilty. This universal guilt, however, is possible only if delight is taken in self-torture (Nietzsche 1994: 2.18) – that is, if it is *desired*. That is why, for Nietzsche, bad conscience survives the death of

God, as it embodies a self-hatred of man in which the difference between theism and atheism is irrelevant. It is also why, for Deleuze and Guattari, Oedipus can replace Christ as the modern figure of guilt, and psychoanalysis can replace the priest as the pedlar of guilty conscience.[19]

Dismantling the face

Faciality creates the resigned, docile and neurotic subjects needed for capitalist assemblages to function. These are subjects whose desires are structured around nameless lacks, who can be manipulated into a perpetual search for fulfilment that passes them from one fetishised object to another, and who are willing participants in their own disciplining and normalisation. The neurotic subject is the politically harmless and occasionally useful form of deviance that capitalism succeeds extremely well in producing, just as, in Foucault's analysis, the delinquent is the prison system's politically harmless and occasionally useful product (Foucault 1977: 277). Nevertheless, just as capitalism produces the very schizophrenia that threatens to overturn it, the means to break apart faciality are found in its very own white wall of significance and black hole of subjectification (ATP 189).

Dismantling the face in the realms of significance and subjectification can be compared to the task of making oneself a body without organs within the stratification of the organism. Just as the latter is often said to be not an organless body but a 'body without organisation',[20] the dismantled face would not be a dissolved face but one without organised facial traits. The facial tic, Deleuze and Guattari declare, represents 'the continually refought battle between a faciality trait that tries to escape the sovereign organisation of the face and the face itself, which clamps back down on the trait, takes hold of it again, blocks its line of flight, and reimposes its organisation upon it' (ATP 188). Facial traits are liberated when they cease to be fixed structural components of a mysterious and omnipresent power and follow their own becomings and lines of flight, linking to others so that 'each freed faciality trait forms a rhizome with a freed trait of landscapity, picturality, or musicality' (ATP 190). The slogan for defacialisation would then be: make your facial tic and facial traits creative. In this way the face ceases to be a redundancy for despotic signification and authoritarian subjectivity, becoming a vehicle for creative experimentation instead.

The dangers of dismantling the face include madness (ATP 188). Deleuze and Guattari touch on this point when discussing defacialisation in relation to the novel, which, they argue, differs from the epic in that it always concerns 'the adventure of lost characters who no longer know their name, what they are looking for, or what they are doing, amnesiacs, ataxics, catatonics' (ATP 173). These characters can, they say, under certain conditions, 'push the movement further still, crossing the black hole, breaking through the white wall, dismantling the face – even if the attempt may backfire' (ATP 173). But positive 'defacialisation' can liberate what Deleuze and Guattari call 'probe-heads' (ATP 190). Probe-heads – *têtes chercheuses* – are homing devices for guided missiles and bombs. They are literally war machines, and they 'dismantle the strata in their wake, break through the walls of significance, pour out of the holes of subjectivity, fell trees in favour of veritable rhizomes, and steer the flows down lines of positive deterritorialisation or creative flight' (ATP 190). Probe-heads are inhuman, but they challenge the inhumanity of the face (ATP 170) with 'strange new becomings, new polyvocalities' (ATP 191). They turn the face itself into a probe-head, a machine of deterritorialisation.

Notes

1. For example: 'The Dogons . . . formulate the problem as follows: an organism befalls the body of the smith, by virtue of a machine or machinic assemblage that stratifies it. "The shock of the hammer and the anvil broke his arms and legs at the elbows and knees, which until that moment he had not possessed. In this way, he received the articulations specific to the new human form that was to spread across the earth, a form dedicated to work . . . His arm became folded with a view to work"' (ATP 41).
2. Lacan's thesis that the unconscious is necessarily structured like a language is challenged by Deleuze and Guattari in *Anti-Oedipus*, where they maintain that this only comes about by way of a stratification of the unconscious whereby desire comes to desire its own repression.
3. Deleuze and Guattari link the regime of subjectification to the figure of the Hebrew God, whose power comes not from his face being omnipresent but rather from its being hidden: 'Faciality undergoes a profound transformation. The god averts his face, which must be seen by no one; and the subject, gripped by a veritable fear of the god, averts his or her face in turn. The averted faces, in profile, replace the frontal view of the radiant face. It is this double turning away that draws the positive line of flight' (ATP 123).
4. 'That is why, at the limit, one can forgo the notion of the sign, for what is retained is not principally the sign's relation to a state of things it designates, or to an entity it signifies, but only the formal relation of sign to sign insofar as it defines a so-called signifying chain . . . The question is not yet what a given sign signifies but to which other signs it refers, or which signs add themselves to it to form a network without beginning or end that projects its shadow onto an amorphous atmospheric continuum. It is this amorphous continuum that for the moment plays the role of the 'signified', but it continually glides beneath the signifier, for which it serves only as a medium or wall: the specific forms of all contents dissolve in it' (ATP 112).
5. 'The infinite set of signs refers to a supreme signifier presenting itself as both lack and excess (the despotic signifier, the limit of the system's deterritorialisation [that is, the limit of the sign's separation from the signified meant to serve as its index])' (ATP 117; see also 112).

6. Deleuze and Guattari include Sartre's 'look' in this critique.
7. This clarification comes in Lacan's 1960s reformulation of the mirror stage (see Fink 1997: 88), though Lacan contends it was part of the original idea: 'In truth, I do not believe that there ever were two phases in what I taught: one phase which is supposed to be centred on the mirror stage, on something highlighted in the imaginary, and then after, with this moment of our history that is located by the Rome report, the discovery which I suddenly made of the signifier' (Lacan unpublished typescript: 25). My thanks to London-based Lacanian analyst Richard Klein for first pointing me to the place of signification in the mirror stage, and to Emma Ingala for pointing me to *Seminar X* as one of the sources.
8. '"You are no longer a child": this statement concerns an incorporeal transformation, even if it applies to bodies and inserts itself into their actions and passions. The incorporeal transformation is recognizable by its instantaneousness, its immediacy, by the simultaneity of the statement expressing the transformation and the effect the transformation produces; that is why order-words are precisely dated, to the hour, minute, and second, and take effect the moment they are dated' (ATP 81).
9. 'An organ-machine is plugged into an energy-source-machine: the one produces a flow that the other interrupts. The breast is a machine that produces milk, and the mouth a machine coupled to it' (Deleuze and Guattari 1983: 1).
10. 'Adolf Wölfli's drawings reveal the workings of all sorts of clocks, turbines, dynamos, celestial machines, house-machines, and so on. And these machines work in a connective fashion, from the perimeter to the centre, in successive layers or segments. But the "explanations" that he provides for them, which he changes as often as the mood strikes him, are based on genealogical series that constitute the recording of each of his drawings. What is even more important, the recording process affects the drawings themselves, showing up in the form of lines standing for "catastrophe" or "collapse" that are so many disjunctions surrounded by spirals' (Deleuze and Guattari 1983: 15).
11. 'From his very earliest infancy, the child has a wide-ranging life of desire – a whole set of nonfamilial relations with the objects and the machines of desire – that is not related to the parents from the point of view of immediate production, but that is ascribed to them (with either love or hatred) from the point of view of the recording of the process, and in accordance with the very special conditions of this recording, including the effect of these conditions upon the process itself (feedback)' (Deleuze and Guattari 1983: 48).
12. 'Our only points of disagreement with Foucault are the following: (1) to us the assemblages seem fundamentally to be assemblages not of power but of desire (desire is always assembled), and power seems to be a stratified dimension of the assemblage; (2) the diagram and abstract machine have lines of flight that are primary, which are not phenomena of resistance or counterattack in an assemblage, but cutting edges of creation and deterritorialisation' (ATP 531 n.39). Against this reading of Foucauldian resistance as being in opposition to power relations – a view common to Deleuze and Guattari and many others – see Widder 2004. On the relation of Foucauldian power and resistance to Deleuze's conception of desire, see Widder 2012: 89–94.
13. In physical chemistry, a dispersion is 'a type of intimate mixture in which one substance is present in a large number of separate small regions distributed throughout another, continuous substance; examples are emulsions (one liquid in another) and aerosols (a solid or a liquid in a gas); also a state of being so distributed' (Simpson and Weiner 1989: vol. 4). In French: 'État d'une solution colloïdale, en suspension dans un mileu où elle est insoluble' (Robert 1993).
14. The asylum physician, for example, did not necessarily have any of the medical expertise suggested by his role: 'It is thought that Tuke and Pinel opened the asylum to medical knowledge. They did not introduce science, but a personality, whose powers borrowed from science only their disguise, or at most their justification . . . The physician could exercise his absolute authority in the world of the asylum only insofar as,

from the beginning, he was Father and Judge, Family and Law – his medical practice being for a long time no more than a complement to the old rites of Order, Authority, and Punishment' (Foucault 1989b: 271–2).
15. In Lacan's (1981: 138–41) terms, this is the distinction between the level of enunciation (what is said) and the level of the statement (the sense of what is said).
16. 'In this sense, discourse ceases to be what it is for the exegetic attitude: an inexhaustible treasure from which one can always draw new, and always unpredictable riches; a providence that has always spoken in advance, and which enables one to hear, when one knows how to listen, retrospective oracles: it appears as an asset – finite, limited, desirable, useful – that has its own rules of appearance, but also its own conditions of appropriation and operation; an asset that consequently, from the moment of its existence (and not only in its 'practical applications'), poses the question of power; an asset that is, by nature, the object of a struggle, a political struggle' (Foucault 1989a: 120).
17. Nietzsche proposes that 'within the original tribal association – we are talking about primeval times – the living generation always acknowledged a legal obligation towards the earlier generation, and in particular towards the earliest, which founded the tribe'; this duty becomes a 'conviction . . . that these have to be paid back with sacrifices and deeds: people recognize an indebtedness [*Schuld*], which continually increases because these ancestors continue to exist as mighty spirits, giving the tribe new advantages and lending it some of their power' (Nietzsche 1994: 2.19). As the community becomes stronger, the debt increases and the ancestors grow in stature, eventually becoming gods themselves. Christianity's emergence within the universal empire of Rome would then entail infinite debt: 'The advent of the Christian God as the maximal god yet achieved, thus also brought about the appearance of the greatest feeling of indebtedness on earth' (2.20). All this would suggest that with God's death and modern atheism's emergence, guilt would dissipate. But here Nietzsche abandons the hypothesis, declaring that 'I have so far intentionally set aside the actual moralisation of these concepts . . . and . . . I actually spoke as though this moralisation did not exist, consequently, as though these concepts would necessarily come to an end once the basic premise no longer applied, the credence we lend our "creditor," God. The facts diverge from this in a terrible way' (2.21).
18. Deleuze explains in his work on Nietzsche how the forces of the slave, forces of *ressentiment*, defeat powerful and active noble forces without ceasing to be weak, in these same terms. Weak forces 'do not form a greater force, one that would be active. They proceed in an entirely different way – they decompose; *they separate active force from what it can do*; they take away a part or almost all of its power' (Deleuze 1983: 57).
19. 'Transgression, guilt, castration: are these determinations of the unconscious, or is this *the way a priest sees things?* Doubtless there are many other forces besides psychoanalysis for oedipalising the unconscious, rendering it guilty, castrating it. But psychoanalysis reinforces this movement, it invents a last priest' (Deleuze and Guattari 1983: 112).
20. I am unsure of the origin of this now fairly common way of describing the body without organs, but the earliest use of which I am aware is Best and Kellner 1991: 90.

Chapter 8

'What Happened Next?': Hjelmslev's Net, Arachne's Web and the Figure of the Line

Helen Palmer

Introduction: lines and lives

The figure of the line is clearly of huge importance in the 'Three Novellas' plateau, but it is also a motif that runs not just through this section but through the whole of *A Thousand Plateaus*. This is the most explicitly literary discussion in the book, but the discussion points both inwards and outwards to reveal the lines that power these particular instances and happenings. This chapter thinks through the beginnings of a philosophy and politics of the line through its uses in Plateau Eight, tracing the work of some thinkers who inspired Deleuze and Guattari and their systems of lines, nets, networks and webs.

As Deleuze and Guattari say in Plateau Eight, 'we are made of lines' (ATP 194). Lines are important because they constitute the articulation of a limit, which is both the placing of the limit and the breaking of that limit. The figure of the line is a geometrical rendering of double articulation; it expresses both liberation and constriction simultaneously. The figure of the rhizome which opens *A Thousand Plateaus* is the primary lineament of the book, but the systems of stratification, segmentarity and flight are expressed as lines throughout. 'Unlike a structure, which is defined by a set of points and positions, the rhizome is made only of lines; lines of segmentarity and stratification as its dimensions, and the line of flight or deterritorialisation as the maximum dimension after which the multiplicity undergoes metamorphosis, changes in nature' (ATP 21). This multifarious nature of the line is important in multiple ways; it expresses division and measurement as well as abstraction and escape. The reason why this is important for life is that these lines are not just metaphorical; they are real. Lines make bars on cages; they make limbs which make movements; they make marks on a page which form letters and sentences; they intersect to form webs and nets. As Deleuze and Guattari say in Plateau Three, 'The Geology of Morals': 'There is no "like" here, we are not saying "like an electron", "like an interaction", etc. The plane of consistency is the abolition of all metaphor; all that consists is Real' (ATP 69). Rather than being 'like' lines, we actually *are* composed of lines. The relationships we have to these multiple types of lines is the same as the relationship we have to the things we make and the things we become. This is the emancipatory aspect of the line; the line of becoming. Deleuze says the following in *Dialogues II*:

> As Lewis Carroll says, it is when the smile is without a cat that man can effectively become cat as soon as he smiles. It is not man who sings or paints, it is man who becomes animal, but at exactly the same time as the animal becomes music, or pure colour, or an astonishingly simple line . . . Everything which becomes is a pure line which ceases to represent whatever it may be. (Deleuze and Parnet 1987: 73–4)

Everything that becomes is a pure line, because becoming is something that goes beyond representation. If the 'pure line' discussed here ceases to represent whatever it may be, we need to ask what it does beyond representation. The pure line Deleuze is talking of is the figure of the abstract line; the 'pure and empty form' which is a motif throughout his work. Among multiple other concepts, figures and movements, the simultaneous movements of deterritorialisation and reterritorialisation discussed throughout *A Thousand Plateaus* can be understood in terms of abstraction. But what about the lines which Deleuze and Guattari specifically talk about in Plateau Eight? These lines trace much more than narrative events; various thinkers inspire the thinking of lines in this plateau and the pattern that these lines of life and language make. The lines discussed in this plateau are equally lines of writing, lines of life, spatiotemporal coordinates, lines *between* other lines, and many others. The conjunctive nature of these lines forms the basis of Deleuze and Guattari's analysis of the three novellas.

Three types of line make up the gradation set out in this schema, and they correspond to varying dimensions, vectors and modes of being. The 'rigid, clear-cut segmentarity' is composed of expectations; of societal norms; of linear, predictable progression, of time measured out evenly by social events and stratification. 'There are at least three of them: a line of rigid and clear-cut segmentarity; a line of molecular segmentarity; and an abstract line, a line of flight no less deadly and no less alive than the others' (ATP 197). If we were to use literary conceptual personae, T. S. Eliot's unfortunate Prufrock is a particularly apt conceptual persona for a life of rigid segmentarity.

> For I have known them all already, known them all;
> Have known the evenings, mornings, afternoons,
> I have measured out my life with coffee spoons;
> I know the voices dying with a dying fall
> Beneath the music from a farther room.
> So how should I presume? (Eliot 1972: 13)

The segmented existence here is measured out by the linear progression of time and a sense of predictability and fixity. The listing of temporal markers and repeated words, 'known them already, known them all', 'evenings, mornings, afternoons', creates the feeling of monotony and tedium. Prufrock gives no sense of being able to escape this measured, impotent existence, nor of even desiring to do so.

One contentious line which is used to divide and categorise our existence in the world is the binary line of gender, which is useful for illustrating the second line in Deleuze and Guattari's schema. The line of 'molecular segmentarity' is perched in between the extremes of rigidity on the one hand and deterritorialisation on the other. This line is supple, rather than rigid, and allows for micro-transformations to be made:

> it is a *line of molecular or supple segmentation* the segments of which are like quanta of deterritorialisation. It is on this line that a present is defined whose very form is the form of something that has already happened, however close you might be to it, since the ungraspable matter of that something is entirely molecularised, traveling at speeds beyond the ordinary thresholds of perception. (ATP 196)

Again using literary analogies, as a fictional conceptual persona for molecular segmentarity we might think of someone like Virginia Woolf's Orlando. Orlando lives a segmented aristocratic existence according to the time in which he or she currently finds herself/himself, and abides by the gendered rules without question despite her/his awareness of the arbitrariness of the division.

> She remembered how, as a young man, she had insisted that women must be obedient, chaste, scented, and exquisitely apparelled. 'Now I shall have to pay in my own person for those desires', she reflected; for women are not (judging by my own short experience of the sex) obedient, chaste, scented, and exquisitely apparelled by nature. They can only attain these graces, without which they may enjoy none of the delights of life, by the most tedious discipline. (Woolf 1978: 98)

The lines, segments and ideological constraints presupposed by this extract are multiple. And yet Orlando's shifting gender provides a perspective on these constraints which is unique in its suppleness, despite the fact that the event of switching genders is never explicitly addressed. The expectations and roles are clear, and the binary division is upheld despite the character's ability to move freely within both masculine and feminine prescribed territories.

Finally, the line of flight, or line of absolute deterritorialisation, is the most extreme of the three lines. To use any model of extensive gradation leads us into problematic territory in Deleuze and Guattari's philosophy; the increase or acceleration involved in the gradation/continuum of the three lines is of an intensive nature. The most intensive, then, of the three types of line is the line of flight. Literary-conceptual personae for this line of flight are characteristically more difficult to identify, because any identities would be plural or unstable by nature; they might even express a disavowal of a unified voice or subject entirely. The disembodied a-subjective spluttering polyvocal voice(s) of Rachel Zorn's transformation of the Dada manifesto might qualify as a contender for a literary-conceptual persona for the line of flight:

> Negrigrigrigriiillons 7838 hair 8181 children 1_21 suck 3243
> In it dans les nuuuuu a aaaages 5645 and thick darkness 282_
> I hoped to find a 'Tahiti' like Gauguin for my painting
> Has Dada ever spoken to you about sleeping with Israel?
> How happy I felt as I left the Ministry of Absorption
> Bearing a new name OVERTURNED BY WHOM? DADA
> One shouldn't let many words out je déchiiiiiiiire
> Dogs 361_ and the fowls 57_5 of the heaven
> The key to a house and a small suitcase
> Someone walks on your feet. It's Dada (Zorn 2012: 437)

The intertextual allusions are many; the trajectory is apparently aleatory; the voice is splintered, multiple and has lost all sense of unity. It is a polyvocal, almost cacophonous line in the process of becoming, and yet of course the references are knowingly chosen and the neologisms carefully constructed. This passage demonstrates the anarchic potential of literary and linguistic lines of flight, through the simultaneous processes of abstraction from and affixation to spheres of meaning and world construction. The line of flight is a line of becoming.

These literary personae are particularly relevant for a number of reasons. First and most simply, they are the most relevant because they are illustrative of the way that the lines of writing become more and more abstract. What this means is that the notion of the stable, unified, authoritative voice as speaking subject becomes more eroded. Secondly, they are useful because they illustrate how the deterritorialisation process occurs in both the *content* and the *expression* in each example; or rather, it demonstrates the reciprocity of content and expression. We can observe that Prufrock's rigid segmentarity is expressed through the poetic outlining of a life meted out by regular, mundane objects and markers of time; Orlando's microtransformations are expressed by shifts through the invisible yet present binary segmentation of gender and the gentle questioning of convention which accompanies the shifts, alongside the moments when the boundaries are challenged and Orlando betrays a characteristic of his/her opposing gender. The line of flight in Zorn's text above is highly charged and complex, effecting multiple sensations and occupying several intertextual locations simultaneously at the same time as transforming itself as it moves through different time zones. It is productive of something entirely other than itself.

Time

The process of traversing the lines, from rigid to supple to abstract, is a simultaneous process of intensification, acceleration, destratification and deterritorialisation. Linked to this in the 'Three Novellas' plateau there is an important relationship to temporality. The use of fiction already presupposes at least two temporal dimensions; we have the fictive past to which the 'What happened?' of the title of the plateau refers, and we have the supposed present of the movement of language in real time. There are, however, many further temporal complexities surrounding these. The three fundamental dimensions of time haunt the beginning of this plateau, although as Deleuze and Guattari point out, it would be a mistake to equate past, present and future directly with the novella, the novel and the tale. The reason why it is a mistake to merely align the novella with the past, the novel with the present and the tale with the future is to do with movement and stasis, and also with temporal placing. The type of linguistic temporality presented in this discussion of the three novellas in question occupies a space-time which requires not only both questions 'What happened?' and 'What is going to happen?', but the operation of differentiation between the two. If we think about the difference between the question which Deleuze and Guattari ask of the tale, 'What is going to happen?' and the question which they ask of the novella, 'What happened?', we are thinking along the lines of a Deleuzian time consciousness, which is to do with maintaining an awareness of the difference between the supposed 'now' and all pasts and futures.

These two questions, 'What happened?' and 'What is going to happen?', reverberate around several of Deleuze's works, such as in *Negotiations* when he is discussing his own philosophical practice of personifying concepts and giving them proper names. This is important when we think about the discussion in the 'Three Novellas' plateau, where we see this process in reverse – the characters of the novellas become de-personified – they become mere lines or segments, forces of liberation or of blockage. In *Negotiations* Deleuze says: 'Philosophy's like a novel. You have to ask "What's going to happen?" "What's happened?" Except the characters are concepts, and the settings, the scenes, are space-times' (Deleuze 1995a: 140–1). It is clear that concepts are characters for Deleuze, but rather than merely settings, I think that the operation of 'depersonalisation' taking place with these character-concepts or conceptual personae results in 'space-time' becoming a character in itself. Literary scholars might call the perception of space-time as a character anthropomorphisation or personification, but more generally this is an operation of deterritorialisation. Deterritorialisation is what is required for the transition from one type of line to another.

The form of the secret

Deleuze and Guattari describe the novella as being linked to the form of the secret. Just like the other ways in which the literary forms are defined, this description also pertains to a particular type of complex temporality. In *The Logic of Sense*, Deleuze spends a long time setting out the distinction between *Chronos* and *Aion* as the two forms of time, and then turns to convincing us that the *Aion*, which is presented as a straight line traced by an aleatory point, encompasses both *Chronos* and itself. Particularly significant for this discussion are Deleuze's descriptions of the *Aion* as a straight line (Deleuze 1990b: 62–5), and also as the 'pure and empty form of time' (Deleuze 1994: 122, 266). The way this is described according to its formal dimension is precisely the way in which the secret which powers the novella is described in this plateau: 'the novella relates, in the present itself, to *the formal dimension of something that has happened*, even if that something is nothing or remains unknowable (ATP 214). To use Deleuze's terminology from *The Logic of Sense*, we could say that the novella relates to the *sense* of something that has happened. The unknown or unknowable secret powers the narrative, and it operates in the same way as the pure and empty form of time – a straight line traced by an aleatory point.

The figures of line and form are linked through a common thread of abstraction. We abstract ourselves so that the lines become perceptible, as does sense, or the infinitive, or the purport to use Hjelmslev's terminology. But this abstraction process goes both ways, as theorists of the avant-garde know very well. We lose and we gain at the same time. In the words of futurism scholar Marjorie Perloff, 'there can hardly be rupture without a compensatory addition; to cut out X inevitably means to make room for Y' (Perloff 2003: 115). As with the literary examples quoted earlier, the subtraction of particularities, quantifiable segments, identities or categories occurs at the same time as an addition of a new dimension or locus of being: a reterritorialisation. So when the Cheshire cat loses the smile, simultaneously the man becomes the cat when he smiles. In *The Logic of Sense* Deleuze outlines this when he talks about 'the simultaneity of a becoming whose characteristic is to elude the present' (Deleuze 1990b: 1). The simultaneous movements of deterritorialisation and reterritorialisation – of the smile on the cat, for example – can be understood in terms of becoming.

Lines in action: nets, webs, axes and margins

In the post- or even anti-Saussurean landscape of the 1970s, unlike thinkers such as Baudrillard who saw in Hjelmslev a similar ideology of signification to Saussure himself, Deleuze and Guattari saw a sharp difference and departure from Saussure. In *Anti-Oedipus* Deleuze and Guattari state this very clearly: 'We believe that, from all points of view and despite certain appearances, Hjelmslev's linguistics stands in profound opposition to the Saussurean and post-Saussurean undertaking' (Deleuze and Guattari 1983: 242). Their reasoning behind this is based on what they see as the elimination of any hierarchy within the orders or levels of language in favour of an immanent linguistics.

> Because there no longer occurs a double articulation between two hierarchised levels of language, but between two convertible deterritorialised planes, constituted by the relation between the form of content and form of expression. Because in this relation one reaches figures that are no longer effects of a signifier, but schizzes, points-signs, or flows-breaks that collapse the wall of the signifier, pass through, and continue on beyond. (Deleuze and Guattari 1983: 242)

What Hjelmslev destroys in the Saussurean system is the hierarchy and the directionality of signification. Hjelmslev upholds the mutual presupposition of expression and content, which functions, in Gary Genosko's words, as a 'prophylaxis against signifier fetishism'. As Genosko states, Deleuze and Guattari champion Hjelmslev because their language in his system is both an inclusive and an intensive continuum (Genosko 1998: 179). There is no hierarchy of signifier over signified, and instead we see a series of reciprocational relationships.

In *Language: An Introduction*, Hjelmslev differentiates between the different types of constituent parts of a text and how they relate to one another. There are first *implicational* and *non-implicational* relations. Implicational relations imply that one constituent part necessarily presupposes the other, whereas non-implicational relations do not. Within *implicational* relations Hjelmslev differentiates between reciprocal or unilateral. While within *reciprocal* implicational relations one element may presuppose the other and vice versa, *unilateral* implicational relations may not operate either way round; one element may presuppose the other but it does not work the other way round. Hjelmslev uses the term 'husband' as an example of a reciprocal implicational relation. The presupposed entity of the wife here is '*latent*'; her existence is presupposed even if she is not present. Conversely, Hjelmslev uses the example of chess to illuminate a unilateral implicational relation: 'the king is implied by all the other pieces – if the king is mated, all his men are captured and the game is over – but not vice versa' (Hjelmslev 1970: 99). It is the reciprocal implicational relations which lead us to the most famous distinction within language which Deleuze and Guattari take from Hjelmslev: the content plane and the expression plane. These planes are then further divided into smaller and smaller elements that we recognise as constituent linguistic building blocks: paragraphs, sentences, words, consonants and smaller particles ad infinitum. What is interesting about these categories for Hjelmslev is that 'the substitution of one member for another can entail a difference in the opposite plane of language'. The test to see whether changes occur across both categories for Hjelmslev is called a *commutation* test, and leads to his overall definition of language itself as '*a structure in which the members of each category have mutual commutation*' (Hjelmslev 1970: 100–1). It is clear that this is a schema of high abstraction, and adds extra lines to a structure of signifier and signified which we are much more familiar with. Gary Genosko calls Hjelmslev's glossematics an 'arid algebra of language', yet acknowledges that this aridity was precisely what Guattari used to serve his 'pragmatics of the unconscious' (Genosko 1998: 175). Taking into account the give-and-take nature of abstraction, however, there is a simultaneous abundance of materiality in the becoming-arid, or becoming-algebraic, of language. In both Hjelmslev and Deleuze and Guattari there is a gesture towards an intensified linguistic materiality here that is both more abstract and more concrete; an immanent linguistics.

Lines can be followed, traced or unearthed in a number of ways. In contrast to a *genealogy*, Claire Colebrook calls Deleuze's *geology* of morals 'an attempt at a grammar of space: different series, planes, territories, paths and maps' (Colebrook 1999: 132). If we reverse the concept of a grammar of space, perhaps we get a geometry of language. Among other things, the structuralist project was one attempt at a kind of geometry of language. It is clear that there are various linguistic geometries that inform the thinking of lines in this plateau. There is a linking of geometries and archaeologies of language, and an ongoing dialogue with structuralism that can be seen in both *Anti-Oedipus* and *A Thousand Plateaus*. At several places throughout *Capitalism and Schizophrenia* we see a sharp differentiation between Saussurean structuralism and the glossematics of Hjelmslev. In his *Prolegomena to a Theory of Language*, Hjelmslev departs from Saussure. Rather than the signifier/signified structural relation found in Saussure's *Course in General Linguistics*, Deleuze and Guattari prefer Hjelmslev's glossematic relation of expression/content. Hjelmslev's differentiation between expression and content within a linguistic sign is then further differentiated into expression-form and content-form, and expression-substance and content-substance. The reciprocal relations between these lines form the glossematic 'net'.

Hjelmslev's term 'purport' from the *Prolegomena* operates along similar lines to Deleuze's 'sense' of the *Logic of Sense* era, with some important differences. Hjelmslev defines purport as

> a principle that is naturally common *qua* principle to all languages, but one whose execution is peculiar to each individual language – this factor will be an entity defined only by its having function to the structural principle of language and to all the factors that make languages different from one another. (Hjelmslev 1961: 50)

It is described as the 'thought', the 'amorphous "thought mass"' and even, rather poetically for Hjelmslev, the same handful of sand formed in different patterns and 'the cloud in the heavens that changes shape in Hamlet's view from minute to minute' (Hjelmslev 1961: 52). When feigning madness to Polonius, Hamlet appears to see various different animal shapes in the same cloud. There is much here to compare with Deleuze's sense, which is defined in *The Logic of Sense* thus: 'sense, *the expressed of the proposition*, is an incorporeal, complex, and irreducible entity, at the surface of things, a pure event which inheres or subsists in the proposition' (Deleuze 1990b: 19). Deleuze's description of sense as *aliquid* immediately calls to mind Hjelmslev's description of purport as the *amorphous* thought-mass, but there are some important differences in these characterisations. Deleuze's sense only inheres within the proposition just as Hjelmslev's purport only becomes a substance through form; the reciprocal relations are the same, but the focal points of the processes are different. Hjelmslev's purport is unformed matter, whereas Deleuze's sense is incorporeal.

Building on the terminology developed from Hjelmslev, Deleuze and Guattari find additional ways to describe the reciprocal relation between structural elements in this plateau and in others, drawing on thinkers such as Fernand Deligny. Guattari in particular is very influenced by the work of Deligny, and the thinking of lines which we see all the way through *A Thousand Plateaus* is an interesting conflation of Deligny's conception of the network and Hjelmslev's conception of the net (among lots of other influences). In this plateau, Deleuze and Guattari draw on Deligny's use of maps to chart the walking movements, perceptions and gestures of autistic children in his clinical practice. It is the lines that map us rather than us who map the lines. 'They compose us, as they compose our map. They transform themselves and may even cross over into one another' (ATP 187). These lines are *not* linguistic or structural in essence, though we impose language, structure and other potentially segmentary forces on to the lines, which 'could equally be the lines of a life, a work of literature or art, or a society, depending on which system of coordinates is chosen'.

It is helpful to look more closely at Deligny's work on lines, webs and networks to see the ways in which he sees lines as inflecting, intersecting and determining one another. For Deligny, a network is 'a mode of being' (Deligny 2015: 33). A network necessarily consists of reciprocally determined elements and lines. Deligny draws out and highlights the potential for the network to operate counter to the dominant ideology or arborescent organisation; a network is rhizomatic. Networks emerge as underground warrens; as communities and links forged through shared desires for change and rupture; as systems of refusal or disobedience. As Deligny points out, networks proliferate at times in history when intolerable events have taken place. 'The disarray of the authorities confronted with a network is actually remarkable. Dissidents sometimes manage to play this instrument – the network – with such astonishing virtuosity that it might be deemed a reflex' (Deligny 2015: 48). These are lines of rhizomatic organisation and growth, they are lines of life but they are also lines of writing. Deligny links his thinking of the network to the action of writing as the spinning of a web.

> The fact remains that there is the act of writing and there is the what. The what, the contents of the book, what it will say, what is written about is obviously the essential thing; what remains is the act of writing, which is Arachnean. You can look at ten thousand, a hundred thousand hands writing: they all do the same thing. There are nonetheless some differences between the spider and the act through which the fingers of a hand – turned into legs – and the palm – turned into a body – write; the thread of words does not emerge from spinnerets located at the base of the wrist; we have had to learn to write. (Deligny 2015: 48)

We could say that the 'act' of writing and the 'what' correspond to the content and expression planes in Hjelmslev's terminology, but how exactly does the hand operate as a network? In order to answer this question, we can look at Deligny's description of the network of lines on the skin of the hand.

> the lines that we have on the palms of our hands do not structure the hands as do the bones that can be seen on x-rays; the lines on the hand seem to be made by chance, and the skin of a closed hand makes folds that could be distributed differently, since the palm of each hand has its own way of folding; this is not the case; these lines follow similar patterns with subtle nuances and are even accompanied by secondary lines that are not necessary for the folds; put another way, they have no rational purpose; the fact remains that their persistence is remarkable; such is also the case with the Arachnean; nothing more than a network of lines that are somewhat tangled according to forms that in fact do not structure the network . . . (Deligny 2015: 80)

The lines formed from creases on the hand do not correspond to the skeleton; these lines have no rational function and differ in every human being. Just like a network and like our hands, we manifest in different ways. A hand is like a language. The folds and creases of our hands are our expression and the bones are our content, and the two are reciprocally related. This description goes some way to illustrate the ways that meanings are transmitted across different series, figures and dimensions in *A Thousand Plateaus*.

It is worth exploring further how human or indeed posthuman subjects can produce themselves through or with the lines Deleuze and Guattari speak of. It is relatively easy to conceive of actual, lived examples of molar and molecular segmentarity, but perhaps more challenging to think of examples of lines of flight. One way we might think about this is in terms of the organisation of subjectivity. Rosi Braidotti has something to say about this:

> The marginal subjects who inhabit the multiple locations of devalued difference have their own task cut out for them, insofar as they too often tend to be caught in dialectical relationships of submission, frozen by the paralysing gaze of the master – hating him or her and envying him or her at the same time. For instance, in order to shift from this dialectically binding location, the feminist subject needs to activate different counter-memories and actualise alternative political practices. Becoming-nomadic means that one learns to reinvent oneself and to desire the self as a process of qualitative transformation. Becoming-minor rests on a non-unitary yet politically engaged and ethically accountable vision of the nomadic subject. Both the Majority and the minorities need to overcome the Dialectic of Majority/Minority or Master/Slave and untie the knots of envy (negative desire) and domination (dialectics) that bind them so tightly. In this process, they will necessarily follow asymmetrical lines of becoming, given that their starting positions are so different. For the Majority, there is no possible becoming-other than in the undoing of its central position altogether. The centre is void; all the action is on the margins. (Braidotti 2013a: 344–5)

Each process prefixed with 'becoming-' denotes a different kind of line of flight. Braidotti's work is very useful in allowing us to see how strands of Deleuze and Guattari's thought can begin to be mobilised. So this extract shows how in her nomadic ethics, the feminist subject affirms herself through following what she describes as asymmetrical *lines of becoming*. Her emphasis on voiding the centre can similarly be seen in various places. For example, the centre must be voided when achieving the 'critical distance from the dominant vision of the subject' which is how Braidotti describes the process of defamiliarisation. 'The post-anthropocentric shift away from the hierarchical relations that had privileged "Man" requires a form of estrangement and a radical repositioning on the part of the subject. The best method to accomplish this is through the strategy of defamiliarisation or critical distance from the dominant vision of the subject' (Braidotti 2013b: 88). Braidotti demonstrates how lines of flight can be sourced in gendered or raced spaces, and that cartographies and conceptual personae are part of these figurations. The processes of becoming-woman, becoming-other, becoming-earth or becoming-imperceptible are all examples of lines of flight which Braidotti describes, and come to life through figurations. Prufrock, Orlando and Zorn's reworked Dada manifesto are all examples of figurations of the different types of lines. 'A figuration is the expression of alternative representations of the subject as a dynamic non-unitary entity; it is the dramatisation of the processes of becoming' (Braidotti 2013b: 164). The three novellas chosen by Deleuze and Guattari in this plateau also present figurations of the different types of lines. So let us now turn to one of the novellas discussed by Deleuze and Guattari in Plateau Eight and focus on the young female telegraphist in *In the Cage*, and then to a fourth novella, *Girl Meets Boy*.

In the Cage

The segmented existence described in Henry James's *In the Cage* proposed by Deleuze and Guattari cannot be considered independently of the concepts of segmentarity discussed in other sections of the book. Segmentarity is a force of rigidity, or rather a blockage to an emancipatory or abstracting force, clearly perceptible in the predictable and segmented life of the telegraphist. Literally represented by the bars of the cage in which she sits at her job for so many prescribed hours of the day, James's heroine is imprisoned and is nevertheless able, through her narrative voice, to express and sustain throughout the novella an entirely different inner world. The 'conjugation' expressed by the heroine's fiancé is of a different type to the 'conjunctive' logic expressed by Deleuze and Guattari everywhere in this book but particularly at the beginning in the Rhizome section: 'Always follow the rhizome by rupture; lengthen, prolong and relay the line of flight; make it vary, until you have produced the most abstract and torturous of lines of *n* dimensions and broken directions. Conjugate deterritorialised flows' (ATP 11). The grocer and the telegraphist, the man and the woman, are molar segments that slot together without any independent thought, creation or expression.

The distinction between doubles and couples in Deleuze and Guattari's discussion of James's novella is particularly significant for thinking about the different kinds of lines. We know from Deleuze and Guattari that in their system, the Couple, the Double and the Clandestine map on to rigid segmentarity, supple segmentarity and line of flight, respectively. 'Between the Couple of the first kind of segmentarity, the Double of the second, and the Clandestine of the line of flight, there are so many possible mixtures and passages' (ATP 227). In James's story, the protagonist and her fiancé are a couple. Their relation is described as 'intrinsic'; the aggregates that determine their reciprocity are easy to classify. They slot into easily identifiable categories. The heroine and the gentleman customer with whom she becomes obsessed, however, are described as doubles. The segmentation which takes place in this 'doubling' is of a different kind; it is described as molecular or supple segmentation: 'the quanta of deterritorialisation'. Pointing towards something not-quite-expressed but gestured towards, this segmentation is expressed only formally, since, as Deleuze and Guattari state, 'the ungraspable matter of that something is entirely molecularised, traveling at speeds beyond the ordinary thresholds of perception'. Our heroine cannot speak in definitive terms about her 'alternate self' waiting for her after she finishes work. 'She did last things or pretended to do them; to be in the cage had suddenly become her safety, and she was literally afraid of the alternate self who might be waiting outside. *He* might be waiting; it was he who was her alternate self, and of him she was afraid' (James 1919: 96). The gentleman is emblematic of another existence altogether, but an impossible existence. Ultimately in this novella there *is* a partial answer to the question 'What happened?' in terms of the molecular relation between the telegraphist and the telegraph sender. Nothing happens. What Deleuze and Guattari call the form of the secret dissolves; everybody slots into their pre-defined segments and carries on just as if nothing has happened because nothing has. Nothing has happened but everything has changed. The fact that we are never told the exact nature of the secret is important; it is the *form* of the secret that interests Deleuze and Guattari here. The form of the secret is a narrative line itself, and is the novella's motivational force. The fact that the secret's form never becomes materialised is also important. The molecular relation between the heroine and the telegraph sender is 'dissolved in the form of the secret – because nothing happened'. And yet this is not the full answer. The dissolution of the molecular relation between the telegraphist and the telegraph sender becomes something more extreme; Deleuze and Guattari posit that the heroine achieves 'a kind of absolute deterritorialisation' (ATP 197). There has been an encounter, an acknowledgement and a retrenchment. A shift has occurred only at the level of thought and perception. The lines from James which Deleuze and Guattari quote at this point are from a French translation and quite different from the English, but a few lines before this in James's text the epiphanic moment is described retrospectively thus: 'It had been an abject little exposure of dreadful impossible passion' (James 1919: 99). This line is the Clandestine itself; the form of the secret in which nothing has happened but a seismic shift has occurred.

Girl Meets Boy

The following section is a reading of another novella: *Girl Meets Boy* by Ali Smith, a modern retelling of Ovid's myth of Iphis and Ianthe from the *Metamorphoses*. The discussion is framed around the interplay between the two questions 'What happened?' and 'What is going to happen?', which form a kind of refrain in Plateau Eight. We can read this novella in terms of the philosophy and politics of lines, just as Deleuze and Guattari do with the stories by James, Fitzgerald and Fleutiaux.

The first line of the novella immediately presents a challenge to the conventional binary stratification of gender. 'Let me tell you about when I was a girl, our grandfather says' (Smith 2008: 3). This statement begins Ali Smith's novella *Girl Meets Boy*, set in Inverness in 2007, about a romance between the disillusioned employee of a competitive bottled water company and a political activist who tags themself Iphis and stages performative protests against the local segmentary forces of patriarchy and capitalism while scandalising local residents through their problematisation of gender. So, what is the form of the secret in this novella? In the words of Deleuze and Guattari, 'whatever could have happened, even though everything is and remains imperceptible, in order for everything to be and remain imperceptible forever' (ATP 194)? One segmented dividing line which provides a potential direction for this question is gender. Its disruption can be found everywhere, between the lines of writing, the lines of life, even, to quote Deleuze and Guattari again, along 'the lines productive of the variation of the line of writing itself'. This is particularly evident in this novella. My argument is that in Smith's text, the straight line traced by the aleatory point is the event or the formal dimension of gender. It can be read like Deleuze's Aion. The adult narrator recalls watching the game show, *Blind Date*, in her childhood, with its pantomime sliding door as the very literalisation of the division between male and female. The back-and-forth motion of this sliding door separating the contestants is emblematic of the oscillations between the opposing forces of rigid segmentarity and deterritorialisation perceived everywhere in this text. The actions of deterritorialisation, the political lines of protest drawn, and the ensuing lines of punishment drawn up, from the angry lines etched out of the golf course green in acid saying NO VOTES NO GOLF, to the bars in the prison cell blocking freedom and the analogous penal function of the force-feeding tubes entering the body of the hunger-striking activist, all operate simultaneously while the gender boundaries are subjected to a forceful linguistic challenge. The sister of our protagonist inhabits a self-built prison, a completely rigid and segmented life which is evidenced immediately and physically in the very typography of the novella, in her ritual enactment of closing and sealing off her utterances in parentheses. Everything in this character's life is monitored and controlled, from the ingestion and expulsion of food from her starved body, the miles she treads and the calculation of calorie loss versus intake, the brands on her sportswear and the type of life she buys into with these brands, the power lines linking her and the misogynistic male members of the company. The disruption of gender is the form of the secret which enables this character to reach an epiphanic moment and break down some of the bars she has constructed around herself.

The fact that the process of deterritorialisation retains territorialisation within the word rather than disavowing it entirely is important. Literary and linguistic expressions of this can help here too, particularly when thinking about the ways in which we can realise our own position within these strata in order to free ourselves. Sara Ahmed discusses this gendered, raced process in another novel:

> How can one be disturbed by one's own arrival? The familiar is that which receives to those who inhabit it. To become estranged from the familiar is thus to have it revealed to you. The familiar is disclosed in the revelation of your estrangement. (Ahmed 2010: 86)

Describing a scene in Andrea Levy's 1999 novel *Fruit of the Lemon*, Ahmed is discussing a moment which takes place when Faith Jackson, a black British girl whose parents have migrated to England from Jamaica, realises the lines of rigid segmentarity which block and free her. At such moments it is a question of agency and power; whether a human subject chooses their own estrangement or whether this has been something imposed on them circumstantially. Going back to *Girl Meets Boy*, we see numerous examples of linguistic enactments of such moments. These moments are the most highly charged when the linguistic defamiliarisation occurs across both planes; of expression and content. Thinking back to Braidotti's description of defamiliarisation as a critical distance from the dominant vision of the subject, one significant moment in Smith's narrative takes place when the protagonist breaks out of her own segmented cage precisely by seizing its bars and declaring her own position in order to be liberated from it.

> Listen, world out there, slow-passing beyond train windows. I'm Imogen Gunn. I come from a family that can't be had. I come from a country that's the opposite of a, what was it, dominant narrative. I'm all Highland adrenaline. I'm all teuchter laughter and I'm all teuchter anger. (Smith 2008: 129)

The line of language *itself* vibrates and hesitates, simultaneously unsure of itself and defiantly bold. There is more expressed in the self-interrupting, self-doubting 'what was it' than in any of the rest of the fragment quoted above. The protagonist feels the very fibres that make up her being, emotional, cartographic, geographic, visceral, political, and affirms and houses them. There are lines linking her to her place and her past. She acknowledges the hesitancy and retains it, performs and owns it. The result is a powerful declaration of emancipated subjectivity.

Deleuze and Guattari state in *A Thousand Plateaus* that true creation only takes place during a line of flight. A line of flight is enacted over the course of *Girl Meets Boy*, and this is illuminated in various ways. In one climactic section of the narrative, some kind of literal and metaphorical metamorphosis or becoming takes place, like an androgynous *Alice in Wonderland*, and is composed, quite fittingly, entirely of questions. Another section is almost Joycean in its free-flowing stream of subconsciousness:

> I was a she was a he was a we were a girl and a girl and a boy and boy, we were blades, were a knife that could cut through myth, were two knives thrown by a magician, were arrows fired by a god, we hit heart, we hit home, we were the tail of a fish were the reek of a cat were the beak of a bird were the feather that mastered gravity were high above every landscape then down deep in the purple haze of the heather were roamin in a gloamin in a brash unending Scottish piece of perfect jigging reeling reel can we really keep this up? (Smith 2008: 103)

Some may feel that to analyse the intersecting lines and segments that make up this extract might detract from the overall lyricism of the passage, but if we were to sum up its movement briefly: here we have an excellent demonstration of how language, temporality, content and expression are bifurcated, intersect, break, become dynamic and other and take flight.

Content and expression both take flight here. We see the conjunctive logic performed at a lexical, syntactical and semantic level in this whirling jigging reeling reel – the musical reel is another line here. Parataxis is the quintessential conjunctive and poetic form. Becoming-she, he, interchangeably, and ending with the form of the question which does not require an answer because an answer would be teleological, and this affirmation of queer becoming resists teleology.

Towards the end of the novella, what is described as 'the old spectrum' is something that has become obsolete, because once the characters have become deterritorialised they are able to perceive an entirely new spectrum altogether. It is not a question of a difference in degree; a transversal shift has occurred. And of course we shouldn't forget the narrative source of this story, the myth of Iphis and Ianthe, and the intermingling lines of narrative which intertwine with the new ones, and the retelling that is the narrative line itself retold again, and then again within the fictive frame. Ovid's *Metamorphoses* is, of course, the overall source for this novella, and there is no better ancient figurehead than the irreverent creator of shape-shifting amoral parables, except perhaps Heraclitus, whose river flows through the conclusion to the novella in a song described as 'the song of the flow of things', an undammed force of creativity and vitalism.

It is without doubt that the lines described in this plateau are political in nature. 'Individual or group, we are traversed by lines, meridians, tropics, and zones marching to different beats and differing in nature' (ATP 202). The figure of the line is particularly significant because of its multi-directionality; it both constrains and liberates. An important trap to avoid, however, is to imagine the gradation of lines as becoming 'better' as they become deterritorialised. The danger of absolute deterritorialisation is palpable throughout the plateau, and the level of danger increases proportionally to the level of deterritorialisation. We might echo Deleuze and Guattari's question:

> why is the line of flight, even aside from the danger it runs of reverting to one of the other two lines, imbued with such singular despair in spite of its message of joy, as if at the very moment things are coming to a resolution its undertaking were threatened by something reaching down to its core, by a death, a demolition? (ATP 205–6)

Reterritorialisation is not mentioned in this plateau but is often mentioned elsewhere as the necessary and complementary 'flipside' to deterritorialisation when a line of flight occurs on a stratum (ATP 60). A new, intensified locus of territorialisation must be found to avoid the 'despair' mentioned above. The result is free-fall into a groundless, undifferentiated abyss. So while it is clearly important to develop an awareness of the lines of power and desire which our movements express in order to break out of rigid segmentary forces, we need to simultaneously hold on to 'just a little order to protect us from chaos' (Deleuze and Guattari 1994: 201). The form of the novella is a complex, intensive line in itself, and allows us to perceive potentially invisible forces, vectors and stratifications through the lives of the characters and the paths they follow, and the types of lines that map their narrative journeys.

Chapter 9

Micropolitics and Segmentarity

Eugene W. Holland

Few plateaus demonstrate the Deleuzian principle of difference in repetition more than the 'Micropolitics and Segmentarity' plateau, which appears directly after the 'Three Novellas' plateau in the middle of *A Thousand Plateaus*. Not only do these two plateaus treat many of the same themes – notably the three kinds of lines: lines of rigid segmentarity, lines of supple segmentation and lines of flight – but they also trace the same trajectory, moving from an exposition of the three lines to a discussion of their dangers. Yet this very repetition serves to highlight a key difference: the displacement from a focus on the personal, the existential and the literary in the preceding plateau ('lines of writing conjugate[d] with other lines, life lines' [ATP 194]), to a focus on the social, the political and the anthropological in 'Micropolitics and Segmentarity'.

In earlier plateaus, segmentation was generally presented as a synonym for stratification (or as a mode of stratification), and, more importantly, as a characteristic feature of the passional-subjective, authoritarian post-signifying regime of signs that distinguishes the post-signifying regime from the despotic, signifying regime of signs:

> signifiance and subjectification are semiotic systems that are entirely distinct in their principles and have different regimes (circular irradiation versus segmentary linearity) and different apparatuses of power (despotic generalised slavery versus authoritarian contract-proceeding). (ATP 181–2)

In contrast with a generalised slavery under the direct command of the despot-god, passional subjectification operates with the face of God averted, so that the subject's line-of-flight away from it now takes on a positive value and the linear, segmented form of a series of 'proceedings': '[the] relation to God is passional and authoritative rather than despotic and signifying; he anticipates and detects the powers [*puissances*] of the future rather than applying past and present powers [*pouvoirs*]' (ATP 124). The line-of-flight now operates 'by the linear and temporal succession of finite [segmented] proceedings' (ATP 120), rather than merely jumping from point to point on the concentric circles surrounding the despot. The introduction in *A Thousand Plateaus* of this fourth regime of signs (these regimes being roughly comparable to the three modes of libidinal production presented in *Anti-Oedipus*) contributes to the wholesale transformation of Deleuze and Guattari's analysis of fascism, as we will see towards the end of this chapter: this explains the date of the 'Micropolitics and Segmentarity' plateau (1933), which marks the moment when Hitler's Nazi war machine finally succeeded in taking over the German state apparatus and became macropolitical. But the development of the sociological and anthropological side of the concept of segmentarity also contributes crucially to what may be the most important, explicitly political new concept in all of *A Thousand Plateaus*: micropolitics. In addition to examining some of the sources for this concept, this chapter will outline the analysis of power dynamics it entails, and demonstrate its relevance for events such as May '68 and the Occupy movement. In later plateaus, the analyses of lines and flows presented in 'Micropolitics and Segmentarity' enable Deleuze and Guattari to specify the power dynamics of the state and of capital, and to highlight a crucial distinction between connections of flows, which can be revolutionary, and the conjugation of flows that characterises capitalist axiomatisation. But first and foremost, the 'Micropolitics and Segmentarity' plateau stages an intervention in the field of political anthropology.

Segmentarity

This plateau intervenes in political anthropology in order to transform the very concept of 'segmentary society', as it is customarily used in that field to distinguish between stateless, 'primitive' societies and societies centred on the state. This issue is a major concern of Deleuze and Guattari throughout both volumes of *Capitalism and Schizophrenia*, where their intent is twofold: to eliminate any 'evolutionism' that would construe the state as emerging spontaneously from 'primitive' society as it got bigger and more complex, and to insist nonetheless on a close relationship between the two social forms, such that stateless societies are understood to possess mechanisms by which to ward off the emergence of the state, while the state aims to capture stateless societies and overcode their social relations to its own ends (securing and increasing its command over territory and the payment of tribute). Conventional political anthropology characterises segmentary society as a group of extended families or clans that share a given territory without any one clan or person dominating the others or achieving centralised control over the entire space.[1] Such a group is 'held together principally by likenesses among its segments', which are defined primarily by kinship relations and have 'no permanent organised confederation' (Sahlins 1961: 325–6). State society, by contrast, involves both the differentiation and specialisation of subgroups (social division of labour) and the exercise of power over the entire space and the people inhabiting it by a central authority-figure or structure.

Deleuze and Guattari reject the terms of this dichotomy: *all* societies are segmented; 'the human being is a segmentary animal' (ATP 208). So instead of distinguishing between segmentary ('primitive') and non-segmentary (centralised, state) societies, they propose three forms of segmentation, all of which appear (in varying mixtures) in all human societies: binary, circular and linear. And it is now the two *modes* of these three forms of segmentation – rigid and supple, or molar and molecular, arborescent and rhizomatic – that serve to distinguish different types of society. Having proposed this new categorical distinction between supple and rigid segmentarity, however, Deleuze and Guattari insist (characteristically) that it is an analytic distinction, and that all societies in fact exhibit both modes, but in differing proportions or configurations:

> Primitive societies have nuclei of rigidity or arborification that as much anticipate the State as ward it off. Conversely, our societies are still suffused by a supple fabric without which their rigid segments would not hold. Supple segmentarity cannot be restricted to primitive peoples. It is not the vestige of the savage within us but a perfectly contemporary function ... Every society, and every individual, are thus plied by both segmentarities simultaneously: one molar, the other molecular. The configurations differ, for example, between the primitives and us, but the two segmentarities are always in presupposition. In short, everything is political, but every politics is simultaneously a *macropolitics* and a *micropolitics*. (ATP 213)

Political analysis must therefore proceed on both levels simultaneously, always taking both macropolitics and micropolitics into account, even or especially when the differences in configuration between supple and rigid modes of segmentarity are used to distinguish stateless from state societies.

Take circular segmentation, to begin with. In stateless societies, circular segmentation *ends* with the extended family or clan, which envelops other, smaller segments, whereas in modern state societies, circular segmentation *begins* with the nuclear family and extends outward from there to neighbourhood, city, county, state and nation. More important, the sub-segments of a stateless society are more or less equal in size and lack of power: clan circles coexist within a tribe on a horizontal plane, as it were, but are not concentric with one another. The circular segments in state society, by contrast, vary in size (getting larger and larger as one moves outward from the smallest circle, the nuclear family) and they are, to a greater or less degree, concentric: the more authoritarian a society, the greater the degree of alignment or resonance among its concentric circles, at the power centre of which lies the despot, god, or leader. State societies thus foster monotheism, while stateless societies are polytheistic or animistic (ATP 211). But Deleuze and Guattari get even more specific: the role of the shaman in stateless societies is to forge temporary alignments among the various segments, on a case-by-case basis when needed; this is a supple mode of circular segmentation. But in state societies, the alignment of concentric segments is permanent, structural and more or less rigorously enforced:

> The segmentarity becomes rigid, to the extent that all [segment] centres resonate in . . . a single point of accumulation . . . The face of the father, teacher, colonel, boss, enter into redundancy, refer back to a centre of significance that moves across the various circles and passes back over all of the segments. (ATP 211)

The category of rigid segmentarity thus overlaps with the categories of facialisation, striated space, arborescent form and molar organisation which serve to characterise state society in other plateaus.

Binary segmentation, too, operates in both supple and rigid modes. Rigid binary segmentarity is characteristic of the faciality machine analysed in the 'Faciality' plateau (although the term segmentation rarely appears there). Here, rigid segmentarity takes dualisms (regarding gender, wealth, etc.) as a point of departure for two kinds of hierarchising operation: bi-univocalisation and binarisation. Bi-univocalisation divides populations into two mutually exclusive groups, and privileges one over the other (man over woman, rich over poor, etc.). Binarisation erects a standard against which all that is non-standard is measured (white or not, and if not what complexion; adult or not, and if not what age; etc.). Primitive segmentation, by contrast, produces dualisms only as a by-product of larger operations – as when a matrimonial pairing (man/woman) results from a complex of exchanges involving at least three clans within a tribe (ATP 210).

It is linear segmentation, however, that turns out to be the most significant of the three forms and to occupy most of the plateau, partly because of the way the 'Micropolitics and Segmentarity' plateau, as we have seen, builds on the analysis of the three kinds of 'life lines' presented in the preceding 'Novellas' plateau, and partly because of its relation with overcoding. By means of the former, the dualism of rigid vs. supple segmentarity is itself undone, with the introduction of the notion of a 'quantum flow' that subtends both modes of segmentation – just as, in the 'Novellas' plateau, lines of flight or rupture can be detected beneath both the break lines of rigid segmentarity and the crack lines of supple segmentation (ATP 200). Now, instead of a dual classificatory schema (stateless societies with supple segmentation vs. state societies of rigid segmentarity), the tripartite schema enables a dynamic analysis of power relations pertaining to all kinds of societies, as we will see below. Supple segmentation henceforth appears as a battleground of struggle between rigid state stratification on one side, and quantum flows that are impossible to capture in their entirety, on the other. With respect to economics, for example, rigid segmentarity appears in the actions of state-sanctioned central banks, which issue and validate currency; supple segmentation characterises the aggregate of exchanges actually transacted via the medium of money; and both of these depend on the quantum flows of desire for enjoyment in abundance, only some of which get captured and converted into commercial transactions.

Linear segmentation is thus presented in terms of the two 'simultaneous states of the abstract Machine' (ATP 223), or the two basic types of abstract machine (Deleuze and Guattari appear indifferent as to which of these formulations is preferable): the abstract machine of overcoding, which produces rigid segmentarity, and the abstract machine of mutation, which operates by decoding and deterritorialisation and steers lines of flight along 'submolecular' quantum flows (ATP 223). (These two abstract machines produce the dynamics called 'paranoid' and 'schizophrenic' in *Anti-Oedipus*.) Supple segmentation henceforth occupies 'a whole [intermediary] realm of properly molecular negotiation, translation, and transduction', where on one side, molar segmentarity loses its rigidity and on the other, quantum flows lose their mutability. Macropolitics involves rigid segmentarity, while micropolitics involves lines of supple segmentation and/or quantum flows. (Here again, Deleuze and Guattari appear indifferent or ambiguous as to whether micropolitics concerns supple segmentation, quantum flows, or both; see ATP 199, 213, 216, 217, 218 and *passim*. In what follows, micropolitics will refer to both.) So the abstract machine of overcoding produces rigid lines, makes their centres resonate, striates space (replacing coded places with homogeneous space), and becomes actualised in re-territorialising state assemblages, while the abstract machine of mutation draws lines of flight by decoding and deterritorialising, assures the creation-connection of quantum flows, and erects war machines or metamorphosis machines on its lines of flight.

The series of proceedings comprising the life lines of many North Americans, for example, includes a linear segment called the college years that occurs after the family segment (childhood and early adolescence) and before the full-time employment or career segment. The axiomatising abstract machines of capital and the state overcode this segment primarily as vocational training: disciplined investment in human capital by state-accredited institutions and certified by grade-point averages and diplomas. The same segment, however, fosters immeasurable flows of decoded and deterritorialised desire – desire freed from the Oedipal authority of the family, and not yet subject to that of the boss; the abstract machine of mutation draws multiple lines of personal and collective experimentation, which may go so far, in certain circumstances (e.g. May '68, the South Africa divestment campaign, Occupy), as to mobilise war machines aimed against capital and/or the state. In between these two abstract machines lies the intermediary realm of supple segmentation, where multiple life-choices are made subject to a wide assortment of forces – choices such as which electives to take and what to major in, which extra-curricular activities to participate in, whether to join the campus chapter of a fraternity or the Democratic Socialists of America, and so on; such choices may be made under the influence of a charismatic teacher or classmate, or the latest collegiate fad or current events, as much as lingering pressure from parents and anticipation of possible future career-paths. This intermediary realm is, of course, not immune to overcoding: the state funds Foreign Language and Area Studies in particularly sensitive languages; corporations regularly sponsor research in especially promising fields. And the result is that life-choices are shaped by the specific disciplinary contents of state- or corporate-sponsored rigid segmentarity. More recently, however, axiomatising control has been exerted directly on the quantum flows of desire: neoliberal capitalism forces students into debt so that the fear of future financial failure narrows their life-choices, independent of any specific sponsored content. The college-years segment thus displays the interplay of rigid segmentarity, supple segmentation and quantum flows of desire and fear as it varies historically with the changing relations of political and economic forces.

Having laid out this new conception of segmentarity and the pivotal place within it of supple segmentation, between the abstract machines of overcoding and mutation, Deleuze and Guattari address four possible misunderstandings to be avoided in their proposed transformation of political anthropology. The first is the notion that the radical qualitative difference between the two abstract machines would preclude their interaction. In fact (and more obviously when formulated as the 'simultaneous states' of a single abstract machine [ATP 223]), overcoding and mutation are understood always to operate in tandem, in varying proportions, producing constant negotiation and oscillation between the molecular and the molar on any given set of lines. A second mistake would be to consider the difference between rigid and supple segmentation to be a matter of size, as if supple segmentation involved small segments and rigid segmentarity large ones. In fact, even when supple segmentation involves matters of detail and operates in small groups, it is no 'less coextensive with the entire social field' than rigid segmentarity. By extension (and thirdly), supple segmentation is not an imaginary or individual matter: it is just as Real and as thoroughly social as rigid segmentarity. Finally – and in consonance with the final line of the book: 'Never believe that a smooth space will suffice to save us' (ATP 500) – supple segmentation is not necessarily preferable to rigid segmentarity; we must not believe 'that a little suppleness is enough to make things "better"' (ATP 215). (This qualification is especially important to the revised understanding of fascism presented in *A Thousand Plateaus*.)

In order to dispel the idea that any one of the lines is simply better than the others, Deleuze and Guattari end the 'Micropolitics and Segmentarity' plateau (as they did the 'Three Novellas' plateau) with an analysis of the dangers entailed in each of the three lines (ATP 227–31). The danger of the rigid line is that we actually desire it, out of fear; it is not something (only) imposed upon us: we crave it for the comfort and assurance its very rigidity provides. 'The more rigid the segmentarity, the more reassuring it is for us' (ATP 227). The danger of the line of flight is that it can, under certain conditions, become a line of pure abolition – as when a 'war machine has reached the point that it has no other object but war, [and] substitutes destruction for mutation' (ATP 230). The danger of the supple line, finally, is that it harbours operations of power just as much as the rigid line does, although in different and perhaps unexpected forms – and indeed theorising power is one of the most important contributions the 'Micropolitics and Segmentarity' plateau makes to political philosophy.

Micropolitics

Deleuze and Guattari share credit for the concept of micropolitics with Michel Foucault. Indeed, they explicitly invoke 'Foucault's analysis of "disciplines" or micropowers (school, army, factory, hospital, etc.)' (ATP 224) in their discussion of the molecular operations of power on lines of supple segmentation. But they go on to relate molecular power to molar power and to the quantum flows subtending both, all in terms of something like a unified field theory of power hinging on the operations of conversion-segmentation and capture, which are further developed in the 'Apparatus of Capture' plateau later in the book, and also inform Deleuze's analysis of the more recent type of power in what he called 'control societies.'[2]

Power converts flows into segments, as best it can, and operates in three overlapping zones:

1) its zone of power, relating to the segments of a solid rigid line;
2) its zone of indiscernibility, relating to its diffusion throughout a microphysical fabric (i.e. through lines of supple segmentation); and
3) its zone of impotence, relating to the flows and quanta it can only convert without being able to control or define. (ATP 226)

Despotism, not surprisingly, provides (later, in the 'Apparatus of Capture' plateau) one of the clearest examples of the operations of central power, in its extraction of tribute from conquered peoples. In stateless societies, the value of surplus goods is determined among clans within tribes or among tribes via negotiation on the basis of polyvocal codes: this is supple segmentation, with each clan or tribe having its own local centre of evaluation operating on the same plane as the others, with which it enters into negotiations as equals. But the despotic state proceeds by overcoding, issuing currency into which local goods must be converted so as to pay tribute to the despot: this is rigid segmentation, with a single centre of evaluation (the despot) dominating and overcoding all the others in order to capture surplus once it has been converted into monetary form. The quantum flow of the production of goods remains, of course, completely beyond the despot's control in its zone of impotence (being dependent on the vagaries of the weather and harvests, the abilities and good will of conquered peoples, etc.), and even the collection of tribute payments occupies a whole zone of indiscernibility of intermediary (supple) power relations, with producers trying to deceive the despot's tax-collectors, and they in turn trying to defraud the despot.

The relations of central power to indiscernibility and impotence via the mechanisms of conversion and capture are particularly significant in connection with an important clarification of the first-approximation imagery Deleuze and Guattari had employed earlier in the plateau to characterise central power: it no longer occupies the central point of concentric circles, but serves as a resonance chamber:

> the common central point is not where all the other points melt together, but instead acts as a point of resonance on the horizon, behind all the other points. The State is not a point taking all the others upon itself, but a resonance chamber for them all. (ATP 224)

In this way, all the various institutions within the state are guaranteed a presumptive (not relative) autonomy from one another and from the state, as local power centres, while their variable tendency to operate in consonance with one another accounts for the (variably) achieved consistency of what we might call the 'state-effect' and even the appearance of the state having agency.[3]

While rigid segmentarity epitomises the operations of despotic state power, it also appears in state-forms of thought, royal linguistics and the pipe-dreams of logical positivism. Notoriously, Plato's theory of forms erects a gold standard of rigid meaning to which the multifarious (more supple) uses of words by various speakers in actual situations is expected to conform. Subsequently and more generally, languages become 'major' languages when the propriety and meaning of statements and words are determined from on high by the rigid standards of grammars and dictionaries, to which the dynamic expression of existential states and successful communication among speakers are expected to conform. Deleuze and Guattari's linguistics plateaus work to overturn the rigid segmentarity of major languages and royal linguistics in favour of more supple forms of segmentation (such as pragmatism), as these are informed in turn by encounters with the forces of chaos lying outside language, well beyond its control.

The three zones of power also appear, finally and perhaps most importantly, in the operations of capital. In much the same way that the despot issued currency to capture flows of surplus goods converted into tribute payments, capital issues credit money in order to capture flows of surplus value, based on correlated segmentations of labour time, wage payments, production output, commodity prices and other factors of production and consumption:

> Not only does each line have its segments, but the segments of one line correspond to those of another; for example, the wage regime establishes a correspondence between monetary segments, production segments, and consumable-goods segments. (ATP 212)

The convertibility of all these factors into one another through the medium of money is the constant preoccupation of monetary and fiscal policy, branding and marketing strategies, education and job-training, and so on. Now it could be argued (not without reason) that capital is no longer a centralised power structure, and that it no longer operates via rigid segmentarity at all, particularly since the dollar as a global currency was taken off the gold standard and allowed to float against other currencies. The extent to which this is the case suggests the degree to which global capital has indeed become a war machine, as Deleuze and Guattari propose in the 'Apparatus of Capture' plateau. But they also insist that capitalism still has a central axiom – the conjugation of liquid wealth and unqualified labour power – around which other axioms revolve (and come and go), and that it issues credit and employs labour in a system where the value of commodities is not determined via the dynamic regulation of supply and demand among equal trading partners in a free market, but in terms of the amount of labour power embodied in them in unfree capitalist markets that are constrained and deformed by primitive accumulation, so that a differential surplus can be extracted from them and captured for the sake of capital accumulation.

Here, too, Deleuze and Guattari are even more specific about the operations of central power, particularly regarding the relation between rigid segmentarity and quantum flows as it plays out in the middle ground of supple segmentation: they invoke a key distinction between the *connection* of flows and the *conjugation* of flows. Under propitious circumstances, the connection of flows boosts their intensity and accelerates their rates of decoding and deterritorialisation; the result is greater than the sum of the parts, and can even become revolutionary. The conjugation of flows, by contrast, reduces their potential, 'performs a general reterritorialisation, and brings the flows under the dominance of a single flow capable of overcoding them' (ATP 220) – which is precisely the result of the power that banks exercise by issuing flows of credit money, as we have seen. The further complication is this, and it arises from the pivotal location of supple segmentation between rigid segmentarity and the quantum flows: in this location, connection and conjugation are in fact two sides of the same process. Capital cannot conjugate factors of production without connections emerging at the same time among the flows. Hence the profound ambiguity of capitalism, on which Deleuze and Guattari have always insisted, starting with *Anti-Oedipus* (where connection and conjugation first appeared, as the first and third passive syntheses of the unconscious).

To translate from the terminology of segmentation into the terms of the 'Capture' plateau, capitalist axiomatisation ceaselessly conjugates denumerable (i.e. rigidly segmented) sets of factors of production in its pursuit of surplus value, yet at the same time that very axiomatisation generates non-denumerable sets of flow connections that escape capitalist control altogether. One of the payoffs, then, of the theory of power presented in the 'Micropolitics and Segmentarity' plateau is the revolutionary political imperative that echoes dramatically at the end of both the 'Nomadology' plateau and the 'Capture' plateau: 'bring connections to bear against the great conjunction of the apparatuses of capture or domination' (ATP 423); 'Every struggle is a function of ... undecidable propositions and constructs *revolutionary connections* in opposition to the *conjugations of the axiomatic*' (ATP 473). This imperative to construct revolutionary connections is all the more critical (and perhaps all the more fraught) in light of the hypothesis Deleuze presents under the rubric of control societies, according to which contemporary neoliberal capitalism, functioning more like a war machine than a central power, axiomatises quantum flows more and more immediately, without the need for much segmentation at all.

What Deleuze and Guattari call the 'undecidability' of propositions at the end of the 'Apparatus of Capture' plateau (quoted above) arises from the inseparability of connection and conjugation as two sides of the same process, 'the coexistence and inseparability of that which the system conjugates, and that which never ceases to escape it following lines of flight that are themselves connectable' (ATP 473) – and this leads to another of the payoffs of Deleuze and Guattari's theory of power and segmentation. For the inseparability of connection and conjugation in processes of capture and segmentation is the reason they call supple segmentation 'the zone of indiscernibility' to begin with. And insofar as this zone constitutes the battleground of struggle between the abstract machines of overcoding and mutation, two very different forms of power are always in play and at stake there, which Deleuze and Guattari (following Spinoza) call *puissance* and *pouvoir*: power-with versus power-over; the power of change arising from and increasing with connections among quantum flows, versus the power to conjugate, arrest and dominate the flows.[4] It is because the zone of indiscernibility is the site of this key power struggle that Deleuze and Guattari attach such importance to micropolitics – even while they remind us that the 'molecular escapes and movements [comprising micropolitics] would be nothing if they did not return to the molar organisations to reshuffle their segments, their binary distributions of sexes, classes, and parties' (ATP 216–17).

The key distinction between power-over and power-with overlaps with another concept that is new to the second volume of *Capitalism and Schizophrenia*: the war machine. While it is true that war machines do in certain specific circumstances make war, their essential characteristics are that they operate by means of a very particular kind of social cohesion (horizontal power-with rather than vertical power-over), and that they produce change; in this respect, they would be better known as 'mutation machines' (ATP 229) or, as Paul Patton has suggested, 'metamorphosis machines' (Patton 2000). In order to evoke the kind of social relations characteristic of mutation machines, we can draw on Deleuze and Guattari's distinction between pack and herd animals. Herd animals form an undifferentiated mass, and they all follow a single leader (who in this respect has power over them); this, for Deleuze and Guattari, is the epitome of the state form of social relations. Pack animals such as wolves can interact very differently: for wolves on the hunt, there is a significant degree of role specialisation, and the pack operates via the collective coordination of members' activities rather than via obedience to a single leader.

(While it is true that the dominant alpha-male and alpha-female of a wolf pack unilaterally determine the distribution of food *after* the hunt – as well as the distribution of mating opportunities, for that matter – they do not serve as leaders of the hunt itself, which operates instead via the power-with of horizontal coordination rather than the power-over of hierarchical command.) The kinds of change produced by mutation machines, meanwhile, vary widely. Deleuze and Guattari even go so far as to say that the war machine 'exists only in its own metamorphoses; it exists in an industrial innovation as well as in a technological invention, in a commercial circuit as well as in a religious creation' or 'in specific assemblages such as building bridges or cathedrals or rendering judgments or making music or instituting a science, a technology' (ATP 366). Finally, and perhaps most important, mutation machines operate via contagion, enthusiasm, *esprit de corps* and solidarity rather than strict obligation or duty (ATP 241–9, 267–9, 278, 366–7, 384, 390–3).

May '68 and Occupy

Two historical events demonstrate the heuristic value of micropolitics and the war machine: the events of May '68 and Occupy Wall Street. There is no question that much of what happened during the events of May 1968 in France can be accounted for only in terms of enthusiasm and contagion rather than duty: a small student protest against corporate sponsorship of war gradually spread to become a general strike against the dissatisfactions of French society as a whole. The Occupy Wall Street movement of 2011 (OWS), in a similar way, spread rapidly to cities and campuses around the country, and eventually to groups and places around the world. It operated by contagion rather than by obedience to a single leader, or even to a single platform or programme. OWS also quickly developed both a remarkable degree of role specialisation and very effective horizontal modes of cooperation and coordination. And although it was initially conceived and organised by an identifiable group of activists (as was the initial French student protest), it very quickly grew beyond the bounds of anything they had imagined, and certainly grew far beyond anything they could control.

Yet the fact that OWS can be said to have taken the form of a mutation machine does not make it a panacea: the contemporaneous right-wing Tea Party movement operated according to quite similar dynamics – although it did benefit from funding from the likes of the Koch brothers and from media hype provided by the likes of Fox cable news. Ultimately, then, the form of organisation or the social dynamics of a given group says relatively little about the content of their positions or activities. The value of the concept of the war machine is rather that it directs our attention to the manner in which these social groups or movements actually operate: as war machines. And in May '68, OWS and the Tea Party movements, we have chosen rather extreme examples: it may be that elections in so-called liberal or representative democracies are always won or lost on the basis of which party can mobilise more numerous and more energetic war machines on its behalf – from student volunteers going door-to-door, to volunteer housewives stuffing envelopes, to donors and campaign operatives themselves. Much like the stock market, electoral politics depends far more than is usually recognised on the kind of enthusiasm and contagion that are key micropolitical elements of the war machine.

Since war machines operate on the Right as well as the Left, and everywhere in between, the fact that OWS took that form, or started out that way, cannot be considered decisive in evaluating its impact. But the same was true of the events of May 1968 for Deleuze and Guattari: within the span of a few months, the French movement had been re-absorbed into macropolitics as usual, with President de Gaulle receiving broad-based and strong support in the ensuing elections. But that does not mean nothing changed on the level of micropolitics. In a famous 1984 magazine article (later republished as an essay in Deleuze 2006: 233–6), Deleuze and Guattari describe deep-seated effects on countless individuals, for one thing – in a portrait that might just as well suit a generation of young Americans who would soon participate in OWS:

> The children of May '68, you can run into them all over the place, even if they are not aware who they are, and each country produces them in its own way. Their situation is not great. These are not young executives. They are strangely indifferent, and for that very reason they are in the right frame of mind. They have stopped being demanding or narcissistic, but they know perfectly well that there is nothing today that corresponds to their subjectivity, to their potential of energy. (ATP 235)

And for another thing, the kind of movement that May 1968 was gets registered in the concepts (such as the war machine, micropolitics, etc.) that Deleuze and Guattari (and others) created in order to better understand it and hopefully relay its potential to future generations. Finally, even when a social movement produces no apparent immediate results – as was the case with May 1968, and appears to be the case with OWS as well – it may have produced what Deleuze and Guattari call 'incorporeal transformations' whose real or corporeal effects only become apparent at some later time. Incorporeal transformations often accompany the kind of speech acts Austin called 'performatives' – acts that transform the status or condition of someone or something without affecting them physically. Thus a judge's sentence does not in and of itself physically kill a condemned person on the spot: it produces an incorporeal transformation, changing that person's social and legal status from accused to condemned, which only later, barring unforeseen mitigating circumstances or disruptions, leads to corporeal death. But history is rarely (if ever) as clear-cut as a judicial proceeding: incorporeal transformations may occur without our even being aware of them at the time, such that it is only later that we ask 'What happened?' – what must have happened x months or y years ago to lead up to the unforeseen changes we are witnessing today? This is, of course, precisely the micropolitical question that Deleuze and Guattari associate with the novella genre. In their magazine article, Deleuze and Guattari even went so far as to claim that 'May '68 did not take place' ('Mai '68 n'a pas eu lieu'); they characterise it instead as a 'visionary phenomenon' and a 'pure event' whose realisation depends on society's ability to develop macropolitical 'collective agencies of enunciation' to institutionalise the changes foreseen by the event: 'French society has shown a radical incapacity to create a subjective redeployment on the collective level, which is what '68 demands' (ATP 234). But the fact that no such agencies were found in the two decades following May 1968 doesn't mean that they will not develop in the future. And in the same way, the micropolitical incorporeal transformations put into motion by OWS may yet bear fruit; there can be no question that the movement has already completely transformed the social meaning of an otherwise anodyne figure, 'the 99%', at least.

Sources of the concept of micropolitics

The theory of micropolitics based on the concepts of segmentary power and capture presented in *A Thousand Plateaus* builds on and Deleuze and Guattari's earlier works – notably Deleuze's insistence on the passive nature of the temporal syntheses in *Difference and Repetition* and Deleuze and Guattari's insistence on the passive syntheses of the unconscious and the difference between unconscious and preconscious investments in *Anti-Oedipus*. We have already seen that the state is not to be construed as an actual centre-point of concentric circles, but rather as a resonance chamber producing something like a state-effect (ATP 224); the state sustains a specific mode of interaction of other entities, acting as a stimulus to or catalyst of their consolidation and amplification within the rigid limits set by its molar organisation. In the same vein, Deleuze and Guattari maintain that segmentation itself is produced by abstract machines; power centres merely work to capture segments in the assemblages effectuating the abstract machine as best they can, by 'continually adapt[ing] variations in mass and flow to the segments of the rigid line, as a function of a dominant segment and dominated segments' (ATP 226). That is why they insist that 'power centres are defined much more by what escapes them or by their impotence than by their zone of power' (ATP 217). The result is that

> micropolitics is defined not by the smallness of its elements but by the nature of its 'mass' – the quantum flow as opposed to the molar segmented line. The task of making the segments correspond to the quanta, of adjusting the segments to the quanta, implies hit-and-miss changes in rhythm and mode rather than any omnipotence; and something always escapes. (ATP 217)

Like consciousness, representation and interest with respect to the passive syntheses in earlier works, segmentary power operating via capture is always one step behind the differential interplay of forces on which it depends, and which in this formulation takes place in the micropolitical zone of indiscernibility.

The difference between the 'classes' and the 'masses' aptly illustrates the relations between the macropolitics of rigid segmentarity and the micropolitics of supple segmentation. Importantly, these categories designate two different 'systems of reference' (ATP 221), not two distinct groups of people; the same individual or group of people can be considered from the point of view of class (macropolitically) or that of mass (micropolitically). A single political struggle can thus assume two very different aspects, depending on whether it is considered from a molar or a molecular perspective – to the point that even what counts as victory or defeat for a given struggle can differ according to the perspective adopted (ATP 221). In this connection, Deleuze and Guattari invoke the micro-sociology of Gabriel Tarde: Marx and Emile Durkheim are sufficient to deal with the macropolitics of classes and other rigid collective representations; Tarde's micro-sociology is required to deal with the 'subrepresentative' realm of masses and the quantum flows of belief, desire and fear that govern them.

> Representations already define large aggregates, or determine segments on a line; beliefs and desires, on the other hand, are flows marked by quanta, flows that are created, exhausted, or transformed, added to one another, subtracted or combined. (ATP 219)

Micropolitics concerns the emergence and spread of beliefs, fears and desires among masses rather than the recognition and representation of interests by and for classes; its lifeblood is the dynamics of imitation and contagion rather than conviction and consent.[5] Deleuze and Guattari's analysis of the events of May '68 provides a textbook example: everything of significance took place on the level of micropolitics, as disaffection spread unpredictably and contagiously from students, to workers, into practically all corners of French society, while all its representative macropolitical institutions (unions, government) were at first completely unaware of what was happening, and even afterwards remained largely unaffected by it. Macropolitics operates in terms of binarised choices and measured decisions, but real movement takes place in the zone of indiscernibility of micropolitics.

In addition to Tarde and Foucault, Deleuze and Guattari acknowledge Kafka as another great analyst of micropolitics (and in fact, their book on Kafka and minor literature [1986] contains the first use of the term in their work). What Kafka's fiction shows is that beneath the formal, molar power structure of any institution (school, army, college, prison, family, etc.) lies a vast sea of constantly shifting molecular relations of force that do not (or not always) follow the rigid lines of the institution's organisational chart, but instead cause them to waver, oscillate, reverse polarity or branch off in unforeseen directions. For micropolitics, the key to understanding the operations of power is 'no longer The Schoolmaster but the [hall] monitor, the best student, the school dunce, the janitor, etc. No longer the general but the junior officers, the noncommissioned officers ...' (ATP 224–5). The zone of micropolitics, it could therefore be said, is where matters ultimately get decided, even if it is not where formal political decisions actually get made (ATP 222).

The micropolitics and macropolitics of fascism

A final payoff of Deleuze and Guattari's theory of micropolitics is the transformed understanding of fascism it entails, along with its suggestive insights into contemporary neoliberal capitalism. In *Anti-Oedipus*, as John Protevi has shown, fascism was associated with despotism and paranoia, and was characterised as a fixation of images on the body without organs; it was diametrically opposed to the free flow of images characteristic of (potentially) revolutionary schizophrenia.[6] In *A Thousand Plateaus*, by contrast, fascism is characterised as a war machine, and indeed as a war machine that takes over the state apparatus rather than being captured by it (as is typically the case). Unlike despotism and totalitarianism which are

> quintessentially conservative ... fascism ... involves a war machine. When fascism builds itself a totalitarian State, it is not in the sense of a State army taking power, but of a war machine taking over the State. (ATP 230)

Microfascism, in a word, precedes macrofascism (ATP 228): the fate of Germany was decided micropolitically in the zone of supple segmentation before Hitler finally took over the state apparatus as dictator – hence the significance of 1933 in the plateau's title, the pivotal year of Hitler's ascendancy.

Deleuze and Guattari here return to the question (posed before them by Spinoza and Reich, among others, as well as in *Anti-Oedipus*) of why people crave their own oppression. Explanation in terms of the fixation of images on the body without organs no longer suffices: Nazi fascism was not the 'generalised slavery' (ATP 181) of a despotic signifying regime, but an extremely popular set of post-signifying 'proceedings' which held a positive and attractive valence for the majority of German people – at least for a while. From the start, that is to say, it involved the anticipation and detection of powers (*puissances*) of the future, rather than the reapplication of powers (*pouvoirs*) from the past (ATP 124). In a remarkable study comparing the 'Three New Deals' of Roosevelt, Hitler and Mussolini, Wolfgang Schivelbusch has shown just how much the Nazis did for Germany before the war, through rapid acceleration of the development of productive forces and massive integration of unemployed and underemployed populations into the workforce, along with the equally rapid expansion of consumerism (e.g. the Volkswagen), and the provision of education and enhanced medical care to most of the German population.[7] And yet with the start of the war, it would appear, everything goes bad: 'arms expansion replaces growth in consumption', as Deleuze and Guattari do not fail to note, and 'investment veers from the means of production toward the means of pure destruction' (ATP 231).

But in fact, everything went bad from the very start – demonstrating that popular power-with (*puissance*) is not a panacea, any more than supple segmentation is simply better than rigid segmentarity. Well before the beneficent macropolitics of the Nazi state surveyed by Schivelbusch, the Nazi rise to power took place in the micropolitical zone, largely through the activities of marauding bands (war machines) of thugs and assassins who systematically intimidated and ruthlessly eliminated all opposition. This is the danger identified by Deleuze and Guattari of power operating through supple segmentation, before, beneath or totally independent of the power of rigid segmentarity operating in the resonance chamber of the state:

> supple segmentarity brings dangers of its own that do not merely reproduce in small scale the dangers of molar segmentarity, which do not derive from them or compensate for them . . . microfascisms have a specificity of their own that can crystallise into a macrofascism, but may also float along the supple line on their own account and suffuse every little cell. A multitude of black holes may very well not become centralised, and acts instead as viruses adapting to the most varied situations . . . Interactions without resonance.

> Instead of the great paranoid fear, we are trapped in a thousand little monomanias, self-evident truths . . . [that] no longer form a system, but are only rumble and buzz, blinding lights giving any and everybody the mission of self-appointed judge, dispenser of justice, policeman, neighbourhood SS man. (ATP 228)

So not only was the Nazi movement popular and populist, it was also forward-looking, mobilising the molecular power (*puissance*) of the future in its line of flight from the humiliations of German power (*pouvoir*) following from the First World War. How could it have gone so horribly wrong – from the start? How does a line of flight become a line of pure abolition, of death and destruction?

Deleuze and Guattari are adamant that they are *not* 'invoking any kind of death drive' as an explanation: 'There are no internal drives in desire, only assemblages. Desire is always assembled' (ATP 229). And assemblages undergo mutations. As Deleuze and Guattari explain later (in the 'Apparatus of Capture' plateau), in order to maintain the accelerated pace of economic development and avoid crises of overproduction, the Nazi regime militarised the economy; and then in order to maintain popular support even as guns were replacing butter, it reverted to the (despotic) measures of instilling fear (e.g. the Red menace) and punishing scapegoats (e.g. communists, Jews).[8] The power of supple segmentation in the micropolitical zone, then, can be just as dangerous as the power of rigid segmentarity in the macropolitical zone, as the evolution of Nazism shows as it moves from microfascisms to macrofascism proper, as its 'molecular movements return to the molar organisations to reshuffle their segments' (ATP 216–17). In the terms of the 'Becomings' plateau and *What is Philosophy?*, it is always an open question whether the becomings that emerge in the realm of micropolitics will succeed or fail in affecting policy and generating lasting historical change at the level of macropolitics – for better or for worse.

This analysis of fascism, along with the theory of micropolitics subtending it, can give us additional insight into the 'control society' of contemporary neoliberal capitalism. It functions to some extent more like a war machine than a central power, as we have already suggested, in that it axiomatises quantum flows more and more immediately, without the need for much rigid segmentation at all. We also saw that segmentation becomes predominantly linear (rather than circular) in post-signifying regimes, inasmuch as passional subjectification operates with the face of God turned away, so that the subject's line of flight away from it takes on a positive value and the linear, segmented form of a series of 'proceedings': the subject now 'anticipates and detects the powers [*puissances*] of the future rather than applying past and present powers [*pouvoirs*]' (ATP

124). Neoliberalism is the ultimate turning away of the secular face of God (i.e. society, or the welfare state) – launching each of us alone, without support from past or present powers, on to a series of segmented 'proceedings' whose future outcome is totally uncertain, and totally up to us, as individuals. We thus cling out of fear all the more desperately to, and fight against others all the more viciously for, whatever segments we have or can find; molar organisations no longer provide the comfort and assurance of rigid segmentation that might mitigate or compensate for our precarity; macropolitics no longer answers to the disasters of the micropolitical zone. And at the same time, the axioms of capital reach past or though 'us' and our segments, plugging more and more directly into the living flows of our deepest fears, beliefs and desires as 'individuals' – capturing, converting or perverting them as need be to keep pace with the accumulation imperatives of the global capitalist war machine. At this scale, Nazi fascism seems like child's play, or at most a warm-up exercise. Yet there always remains

> a fundamental difference between living flows and the axioms that subordinate them to centres of control and decision making, that make a given segment correspond to them, which measure their quanta. [And so] the pressure of the living flows, and of the problems they pose and impose, must be exerted inside the axiomatic, as much in order to fight the totalitarian [or neoliberal] reductions [of e.g. welfare state axioms] as to anticipate and precipitate the additions, to orient them and prevent their technocratic perversion . . . (ATP 464)

We must never believe that the suppleness of micropolitics will suffice to save us from catastrophe, but we should nevertheless recognise that its zone of indiscernibility is where alternatives to catastrophe emerge. The promise and challenge of the concept of micropolitics is to be able to detect and recognise them, so as to bring the pressure of living flows and their connections to bear against the great conjunction of the apparatuses of capture or domination.

Notes

1. For the classic formulation of segmentary society, see Evans-Pritchard 1940.
2. 'Postscript on Control Societies' in Deleuze 1995a: 177–82.
3. For a Deleuze and Guattari-inspired critique of the state as agent, see DeLanda 2006.
4. While *puissance* is often translated as 'power-to', I here use 'power-with' in order to emphasise the 'and . . . and . . . and . . .' logic (so dear to Deleuze and Guattari) of the connective synthesis and to highlight its importance to the war machine (discussed in the next paragraph), which is chiefly a form of social organisation, whatever the aims of its activity. For more on the distinction between power-with and power-over, see Holland 2011: esp. 67–72.

5. On the 'affective turn' and its claims to supersede the focus on consent in hegemony theory, see Beasley-Murray 2010; Day 2005.
6. Protevi 2000. For a different view, see Holland 2008b.
7. Schivelbusch 2006: 169–83, esp. 171–2. See also Poulantzas 1974: esp. 99–100.
8. For a painstaking and comprehensive schizoanalytic account of Nazi microfascism, see the two volumes of Theweleit 1987–89.

Chapter 10

Memories of a Deleuzian: To Think is Always to Follow the Witches' Flight

Simon O'Sullivan

I want to organise my reading of the 'Becoming' plateau, the longest of *A Thousand Plateaus*, around three different takes on philosophy, or, at least, three takes on the plateau's relationship to philosophy: 1) philosophy and non-philosophy; 2) philosophy as a way of life; and 3) philosophy as fictioning. I also want to use some of the remarks Deleuze and Guattari make in their final collaboration, *What is Philosophy?*, as a way in to thinking about these themes.

Philosophy and non-philosophy (or relations with an outside)

In terms of its explicit philosophical resources, the 'Becoming' plateau, as evidenced in some of the subtitles of its different sections, draws especially on Bergson (not least in the titling of the sections as 'Memories') and Spinoza – and, invariably, on Deleuze's own previous writings on these two. So, in 'Memories of a Bergsonian' we have the explicit linking of the concept of becoming with the Bergsonian idea of 'a coexistence of very different "durations", superior or inferior to "ours", all of them in communication' (ATP 238). We also find the idea of a creative evolution – or involution – that follows from this: 'to involve is to form a block that runs its own line "between" the terms in play and beneath assignable relations' (ATP 239). It is in this sense that becoming has a reality that is specific to it outside of any fixed terms (subjects or objects) that it passes between. The idea of becoming as a communication, at least of a sort, between different durations is returned to in the final section of the plateau (on music) with Messiaen and his 'multiple chromatic durations' that involve 'relations between the infinitely long durations of the stars and the infinitely short ones of the insects and atoms' (ATP 309). It is in this sense of being able to express different durations that becoming-music is the privileged form of becoming (at least, within art per se).

In 'Memories of a Spinozist I' we find the well-known Deleuze–Spinoza thesis about the elements of life being 'distinguished solely by movement and rest, slowness and speed' (ATP 254), with a definition of the plane of nature as abstract machine or 'single abstract animal' that constitutes a unity of this multiplicity (this being Deleuze's univocity) (ATP 255). 'Memories of a Spinozist II' concerns itself with Spinoza's equally infamous ethical question – 'What can a body do?' – and with the definition of this body as a particular degree of power itself defined by its capacity to affect and be affected. In many ways these two Spinozist principles – that a body is constituted by relations of slowness and speed that themselves define its capacity to affect and be affected – are the key philosophical themes of the plateau, but only if they are thought outside of a strictly 'human' ethics (tied as this can be to a 'molar' form) and in terms of the possibilities for more inhuman transformations (hence, as we shall see, the interest in sorcery, but also drugs).

So far so good. But clearly Deleuze already lays out much of the Bergsonian and Spinozist material elsewhere, not least, again, in his monographs on them. What then characterises the particular use of these philosophical resources in the 'Becoming' plateau (and, indeed, in *A Thousand Plateaus* more generally)? On the one hand it is simply that they are brought together. *A Thousand Plateaus*, if nothing else, is a grand work of philosophical synthesis (Nietzsche being the third key philosophical element). But, again, this is also the case with a book like *Difference and Repetition*, to say nothing of the first volume of *Capitalism and Schizophrenia* which also involves a complex synthesis of Freud and Marx, but also Spinoza and Nietzsche.

In fact, even a cursory glance at the three sections I have already mentioned shows that it is the heavy use of examples – from literature in particular, but also other 'non-philosophical' perspectives – that constitutes perhaps the major difference between *A Thousand Plateaus* and other works signed Deleuze, and, indeed, Deleuze and Guattari (these non-philosophical resources are also evident in the book's extensive footnotes). So, in the short Bergson section there are references to Lévi-Strauss and vampires, Jung and the C-virus. And in the first section on Spinoza we find references to Cuvier, Geoffrey, Von Uexküll, but also to the fact that 'Children are Spinozists' (ATP 256).

In the second Spinoza section ticks, horses and dogs – a whole bestiary that is characteristic of *A Thousand Plateaus* as a whole – accompany the human figures. Indeed, the animal is very much the manifest subject matter of this plateau, which begins with a critique of the classificatory impulse of the sciences (including the human sciences), and especially their obsession with series (involving an analogy of proportion) and structure (involving an analogy of proportionality), before developing the key idea of becoming-animal. As Deleuze and Guattari remark in this earlier section – 'Memories of a Naturalist' – their meditation on the animal is not, however, simply a zoology in so far as 'the relationships between animals are bound up with the relations between man and animal, man and woman, man and child, man and the elements, man and the physical and microphysical universe' (ATP 235). Becoming-animal is part of a processual series that, in fact, begins with becoming-woman but leads, as we shall see, into something altogether more alien.

Certainly then these various examples 'flesh out' the philosophical architecture. They animate the concepts. But, I think, something else is also at stake here: namely, the gesturing to an outside of philosophy per se. *A Thousand Plateaus*, although clearly a work of philosophy (and a great work at that), cannot be reduced to this (or, at least, it cannot be reduced to philosophy as it is typically understood). It mobilises other resources (and, again, offers perspectives from outside philosophy), and in so doing has a traction on reality that is different to philosophy's own more restricted terrain of operation. In part this no doubt explains some of its attraction to non-philosophers, not least artists: it operates as both toolbox and construction site, but also as case study of a creative work in and of itself.

In *What is Philosophy?*, a book that is as much a reflection on their own philosophy as it is on that of others, Deleuze and Guattari draw attention to the importance of a non-philosophical outside for philosophy, an outside from which philosophy finds its inspiration and, indeed, its very 'ground'. In the chapter on 'The Plane of Immanence' they write:

> Precisely because the plane of immanence is prephilosophical and does not immediately take effect with concepts, it implies a sort of groping experimentation and its layout resorts to measures that are not very respectable, rational or reasonable. These measures belong to the order of dreams, of pathological processes, esoteric experiences, drunkenness and excess. (Deleuze and Guattari 1994: 41)

There is some ambiguity here, as the laying out of a plane of immanence is also identified as one of the three moments of philosophy (alongside the invention of conceptual personae and the construction of concepts). Indeed, the plane of immanence is what Deleuze, in *Difference and Repetition*, names the 'image of thought': not so much a concept as the very image of what thinking is (or might be). This is, then, not philosophy as typically understood – as solely rational (or discursive) programme, but something more intuitive and, as Deleuze and Guattari remark, diagrammatic (I will return to this below). Could we make the claim that there is something inhuman about this 'groping experimentation', something that itself involves a kind of becoming-animal (when this is understood, as we shall see, as a deterritorialisation from more fixed and molar forms)?

Although clearly containing more than a few examples of concept creation, *A Thousand Plateaus*, it seems to me, is concerned – especially at certain points in the 'Becoming' plateau – with inventing a new image of thought, and, as such, with a certain kind of pre-philosophical practice. The processes it describes, and itself initiates, do not proceed solely by reason, nor is the book itself about the human in what we might say is its habitual form. *A Thousand Plateaus* is not for us as we are typically constituted in this sense, but for something we might become (or for the molecular collectivity – the becomings – that we are 'behind' this molar self).

In a Spinozist sense, *A Thousand Plateaus* is also itself composed of different speeds, which gives it, for this reader at least, a certain affective charge (and, as far as this goes, the question of how we encounter this book is crucial – in Spinozist terms, whether it fundamentally 'agrees' with our own affective make-up). We might even say that its form (the plateaus) – including the style in which it is written (the very syntax it uses) – performs its content (and it is this, I think, that partly makes it so compelling). All of this has been remarked on before, but it bears restating here: in reading one enters into a kind of becoming with *A Thousand Plateaus* (providing one is 'open' to that possibility).

At the very end of *What is Philosophy?* there is a further discussion of thought's relation to a negative that concerns and comprehends it, where each of the planes (of thought) – philosophy, art, science – confronts a chaos that always and everywhere shadows them (in fact, in *What is Philosophy?*, thought itself is characterised as a chaoid, or chaos given a certain consistency). Although this final collaborative work is often identified as solely Deleuze's (signed with both names as an act of friendship), it is really Guattari, in his solo work, who develops this idea of thought as a relationship between chaos and consistency (or, in Guattari's terms, chaos and complexity) itself determined by different speeds (hence, the very idea of *Chaosmosis*).[1] Philosophically speaking, Guattari flattens Deleuze's actual-virtual topology – the Bergsonian cone of memory that plays such an important role in Deleuze's work before *Capitalism and Schizophrenia* (the virtual remains in Guattari's work, but it is less Bergsonian). The 'Becoming' plateau, I think, especially evidences this move to a radical horizontality.

It is also in these last pages of *What is Philosophy?* that we find a tantalising reference to François Laruelle and the idea that philosophy might need a non-philosophy that comprehends it (just as art might require a non-art and science a non-science).[2] Certainly elsewhere Deleuze has remarked on how philosophy itself can elicit both a philosophical reading and a non-philosophical one (see Deleuze 2012). Clearly one of the functions of this edited collection is to focus attention on the philosophical reading (to take *A Thousand Plateaus* seriously as a work of philosophy and position it within the history of that discipline), but, for this reader, the non-philosophical aspect is crucial and if we neglect this we miss something absolutely essential about the book. Perhaps then we might say that *A Thousand Plateaus* demands a certain stereoscopic vision and approach, a reading that is both philosophical and non-philosophical, and that it is precisely this that marks it out as a great work.

What is Philosophy? also closes with some cryptic remarks about how the brain's submersion into chaos allows the extraction of a 'people to come', forms of subjectivity (or even, perhaps, non-subjectivity?) that are wilder, untethered from the cogito. In this place the three forms of thought become indiscernible (just as concepts, sensations and functions become undecidable) (ATP 218). I will return to this question of interference below, but we might note here that it is also these different kinds of interference between different kinds of thought that characterise *A Thousand Plateaus* (and it is in this sense that it is the very last pages of *What is Philosophy?* that most adequately account for the kind of 'philosophy' a book like *A Thousand Plateaus* deploys).

Indeed, returning to the first part of the 'Becoming' plateau, the philosophical memories, as well as being accompanied by those of moviegoers (the first section which introduces the concept of becoming via a becoming-rat contra familial conjugality), naturalists (which lays out the more typical categorisation of natural history via series and structure: nature as mimesis) and theologians (who are pitched against the transportations of demonology and transformations of alchemy), also contain memories of those figures (could we call them conceptual personae?) that operate on and as the cusp between our human and more non-human worlds and that, strictly speaking, are not philosophers at all: sorcerers.

Philosophy as a way of life (sorcery to diagrammatics)

In 'Memories of a Sorcerer I', multiplicity (or the pack) and with it contagion (or 'unnatural participation') is opposed to more typical (and rational) concerns with classificatory characteristics and filiation. Affect

– as a non-human animal intensity – is the means of this non-conceptual 'passage between things' that brings about transformation. Philosophy, if it can still be called as such, is here less to do with knowledge – discursive or otherwise – than with exploring what a given body might become. It is in this sense that becoming involves a kind of ethics. This is 'philosophy as a way of life', or even a 'spiritual exercise' as Pierre Hadot might have it (a kind of modern Stoic philosophy perhaps).[3] In *A Thousand Plateaus* this creative and fundamentally constructive take on philosophy is given different names: pragmatics, diagrammatics (as we shall see), even, simply, schizoanalysis.[4] Not typical philosophy then, but also not simply psychoanalysis when this relies on preset protocols and predetermined schema. Indeed, experimentation is this form of thought's chief modus operandi (and it is this emphasis on experimental encounter, rather than on any rational programme of work on the self, that is taken from Spinoza put simply, and crucially, for Deleuze and Guattari one cannot tell in advance what – or with what – one might be able to become).

A Thousand Plateaus is not simply 'about' the world in this sense (or this 'interpretation' is secondary), but, rather, offers something more programmatic and pragmatic. Certainly, for myself, this constituted the main interest of the book (as opposed to other philosophical works) when I first encountered it. *A Thousand Plateaus* read like a manual of sorts. Going back to it again (for this edited collection), I am struck by the way it still elicits an excitement in me – and a desire to experiment, to explore the possibilities of a mode of existence away from an overly fixed and striated sense of self. Is this kind of confessional, first-person (and affective) reporting appropriate? For myself, in fact, to leave this out – to simply read *A Thousand Plateaus* without letting it impact on a life – is to surrender it to the worst kind of scholarly capture. It is in this respect that I think Foucault's comment in his Preface to *Anti-Oedipus* might be applied to the *Capitalism and Schizophrenia* project in general: the two books are, precisely, an '*Introduction to the Non-Fascist Life*' (Foucault 1984: xiii), when this refers to combating the micro-fascisms that can stymie experimentation, but also, crucially, to the book's intended terrain of operation: life.

In this sense, it seems to me that *A Thousand Plateaus* is also concerned with what Guattari calls the 'production of subjectivity', when this is the production of something specifically different to the standardised models on offer (the atomised individual of neoliberalism), but also to the production of the human per se (understood as a particular historical configuration). Deleuze, in *Difference and Repetition*, writes of 'larval subjects', 'the thousands of passive syntheses of which we are organically composed' (Deleuze 1994: 74), but it is Guattari that really brings this idea of the collectivity that constitutes us – a 'social and mental ecology' – into a more pragmatic realm, especially in foregrounding more fluid analytic modellings (that privilege the encounter) which might allow people to 'resingularise themselves' (Guattari 1995: 6). As such, we might also say – rather obviously – that it is Guattari's knowledge and experience, especially from *La Borde* (itself a realm of heterogenetic encounters – or becomings), that also marks out *A Thousand Plateaus*' singularity as a collaboration, or even, as itself a work of collectivity (the two authors already being several as the opening to *A Thousand Plateaus* remarks).[5]

All of this is no more apparent than in the 'Becoming' plateau which involves mapping out a specifically different individuation of the world (and of the entities within it):

> between substantial forms and determined subjects, *between the two*, there is not only a whole operation of demonic local transports but a natural play of haecceities, degrees, intensities, events, and accidents that compose individuations totally different from those of the well-formed subjects that receive them. (ATP 253)

We might also note Deleuze's own remarks in interview about *A Thousand Plateaus*, which, in some sense, offer a non-philosophical inflection on the above:

> What we're interested in, you see, are modes of individuation beyond those of things, persons or subjects: the individuation, say, of a time of day, of a region, a climate, a river or a wind, of an event. And maybe it's a mistake to believe in the existence of things, persons, or subjects. (Deleuze 1995a: 26)

I will return below to this laying out of different individuations in and of the world, which, in Deleuze and Guattari's account, characterises the sorcerer's perspective.

The key resources in the first sorcerer section are also, again, not philosophical concepts per se, but literature – fiction – with its authors and their invented avatars. Virginia Woolf experiencing herself 'as a troop of monkeys, a school of fish' alongside H. P. Lovecraft's Carter who lives a series of 'human and non-human, vertebrate and invertebrate, conscious and mindless, animal and vegetable' becomings leading to more extreme inorganic – molecular and cosmic – ones (ATP 239–40). Indeed, in the plateau, it is Lovecraft as much as Spinoza who is the thinker of becoming (the philosophical principles are, in this sense, always doubled by these literary examples).

These becomings themselves enter into larger assemblages, or war machines, which are opposed to more typical and molar formations, or the state machine. The war machine (as a name for the multiplicity of individual war machines) occupies a smooth rather than striated space, but also a time without measure (this is addressed more fully in the other central plateau of *A Thousand Plateaus*, '1227: Treatise on Nomadology: –The War Machine' (ATP 351–423)). It is in this sense that becomings are opposed to stasis, but also, more generally, to concepts of Being when these posit an originary and fixed ground. In passing, we might note the importance of Deleuze and Guattari's Nietzsche here (which is itself indebted to Klossowski), and especially the reading of the eternal return in *Anti-Oedipus* as a repetition of difference set against the return of the same. In Deleuze and Guattari's account, Nietzsche lives through a series of becomings or 'intensive states' – only retroactively identifying or claiming them on the basis of affect or felt sensation ('They're *me*! So it's *me*!' (Deleuze and Guattari 1983: 21)).[6] Becoming destabilises any ground, but also undoes the typical subject, naming, as it does, a more processual – intensive – mode of being in the world.

In terms of the use of fiction we might briefly return to *What is Philosophy?* and note Deleuze and Guattari's comments about those intrinsic interferences between the different planes of thought, and, in particular, between philosophy and art. This is the second form of interference after a first, more straightforward one of a particular discipline having a take, from its own perspective, on another (as, for example 'when a philosopher attempts to create the concept of a sensation' (ATP 217)). An intrinsic interference, on the other hand, happens when, for example:

> concepts and conceptual personae seem to leave a plane of immanence that would correspond to them, so as to slip among the functions and partial observers, or among the sensations and aesthetic figures, on another plane . . . These slidings are so subtle . . . that we find ourselves on complex planes that are difficult to qualify. (Deleuze and Guattari 1994: 217)

Are not these 'complex' planes also the plateaus of *A Thousand Plateaus*, made up as they are by these slips and slidings – a blurring even – between the three great forms of thought? Certainly the 'Becoming' plateau, in its deployment of aesthetic figures *as* conceptual personae, involves precisely this grey zone between concept and affect.[7]

In 'Memories of a Sorcerer II', the first principle of multiplicity and contagion is doubled by a second: alliance with something more singular: the anomalous, understood as that which borders the pack. Again, literary examples are crucial in helping define this principle: Captain Ahab's complex relation with Moby Dick (the 'white wall') and Josephine, the privileged mouse singer of Kafka's mouse society. Philosophically speaking, these literary examples are doubled by a more abstract definition of multiplicity as constituted by its boundaries and borders, by 'the lines and dimensions it encompasses in "intension"' (ATP 245). The anomalous is the border of this multiplicity, the line of flight, or 'cutting edge of deterritorialisation' (ATP 244). But even in these more abstract definitions, the implication, it seems to me, is that this is a programme for life: one needs to find one's own anomalous – to follow a line of flight. Literature itself operates as a kind of manual in this sense, or at least offers up case studies for a lived life. And the philosophy itself – the invention of concepts (for example of an 'intensive multiplicity') – is precisely experimental and, once again, pragmatic (what will this concept allow one to think?).

In 'Memories of a Sorcerer III', becoming-animal is placed in sequence, with becoming-woman on the near side and becoming-molecular, ultimately, becoming-imperceptible, on the far side (I will return to becoming-women below.) Once again Lovecraft, this time alongside Carlos Casteneda, is the writer deployed, but Deleuze and Guattari also point to science fiction in general as a genre 'on' becoming: 'science fiction has gone through a whole evolution taking it from animal, vegetable, and mineral becomings to becomings of bacteria, viruses, molecules, and things imperceptible' (ATP 248). At its best, science fiction operates as philosophy's own forward-hurled probe-head in this sense, at least when this philosophy is defined as itself future-orientated and as a creative and constructive pursuit.

Again, philosophically speaking, this becoming as multiplicity 'is defined by the number of dimensions it has; it is not divisible, it cannot lose or gain a dimension *without changing its nature*' (ATP 249). Deleuze and Guattari continue:

> Since its variations and dimensions are immanent to it, it amounts to the same thing to say that each multiplicity is already composed of heterogeneous terms in symbiosis, and that a multiplicity is continually transforming itself into a string of other multiplicities, according to its thresholds and doors. (ATP 249)

Indeed, for Deleuze and Guattari, this multiplicity is always in the process of becoming something else, always differing from itself.

We might say then that the 'Becoming' plateau draws out a kind of programme, again of transformation, dependent on this very particular and precise ontology, but developed through aesthetic figures (as conceptual personae) that 'live' these transformations. This is not exactly a therapeutics (at least, not in terms of producing a cohesive and centred subject), but it is certainly a form of practical analysis, when this is also understood as involving a kind of ethico-politics (or molecular politics in Guattari's sense). In fact, in the plateau, becoming is aligned more explicitly with schizoanalysis insofar as both are described as an experimental pragmatics, to do with locating a 'line of escape' from more striated space-times ('a new borderline, an active line that will bring other becomings . . .' (ATP 251)). Becoming is pitched against 'the great molar powers' that restrict the possibilities of transformation: 'family, career, and conjugality' (ATP 233). This is dealt with in more detail in other plateaus (in particular 'November 28, 1947: How Do You Make Yourself a Body without Organs?' (ATP 149–66)), but in the 'Becoming' plateau it is given its most abstract, but also worked out and, indeed, philosophical form.

There is also another practice laid out here, of diagrammatics, that itself informs the criteria for this experimentation:

> If multiplicities are defined and transformed by the borderline that determines in each instance the number of dimensions, we can conceive the possibility of laying them out on a plane, the borderlines succeeding one another, forming a broken line. (ATP 251)

Deleuze and Guattari continue: 'Far from reducing the multiplicities' number of dimensions to two, the *plane of consistency* cuts across them all, intersects them in order to bring into coexistence any number of multiplicities, with any number of dimensions' (ATP 251). Indeed, 'all becomings are written like sorcerers' drawings on this plane of consistency' (ATP 251). Once again Lovecraft becomes the writer most capable of expressing this multi-dimensional, but flat plane, although D. H. Lawrence's apparently less cosmic writings, on the tortoise for example, also foreground this particular form of abstraction – or practice of diagrammatics ('Lawrence, in his becoming-tortoise, moves from the most obstinate animal dynamism to the abstract, pure geometry . . . he pushes becoming-tortoise all the way to the plane of consistency' (ATP 251)).

Deleuze and Guattari also call this plane the 'Planemon, or the Rhizosphere, the criterium . . . At *n* dimensions, it is called the Hypersphere, the Mechanosphere': 'It is the abstract figure, or rather, since it has no form itself, the abstract Machine of which each concrete assemblage is a multiplicity, a becoming, a segment, a vibration. And the abstract machine is the intersection of them all' (ATP 252). Once again this is the univocity of Spinoza (individual modes as different expressions of the same substance) mediated through Bergson (the multiplicity of different durations in communication), but it is Woolf – 'who made all of her life and work a passage, a becoming' – and her book *The Waves* that best shows this abstract machine at work (and ends the sequence of memories of a sorcerer) (ATP 252).

We have here an abstract and speculative perspective (a kind of external point of view) which is then accompanied by something more experiential and experimental (a becoming that is firmly in and with the world). It is this conjunction of the abstract and concrete – of being apart from but also a part of the world – that defines this plateau (and indeed, *A Thousand Plateaus* more generally).⁸ Could we not also reframe this as a conjunction – or interference – between philosophy and fiction, when both, each in their own way, announce a different individuation in and of the world from typical subjects and objects, but also from different perspectives? In fact, it seems to me that we might say that, in the 'Becoming' plateau, fiction becomes philosophy, but also that philosophy operates as itself a kind of fiction (the different memories of the plateau – which Deleuze and Guattari later rename becomings – are themselves philo-fictions in this sense).⁹

Philosophy as fictioning (becoming-imperceptible . . . becoming-world)

'Memories of a Haecceity', the section that follows directly on from the two Spinoza sections, concerns itself more explicitly with these different philo-fictions, or different individuations in and of the world.¹⁰ Deleuze and Guattari use a term from Duns Scotus, 'haecceity', which names a certain 'thingness' (or 'here and nowness') that is irreducible to subjects or objects per se. In fact, any given body (including, as the above quote from the interview with Deleuze suggests, seasons and weather systems, certain times of the day, but also, in fact, the subject themselves) can be understood as a haecceity, defined – in a return to Spinoza – by a longitude (relations of speed and slowness) and latitude (the capacity to affect/be affected).

Once more, literature is drawn in as 'lived' example of this particular fictioning of the world – Charlotte Brontë, Michel Tournier, Virginia Woolf – and, following on from this, a particular form of expression or semiotic is mapped out that is appropriate and adequate to this peculiar individuation: 'proper names, verbs in the infinitive and indefinite articles or pronouns' (ATP 263). The proper name, for example, 'fundamentally demarcates something that is of the order of the event, of becoming or of the haecceity. It is the military men and meteorologists who hold the secret of proper names, when they give them to a strategic operation or a hurricane' (ATP 264).

We also find in this section of the plateau the distinction that Deleuze develops in his single-authored works between *Aeon*, 'the indefinite time of the event', and *Chronos*, 'the time of measure that situates things and persons' (ATP 262). We might say that *A Thousand Plateaus*, and the 'Becoming' plateau in particular, is concerned specifically with the forms of individuation of *Aeon*. 'Memories of a Plan(e) Maker' – the next section of the plateau – concerns itself with what we might call the terrain of these haecceities, and more specifically the relation of transcendence and immanence, or the plane of organisation ($n+1$) and the plane of consistency ($n-1$). The latter has no supplementary dimensions, no hidden principles – everything is, as it were, on the surface. Here it is Kleist ('everything with him, in his writing as in his life, becomes speed and slowness' (ATP 268)) alongside Nietzsche who best constructs this plane (for it is never a question of discovering a ready-made plane of consistency, but of making one), though it is also, again, music (for example, with Boulez and Cage) that best expresses the two planes (and their necessary interaction).[11] (Artaud is also footnoted as distinguishing between the two planes – one 'denounced as the source of all illusions' (ATP 542).)

We also find here something that is characteristic of *A Thousand Plateaus* in general (and, in this respect, marks a key difference from the more accelerationist tone and orientation of *Anti-Oedipus*): the issue of caution.[12]

> But once again, so much caution is needed to prevent the plane of consistency from becoming a pure plane of abolition or death, to prevent the involution from turning into regression to the undifferentiated. Is it not necessary to retain a minimum of strata, a minimum of forms and functions, a minimum subject from which to extract materials, affects, and assemblages? (ATP 270)

A Thousand Plateaus is concerned with strategy in this sense – and, indeed, with the maintenance of a subject, at least as a minimum consistency or territory from which to deterritorialise. Deleuze and Guattari write more about the dangers of absolute deterritorialisation (and destratification) in other plateaus, especially, again, 'November 28, 1947: How Do You Make Yourself a Body without Organs?' (where they argue that it is only 'through a meticulous relation with the strata that one succeeds in freeing lines of flight' (ATP 161)) but certainly the 'Becoming' plateau is also concerned with this 'art of dosages'.

If the 'Memories of a Sorcerer' sections are, for this reader at least, the key sections of the first part of the 'Becoming' plateau (not least as they concern themselves with a minimum subject of becoming), then 'Memories of a Molecule' is the key section of the latter part and takes us away from the human subject per se. Here we get a more explicit account of how becoming actually operates, not via mimesis or imitation but by the extraction of 'particles' (asignifying and intensive) that follows from the establishing of 'zones of proximity' (which itself follows from the establishment of one's territory (which, in turn, defines one)):

> Starting from the forms one has, the subject one is, the organs one has, or the functions one fulfils, becoming is to extract particles between which one establishes the relations of movement and rest, speed and slowness that are *closest* to what one is becoming, and through which one becomes. (ATP 272)

It is in this sense, as Deleuze and Guattari remark, that the process of becoming is desire, when this names a whole assemblage of elements in contact and communication (something in you desires to become something else . . . and begins to adjust its speeds . . . establishes a zone of proximity . . . it then, as it were, slips in among things . . .).[13]

We are given the example of a becoming-dog (for example, when a child plays at 'being' this animal): 'Do not imitate a dog, but make your organism enter into composition with *something else* in such a way that the particles emitted from the aggregate thus composed will be canine as a function of the relation of movements and rest, or of molecular proximity, into which they enter' (ATP 274). It is in this sense that becoming-animal does not necessarily involve any likeness to an animal (though it may), but rather a capture of certain kinds of affect (the particles) that, ethologically speaking, characterise a given animal (understood as a set of capacities to affect and be affected).[14] All becomings are molecular in this sense (though they might take on a certain molar 'appearance', this is always a secondary effect of becoming).

At stake in this section is also, again, the key idea of a sequence – or series – of becomings, beginning with becoming-women and ending with becoming-imperceptible. Becoming-women is simply, for Deleuze and Guattari, the privileged threshold or doorway through which one embarks upon other becomings – and moves ever further from molar forms. Women as much as men must become-women in this sense (Deleuze and Guattari take time to pre-empt some of the possible feminist responses to this particular idea, but it is true that a certain form of femininity, or at least microfemity, is privileged (as closer to the situation of desire), and once again it is Woolf who best expresses this state of becoming). It is in this sense that the girl – introduced as 'fugitive being' in the previous section of the plateau – is the key conceptual persona of the second part of the plateau ('What is a girl, what is a group of girls? Proust at least has shown us once and for all that their individuation, collective or singular, proceeds not by subjectivity but by haecceity . . . They are pure relations of speeds and slownesses, and nothing else' (ATP 271)).

The furthest reaches of the series (although there is no ultimate *telos*, there is a tendency to increasing dissipation) can be broken down into three aspects: a becoming-imperceptible (towards the anorganic), a becoming-indiscernible (towards the asignifying) and a becoming-impersonal (towards the asubjective). Ultimately, to follow these is to become like everyone else, not in a reduction of singularity, but in the sense of a kind of invisibility in the world – or, more accurately, a kind of becoming-world: 'becoming everybody/everything, making the world a becoming, is to world, to make a world or worlds, in other words, to find one's proximities and zones of indiscernibility' (ATP 280).[15]

It is in this sense that drugs are an important, if ultimately limited, technology of experimentation, involving 'modifications of speed', or, more simply, changes in perception (they allow the hitherto imperceptible to be perceived) (ATP 282). As Deleuze and Guattari remark earlier in the 'Becoming' plateau, drugs have, in this sense, changed the 'perceptive coordinates of space-time' even in non-users (ATP 248). Drugs can also eliminate, at least temporarily, forms and subjects (they undo the plane of organisation). It is here that Deleuze and Guattari posit a 'pharmocoanalysis' that would be concerned with an unconscious of these impersonal microperceptions. This is not an unconscious to be discovered, but, again, one to be constructed.[16] Indeed, following Spinoza, there is not so much a conscious/unconscious dualism here (or bar between the two) as a sliding scale. This is something Deleuze returns to in his later book on Leibniz with the idea of a 'dark background' from which 'clear and distinct' perceptions foreground themselves, but we might also say that the idea of a kind of plenitude of virtualities as yet unactualised characterises Deleuze's other writings, on cinema for example, with the latter operating as precisely an 'actualising machine'.[17] In fact, this actual/virtual relation is, I think, an isotope of a broader finite/infinite one that has always been a key concern of philosophy (and, indeed, religion). Deleuze might be said to posit a continuum between these two – the finite and infinite – in place, again, of any bar or gap – and it also this, I think, that constitutes the importance of both Bergson and Spinoza for Deleuze, as well as his difference from other post-Kantian thinkers. It is also this that gives his writings their pragmatic and transformative character (we can always become more than what we already are).

Once again, however, this foregrounding of perceptive and psychic experimentation holds its dangers (as expounded by the two key conceptual personae – or 'probe-heads' – when it comes to the pharmacological, Artaud and Michaux): either the black hole, the line of abolition, or 'a segmentarity all the more rigid for being marginal, a territorialisation all the more artificial for being based on chemical substances, hallucinatory forms, and phantasy subjectifications' (ATP 285).[18] 'Drug addicts may be considered as precursors or experimenters who tirelessly blaze new paths of life, but their cautiousness lacks the foundation for caution' (ATP 285). Drug use, we might say, does not involve an adequate (or sustainable) programme of construction.

'Memories of a Secret' likewise addresses the question of imperceptibility in relation to the secret, understood as (hidden) content, but also as constituting a form itself. Deleuze and Guattari discuss secret societies and their necessary coexistence within society, but also return to both the figure of the girl (as secret) and, indeed, the war machine (as that which invents/occupies a different space-time – or operates *as* secret). Once more, artists are the pre-eminent thinkers of the secret, especially in their deployment of a secret rhythm, a secret line and so forth (with Henry James laying out a kind of metanarrative of the passage of the secret from content to form).

In the penultimate section of the plateau, 'Memories and Becomings, Points and Blocks', becoming is opposed to memory, and also history. Becomings are, to follow Nietzsche, untimely. They are both in and out of time, or irreducible to the conditions that allow for then. It is in this sense that becomings are also always minoritarian, when the major names a model, or standard, that is, precisely, historical ('women, children, but also animals, plants, molecules, are minoritarian' (ATP 291)).[19] Becomings then proceed not by memory but by blocks, for example 'blocks of childhood' that do not involve a regression to the child that one was, but an experimental becoming-child (it is in this sense that Deleuze and Guattari see a homology between Spinoza and children).

In this section, in an echo of the previous discussion of the two planes, two systems are counterposed: First, the punctual, which proceeds by points (with any lines present subordinated to the latter): 'These systems are arborescent, mnemonic, molar, structural: they are systems of reterritorialisation' (ATP 295). And the second multilinear with a privileging of the line over the point ('Free the line, free the diagonal' (ATP 295)). In fact, the multilinear might utilise a punctual system in order to break and go beyond it, just as becoming utilises history but is not of it. *A Thousand Plateaus* never simply privileges the rhizome over the root, the smooth over the striated and so forth, but always, again, articulates this in terms of strategy. Always the consolidation of a territory before deterritorialisation. Always the opening up of a smooth space from within the striated (and, inversely, always the dangers of deterritorialisations being reterritorialised, of smooth space becoming striated). Experimentation, we might say, necessarily involves this working out of proportions. A neither moving too slow or too fast.

That said, becoming does mean leaving a given territory, following an aberrant line and then constructing a new territory. Becoming, ultimately, is creation in this sense. As Deleuze and Guattari remark, 'Creations are like mutant abstract lines that have detached themselves from the task of representing a world, precisely because they assemble a new type of reality that history can only recontain or relocate in punctual systems' (ATP 296). Becoming, we might say, is a kind of world-building technology.

In contradistinction to drugs, and in the final section of the plateau, becoming-music once again becomes the pre-eminent (and most successful) example of becoming (even more so than painting, which involves its own deterritorialisation, of faces and landscapes). In music's case, it is the deterritorialisation of the refrain that defines a becoming-music that itself processes through a series, from becoming-women to becoming-child to becoming-molecular. It is also here that we return to the Bergsonian memories I began my own commentary with and the idea of a coexistence of different durations and, indeed, of a passage between them. Deleuze and Guattari make some compelling remarks in these last pages of the plateau about how 'A becoming-insect has replaced becoming-bird, or forms a block with it' (ATP 308). They continue: 'The insect is closer, better able to make audible the truth that all becomings are molecular' (ATP 308). But, we might add, music can also progress to more inorganic durations and with this the production of other, stranger forms and rhythms as yet unknown. Becoming operates as a passage between then, but also names this construction and expression of a different individuation in and of the world. If this account of becoming is philosophy (one which, as I hope I have conveyed, involves its own becomings), then it is of a very strange kind. An untimely philosophy that might use its own history (that is, the history of philosophy), but only as a set of conditions from which to depart. A philosophy that does not necessarily respect preset and predetermined terms and protocols (though it has its own rules), or indeed clearly demarcated subjects and objects (though it has its own individuations). It is philosophy as a fundamentally experimental and constructive – and affirmative – pursuit. Might we even say that it is philosophy as a form of fictioning, when this ultimately names the production of a new kind of reality from within this one?

Notes

1. See especially Guattari 1995: 110–13.
2. In fact, although sympathetic, the issue of other 'non-' forms of thought is a point of difference with Laruelle. As Deleuze and Guattari remark in the footnote: 'François Laruelle proposes a comprehension of nonphilosophy as "the real (of) science", beyond the object of knowledge ... But we do not see why this real of science is not nonscience as well' (Deleuze and Guattari 1994: 234 n.16). Deleuze and Guattari also footnote Laruelle in 'The Plane of Immanence' chapter when suggesting that 'the nonphilosophical is perhaps closer to the heart of philosophy than philosophy itself, and this means that philosophy cannot be content to be understood only philosophically or conceptually, but is addressed essentially to nonphilosophers as well' (Deleuze and Guattari 1994: 41).

3. See Hadot 1995: 81–125. In relation to positioning Deleuze and Guattari's philosophy as 'a way of life' see Chapter 5, 'Desiring-Machines, Chaoids, Probe-heads: Towards a Speculative Subjectivity (Deleuze and Guattari)' of my *On the Production of Subjectivity* (O'Sullivan 2012: 169–202), and, specifically in relation to *A Thousand Plateaus*, the section on 'Probe-heads Against Faciality' (187–202). In relation to Hadot and Deleuze, see May 2000.
4. See, in particular, the discussion in '587 BC–AD 70: On Several Regimes of Signs' (ATP 111–48), which gives more detail on pragmatics as the practice of translation and transportation of statements between different regimes, but also as the creation of new 'unknown statements': 'even if the result were a patois of sensual delight, physical and semiotic systems in shreds, asubjective affects, signs without significance where syntax, semantics, and logic are in collapse . . . cries-whispers, feverish improvisations, becoming-animal, becoming-molecular, real transsexualities, continuums of intensity, constitutions of bodies without organs' (ATP 147).
5. On a purely theoretical, if not philosophical, level, *A Thousand Plateaus* evidences a particularly productive entanglement of Guattari's more therapeutic modellings with Deleuze's more strictly conceptual work. It is in this sense that I think the project of attempting to disentangle – or 'wrench' – a 'pure' philosophical (or, indeed, scientific) Deleuze from Guattari (as in Manuel DeLanda's project of reconstruction, *Intensive Science and Virtual Philosophy* (see especially DeLanda 2002: 1–7)) misunderstands the very nature – and thus the productivity – of collaboration.
6. And Nietzsche here is doubled by Schreber who also goes through this series of '*nervous states*', 'becoming a women and many other things as well, following the endless circle of the eternal return' (Deleuze and Guattari 1983: 19).
7. And no doubt a different reading of the 'Becoming' plateau might foreground the interference between science and philosophy, especially around the concept of 'intensive multiplicity'.
8. As evidenced in the title of the final chapter of *A Thousand Plateaus*, 'Conclusion: Concrete Rules and Abstract Machines' (ATP 501–16).
9. In fact, this is to follow Deleuze when he remarks in the Preface to *Difference and Repetition*: 'A book of philosophy should be in part a very particular species of detective novel, in part a kind of science fiction' (Deleuze 1994: xx). For a compelling example of a book that uses Deleuze and Guattari (and not least the concept of becoming) in a more pronounced philo-fiction, see Negarestani 2008. I attend further to a kind of practice that results from interference between philosophy and fiction in my forthcoming book *Mythopoesis / Myth-Science / Mythotechnesis: Fictioning in Contemporary Art* (Burrows and O'Sullivan 2018).
10. In his own commentary on the 'Becoming' plateau, Eugene Holland points to an interesting ambiguity here – when the plateau moves from the memories of human figures to those of objects. As he suggests, this might point to the author's own memories – of haecceities, molecules and so forth – but also to the stranger and more compelling idea that these non-human and inorganic entities might themselves have memories (or becomings): 'But if the earth can think (as per the title of the Geology plateau), why can't molecules remember?' (Holland 2013: 103). Again, it is in this sense, it seems to me, that *A Thousand Plateaus* is itself a kind of philo-fiction.
11. In terms of this construction project we might turn to Deleuze and Guattari's remarks in 'November 28, 1947: How Do You Make Yourself a Body without Organs': 'The field of immanence or plane of consistency must be constructed. This can take place in very different social formations through very different assemblages (perverse, artistic, scientific, mystical, political) with different types of bodies without organs' (ATP 157). The relation of construction to expression is complex, but what one can say (and here I am explicitly following Eric Alliez's take on Deleuze and Guattari's philosophy) is that it is only through a construction of some kind (which is to say a practice) that expression can take place (see in particular Alliez 2004: 85–103). Brian Massumi's

'Introduction: Like a Thought' to *A Shock to Thought* also attends to the importance of the concept of expression for Deleuze and Guattari, and, of relevance here, the connection of this concept to becoming when this names expressive processes (and practices) of actualisation (Massumi 2002: xiii–xxxix).
12. For a precise diagnosis of this difference (and an argument for the superiority of *Anti-Oedipus*), see Land 2013 (and, indeed, his other essays of the 1990s).
13. It is in this sense that Deleuze talks of his interest in surfers and their relation to the wave in the 'From A to Z' interview with Claire Parnet (Deleuze 2012), but also, more philosophically speaking, that he links learning to swim with the movement from the First to Second kind of knowledge in his seminar on Spinoza (we learn to compose our body, with its particular relations of speed and slowness, with those of the wave: we are no longer subject to the wave but have, as it were, understood and thus 'conquered' (or formed a common notion with) this element of the world) (Deleuze 1978).
14. It is in this sense that 'A racehorse is more different than a workhorse than a workhorse is from an ox' (ATP 257).
15. Michel Tournier's *Robinson*, at least as Deleuze reconstructs the story in one of the appendices to *Logic of Sense* (Deleuze 1990b: 301–20), offers a fictional case study of this becoming-world (see also the section 'Becoming world' in O'Sullivan 2006: 95–7).
16. In connection to the construction of a molecular unconscious (in an analytic sense), especially in relation to 'other, non-human, animal, vegetable, cosmic, abstract machine becomings', see the section 'Unconscious versus libido' in Guattari 2013: 29–31.
17. See, in particular, Deleuze 1993: 85–99. And, in relation to cinema opening up different space-times, see especially Deleuze 1989.
18. Deleuze and Guattari define 'probe-heads' (in relation to becomings) in the plateau 'Year Zero: Faciality' (ATP 167–91): 'Beyond the face lies an altogether different inhumanity: no longer that of the primitive head, but of "probe-heads"; here, cutting edges of deterritorialisation become operative and lines of deterritorialisation positive and absolute, forming strange new becomings, new polyvocalities' (ATP 190–1).
19. For more detail on this idea of becoming as minoritarian (and a politics that might lead on from this), see O'Sullivan 2016.

Chapter 11

Of the Refrain (The Ritornello)

Emma Ingala

'A child in the dark, gripped with fear, comforts himself by singing under his breath. He walks and halts to his song. Lost, he takes shelter, or orients himself with his little song as best as he can' (ATP 311).[1] This passage, probably one of the most quoted of the book, opens and sets the tone of the chapter '1837: Of the Ritornello'.[2] These lines have garnered attention mainly because it is easy to identify with the affective atmosphere they depict. In moments or spaces of disorientation, when we are 'in the dark', we may try to appease ourselves by humming a tune, clapping our hands or tapping our fingers. With this scene, the ritornello is initially portrayed as a sort of rhythmic reaction that constitutes a reassuring resource, a protective mechanism, an antidote against fear and chaos.

The rhythmic condition of the ritornello is already patent in its etymology: from the Italian *ritorno*, it is something that returns, a little return. Coined originally as a musical term, it designates the recurrence (either simple reproduction or variation) of a phrase or fragment within a piece. In everyday French, *ritournelle* also alludes to rudimentary songs for children and, more broadly, to an insistent repetition. Drawing from this last sense, Jacques Lacan turned the word into a psychoanalytic concept to denote the repetitive or stereotypical formulas that appear in psychotic language and which break with common discourse by stopping signification, grammar or meaning (Lacan 1993: 33). This is probably the source of Guattari's first employment of the ritornello in his 1956 clinical report 'Monograph on R. A.'[3]

Deleuze and Guattari acknowledge that the ritornello is initially a 'properly musical content' (ATP 301), hence the privilege of sound and the multiple references to music throughout the eleventh chapter of *A Thousand Plateaus*.[4] Nevertheless, this chapter is not about music. Like the rest of the book, it is about 'philosophy, nothing but philosophy, in the traditional sense of the word' (Deleuze 2006: 176, translation modified). Indeed, when asked by Didier Eribon about their famous definition of philosophy as concept-creation and their own contribution to it, Deleuze and Guattari responded: 'The ritornello, for example. We have formulated a concept of the ritornello in philosophy' (Deleuze 2006: 381, translation modified).[5] This interview was published under the even stronger formula 'We Invented the Ritornello', and while this title captures the importance that Deleuze and Guattari attribute to this creation, it misses the core novelty of it: it is not that they invented the ritornello per se, but that they invented this concept *in philosophy*, that they forged a properly philosophical concept, a philosophical ritornello.[6]

For Deleuze, concepts are not created on a whim, but are rather the result of a pressing problem. Concepts fulfil functions within fields of thought (Deleuze 2006: 349); for example, the concept of substance serves, for a certain ontology, the function of supporting properties ('red' or 'heavy' are always predicated *of* a substance). In this sense, the creation of the concept of the ritornello in philosophy is called for by an encounter that exposes the need for a certain function or functions to be fulfilled. In the climate of fear and darkness that opens the eleventh chapter of *A Thousand Plateaus*, the purpose of the ritornello seems to be to provide protection, even if it is in a playful way. This is certainly one of the main functions of the ritornello for Deleuze and Guattari, but it is not the only one. In the chapter devoted to it, the ritornello is presented as a combination of three dynamisms: the determination of a centre, the tracing of a circle around the centre, and the opening of the circle. While the first two are designed to create and protect a familiar territory, the third is a vector towards the unfamiliar, towards change and novelty. The originality of the approach adopted in *A Thousand Plateaus* resides in its understanding of the complex relation between the familiar and the unfamiliar. Rather than naively choosing one of these over the other, it recognises the importance of regulating the passages and dosages of familiarity and unfamiliarity, which in Deleuze and Guattari's universe take the forms of identity and difference, territorialisation and deterritorialisation, striated space and smooth space, or state apparatus and war machine. The ritornello is, in this context, the site where this regulation takes place and the concept that shapes what Deleuze and Guattari call an 'art of caution' (*art de la prudence*) (ATP vi): an ethics of quantities, passages and dosages.

To develop this, I will examine the philosophical consequences and the scope of the regulatory function of the ritornello through two different, but interrelated, lines of analysis. In the first part, I follow Deleuze and Guattari's threefold characterisation of the ritornello (centre, circle and opening of the circle). In the second, I consider how the ritornello combines the three aspects identified in the first part to fulfil three regulatory functions: 1) it is the *a priori*, meaning the genetic condition, of space and time and, through them, of subjects, individuals and societies; 2) it shows how difference and repetition complement one another, while also clarifying their relationship to identity; and 3) it resolves the problem of consistency, of how heterogeneous things can be kept together.

The three aspects of the ritornello

As we have seen, the chapter 'On the Ritornello' does not begin with a definition; in fact, the question 'What is a ritornello?' is not explicitly raised until almost the end (ATP 348). Deleuze and Guattari first provide a multi-layered portrait that is graphic and affective rather than conceptual. This is because the ritornello is a concept that (somewhat paradoxically) deals with, among other things, a pre-conceptual experience, with the moment before concepts are created to pacify the forces of chaos by structuring the world into familiar territories. To explore this, Deleuze and Guattari employ a prolific lexicon and imagery borrowed from music, geography and ethology. However, if we take seriously their statement that they invented the ritornello 'in philosophy', this detour through other disciplines cannot be understood as a movement away from philosophy; it is, on the contrary, the constituting point of philosophy as the creation of concepts. In *What is Philosophy?*, Deleuze and Guattari explain that concepts are never created from nothing; instead they originate from other concepts in 'zones of neighbourhood' (Deleuze and Guattari 1994: 19) or thresholds of indiscernibility, which are regions where boundaries are suspended. In this particular case, a musical notion such as 'ritornello' becomes, in its zone of neighbourhood, at the same time geographical, ethological and philosophical. This is why Deleuze and Guattari always warn that their use of geographical and musical concepts is not metaphorical or figurative, but literal.[7]

The ritornello is characterised for the first time in the chapter by its role: 'it is territorial, is a territorial assemblage' (ATP 312). The main function of the ritornello is to create and demarcate a territory. Assembling a territory, according to Deleuze and Guattari, has three aspects that appear in the table of contents of the book as three settings: 'in the dark, at home, towards the world'. Against the inclination to consider the three scenes teleologically, as successive moments in an evolution, Deleuze and Guattari insist on their entwinement. *In the dark*, the territorialising function of the ritornello is to provide protection and orientation through the creation of a centre; *at home*, the ritornello delineates around that centre a circle or perimeter that erects the boundaries of one's own house and territory; *towards the world*, the ritornello reveals its power to break through the circle and project vectors abroad. These three aspects can also be understood as three different perspectives on the assemblage: in the dark, we are dealing with an infra-assemblage, as the ritornello intervenes to arrange a yet unassembled space; at home, the ritornello focuses on the inside of the assemblage, on the intra-assemblage; and, finally, towards the world, the forces of the ritornello push outwards, towards other assemblages, so the perspective is that of the inter-assemblage. Lastly, Deleuze and Guattari offer another characterisation of these three aspects in terms of the forces they deal with: forces of chaos, forces of the earth and cosmic forces.

In the dark

Let us go back to the frightened child in the dark singing to soothe himself. Evidently, the safety provided here by the ritornello cannot be conceived in terms of a physical protection against the potential attack of monsters huddled in the shadows. Rather, it must be understood as a modulation of space. In the same sense, and to borrow from a well-known psychoanalytic example that for Deleuze and Guattari also qualifies as a ritornello, the child who repeatedly chants '*Fort!-Da!*' while throwing away and bringing back a wooden reel is not actually mastering his mother's absences and presences, nor substituting signifiers for things (as Lacan interpreted), but inflecting his space against chaos.[8] The experience of chaos is not so much that of a mere disorder as that of a non-dimensional state, of pure and formless undifferentiation,[9] a non-space or a non-time with no points of reference and no localisations; hence the disorientation. Such is the (non-)status of chaos that in *The Fold* Deleuze even characterises it as non-existent (Deleuze 1993: 76). In *What is Philosophy?*, chaos is portrayed as the infinite speed with which determinations take shape and vanish, to the extent that it is impossible to make distinctions or connections between them (Deleuze and Guattari 1994: 42). Chaos results from 'infinite speeds that blend into the immobility of the colourless and silent nothingness they traverse' (Deleuze and Guattari 1994: 201). The ritornello operates in this initial scene as a principle of order that confronts chaos by establishing a centre. The designation of a centre entails the institution of a landmark or point of reference and, with it, of a minimum system of coordinates to orientate oneself. In the example, the ritornello is a little song, but it might be any resource capable of creating a rhythm. In this case, rhythm is what transforms the amorphous scream and shiver of fear into chant and dance by introducing remarkable points of reference into an otherwise homogeneous medium.

Deleuze and Guattari understand rhythm in a specific way: it is not cadence or metre, that is, a stable (regular or irregular) unit of measure. While metre is dogmatic because of this stability, rhythm is critical. In other words, rhythm is not registered in the domain of resemblance, measure, identity and equality; rather, rhythm is difference, the 'Unequal or the Incommensurable' (ATP 313). Rhythm is not reproduction of the same; it is repetition of difference. The child in the dark is not, therefore, searching for a measure or identity to hold on to, because what is scary about chaos is not its inequality or difference, but its absolute undifferentiation, the equivalence of all of its points. Rhythm protects from chaos through the establishment of an inequality or a difference that can then become a landmark. Admittedly, this rhythmicity remains ambiguous in so far as, while it breaks with the regularity of chaos, it can end up establishing another kind of regularity. In this respect, even if the rhythm of the ritornello operates through difference, it is always in danger of degenerating into the mechanical reproduction of the same (metre). When the ritornello loses its differentiating power it becomes a litany, what Deleuze and Guattari call a ditty (*rengaine*). This is a bad usage of the ritornello or a 'mediocre or bad' ritornello (ATP 349). Nonetheless, the issue when in the dark is not yet to prevent the solidification of identity, but to create difference.

The image of the frightened child must not mislead us into thinking that there is a fully constituted subject before the encounter with chaos, that this subject experiences fear and then acts against it with the ritornello. The subject, on the contrary, is a consequence of this action, of how this action is accomplished. Before the action, there is no interiority, no self, and hence no opposition between an inner fear and an outer threat; there is just an undetermined and pre-conceptual affect, pure imbalance that we will later identify as fear. It could be objected that affects are always states of an already given individual, but Deleuze and Guattari conceive of affects as pre-individual and impersonal relations.[10] The second dynamism of the ritornello (*at home*) is the delineation of a circle or perimeter around the centre created by the first dynamism. This circle establishes a home and, with it, the distinction between interiority and exteriority that did not exist in the chaotic darkness. In this sense, as with any trauma, it is only *a posteriori* that we manage to speak about what happened and to shape it through a narrative; it is only in hindsight, when there is a child and a home, when the child is at home, that he can explain his fear of the dark. There is hence no temporal linearity, but enjambment between the different aspects of the ritornello. Furthermore, if the child can leave the darkness, it is because he already presupposes a home, even if he does not have one yet. The child is on his own, and that is one of the reasons for his fear, but he is not alone: if he is able to have recourse to a ritornello, to a little song, it is because somebody or something has already a home and taught him how to sing. The child is alone and not alone at the same time: on the one hand, humming in the dark is a private and even intimate act, not designed to delight an audience but to protect and orient oneself. But, on the other hand, there would not be such an act without a community, a culture or a symbolic order (and even a nature) from which to draw that first ritornello, even if it is to sing it differently (see Sauvagnargues 2013: 47). For this reason, the first aspect of the ritornello (*in the dark*) presupposes the second (*at home*).

At home

'Everyone, at every age, in the smallest things as in the greatest challenges, seeks a territory, tolerates or carries out deterritorialisations, and is reterritorialised on almost anything – memory, fetish, or dream. Ritornellos express these powerful dynamisms' (Deleuze and Guattari 1994: 67–8). The universality of the ritornello, combined with its genetic potential, is what turns it into a transcendental category,[11] into an *a priori*. So far, in the dark, we have seen how an elementary self is set in space and time through the establishment of a basic cardinal point. This process was only possible because somewhere else there were houses and cartographies. The second aspect of the ritornello is where Deleuze and Guattari explain the formation of a home or a *chez-soi*, that is, a place for the self to dwell, which is the place where the self strictly speaking comes to be.

The first arrangement of space and time produces what Deleuze and Guattari, following Gilbert Simondon, call a 'milieu' (Simondon 2005: 63–4). A milieu, broadly understood as the environment of life, is an operation that selects and extracts components from the otherwise undifferentiated chaos. The first component selected functions as a centre. This privileged component distinguishes a particular milieu from other milieus and from chaos. Deleuze and Guattari thus define the milieu as 'a block of space-time constituted by the periodic repetition of the component' (ATP 313) that serves as a stabilising centre. In this way, a milieu responds to chaos through rhythm, which is to say through differentiation. Nevertheless, a milieu is not yet a home. The child singing in the dark or throwing and pulling back a little toy might feel relieved with the rhythmicity of his action, with the interruption of a frightening grey zone, but he is not yet at home. A home requires, on top of a centre, a perimeter around it; not only a landmark, but a whole appropriation and organisation of space. In other words, a home requires a territory. Ethology teaches Deleuze and Guattari that while all animals have a milieu, not all of them have a territory, and that expression is what turns a milieu into a territory or a home. Milieus have components that fulfil certain functions. For example, the colour of plumage or a birdsong can serve the function of courtship. A milieu develops into a territory when these components are seized, stripped of their function and transformed into purely expressive components: colour and song now just mark a territory. In this sense, the territorialising act of appropriating a milieu is the performative act of expressing this appropriation. The child's song becomes pure expression as it is no longer submitted to the function of establishing a centre; the child is no longer singing to calm down, but to mark his territory, his spot. It should be noted that, in the same way that there is no prior self, territory is not given in advance, waiting for the expressive act to seize and mark it; on the contrary, the fence and sign create the territory. Expression, for Deleuze and Guattari, is anything that can become a mark, index or placard of a territory, but it can also adopt more sophisticated forms. When the rudimentary expressive marks enter into complex relations with one another and stop being pure indicators, they become the territorial motifs and counterpoints that define the style of each territory.

Deleuze and Guattari provide a number of examples of this second aspect of the ritornello. There is the child who hums while doing her homework, the housewife singing to herself while doing the chores, and the radio or TV nobody in the house pays attention to, but whose mission is to emit noise that demarcates the threshold of the home. At a certain point in the chapter, the examples refer to animals (birds, fish, tortoises . . .), which when taken together with the TV and the radio example remind us that, even if the fundamental operation of the territory is expression, it is not anthropomorphic. This means that expression must not be understood according to the structuralist and linguistic paradigms as signification or symbolisation, but as an a-signifying semiotics that humans share with animals (see Sibertin-Blanc 2010a). This leads Deleuze and Guattari to suggest that art, conceived primarily as expression, is not exclusively human (ATP 316–17).[12]

Towards the world

Although the ritornello functions primarily as rhythm, that is, as the repetition of a difference, it accomplishes its protective task against chaos by creating through this repetition a number of identities or familiar references: first of all, a centre or landmark; around it, a territory or a home;

and, through the first two, the subjects and the community inhabiting the assembled space. In this sense, for those acquainted with Deleuze's previous work, especially *Difference and Repetition* (first published in 1968), the promotion of the ritornello as a homebuilder might sound at odds with the premises of his philosophy of difference. Very briefly, Deleuze's purpose in *Difference and Repetition* was to explore the possibility of thinking, which for him was to think difference in itself, to think beyond any familiarity. The history of philosophy had been mostly unable to do this, since differences were usually regarded through the filter of prior identities. Deleuze called this operation 'the image of thought' (see Deleuze 1994: ch. 3), and linked it to common sense and tradition. He did not consider this understanding to entail thinking, but mere re-cognising, re-producing and re-presenting. The only way to think difference in itself was, for Deleuze, to eliminate the image of thought and achieve a 'thought without image' (Deleuze 1994: 132), namely, a thought stripped of any identity, familiarity or presupposition. In this context, the ritornello seems to be an image of thought devised to protect against a thought without image, against the anxiety produced by the absence of images, by the unrecognisable and unfamiliar. While in *Difference and Repetition* Deleuze invited us to confront the realm of difference without any mediation or shield, in *A Thousand Plateaus* the ritornello appears initially as a most wanted mediation or shield against chaos. There is certainly a change in the appreciation of the image of thought, whose inevitability and, to an extent, desirability Deleuze ends up accepting. This is explicit in *A Thousand Plateaus*, where 'noology', understood as the study of the different images of thought (ATP 376), is proposed as a prolegomena to philosophy, but it becomes more accentuated in the latter works, where Deleuze and Guattari identify some of their key concepts, such as rhizome or plan of immanence, with the image of thought.[13] In an interview from 1988, Deleuze defines the image of thought as a 'system of coordinates, dynamics, orientations' (Deleuze 1995a: 148). This description is close to the ritornello.

Nevertheless, the new appraisal of the image of thought and the invention of the ritornello must not be understood to entail an abandonment of the philosophy of difference or a resignation to identities and familiarity. The combat against the solidification of identities is particularly clear in Deleuze's *Francis Bacon. The Logic of Sensation*, published one year after *A Thousand Plateaus*. Here, Deleuze acknowledges the importance of undertaking a propaedeutic work before starting to paint: all the identitarian presuppositions ('ready-made perceptions, memories, phantasms')[14] that overpopulate the painter's head and, virtually, the canvas on which she is about to paint must be eliminated in order for the painter to create something more than mere figuration or re-presentation. These presuppositions are clichés, and can only be overcome, Deleuze states, if the painter embraces the chaos; yet the painter must also make sure she gets out of the chaos (see Deleuze 2003: 103).

The project of combating identities and clichés through immersion in chaos seems at first sight to contradict the project of protecting against chaos through the creation of a familiar home. However, in the ritornello both projects work together, balancing each other. Whereas the first two aspects of the ritornello are concerned with fighting against chaos and, for that purpose, with delineating and maintaining the borders of a home, the third aspect of the ritornello (*towards the world*) ensures that the home does not become a jail, that borders can be overstepped and other territories created. If this third aspect is not activated, the ritornello is in danger of turning from a rhythmic repetition into a mechanic reproduction, into a ditty (*rengaine*) or cliché. At the same time, the first two aspects prevent the third aspect from casting the subject into chaos with no protection whatsoever, and provide landmarks to get out of it. In this regard, the function of the ritornello is to manage the distance between chaos and clichés. The ritornello, like clichés, is initially inherited from others and creates familiarity to keep chaos away; unlike clichés, however, it operates primarily through difference and its repetition and not through identity and its reproduction, while its third aspect guarantees a certain amount of chaos able to subvert the familiar.

'Towards the world', therefore, means towards an outside of the familiar territory, an outside of home and the self; it entails a deterritorialisation of the well-known territories and an invocation of different ones. The third aspect of the ritornello opens a crack in the circle created by the second aspect, and shoots through the crack what Deleuze and Guattari call 'lines of flight' (e.g. ATP 9), namely, vectors of change and novelty. Under this third aspect, the ritornello is no longer a song that creates and delimits a home, but a tune encouraging those who sing it to venture outside. This adventure outside the circle of familiarity is neither a mere regression into chaos, nor a simple opportunity to refurbish the house. Deleuze and Guattari consider it to be the chance to go beyond the territories to what they call the 'cosmos' (e.g. ATP 312), a non-chaotic outside. In Paul Klee's words, cited in *A Thousand Plateaus* as an example of this third aspect of the ritornello, it is the chance to render visible non-visible forces (ATP 342).

Again, it must be noted that 'In the dark, at home, towards the world' do not register a linear account of the progression from chaos to cosmos. Instead, these three aspects are interlaced processes without a beginning or an end. In the same way as the second aspect was already presupposed in the first, the third aspect is already presupposed in the second.

A territory cannot be established without previously deterritorialising a number of functions in the milieu, without deterritorialising the function of a component in order to reterritorialise it as an expression. Besides, as we have seen, the aspects counterbalance each other, preventing the ritornello from either plunging into chaos or degenerating into a cliché. This regulative function of the ritornello operates through three philosophical problems that I examine in the next section: space and time, difference and repetition, and the problem of consistency.

The ritornello 'in philosophy'

Space and time

Towards the end of the chapter, Deleuze and Guattari present the ritornello as an *a priori* form. The ritornello appears as the condition of possibility, or rather as the condition of genesis,[15] of space and time. There is space and time because the ritornello introduces modulations, landmarks and differences in an otherwise undifferentiated and non-dimensional chaos. By inflecting space and time, the ritornello is also the *a priori* of the processes of subjectivation and individuation, since subjects and individuals become such through the determination of and their association with a time and place, an 'hour and (a) territory' (Zourabichvili 2012: 134). This particular understanding of space and time as effects and not as *a priori* forms of sensibility entails a reversal of Kant's formulation. However, for this reversal to take place, both the notion of *a priori* and the concepts of space and time must be conceived in a specific way. First, the *a priori* Deleuze and Guattari postulate is not general but concrete, something only applicable and fully determinable in each case (like the little song of the example), and as such it is not an empty form lodged in a transcendental subject, but that which triggers the processes of subjectivation. Secondly, space and time for Deleuze and Guattari are not abstract, but lived, inhabited, habitual and particular dimensions; they are the space and time we dwell in (see also Guattari 2011: 107) (as the space and time that result from singing a song in the dark). Instead of static coordinates, space and time are never-ending processes of spatialisation and temporalisation, processes that mould our milieus, territories and chronologies. This reversal of the status of space and time is one of the reasons why Deleuze and Guattari insist that *A Thousand Plateaus* is a post-Kantian book (Deleuze 2006: 309).

Despite rhythm being concerned with time intervals, in the chapter on the ritornello the spatial perspective is privileged – as it is in general in Deleuze and Guattari's geophilosophy (see Antonioli 2003: 8). The account of the ritornello is structured around the arrangement of a territory and its further deterritorialisations, around the creation, organisation and transformation of space from a uniform chaos. Deleuze and Guattari explain how space results from the action of a ritornello (establishment of a centre, delimitation of a perimeter or circle around it, and aperture of the circle), and how a ritornello is therefore the *a priori* of space. Without ritornellos, we are in the dark. However, despite giving prominence to space, at the end of the chapter the ritornello is also presented as the *a priori* of time. 'The ritornello fabricates time . . . Time is not an a priori form; rather, the ritornello is the a priori form of time, which in each case fabricates different times' (ATP 349). Time is produced when a ritornello institutes intervals and cuts in an otherwise homogeneous and timeless continuum. These intervals are created through the repetition of a difference (through, for example, the repetition of a bell stroke or, more elaborately, of a whole song, or of a transition from day to night), and this repetition establishes a difference between 'now' and 'then'.

Space and time, as processual dimensions generated by the rhythm of a ritornello, converge in the notion of habit.[16] 'Habit' has a double sense: on the one hand, it means the repetition in time of a routine or behaviour pattern; on the other hand, it is related to 'inhabit', to habitation, to the act of dwelling in a space. The ritornello is the *a priori* of space and time because it renders them habitable, because it creates and curbs them through the enactment of habits, that is, through the repetition of spatiotemporal landmarks and demarcations against the undifferentiation of chaos. The ritornello is a machine of producing habits, of producing through them space and time, and, finally, of producing subjectivity. Because the ritornello always comprises vectors of deterritorialisation, the notion of 'habit' or 'habitation' cannot be understood in purely identitarian terms; rather, a habit is not the repetition of the same, but the 'harnessing or the "preservation" of a difference' (Zourabichvili 2012: 113).

Difference and repetition

Through the concept of the ritornello, Deleuze and Guattari re-engage with the discussion of the relation between difference and repetition. Indeed, this re-engagement is so substantial that François Zourabichvili chose the subtitle 'difference and repetition' for the entry 'Ritornello' in his *Vocabulary of Deleuze* (Zourabichvili 2012: 205). As we have seen, the ritornello is a rhythmic repetition of differences that engenders a number of more or less stable identities under the form of assemblages, milieus, territories, individuals, selves, subjects, societies, communities and so on. At the same time, to the extent that it is made up of differences, the ritornello always contains the potential to undo these identities. The ritornello is conceptually between chaos and cliché and fighting against both on two fronts: on the one hand, it produces difference, which in turn crystallises in identities, to confront the undifferentiation of chaos; on the other hand, it produces difference, which in turn subverts the established identities, to avoid the instauration of clichés. A bad use of the ritornello stops the production of differences and stagnates in identities, or collapses into pure chaos when it loses all of its landmarks.

The ritornello is, for Deleuze and Guattari, a perfect example of how difference and repetition are entwined dynamisms. Even if common sense inclines us to think that repetition belongs to the realm of identity, sameness and generality, and difference to that of the dis-similar, singular and particular, repetition and difference are two sides of the same process. Repetition is always repetition of a difference, the 'power of difference' (Deleuze 1994: 302). A repetition of the same is not a repetition, but a mechanical reproduction, and when a ritornello stops repeating and starts reproducing, it becomes a ditty (*rengaine*). *A Thousand Plateaus* insists on the importance of difference to the ritornello: 'It is the difference that is rhythmic, not the repetition, which nevertheless produces it: productive repetition has nothing to do with reproductive meter. This is the "critical solution of the antinomy"' (ATP 314).

The ritornello operates through at least two repetitions: every ritornello is already the repetition of other ritornellos; no ritornello is created *ex nihilo* (Sauvagnargues 2013: 54) and there is no first ritornello. Each also continuously repeats itself and is never a one-off event. In this sense, the ritornello is a phenomenon of return, although the idea of return must be thought once again in a very specific way. The three aspects of the ritornello describe a striking repetition that, far from having a beginning or an end or proceeding linearly, entails an aberrant circularity of infinite variations. The darkness is not the beginning of the process and the 'beyond the circle' is not the end; these aspects are entwined, altering the order, simultaneously or successively, in an open-ended and undulatory movement. As Zourabichvili puts it, 'there is no arrival, there is only ever a return, but returning must be thought of as the reverse or the flipside of departing, and it is at the same moment that we both depart and return' (Zourabichvili 2012: 206). This depiction of the ritornello situates it close to Nietzsche's eternal return, at least on Deleuze and Guattari's reading of it.[17] Like the eternal return, the ritornello is a selection device: it selects what is going to return, namely difference.

Nevertheless, the difference promoted by the ritornello is not as radical as a thought without image, as a pure difference without identities or representations. The notion of the ritornello reintroduces a specific degree of representation to protect us from the dangers of an open confrontation with chaos. In *Difference and Repetition*, repetition was opposed to representation: 'repetition differs in kind from representation, the repeated cannot be represented' (Deleuze 1994: 18). Now, however, this opposition is somewhat relaxed, and repetition and representation are combined. While the ritornello is a repetitive response to un-representable chaos, it produces a certain amount of reassuring representation. This duplicity introduces the problem of quantities, and turns *A Thousand Plateaus* into 'a book on ethics' (Foucault 1984: xiii): how much reassuring representation should we admit before falling into the cliché? How far should we venture outside the circle before allowing the chaos to destroy absolutely everything? The problem of consistency deals with these issues.

The problem of consistency

The problem of consistency initially concerns the topic of space and time. Space and time, as we dwell in them, must be engendered. But they must also endure and become consistent; that is, hold together their heterogeneous elements instead of falling into unconnected fragments. The ritornello is, as we have seen, the solution to this question: its repetition holds together the heterogeneous elements – the refrain that holds together the different parts of a song, or the song that holds together the little child and his precarious newfound centre, or the repetition of a certain habit that allows a subject to constitute herself and her home.

However, the matter is not as simple as this. Homogenising a set of heterogeneous components will not make them consistent, since consistency requires that the heterogeneous components be held together in a way that maintains their heterogeneity. The problem of consistency is rather an issue of dosages and quantities of identity and difference, territory and deterritorialisation, inside and outside. The ritornello is the site of this calculation. A consistent assemblage requires sufficient difference to maintain the heterogeneity of its elements, but not so much that it regresses to the homogeneity of chaos. It also requires enough identity to glue together the heterogeneous components, but not so much identity to produce uniformity. This problem of consistency leads Deleuze and Guattari to elaborate, in *A Thousand Plateaus*, an ethics of prudence that aims to regulate the dosages. 'Ethics' is here understood as intimately related to *nomos*, the unwritten law that distributes space. Ethics is about creating a home, an *ethos*, an abode (ATP 312). This ethics prescribes caution and prudence, but cannot determine once and for all the dosages of homeliness and unhomeliness used to organise the habitation. These dosages must always be settled in accordance with the specific problem encountered and the particular circumstances.

The ethics of prudence can also be explained in geographical terms. In this respect, the ritornello would be the art of managing distances and passages, of setting frontiers and checkpoints: how far or how close a territory should erect its boundaries, how to keep at a distance both the forces of chaos and other territories, allowing and regulating at the same time certain passages towards them in order to produce change. The ritornello 'is less a question of evolution than of passage, bridges and tunnels' (ATP 322). And Deleuze and Guattari's prescription is once again crystal clear: prudence and sobriety (ATP 344); neither to venture without any protection into the outside, nor to remain on the inside mechanically reproducing clichés. At no point, then, does *A Thousand Plateaus* encourage us to completely abandon identity and embrace an unrecognisable pure difference;[18] on the contrary, the invitation is to determine in each case how much identity and how much difference we require in order to think and act.[19] The end of the chapter 'On the Ritornello' reveals to what extent Deleuze and Guattari try to protect themselves against a number of dangers, and how difficult they find it to be 'strong enough' (ATP 350). These dangers adopt different figures (black holes, closures, paralysis, madness, death . . .), but are all manifestations of an excess or a defect, of too much familiarity or unfamiliarity, identity or difference, territory or deterritorialisation.

The relationship between the state apparatus and what Deleuze and Guattari call the war machine is a perfect example of how this art of dosages works.[20] The space of the political is shaped by a permanent tension between these two instances, which could be understood, for our present purpose, as the institutional infrastructure of a system of power (state apparatus) and as the extra-institutional claims, criticisms and expectations of, for example, the streets (war machine). An imbalance in their combination leads to fatal consequences: an excess of war machine might fall into fascism, as an excess of state apparatus can end up in totalitarianism (ATP 230). Both elements are required to contain the excess of each other. Deleuze and Guattari's conception of the political space is, therefore, not based on a utopian appeal to a pure outside of the state,[21] nor is it based on the choice of one pole or the other. They understand the functioning of the political as a determination of how much inside and how much outside is required in each circumstance.

To conclude, the problem of consistency reveals the particular problematic field of the philosophy of *A Thousand Plateaus* and the ritornello.

This problematic field is no longer designed by the difference between 'up' and 'down' and its multiple concretisations: essences and appearances, soul and body, reason and passion, bourgeoisie and proletariat, and so on. Kant had already denounced this problem as a false problem when his Copernican revolution substituted the apparition/conditions of apparition distinction for the couple essences/appearances (Deleuze 1984: 14). However, Deleuze and Guattari still find in Kant's approach too much verticality or hierarchy, and the problematic field they design is rather a horizontal one, suitable for a theory of immanence. The difference between 'up' and 'down' is replaced by the difference, understood horizontally, between 'inside' and 'outside', while the axiology that considered one of the poles good and the other bad is superseded by a complex appreciation of both instances. 'It is in terms not of independence, but of coexistence and competition *in a perpetual field of interaction*, that we must conceive of exteriority and interiority' (ATP 360). It is not about choosing one or the other, but about combining them, passing from one to the other. The lesson of the ritornello is that thought, existence, politics and art are the result of an undulatory movement between the inside and the outside, of a careful dosing of familiarity and unfamiliarity.[22]

Notes

1. The image of the frightened child has already been evoked in the previous chapter (ATP 299), and an earlier version is found in Guattari's 'The Time of Ritornellos' (Guattari 2011: 107).
2. Following Deleuze's suggestion to the English translators of *Dialogues* (Deleuze and Parnet 1987: xiii), I translate *ritournelle* as 'ritornello' and not 'refrain', as Brian Massumi does in the English version of *Mille plateaux*. '*Refrain*' is also found in French, and is used by Deleuze himself in *Différence et répétition* (Deleuze 1968a: 161, 373; Deleuze 1994: 123, 292) and *Logique du sens* (Deleuze 1969: 39, 59, 73). However, in *Mille plateaux* Deleuze and Guattari choose for their concept the name *ritournelle* and not *refrain* (which does not appear at all in this book). My guiding contention to explain this decision is that there are at least two types of refrains (*refrains*): ritornellos (*ritournelles*) and ditties (*rengaines*). While ritornellos entail a return or a repetition that operates through variation and difference and so have no fixed identity, signification or resemblance, as for instance in Schumann's *Études symphoniques*, ditties (*rengaines*) generally constitute a mechanical reproduction of the same. The ditty would be a 'mediocre or bad' ritornello, a bad usage of the ritornello (ATP 349). Most probably, to avoid the ambiguity inherent to *refrain*, Deleuze and Guattari chose not to use it any longer and instead employed *ritournelle* and *rengaine*. Besides, the word 'ritornello' has explicit resonances and connotations (repetition, return, eternal return . . .) that are more vague in 'refrain'.
3. Guattari, 'Monograph on R. A.' [1956], in Guattari 2015: 36–41. Besides this text, Guattari addresses the ritornello in Guattari 2011; 2013; 2014; and 1995. Guattari, thus, has a record of publications on his own on the topic of the ritornello. For this reason, some commentators have claimed that the ritornello belongs more to Guattari

than to Deleuze. See Dosse 2010: 253. More subtly, other analyses provide insights into which particular aspects of the concept carry Deleuze or Guattari's signature. See Sauvagnargues 2013: 48; Massumi 1992: 151. While these approaches are valuable, I will focus rather on the 'between-the-two'. Indeed, if we follow their own claim, 'they' (and not one or the other) invented the ritornello.
4. Including the year of the title, 1837, which was the year of publication of Schumann's *Études symphoniques*.
5. Even if the definition of philosophy as the creation of concepts cannot be found in *A Thousand Plateaus*, it is already articulated by 1980, as can be seen in this interview.
6. Furthermore, the ritornello does not merely add one more concept to the list; it is a concept about concepts, in so far as concepts themselves are defined as ritornellos. In this respect, the whole task of philosophy as a creation of concepts is intimately concerned with the notion of the ritornello. See Deleuze 1994: 26.
7. See Antonioli 2003: 13; Deleuze and Parnet 1987: 3.
8. Freud 1975: 8–9; Lacan 2006: 262. Deleuze and Guattari's brief account of the '*Fort-Da*' can be found in ATP 299. See also Guattari 1995: 72–6.
9. See Deleuze and Guattari 1994, where chaos is described as an 'undifferentiated abyss'. In *A Thousand Plateaus*, Deleuze and Guattari no longer distinguish between the two senses of differenc/tiation that Deleuze established in *Difference and Repetition* (see Deleuze 1994: 209–10). 'Undifferentiated' here simply means with no differences, with no remarkable points.
10. Gilbert Simondon's theory of individuation is a fundamental reference for understanding the nature of pre-subjective affects. See Simondon 2005. Guattari reaffirms this conception of affects in his text 'Ritornellos and Existential Affects': 'Affect is thus essentially a pre-personal category, establishing itself "before" the circumscription of identities' (Guattari 2013: 203).
11. Deleuze expressed on numerous occasions that he conceived *A Thousand Plateaus* as an attempt to provide a table of categories. See, for example, Deleuze 2015: 78.
12. ATP 316–17. This affirmation does not prevent Deleuze and Guattari from providing their own account of the history of (human) art through three main paradigms corresponding to the three aspects of the ritornello: classic, romantic and modern.
13. Deleuze 1995a: 149; Deleuze and Guattari 1994: 37.
14. Deleuze 2003: 87. See especially chapter 11.
15. For the difference between them, see Smith 2012: 235–55.
16. For an analysis of the relationship between the notions of ritornello and habit, see Holland 2008a.
17. The more than phonological proximity between the eternal return and the ritornello (*ritournelle / retour eternel*) is acknowledged by Deleuze and Guattari themselves. See ATP 343.
18. For a discussion of the relationship between difference and identity in Deleuze's thinking, see Rae 2014.
19. For the prescription of prudence, see for example ATP 161, 270. Deleuze also speaks about an art of dosages in relation to drinking alcohol: see G. Deleuze, 'B comme boisson', in Deleuze 2012.
20. The relationship between the ritornello and state apparatuses is highlighted by Deleuze himself; Deleuze 1995a: 31.
21. Contrary to Pièrre Clastres, Deleuze and Guattari claim that the idea of a society without a state is an 'ethnological dream' (ATP 429).
22. I would like to thank the editors for their remarks, Nathan Widder for his deep and insightful reading and feedback on an earlier version, and Gavin Rae for helping me throughout the whole process of designing and writing this chapter.

Chapter 12

1227: Treatise on Nomadology – The War Machine

Paul Patton

Introduction: one or many concepts

Deleuze and Guattari defined philosophy as the invention of concepts and, as Deleuze commented in an interview, this is what he and Guattari tried to do in *Anti-Oedipus* and *A Thousand Plateaus*: 'especially in *A Thousand Plateaus*, which is a long book putting forward many concepts' (Deleuze 1995a: 136). Several concepts are on display in Plateau Twelve, '1227: Treatise on Nomadology – The War Machine', although exactly how many and how these are related is far from clear. The title of the plateau suggests that it concerns two interrelated concepts, a concept of the nomad or the nomadic and a concept of the war machine. However, it is not obvious that these are in fact two distinct concepts rather than two faces of one and the same concept viewed from a different angle. At times in the course of the plateau the two terms appear to be used interchangeably, or combined in the phrase 'nomad war machine'.

The title suggests that 'nomad' is the more encompassing concept, in the sense that nomadology or the study of the nomadic includes the war machine as a particular case. Such a relationship of inclusion is expressed in Axiom II, according to which 'the war machine is the invention of the nomads' (ATP 380). However, this apparently simple claim only raises further perplexing questions. The plateau makes it clear that neither war machines nor nomads are simply empirical phenomena. Rather, they are abstract machines or processes that can be expressed in different ontological fields (the social, the natural sciences, images of thought, and so on). What then does it mean to say that nomads 'invented' the war machine? This question is complicated further by Deleuze and Guattari's recapitulation of the war machine hypothesis towards the end of Plateau Twelve, where they assert that the war machine has 'many varied meanings' and that it is not something that can be 'uniformly defined' (ATP 422). In particular, in its manifestation in the social field, it is a concept with two distinct 'poles'. The first, the state-inflected war machine, includes those forms of nomad war machine that have embarked upon war against particular states, or those forms of war machine that have been captured by a state and are included among the apparatuses of government. The appropriation of war machines by states and the integration of nomads into the state has been 'a vector traversing nomadism from the very beginning, from the first act of war against the State' (ATP 420). Deleuze and Guattari recount some of the many ways in which throughout history particular states appropriated a war machine, from the 'encastment' of a pre-existing war machine to appropriation proper in the form of a citizen army or a professional military force.

The second pole of the war machine is completely external and unrelated to forms of state. Its primary object is not war but 'the drawing of a creative line of flight, the composition of a smooth space and of the movement of people in that space' (ATP 422). Understood in these terms, the war machine has only an indirect or supplementary relation to war, in contrast to the state-inflected war machine that has war as its object. This is a pure Idea or rather 'the content adequate to the Idea' of an abstract machine that is realised in forms of nomadism, so long as nomadism itself is understood as an abstraction, 'an idea, something real and nonactual' (ATP 420). On this basis, Deleuze and Guattari suggest that a political, scientific or artistic movement can be a potential war machine, precisely to the extent that it draws a plane of consistency in relation to a political, scientific or artistic tradition, a creative line of flight, or a smooth space of displacement. Importantly, they add that 'it is not the nomad who defines this constellation of characteristics; it is this constellation that defines the nomad, and at the same time the essence of the war machine' (ATP 423). This creative pole is for them the essence of the concept. Deleuze and Guattari's resumé of the hypothesis is explicit in stating that it was this pole of the war machine that was invented by nomads. They advance this claim

> only in the historical interest of demonstrating that this kind of war machine was invented [*dans le souci historique de montrer qu'elle fut inventée comme telle*], even if it displayed from the beginning all of the ambiguity that made it enter into composition with the other pole ... (ATP 422, translation modified)

The fact that this creative pole of the war machine has no necessary relation to nomads or indeed to war raises further questions that will be taken up below. Why, if it has no necessary relation to war, is it called a *war machine*? Why the focus on war rather than on the creative potential or the transformative power of such assemblages?

Over and above the fundamental duality of the concept from the point of view of its relation to war, there is another duality between the nomad war machine as expressed in material and social form and its expression in forms of knowledge and thought. This duality may be traced in the origins of the term 'war machine' in a series of Deleuze's conference presentations and texts from around 1972, with reference to two otherwise disparate concerns. The first was a problem of political organisation that confronted left militants and activists across Europe at this time, namely that of finding new forms of revolutionary organisation that would provide some kind of coordination and control of dispersed struggles while avoiding the kinds of party structure that reproduced an embryonic state apparatus. This problem was invoked in the discussion following Deleuze's presentation of 'Five Propositions on Psychoanalysis' at a conference in Milan in May 1972, where he raises the question of why it is that revolutions have tended to go badly. His answer is that, while they need some kind of central instance or 'war machine' of organisation or control, there has not yet been such a machine that did not reproduce the instances of state repression: 'revolutionary parties have constituted themselves as embryonic State apparatuses, instead of forming war machines irreducible to such apparatuses' (Deleuze 2004a: 280). This is the political problem that interests Deleuze and Guattari at this point: the need to find a new mode of unification whereby all kinds of critical discourses and lines of flight can be grafted on to 'a war machine that won't reproduce a Party or State apparatus' (Deleuze 2004a: 280).

The second problem was one that had preoccupied Deleuze for a longer time: how to characterise a form of mobile and creative thought that did not accord with what he called in *Difference and Repetition* the dominant or 'dogmatic' image of thought in philosophy (Deleuze 1994: 131). This problem reappears in his 'Nomad Thought' presentation to the 'Nietzsche Today' conference held at Cerisy-la-Salle in July 1972, where he suggested that, if Nietzsche does not belong in philosophy, perhaps this is because

> he is the first to conceive of another kind of discourse, a counter-philosophy, in other words, a discourse that is first and foremost nomadic, whose utterances would be produced not by a rational administrative machine – philosophers would be the bureaucrats of pure reason – but by a mobile war machine. (Deleuze 2004a: 259)[1]

In *A Thousand Plateaus*, Proposition III develops a contrast between major or state science and minor or nomad science, while Proposition IV outlines a non-state modality of philosophical thought. The distinction between nomad and state thought responds to the problem of whether it is possible to extricate thought from the state model. The affirmative answer refers back to the concept that Deleuze first sketched in 'Nomad Thought'. This involves a form of thought radically external to the state model of thought understood as capture and constitution of a conceptual interiority. If the state model corresponds to what Deleuze earlier called the 'dogmatic' image of thought, then nomad thought is a paradoxical form of thought without image (Holland 2013: 46).

The dual purpose of the war machine concept as a response to a problem of political organisation and a response to a philosophical problem about the nature of thought raises a further question: how successful was the war machine concept as it appeared in *A Thousand Plateaus* in responding to these two problems? Was it an effective means to think a new kind of political organisation and, at the same time, a non-dogmatic, rhizomatic and creative form of thought that did not conform to the traditional image of thought?

Nomads, war machines and smooth space

The thesis that the creative pole of the war machine was the invention of nomads is presented as one axiom alongside other axioms, problems and propositions that make up the 'Treatise on Nomadology'. Plateau Twelve outlines a series of defining characteristics of the war machine by means of Propositions I to IX. Some of these are presented as following from axioms, while others are presented in the form of responses to problems. Although the mode of presentation suggests a rigorous axiomatic structure along the lines of Spinoza's *Ethics*, this form of organisation is more like a playful parody than a genuine attempt at rigour.[2] There is no systematic deduction of propositions from axioms or prior propositions and no reason to suppose that this series of axioms, problems and resultant propositions is either definitive or closed.

Axiom II asserts the relationship of dependence between the war machine and the nomads who invented it, while Propositions V to VIII identify different 'aspects' of both the war machine and nomadic existence, thereby apparently defining the war machine by reference to features of nomadic social and military organisation. These include a relation to smooth space, to a certain kind of numerical organisation, to affects and to metallurgy. Axiom III effectively collapses the two concepts of nomad and war machine into one by asserting that the nomad war machine is a form of expression of which itinerant metallurgy is the form of content. Finally,

Proposition IX affirms a purely contingent relationship between the war machine and war, asserting that the war machine does not necessarily have war as its object but rather the constitution of smooth space: the sole objective of the war machine is the composition of a nomadic people capable of occupying smooth space. It is only when war machines encounter cities, states or other forces of striation that oppose their innermost tendency, the propagation of smooth space, that they adopt war as the means to annihilate such forces. It is at this point that the war machine oscillates towards the other pole of the concept and embraces war. Henceforth, its sole aim is to 'annihilate the forces of the state, destroy the State-form' (ATP 417).

The most important feature that is common to nomadic societies and war machine assemblages is a relation to smooth as opposed to striated space. Striated space is bounded by enclosures and divided by fixed paths in determinate directions. It is produced by forms of state: 'One of the fundamental tasks of the State is to striate the space over which it reigns' (ATP 385). By contrast, nomadic space is a pure surface for mobile existence, without enclosures or fixed patterns of distribution. Whereas the trajectory of inhabitants of striated space 'parcels out' the space to people, 'assigning each person a share and regulating the communication between shares', the nomadic trajectory does something different: 'it *distributes people (or animals) in an open space,* one that is indefinite and noncommunicating' (ATP 380). Although nomads display different patterns of movement to those found in sedentary, migrant or transhumant peoples, it is the relation to smooth space that defines them: 'The nomad distributes himself in a smooth space; he occupies, inhabits, holds that space; that is his territorial principle' (ATP 381).

Neither nomads nor war machines are simply inhabitants or occupants of smooth space: they are active agents who smooth existing spaces. Deleuze and Guattari insist that 'the nomads make the desert no less than they are made by it. They are vectors of deterritorialisation' (ATP 382). So too with the war machine that

> was the invention of the nomad, because it is in its essence the constitutive element of smooth space, the occupation of this space, displacement within this space, and the corresponding composition of people: this is its sole and veritable positive object (*nomos*). (ATP 417)

Other principles of nomadic existence invoked under Axiom II include a constitutive relation to speed, which is intensive, as opposed to movement, which is extensive. Deleuze and Guattari assert, as a matter of convention (in effect, another axiom), that 'only nomads have absolute movement, in other words speed: vortical or swirling movement is an essential feature of their war machine' (ATP 381). Vortical or swirling movement is also a feature of the 'hydraulic' conception of matter identified by Michel Serres in the atomism of Democritus and Lucretius.³ This model

> operates in an open space throughout which things-flows are distributed, rather than plotting out a closed space for linear and solid things. It is the difference between a *smooth* (vectorial, projective, or topological) space and a *striated* (metric) space: in the first case 'space is occupied without being counted', and in the second case 'space is counted in order to be occupied'. (ATP 361–2)

As this example suggests, nomad science shares with nomadism as a social phenomenon a defining relationship to smooth space. It develops in diverse fields a hydraulic, heterogeneous and problematic form of knowledge that is 'bound up in an essential way with the war machine' (ATP 362). The difference between nomad and state sciences then reappears in a variety of different historical moments such as the mathematical techniques employed in the construction of Gothic cathedrals in the twelfth century or bridges in France in the eighteenth and nineteenth centuries. This difference touches on many of the characteristics that define the nomad war machine alongside the relation to smooth space. It is as though nomad sciences resulted from the projection of the characteristics of the war machine into the ontologically distinct realm of abstract knowledge. That is also to say that the war machine is by definition an abstract machine, prior to the distinction between the different attributes of being such as thought, matter or the social field.

Real or stipulative nomads?

From the outset of the discussion of nomad or smooth space, it is apparent that the concept is not derived from the empirical study of nomadic ways of life but rather from mathematical and philosophical sources. Deleuze and Guattari relate the idea of a distribution of people or animals in an open space to the original sense of the Greek *nomos*, which referred to a special kind of distribution in a space 'without borders or enclosure' (ATP 380).⁴ The concept of a space that is indefinite and non-communicating is elaborated in Plateau Fourteen, '1440: The Smooth and the Striated', with reference to the mathematical conception of space developed by Bernhard Riemann. This is a conception of space as a kind of patchwork of local spaces without a homogeneous overall frame, in which the linkages between adjacent spaces can be effected in an infinite number of ways (ATP 485; see also Plotnitsky 2005).

Deleuze and Guattari draw upon anthropological and other accounts of nomadic peoples in order to provide illustrations of nomadic people's distinctive relation to the spatial and geographical environment in which they live, whether desert, arctic or oceanic: their sources include Pierre Hubac's *Les nomades* (1948), José Emperaire's *Les nomades de la mer* (1954), Wilfrid Thesiger's *Arabian Sands* (1959) and Edmund Carpenter's *Eskimo* (1959). In the same manner, they draw on historical sources for the characterisation of the social and military organisation of the nomadic peoples who conquered much of Central Asia and parts of Western Europe: among others, Arnold Toynbee's *A Study of History* (1947), Boris Iakovlevich Vladimirtsov's *Le régime social des Mongols: Le féodalisme nomade*, (1948), René Grousset's *The Empire of the Steppes* (1970) and the anonymous *The Secret History of the Mongols* (1937). However, this empirical material is not the source of Deleuze and Guattari's concepts. The war machine is an abstract assemblage, not to be confused with any concrete social, much less military, apparatus. Similarly, Deleuze and Guattari's nomads are virtual or conceptual objects whose features are settled not by observation, but by definition. As they suggest at the outset of their discussion of the spatiality of nomadic existence: 'the question is what in nomad life is a principle and what is only a consequence' (ATP 380). In terms of the machinic conception of history presented in *A Thousand Plateaus*, historical war machines such as the organisation and equipment of the Mongols are the expression of abstract machines that 'coexist' alongside other machines such as the state machine of capture (ATP 437). In this sense, actual states express apparatuses of capture and particular nomadic societies are expressions of war machinic assemblages, some more so than others. There is no doubt, Deleuze and Guattari suggest, that 'the war machine is realised more completely in the "barbaric" assemblages of nomadic warriors than in the "savage" assemblages of primitive societies' (ATP 359).

Even though the references to real nomads, their history and culture are interspersed with mythological, literary and philosophical sources, along with material from the history of science, Deleuze and Guattari's use of historical examples and ethnographic or quasi-ethnographic accounts of nomad life misleads some readers into supposing that they are engaged in a form of empirical social science. The question of the representational status of Deleuze and Guattari's concept of nomadism lies at the heart of an exchange between Christopher Miller and Eugene Holland.[5] In an influential article, Miller argued that their reliance upon anthropological sources committed them to an 'anthropological referentiality' and that their characterisation of nomadism was corrupted by the primitivism and colonialism of the anthropological sources on which they relied (Miller 1993). In response, Holland noted their insistence that philosophy is not representational, and suggested that the key issue is how they can 'draw upon ethnographic and anthropological sources without representing actual people' (Holland 2003a: 163).

In turn, Miller reiterated his earlier claim that their philosophical concept of nomadism was 'derived from' real nomads and that, as a result, the 'taint of mortal representation remains in *A Thousand Plateaus*' (Miller 2003: 136). However, this criticism is only effective to the extent that Deleuze and Guattari's concept is in some way beholden to truths about real nomads. It is not. The empirical claims made about nomadic existence serve only to demonstrate certain characteristics of the abstract machine that defines nomadism and the war machine such as the relation to smooth space, number, weapons, affects and forms of decoration.

Nomadism and war machinic processes

Proposition VI identifies a certain kind of relation to number and the organisation of people into numerical units as a further defining characteristic of war machinic assemblages and nomadic societies. Deleuze and Guattari suggest that the numerical organisation that has become standard in state and non-state military assemblages came from nomadic peoples and that it involves two complementary operations: first the organisation of people into numerical groups, and second the extraction from those groups of a select number of individuals who then form a special numerical body:

> We believe that this is not an accidental phenomenon but rather an essential constituent of the war machine, a necessary operation for the autonomy of the number: the number of the body must have as its correlate a body of the number. (ATP 391–2)

This special body takes a variety of forms, such as a privileged tribe as in the case of Moses and the Levites, or the firstborn of members of the original groups who then become hostages, as in the case of Genghis Khan's organisation of the Mongols, or the diverse forms of military slavery imposed upon foreigners or members of another religion. In modern armies, there is an echo of this process in the elite fighting units that protect the state against its enemies, including terrorism and the threat of revolt among its ordinary soldiers.

Here too, it is not the historical examples of numerical organisation among nomadic peoples that drives the construction of the concept but an underlying conception of number as directional and dynamic rather than dimensional or metric, which they call 'numbering number'. This implies a form of autonomous arithmetic organisation that appears when things are distributed in space rather than space itself being distributed or divided in some way:

> The number becomes a subject. The independence of the number in relation to space is a result not of abstraction but of the concrete nature of smooth space, which is occupied without itself being counted. The number is no longer a means of counting or measuring but of moving: it is the number itself that moves through smooth space. (ATP 389)

Proposition VII outlines a diverse set of characteristics of both nomadism and war machines. First, a distinction is drawn between weapons and tools that relates the differences between them to the nature of the assemblages to which they belong: weapons are associated with war machines and tools with sedentary work assemblages. In themselves, 'Weapons and tools are consequences, nothing but consequences' (ATP 398). Understood in these terms, there are no intrinsic characteristics that define weapons as opposed to tools, only tendential differences imposed by the assemblages to which they belong. The same physical object such as an axe may serve either as a tool or a weapon. The same animal such as a horse or elephant may function as an element of a war machine that imparts speed or projects force, or as an element of a work machine that transports materials or ploughs the earth. Weapons and tools both involve the application of force, but it is not the same mode of application in each case: weapons are projective, tools are introceptive. Tools involve an expenditure of force as work, confronting resistance and being consumed in the process, whereas weapons involve the exercise of force according to a model of free action where this does not aim at overcoming a resistance so much as impelling the weapon in such a manner that it creates and occupies a smooth space (ATP 397).

Secondly, this section discusses the different kinds of passion mobilised in assemblages of war and work, where 'passions are effectuations of desire that differ according to the assemblage: it is not the same justice or the same cruelty, the same pity, etc.' (ATP 399). Deleuze and Guattari suggest that there is a passional regime of 'feeling' (*sentiment*) associated with work assemblages, in contrast to the passional regime of 'affects' (*affects*) associated with war machine assemblages. Mythology, along with literary sources such as Kleist and various forms of martial art, all point to a relationship of equivalence or interchangeability such that 'Weapons are affects and affects weapons' (ATP 400).

Thirdly, there is a parallel relationship between, on the one hand, work assemblages, tools and signs, especially writing, and on the other hand, nomad war machines, weapons and jewellery, metalwork and other forms of ornamentation attached to, for example, 'the horse's harness, the sheath of the sword, the warrior's garments' (ATP 401). Work, tools and writing are all bound up with forms of state, since in order for there to be work as opposed to free activity 'there must be a capture of activity by the

State apparatus, and a semiotisation of activity by writing' (ATP 401). Jewellery, ornamentation and weapons on the other hand are bound up with nomad war machines. Deleuze and Guattari summarise the argument underneath this proposition by listing the differential traits that distinguish weapons and tools according to whether they form part of a war machine or work assemblage: directionality (projection rather than introception), vector (speed rather than gravity), model of activity (free action rather than work), expression (jewellery rather than signs) and the kind of passion (affect rather than feeling). These disparate characteristics are summed up in the elliptical and composite Proposition VII, which affirms that 'Nomad existence has for "affects" the weapons of a war machine' (ATP 394).

State and war machine

The numbered series of propositions that make up Plateau Twelve continues into Plateau Thirteen, '7000 BC: Apparatus of Capture', which is arranged under Propositions X to XIV although without introducing any additional axioms or problems. Does this imply that the concepts of state and capture also belong to the 'Treatise on Nomadology'? In effect, they are already included to the extent that the initial propositions about the war machine define it by reference to its 'exteriority' in relation to forms of state. Axiom 1 asserts the exteriority of the war machine to the state, while Propositions I to IV assert that this exteriority is 'attested to' by a range of mythological, literary, anthropological, scientific and philosophical sources. The argument for and illustration of the 'exteriority' of the war machine to the state takes up much of the first half of Plateau Twelve. Deleuze and Guattari draw upon these diverse cultural sources to support the idea that there is a fundamental and irreducible difference between states and war machines: 'In every respect, the war machine is of another species, another nature, another origin than the State apparatus' (ATP 352). George Dumézil's study of Indo-European mythology shows that the gods of war do not appear on the same level as those that represent the twin poles of political sovereignty: the magician and the jurist, the despot and legislator (Dumézil 1988). Roman mythology and Shakespearean drama alike present the man of war in a negative light, characterised by his propensity to betray everything and everyone: rulers, laws of God and war, and women. Such negative portrayals of warriors or men of war, like the mistrust that states often have towards their own military forces, are indications of the profound difference between sovereign power and the power of war.

The thesis of the exteriority of the war machine to the state contradicts the Nietzschean hypothesis invoked in *Anti-Oedipus* according to which states originated in the subjugation of a formless people by 'a conqueror and master race . . . organised for war and with the ability to organise'.[6] On the contrary, Deleuze and Guattari argue in *A Thousand Plateaus*, the state in and of itself does not involve a power of waging war: '*The State has no war machine of its own*; it can only appropriate one in the form of a military institution' (ATP 355). The state is an apparatus of capture characterised by a '*power of appropriation*' whose essential operations include, besides capture, the 'policing' of the field of interiority that results (ATP 437). Not only is there no intrinsic relationship between states and war, the oldest forms of state 'do not even seem to have had a war machine' (ATP 417).

Conversely, there is evidence to suggest that in some nomadic societies the conduct of war was a means to prevent the formation of the stable relationships and institutions that might form the basis of state power. Deleuze and Guattari point to anthropological studies such as Pierre Clastres's *Society Against the State* (1989) and Jacques Meunier's *Les gamins de Bogotà* (1977) in support of the idea that some primitive societies and social groups have mechanisms that actively prevent the emergence of a state (ATP 357–8). Clastres's work is invoked again in Plateau Thirteen for its criticism of evolutionary accounts of the emergence of the state from so-called primitive forms of society. Deleuze and Guattari go further by criticising the tendency of Clastres and other ethnologists to ignore the archaeological evidence of ancient empires. They insist that there have always been states coexisting alongside forms of nomadic war machine (ATP 429–30). Nomadism is not an earlier stage of social evolution that preceded sedentary societies but rather 'a movement, a becoming that affects sedentaries, just as sedentarisation is a stoppage that settles nomads' (ATP 430).[7]

This points to the underlying character of the state and war machine as machinic processes. The state is defined by the process of capture whereas the war machine is defined by a process or *power of metamorphosis* (ATP 437). History, for Deleuze and Guattari, is simply the translation of these coexistent becomings into a succession (ATP 430). However, this translation also complicates the empirical exteriority of state and war machine by producing hybrid forms. On the basis of their thesis of the essential bipolarity of the social war machine and its propensity to be appropriated by forms of state, Deleuze and Guattari outline a historical account of the modern evolution of military organisation and technology under the influence of its interaction with capitalism. They suggest that the adoption by modern states of the principle of total war against enemy states and their populations, in combination with massive investments of capital in military institutions and equipment, produced an immense, worldwide war machine of which individual states are no longer anything more than 'the opposable or apposed parts' (ATP 421). This complex configuration appeared first in the form of fascism, with its subordination of the state to the aim of pure war to the point that it becomes suicidal. It then appeared in the form of a worldwide war machine whereby states are 'no more than objects or means adapted to that machine' (ATP 421). Deleuze and Guattari suggest that the global axiomatic of capitalism is bound up with the state-appropriated power of war to the degree that

> the depreciation of existing capital and the formation of new capital assume a rhythm and scale that *necessarily take the route of a war machine* now incarnated in the [financial, industrial and military, technological] complexes. (ATP 466, my emphasis)

They follow Paul Virilio's 'apocalyptic or millenarian' conception of the present as one in which the worldwide war machine now finds its object not in the conduct of war but in the maintenance of an 'absolute peace' of terror or deterrence directed at an 'unspecified enemy'. As well as the economic function served by the 'capitalisation' of value in the form of military technology, this worldwide war machine promotes a new conception of security as 'materialised war, as organised insecurity or molecularised, distributed, programmed catastrophe' (ATP 467).[8] However plausible this scenario may have seemed in the geopolitical circumstances of the Cold War towards the end of the 1970s, it is less convincing in the aftermath of the collapse of the Soviet Union, the rise of China and the re-emergence of archaic war machines fuelled by religious extremism. Far from a situation of absolute peace, the early twenty-first century has seen the proliferation of so-called asymmetric conflicts between military and paramilitary forces along with the threat of major conflicts between states.

War machines, nomad thought and the ambivalent relation to war: why *war* machine?

The irreducible difference between war machines and states allows Deleuze and Guattari to suggest that all forms of opposition to states and to the state-inflected worldwide war machine rely on the invention or constitution of new forms of nomadic war machine:

> each time there is an operation against the State – insubordination, rioting, guerrilla warfare, or revolution as act – it can be said that a war machine has

> revived, that a new nomadic potential has appeared, accompanied by the reconstitution of a smooth space or a manner of being in space as though it were smooth. (ATP 386)

As we saw at the outset, this nomadic potential is the 'essence' of the war machine concept. The fundamental tendency of the war machine is not war but creative displacement, deterritorialisation and the propagation of smooth spaces in which new connections between different forces are possible. At the same time, Deleuze and Guattari suggest, this creative pole of the war machine can and does lead to war, 'but as its supplementary or synthetic object, now directed against the State and against the worldwide axiomatic expressed by States' (ATP 422).

The differences between war machinic processes and forms of state are fundamental. They are also formal. As an apparatus of capture, the state has a certain 'unity of composition' across all its historically variant forms (ATP 360, 427). All states involve the constitution of a milieu of interiority and a centre of appropriation, some thing or some one that appropriates: emperor, monarch, landowner or capitalist entrepreneur. By contrast, war machinic assemblages are 'assemblages of metamorphosis' (ATP 402). As such, defined by their power of metamorphosis, they are inherently plural. The war machine's exteriority to the state is such that

> it exists only in its own metamorphoses; it exists in an industrial innovation as well as in a technological invention; in a commercial circuit as well as in a religious creation, in all flows and currents that only secondarily allow themselves to be appropriated by the State. (ATP 360)

In other words, the war machine is not only a machine of metamorphosis, one that engenders change, it is also a metamorphic machine, one that exists only in multiple and diverse forms. It is not only fundamentally different from the state, in all respects 'of another species, another nature, another origin', it is fundamentally different from itself (ATP 352). The war machine is not only external to the state but external to itself; it is 'a pure form of exteriority' (ATP 354). As such, it is a paradoxical object that is at once identical to and different from itself. The war machine is not the kind of thing of which there can be a concept in the traditional sense of the term, involving a series of features or marks that will determine necessary and sufficient conditions for something to be a machinic process of this kind. Such a differential and essentially plural object is incapable of being captured in a stable concept of this kind. Hence the need to define it by reference to externalities such as the nomads who invented it, or the relations to space, number, technology and affects that distinguish nomadic from sedentary forms of life.

Thinking an object of this kind poses a problem for thought, since as Deleuze and Guattari suggest, this has traditionally been understood in terms of a model borrowed from the state: there is an image of thought that is 'like the State-form developed in thought' (ATP 374). This state-centric conception of thought will be one that aspires to capture phenomena via the constitution of an interiority in thought. It is incapable of thinking a differential object such as the war machine since, as they note, 'it is not enough to affirm that the war machine is external to the apparatus, the war machine must be thought as itself a pure form of exteriority' (ATP 354, translation modified). The solution to this problem calls for another, non-state style of thought. In effect, it calls for 'nomad' thought: a mode of thinking that does not ally itself with a universal thinking subject but with a singular 'race', and that does not ground itself in a totality but is deployed 'in a horizonless milieu that is a smooth space' (ATP 379). This is the style of rhizomatic or nomad thought practised in *A Thousand Plateaus*. It delineates its objects not by conceptual capture but by following paths of conceptual variation. This explains the mode of specification of the war machine that is both differential and deferential (in Derrida's sense of the term), proceeding via an open-ended series of further terms: smooth space, numbering number, free action, affect, non-signifying ornamentation and so on. In this manner the war machine concept is defined by retracing a line of continuous conceptual variation through the various kinds of content addressed in this plateau (Patton 2010: 32–4).

Considered in this light, war machines are not confined to the kinds of assemblage found in nomadic or warrior societies, or indeed to those that have any connection to war. As we saw above, an ideological, scientific or artistic movement can be a potential war machine. The jurisprudential invention of a new form of legal title to land can amount to a war machine against a particular legal apparatus of capture (Patton 2000: 125–31). However, the insistence that it is not war but metamorphosis that is the essence of the war machine only intensifies the strangeness of the concept. How can there be an 'essence' to something that must be thought as a pure exteriority? Why the focus on war? Why choose the violence of war and the characteristics of the warrior as the means to conceptualise whatever is antithetical and opposed to apparatuses of capture?

One possible answer to the question why Deleuze and Guattari chose to name this machine of pure exteriority the war machine might be that, historically, it has been social and military assemblages of the nomad war machine type that have been the most devastating enemies of states. The history of opposition to forms of state has long been a history of warfare, complicated by the fact that states have appropriated forms of war machine to defend themselves, not only against other states but against their internal as well as external nomadic enemies. Modern revolutionary movements have also pursued their opposition to forms of state by military means, sometimes in the form of clandestine or guerrilla warfare. However, this history does not imply that present or future challenges will continue to take military or paramilitary form. Whatever the historical relationship between nomads, war machines and war, these do not exhaust the potential metamorphoses of this abstract machine of exteriority.

Understood in this manner, Deleuze and Guattari's reliance on the war machine concept as a means to think forms of opposition to states that do not themselves reproduce a state apparatus parallels Nietzsche's reliance on the concept of will to power as a means to think life as a perpetual process of self-overcoming. Their comment that the war machine 'comprises something other than increasing quantities of force' alludes to Nietzsche's qualitative and transformative conception of power that is expressed in the destruction of a given body or form of life and its transformation into something else, as opposed to the simple maintenance or increase in the power of a given body or form of life (ATP 422).[9] In its most primitive forms, Nietzsche admits, the will to power is inseparable from 'appropriation, injury, overpowering of the strange and weaker, suppression, severity, imposition of one's own forms, incorporation and, at the least and mildest, exploitation . . .' (Nietzsche 2001: 259). Nevertheless, despite the fact that the will to power for a long time was manifest in forms of bloody confrontation with others or with oneself, it has become increasingly refined in the course of cultural development so that it can now be satisfied by artistic, intellectual or social activities that have no relation to bloodshed or physical pain. Deleuze and Guattari's war machine might be supposed to have undergone a similar evolution:

> Could it be that it is at the moment the war machine ceases to exist, conquered by the State, that it displays to the utmost its irreducibility, that it scatters into thinking, loving, dying, or creating machines that have at their disposal vital or revolutionary powers capable of challenging the conquering State? (ATP 356)

However, there is a significant difference between their concept and Nietzsche's. While it is not implausible to think of power in terms of transformation and metamorphosis, the usefulness of Deleuze and Guattari's war machine concept as a means to think novel forms of social and political creativity is not helped by the reference to war. Deleuze and Guattari's bi-polar concept of the war machine amounts to an effort to combine in one concept the power of metamorphosis and the power that is expressed in the conflict of forces. The arbitrariness of this conceptual combination is nowhere more clearly apparent than in their cavalier treatment of Clausewitz's idea of pure or absolute war, which they transform into that of a war machine that does not have war as its object (ATP 420). Clausewitz defines war as 'an act of violence' whose aim is 'the disarming or overthrow of the enemy' (Clausewitz 1982: 101, 104). Deleuze and Guattari retain the distinction between the pure Idea of war and real wars, but then proceed to apply 'a different criterion than that of Clausewitz' and redefine war as the drawing of a creative line of flight and composition of a smooth space (ATP 420).[10]

This suggests another, more conjunctural reason for calling it a war machine. Foucault's 1976 lectures 'Society Must be Defended' drew attention to the popularity in his own thought and in the milieu of the French left more generally of what he called the 'war-repression' conception of power. According to this schema, power is essentially repressive and a matter of struggle or conflict between opposing forces: 'Power is war, the continuation of war by other means' (Foucault 2003: 15). Foucault's lectures were dedicated to the critical examination of this hypothesis, even if he did not propose an alternative conception of power as action on the actions of others until some years later (Patton 2013). Even though they sought to prioritise a qualitative and transformative conception of power, Deleuze and Guattari's war machine concept retained an association with the history of struggles against the repressive power of forms of state. While it may have resonated with the 1970s left milieu that tended to understand power in terms of the war-repression model, this dimension of the war machine concept may also have contributed to its failure to function in hoped-for ways after the publication of *Mille plateaux* in 1980. Deleuze seems to have come to such a view of many of the concepts produced in *A Thousand Plateaus*. In an interview with Didier Eribon, published after his death in 1995 under the title 'I remember (*Je me souviens*)', he spoke about a 'new functionalism' with regard to concepts that was a feature of the milieu in which the book was written. By this he meant the conception of philosophy as the creation of concepts that function in a given social field, in the way that, for example, Foucault's concept of disciplinary society crystallised a series of problems about the nature of power and its operation in modern European societies. In a melancholic comment about the fate of *A Thousand Plateaus*, which he insisted was the best work he ever wrote, Deleuze suggested that it failed to fulfil its critical ambitions by functioning in this way in France after it was published in 1980: 'The book was perhaps too big. And above all, the times had changed' (Deleuze 1995b: 51).

Notes

1. Elsewhere in the presentation he referred to Kafka's writing as a war machine in German against German and, at the end, returned to the problem of finding some form of unity across the various kinds of social struggle without falling back on 'the despotic and bureaucratic organization of the party or State-apparatus: we want a war machine that would not recreate a State apparatus, a nomadic unity in relation with the Outside, that would not recreate the despotic internal unity' (Deleuze 2004a: 254, 260). His preface to Guattari's *Psychoanalysis and Transversality*, published in the same year, also reproduced this dual orientation of the concept, describing the book as a war machine and making the same point about the kind of unification required of a revolutionary group: it must be '*the unification of a war machine and not that of a State apparatus*' (Deleuze 2004a: 199, 203). On the emergence of the term 'war machine' in relation to the problem of revolutionary political organisation, see also Sibertin-Blanc 2013: 74–5; Lundy 2013.
2. Brent Adkins suggests that this structure 'is surprising because it seems at odds with the critique of "royal science" that occurs here and elsewhere in the book. Perhaps it is a tribute to the structure of Spinoza's *Ethics*. Or, perhaps it is a play on their analysis of capitalism . . .' (Adkins 2015: 192).
3. Deleuze and Guattari refer to Serres 2001.
4. In *Difference and Repetition* Deleuze identified a nomadic distribution of being in terms of 'a completely other distribution which must be called nomadic, a nomad *nomos*, without property, enclosure or measure. Here, there is no longer a division of that which is distributed but rather a division among those who distribute *themselves* in an open space – a space which is unlimited, or at least without precise limits' (Deleuze 1994: 36).
5. Miller 1993; Holland 2003a; 2003b. See also Patton 2000: 117–18; 2010: 34–40.
6. Nietzsche 1994: Book II, Section 17. See Deleuze and Guattari 1983: 192–200.
7. In his presentation to the 'Nietzsche Today' conference in 1972, with reference to Kafka's 'Great Wall of China' and the emergence of Asiatic empires, Deleuze emphasises the difference between the ways in which primitive communities are caught up in the machinery of empire, and the ways in which, on the periphery, they embark on another kind of adventure, displaying another, nomadic kind of unity. 'They enter into a nomadic war machine and become decoded rather than overcoded. Entire groups take off on a nomadic adventure. Archaeologists have taught us to consider nomadism not as an originary state, but as an adventure that erupts in sedentary groups: the call of the outside, movement. The nomad and his war machine confronts the despot and his administrative machine; extrinsic nomadic unity confronts intrinsic despotic unity. And yet they are so interrelated or interdependent that the problem of the despot will be to integrate, internalise the nomadic war machine, while that of the nomad will be to invent an administration for his conquered empire. They ceaselessly oppose one another to the point of indistinguishability' (Deleuze 2004a: 259, translation modified).
8. Deleuze and Guattari refer to Virilio 1976; 1990; 2006.
9. On the priority of this qualitative conception of power in Nietzsche, see Patton 2001: 105–6.
10. Julian Reid attempts to find some justification for this redefinition of war in Clausewitz's comments on the elements of war, in particular the role of chance. See Reid 2003: 67–71.

Chapter 13

7000 BC: Apparatus of Capture

Daniel W. Smith

I

The 'Apparatus of Capture' plateau expands and alters the theory of the state presented in the third chapter of *Anti-Oedipus*, while at the same time providing a final overview of the sociopolitical philosophy developed throughout *Capitalism and Schizophrenia*. It develops a series of challenging theses about the state, the first and most general of which is a thesis against social evolution: the state did not and could not have evolved out of 'primitive' hunter-gatherer societies. The idea that human societies progressively evolve took on perhaps its best-known form in Lewis Henry Morgan's 1877 book, *Ancient Society; Or: Researches in the Lines of Human Progress from Savagery through Barbarism to Civilization* (Morgan 1877; Carneiro 2003), which had a profound influence on nineteenth-century thinkers, especially Marx and Engels. Although the title of the third chapter of *Anti-Oedipus* – 'Savages, Barbarians, Civilized Men' – is derived from Morgan's book, the universal history developed in *Capitalism and Schizophrenia* is directed *against* conceptions of linear (or even multilinear) social evolution. Deleuze and Guattari are not denying social change, but they are arguing that we cannot understand social change unless we see it as taking place within a *field of coexistence*.

Deleuze and Guattari's second thesis is a correlate of the first: if the state does not evolve from other social formations, it is because it *creates its own conditions* (ATP 446). Deleuze and Guattari's theory of the state begins with a consideration of the nature of ancient despotic states, such as Egypt or Babylon. What was the origin of such empires? And how did they acquire their astonishing dominance? Marx proposed a famous answer to the second question: the archaic state is a milieu of interiority that stockpiles the surplus production of the surrounding agricultural communities, constituting a transcendent public power that converges on the person of the despot (Marx 1965: 69–70; cf. Deleuze and Guattari 1983: 194). In the archaic state, primitive codes, with their lineages and territories, are allowed to subsist, but they are overcoded by the state and taken up into its eminent unity. The despotic state is literally a mega-machine, in Lewis Mumford's terms, in which human beings function as its working parts in a kind of 'generalised enslavement' (ATP 456–7). The machine is constructed like a pyramid, with the agricultural communities at its base, the despot at its apex, and a vast bureaucracy in between.

Anti-Oedipus had proposed the term 'overcoding' to describe the basic mechanism of the archaic mega-machine: the coded filiations and alliances of primitive societies are overcoded by a new alliance (of the people with the despot) and a direct filiation (of the despot with his deity) (Deleuze and Guattari 1983: 192, 205). The concept of capture introduced in *A Thousand Plateaus* is meant to provide a more detailed account of the way in which overcoding works. The state is a transcendent 'apparatus of capture' that incorporates everything into its form of interiority through three primary mechanisms – rent, labour and money – which are a variant of the 'trinity formula' analysed by Marx (Marx 1981: 953), and operate through two interrelated operations: *direct comparison* in the form of abstract quantities, and *monopolistic appropriation* in the form of stock.

Ground rent. Rent is a mechanism of capture that incorporates land, or the 'earth', into the state apparatus. But the earth is not a given; if we understand the earth as an abstract general space – the *geo* in geometry, and not the more general notion of Earth [*terre*] sometimes employed by Deleuze and Guattari – we must say that this abstract and striated space was *created* by the apparatus of capture. 'Before' the earth, the land was occupied or territorialised without being measured or divided: there were only the shifting territories of primitive societies (or the smooth spaces occupied by nomadic societies). The genius of the state, in creating the concept of the earth, is to insist that these territories and their occupation coexist in a general and abstract space, a space that belongs to the despot. In turn, it is the constitution of this indeterminate and abstract space that allowed the earth to be divided and portioned out in plots, which were distributed to officials whose title to the land was entirely dependent on their position in the state bureaucracy. There was no private property: the despot was the sole public-property owner, who maintained control over his officials through the imposition of rent. Even when agricultural communities were permitted a certain autonomy, they were subordinated to the state apparatus through the payment of rent.

Such is the origin of geo-metry: the constitution of the earth (*geo*) and its measurement and striation (*metron*) are coexistent. Every year in Egypt, after the Nile floods, land surveyors or 'rope-stretchers' (*hardenonaptai*) would restriate the land; the Greeks called them, precisely, the 'measurers of the earth' (*geo-meters*) (see Serres 1993). The measurement and striation of the earth was the condition for the extraction of rent and tribute, since rent requires a *direct and quantitative comparison* of yields to be drawn between qualitatively different lands. The worst land bears no rent, but it thereby constitutes the lowest element in a cardinal series that allows the other soils to produce rent in a comparative way (differential rent). Ground rent, as an apparatus of capture, creates the conditions for its own operation: rent requires striation, and striation presupposes the earth as a general space. But in creating the earth, the state at the same time creates the transcendent unity to which the earth is subordinated (the despot). States are often seen as territories centred on the palace-temple complex of a capital city, but more properly one must say that the state 'deterritorialises' the surrounding territories and subordinates them to an imperial centre of convergence located outside and beyond them. Ground rent is thus an apparatus through which the earth is captured and made the object of the state's higher unity.

Labour. Similarly, human activity is appropriated by the state in the form of surplus labour, which is stockpiled in large-scale public works projects (pyramids, irrigation projects). The state thus implies a specific mode of human activity that does not exist elsewhere: labour. In primitive societies, strictly speaking, people do not 'work', even if their activities are highly constrained and regulated. Deleuze, following Martial Gueroult, calls this non-labour mode of activity *free action*, which is in continuous variation: one passes from speech to action, from a given action to another, from action to song, from song to speech, from speech to enterprise, 'all in a strange chromaticism with intense but rare peak moments or moments of effort' (ATP 491; Gueroult 1934: 119ff.).

For labour to exist, there must be a *capture* of such human activity by the state apparatus: it is only in the state that activity comes to be compared, linked and subordinated to a common and homogeneous quantity called 'labour'. (This development reached its apex in the nineteenth century with Taylorism and Fordism.) For this reason, 'labour' and 'surplus labour' cannot be said to be independent, as if there were first a necessary labour, and then beyond that a surplus labour. *Labour and surplus labour are strictly the same thing*, and all labour implies surplus labour. The term 'labour' simply applies to the quantitative comparison of activities, a striation of the space-time of human activity, while 'surplus labour' refers to the monopolistic appropriation of labour by the state. The Egyptian pyramids were not constructed by slaves but by conscripted Egyptian labour, and as such they constitute a form of stockpiled activity. In other words, it is surplus labour that constitutes labour as a new mode of activity in the state. There is no labour outside of the state apparatus, and human activity is transformed into labour only in relation to the state.

Money. Finally, just as labour does not exist outside the state, neither does money. Money was not introduced in order to serve the needs of commerce, as if there were first an autonomous domain of 'markets' into which money was introduced to facilitate exchange (Graeber 2011: 44–5). Rather, the converse is the case: money was created by the state to make taxation possible. Money, as an abstract equivalent or unit of account, is an instrument of measure (*metron*) that makes possible a direct comparison between goods and services, which the state can then appropriate in the form of taxes or tribute (Will 1955; Foucault 2013: 133–48; Deleuze and Guattari 1983: 197; ATP 442–3). For this reason, it is money that creates markets, and not vice-versa: the 'economy' presupposes the state. As Litaker observes, money striates space-time through the emergence of markets, which are spaces of commercial exchange that determine the times of production, circulation and consumption (Litaker 2014: 121).

Ground rent, labour and money are the three fundamental aspects of the state's apparatus of capture: ground rent captures the earth, labour captures human activity, and money captures exchange. Put differently, rent, profit and taxation are three forms of *stockpiling*, and each of these mechanisms converges in the person of the despot, who is at once 'the eminent landowner, the entrepreneur of large-scale projects, and the master of taxes and prices' (ATP 444). The apparatus of capture has several distinct characteristics.

First, and most importantly, *the apparatus of capture creates what it captures*. The earth, labour and money are the conditions that make possible rent, surplus-labour (profit) and taxes, but these conditions are themselves created by the state. This is why 'capture' does not simply mean an 'appropriation' of what already exists; both in fact and in principle, the state is only able to capture what it itself creates, or at least what it contributes to creating (ATP 446). The state plays the role of a foundation, but it cannot play this role if it captures what already exists: if something exists before the state, it can exist without the state. For the state to be foundational, *the state must be self-presupposing* (ATP 427), and it is the self-presupposing nature of the state that grounds its monopoly power, its triple possession *in principle* of the totality of the earth, the totality of labour and the totality of money. The monopoly power of the state can be expressed philosophically in several ways: in the language of sufficient reason, *the state is its own ground*; in the language of causality, the state is *causa sui* (Lampert

2011: 157); in the language of Kant, *the state produces its own conditions of possibility* (and thus is in itself unconditioned).

Secondly, the apparatus of capture is primarily a *semiological* process (ATP 445). For Deleuze, every social formation is both a physical system (a manner of occupying space and time) and a 'regime of signs'. In the codes of primitive societies, these signs were inscribed directly on the body in the form of markings (tattoos, circumcisions, incisions, scars, mutilations and so on) that indicated one's inclusion in the social formation – an entire system of 'mnemotechnics' (Deleuze and Guattari 1983: 144–5). If the ancient despotic state was able to overcode these existing codes, it was because it operated with an abstract and externalised semiotics based on numeracy, literacy and money: the development of geometry and arithmetic, the invention of phonetic writing and the issuing of currency. Money is an abstraction that functions as an abstract equivalent for goods and services. Geometry treats the earth as an abstract space in which all places are equivalent. Labour allows for a quantitative and abstract comparison of human activities. Taken together, these three heads of the apparatus of capture create an abstract locus of comparison in which land, goods, services, transactions and human activities are equalised, homogenised, compared, appropriated and stockpiled – all in a single process. In other words, the state operates by abstraction and *is itself an abstraction* (Sibertin-Blanc 2013: 50).

Thirdly, the self-presupposing and abstract nature of the state entails a particular type of *violence*, one that is itself posited as pre-established and pre-accomplished, even if it must be reactivated every day. It is often said that the state has a monopoly on legitimate violence – violence against 'criminals', violence against those who capture something they have no 'right' to capture – which the state self-regulates through the institution of law. But this juridical coding of violence *within* the state takes place within the structural violence *of* the state itself, whose apparatus of capture simultaneously constitutes and presupposes a *right* to capture (ATP 448). The state, as self-presupposing, is itself a kind of originary or primary violence that is always-already present, even if it never actually 'took place' (see Derrida 2002). As such, it is first and foremost in *myth* that the primary violence of the state finds expression, retrojected in an original violence against chaos that, at the limit, never actually occurred, even if it is omnipresent in every mechanism of the state. Hence the appeal to Dumézil's classic analyses of the two poles of sovereignty found in Indo-European myths: the jurist-kings who operate through law and a respect for obligations, but also the terrifying magico-religious sovereign who operates through a *magical capture* that 'binds without combat' (Dumézil 1988: 152; ATP 424–5). The originary violence of the state makes resistance impossible, and it is what gives the state its power (*puissance*): territorial power (monopoly of the earth), economic power (monopoly of labour), monetary power (monopoly of currency) and, ultimately, political power (monopoly of violence).

II

The self-presupposing or self-producing nature of the state leads to a third thesis: *the archaic state had no distinct cause that could explain its 'origin'*. The great archaeologist V. Gordon Childe proposed a well-known theory about the origin of the state (Childe 1951; 2009; cf. Lull and Mico 2011: 180–9): at some point in prehistory, hunter-gatherer groups learned to cultivate grain and raise livestock (the Neolithic revolution), and it was this surplus of agricultural food that is supposed to have made the state possible, with its complex divisions of labour, large economic projects and intricate social organisation (the urban revolution) (ATP 428). In other words, primitive societies eventually reached a threshold in their 'mode of production' that allowed them to pass from an economy of *subsistence* to an economy of *surplus*. Using two complementary arguments, Deleuze and Guattari show that the evidence from archaeology, ethnography and even history does not support this theory.

The first argument comes from the analysis of primitive societies. Pierre Clastres, in his 1974 book *Society Against the State* (Clastres 1989; cf. Clastres 1994), had shown that the absence of a state in primitive societies is not a sign that they were 'backward' societies that had not yet evolved or developed enough. On the contrary, primitive societies are constituted by mechanisms that deliberately *ward off* the apparatus of the state, and actively prevent it from appearing. Clastres identified two such mechanisms: the role of *chiefs*, whose status constantly waxes and wanes, thereby preventing the resonance of power in a single despot; and the function of *war*, which maintained polemical relations of antagonism between segmentary lineages, preventing their convergence in a state apparatus. Clastres had been influenced, in part, by Marshal Sahlins's *Stone Age Economics*, which had shown that hunter-gatherers, far from living at a subsistence level requiring constant toil, were in fact the first affluent society, where the quest for food was intermittent and leisure was abundant (Sahlins 1972; see Clastres 1994). The absence of a surplus did not indicate an inability to develop technical means or overcome environmental obstacles, but was a positive goal, socially valorised. Even the innovations imported by colonialists were utilised, not to increase production but to reduce work time. Sahlins's thesis was anticipated by Marcel Mauss, whose

1925 essay *The Gift* had already shown that the giving of gifts and counter-gifts (potlatch) in primitive societies was a mechanism for warding off the accumulation of wealth (Mauss 1954: 3). In short, anthropologists have identified positive mechanisms in primitive societies that *prevented* the formation of a state apparatus: there is a refusal of the state's apparatus of power as much as a refusal of markets and the economy. Primitive societies, like states, are 'self-validating' (Deleuze and Guattari 1983: 203). If this claim is correct, it makes the appearance of the state even more difficult to explain. How could the state have evolved out of primitive hunter-gatherer societies if these are societies whose very organisation is directed *against* the formation of the state (Sibertin-Blanc 2013: 22)?

The second argument comes from the analysis of the state. The urbanist Jane Jacobs, in the first chapter of her 1969 book *The Economy of Cities*, which is entitled 'Cities First – Rural Development Later', launched an attack on what she called 'the dogma of agricultural primacy' (Jacobs 1970: 3). Jacobs, contentiously, attempted to invert this schema: it is the state that creates agriculture, she argued, and not the converse. She based her conclusions in part on James Mellaart's discovery of Çatalhöyük, a 'proto-town' in Turkey that dates back to Neolithic times (7000 BC – the date given to the thirteenth plateau), and perhaps even further, and which would thus have been in direct contact with hunter-gatherers. Jacobs suggests that it was in such cities that seeds were first gathered, hybridised and finally planted, initially in the soil around the town, and then expanding into the countryside. To explain (and exorcise) the prevalence of the 'agriculture first' dogma, Jacobs draws an analogy with the technologies of electricity (Jacobs 1970: 46). Electricity was invented in cities, yet it is primarily in rural areas that we find the massive installations needed for generating and transmitting electricity: dams, power plants, grids. If human memory did not extend back to a time when the world had cities but no electricity, the archaeological evidence could be interpreted to imply that, initially, there were rural people with no electricity, who then developed dams and power plants, eventually producing a large enough surplus of electricity to make cities possible. We are doing something similar when we claim that an agricultural surplus made the state possible, but the error is clear: we turn the *results* of state activity into a *precondition* for the state.

The French historian Fernand Braudel, in his *Civilization and Capitalism*, took up a modified version of Jacobs's thesis, although he was writing in a different context, analysing the relation between the urban and the rural in fifteenth- to eighteenth-century Europe. Braudel likewise contested the dogma that the countryside 'necessarily preceded the town in time', but argued, not that cities preceded the countryside, but that the two were *reciprocally determined*. 'Jane Jacobs, in a persuasive book, argues that the town appears at least simultaneously with rural settlement, if not before it . . . Town and countryside obeyed the rule of "reciprocity of perspectives": mutual creation, mutual domination, mutual exploitation according to *the unchanging rules of co-existence*' (Braudel 1992: 484, 486: see also Smith, Ur and Feinman 2014: 1532: 'Agriculture and urbanism . . . developed in tandem'). Building on his analysis of the apparatus of capture, Deleuze adopts a variant of Braudel's thesis: not that the state preceded agriculture, but that agriculture and the state were *co-determined*.

> It is the State that creates agriculture, animal raising, and metallurgy; it does so first on its own soil, then imposes them on the surrounding world . . . It is not the State that presupposes a mode of production, it is the State that makes production a 'mode'. The last reasons for presuming a progressive development are invalidated. (ATP 429)

We return to the self-presupposing nature of the state: if the state stocks an agricultural surplus, it is because *it itself creates the conditions that make a surplus possible*.

Deleuze draws on this argument when he assesses Friedrich Engels's famous 1884 book on the *Origin of the Family, Private Property, and the State* (Engels 1972). Engels appealed to several sets of factors to explain the origin of the state: *exogenous* factors, such as the need to organise wars; *endogenous* factors, such as the rise of private property and money; and *specific* factors, such as the emergence of 'public functions' (Deleuze 1979a; cf. ATP 427). But Deleuze shows how each of these factors, far from explaining the emergence of the state, in fact *presuppose* an already-existing state. States can and often do appropriate a war machine for themselves, but such an appropriation presupposes that the state already exists. Similarly, no one has ever indicated a mechanism through which one could move from a communal tribal property to private property, as if one day some exceptional person decided to proclaim, 'This is mine.' On the contrary, archaeology has been able to provide a precise mechanism, assignable if variable, showing how private property was constituted out of a system of imperial public property through *freed slaves* – but this means that the privatisation of property could become a characteristic of the state only if the public property of the archaic state were *already given* (ATP 449, 451). The same is true for the origin of money, which was created not to promote commerce, but for the purposes of taxation, which likewise presupposed an already-existing state. Finally, public functions also presuppose a state: irrigation, for instance, was an agricultural problem that went beyond the capacities of most agricultural communities.

These analyses all point to the same antinomy: on the one hand, the state could not have emerged from the soil of primitive societies, since they are directed *against* the state; on the other hand, the factors typically put forward to explain the emergence of the state (agricultural surplus, the military, private property, money, public works) in fact presuppose an already-existing state. Every explanation of the origin of the state is tautological, presuming what it seeks to explain. How then can we explain the appearance of the state's apparatus of capture, if it was not the result of a progressive evolutionary process, and if it 'leads back to no *distinct* assignable cause' (ATP 427)? Deleuze draws the only possible conclusion: the state appeared in the world fully formed and fully armed, as if it were born an adult, 'a master stroke executed all at once [*coup de maître en une fois*]' (Deleuze and Guattari 1983: 217; cf. ATP 427). But what does it mean to say that the state appeared in the world 'fully formed'?

III

The question of the origin of the state can be posed as both a de facto and a de jure problem. Even if one grants that the state did not evolve from primitive societies, but was a 'master stroke executed all at once', one could still (and legitimately) attempt to search for the first state. Such a search would be complicated by the fact that the criterion for identifying a state or proto-urban formation is *not* a matter of population or size, since 'primitive accumulation' occurs whenever there is an apparatus of capture. 'It is enough for this point of comparison and appropriation to be effectively occupied for the apparatus of capture to function' (ATP 447). But archaeology has continued to push back in time the appearance of the first state, and no doubt it will continue to do so. As Leroi-Gourhan once observed, 'while we may expect to discover evidence of ever older semi-urbanised units going back to the very beginnings of proto-agriculture, the first city will probably never be found' (Leroi-Gourhan 1993: 171). As such, the search for the first state is a kind of *passage to the limit*, and this limit is the point where the question ceases to be a quantitative and de facto question of regression in time, and instead becomes a qualitative and de jure question (ATP 428): the de facto problem of *chronological succession* becomes a de jure problem of *topological coexistence*. If 'the self-sufficiency, autarky, independence, and preexistence of primitive communities is an ethnological dream' (ATP 429), it is because primitive societies and states have always and everywhere coexisted with each other.

The *quid juris* question then becomes that of the relations of coexistence between social formations. Yet if the various social formations analysed in *Capitalism and Schizophrenia* do not represent the *evolutionary stages* of social development, neither can they simply be identified as the *ideal types* of a comparative sociology, despite appearances, since each type functions in a different manner (Silbertin-Blanc 2010b: 114). The concept of the 'primitive', for instance, can be seen as a type whose unity is the *unity of reason*, theoretically subsuming under a single concept a plurality of heterogeneous societies. By contrast, the capitalist type has a unity that is not only theoretical but also historical: it is a *singular universal*, in the sense that it is the result of a historically contingent process that has resulted in the universalisation of its singularity. But Deleuze and Guattari ascribe to the state a unity of a completely different nature: a *real unity* that, whether actualised or virtual, is omnipresent throughout the entire social field, not only in archaic states or modern nation-states, but even in primitive societies 'without a state'.

This brings us to Deleuze and Guattari's fourth thesis: *there has never been but one state*, a thesis that is repeated throughout *Anti-Oedipus* (Deleuze and Guattari 1983: 214, 220, 261) and taken up in *A Thousand Plateaus*. To be sure, Deleuze and Guattari readily admit that in fact there are a plurality of states, and that modern states are very different from the archaic imperial state. But these de facto differences between concrete states find their de jure ground in the ideality of a single state (pluralism = monism), which Deleuze and Guattari call the *Urstaat* (ur- [proto] + *staat* [state]). The *Urstaat* is both a limit-concept and an *Idea*, in the Deleuzian sense. For Deleuze and Guattari, 'the general theory of society is a generalised theory of flows' or *fluxes* (Deleuze and Guattari 1983: 262), and the function of social formations is to *code* these fluxes. The Idea of the *Urstaat*, in turn, lies at the opposite pole of the Idea of a pure flux (schizophrenia): it is the Idea of a completely captured and coded flow, which is 'the eternal model of everything the State wants to be and desires' (Deleuze and Guattari 1983: 217). Thus, the *Urstaat* must not be confused with the archaic imperial state, which simply actualises the *Urstaat* in its 'purest conditions' (Deleuze and Guattari 1983: 198). Rather, the *Urstaat* is 'THE abstraction, which is realised, certainly, in imperial formations ... but takes on its concrete immanent existence in subsequent forms that make it reappear in other figures and under other conditions' (Deleuze and Guattari 1983: 221).

The theory of the *Urstaat* must be read, in part, as Deleuze and Guattari's contribution to the Marxist debates surrounding the status of the 'Asiatic mode of production', which Marx saw as an original mode of production that was reducible to neither the ancient slave mode of production nor the feudal mode of production (see Godelier 1978; Tokei 1979; Anderson 1979). Marx introduced the concept in the *Grundrisse* (Marx 1965: 69–70), referring primarily to India and China, but he abandoned it in *Capital*, and Engels renounced it in *The Origin of the*

Family, Private Property, and the State. During the Stalinist period, it was officially rejected in favour of Marx's theory of five stages (primitive communism, slavery, feudalism, capitalism, socialism) in which the Asiatic mode of production finds no place (Deleuze and Guattari 1983: 219). But the debates never subsided. Is the Asiatic mode of production a weak hypothesis that Marx renounced after his reading of Morgan, as Plekhanov suggested (Plekhanov 1992)? If not, is it an autonomous mode of production? Or simply a 'pseudo-feudal' formation, a transition between the primitive communist mode and the ancient mode of slavery? Or is it the embryonic form of an ancient mode of production that was 'blocked' at a 'phase prior to the evolution of slavery', as Stalin argued, laying down the position that would dominate Soviet Marxism (Stalin 1940)? What Deleuze and Guattari derive from these debates is an extension of the position adopted by Karl Wittfogel in his 1957 book *Oriental Despotism*. Like Trotsky and Bukharin before him, Wittfogel, himself an ambiguous figure (Ulman 1978), likened Stalin to an Eastern potentate and saw his regime as a species of Oriental despotism, embodying the worst aspects of the Asiatic mode of production. In a sense, Deleuze and Guattari agreed: 'We have to go along with Wittfogel when he shows the degree to which modern capitalist and socialist States take on the characteristic features of the primordial despotic State' (Deleuze and Guattari 1983: 229; cf. Deleuze and Guattari 1983: 219n). But they pushed the point further than Wittfogel: they argued that it is not simply modern totalitarian states that resurrect the *Urstaat*; rather, *every* type of state, whether totalitarian or fascist, democratic or capitalist, is a resurrection of the ideal *Urstaat*. '"Asiatic" production, with the State that expresses or constitutes its objective movement, is not a distinct formation; *it is the basic formation*, on the horizon throughout history' (Deleuze and Guattari 1983: 217).

The *Urstaat* addresses several results of Deleuze and Guattari's analysis of the state: the fact that a genesis of the state-form is impossible, since it is self-presupposing and has no 'cause'; the fact that the historical beginnings of the state are unassignable; and finally, the fact that the *Urstaat* cannot be identified with its material manifestations. In one of his few affirmations of Hegelianism, Deleuze writes: 'If there is even one truth in the political philosophy of Hegel, it is that every State carries within itself the essential moments of its existence' (ATP 385; cf. 460). The 'essential' moment is the ideal moment of magical capture, but the *Urstaat* is materialised in a long history of mutations, and as such, it marks the point where the traditional alternative between Hegelian idealism and Marxist materialism becomes undecidable (Sibertin-Blanc 2013: 19, 29). It is for this reason that the *Urstaat* appears to be set back at a remove from what it transects and from what it resects, as though it were giving evidence of another dimension, *a cerebral ideality* [in the Platonic sense] that is superimposed on the material evolution of societies, *a regulating idea* [in the Kantian sense] or principle of reflection (terror) that organises the fluxes into a whole. (Deleuze and Guattari 1983: 219)

But the *Urstaat* is an Idea in the Deleuzian sense: it is an immemorial Idea, *a past that has never been given as such* (second synthesis). If there is but one state, it is because the *Urstaat* is a virtuality or basin of attraction that permeates the entire social field as its foundation or ground (*fondement*), even though it cannot be identified with any of its actualisations.

IV

But the theory of the *Urstaat* confronts an obvious problem with regard to primitive societies. How can one claim that the *Urstaat* is present throughout the social field, even in primitive societies, if such societies actively ward off the state? This leads us to Deleuze and Guattari's fifth thesis: *the Urstaat was active 'before' its existence*. If primitive societies warded off the state, they must have had a 'presentiment' of the state as the actual limit they are avoiding – a limit they could not reach without self-destructing. The manner in which the *Urstaat* is actualised in historical states, in other words, is different from the manner in which the *Urstaat* pre-exists as a warded-off limit in primitive societies. Objectively, Deleuze and Guattari initially explain this phenomenon from a model drawn from physics. If one considers the social field as a field of vectors, one could say that primitive societies are traversed by a centripetal wave that converges on a point x – a point where the wave would cancel itself out and be inverted into a divergent and centrifugal wave, which is a reality of another order (the state) (ATP 565 n.14). The point of convergence marks a *potential* or a *threshold of consistency*, and the convergent wave has the double property of both anticipating it and warding it off. The state is thus 'beyond' primitive groups, but 'beyond' does not mean 'after'. The threshold of consistency has always existed, but it is beyond the limit of primitive societies, which are content to keep that threshold at a distance. We must thus conceptualise the *coexistence* or *contemporaneousness* of these two inverse movements, 'as if the two waves that seem to us to exclude or succeed each other unfolded *simultaneously* in an "archaeological", micropolitical, micrological, molecular field' (ATP 431).

But there is a second issue that comes to the fore here, which is more subjective. Since every exchange of objects requires a way in which one can *compare* the objects of exchange, no political economist can avoid the question, how should one evaluate the criteria of exchange? Responding to this question requires a theory of *collective evaluations*, or what one might call, in a Kantian vein, 'anticipations of social perception' (Deleuze 1979c). In the Marxist theory of labour-value, the way to compare exchanged objects – for instance, an iron axe and a steel axe – is to compare the labour time that is socially necessary for their production, which requires a collective evaluation of both the worker and the entrepreneur using a scientific (or pseudo-scientific) form of quantification. In primitive societies, however, this route is closed off in advance, not because a measure is lacking, but because there is no 'labour time' to be measured. Human activity is in constant variation, and there is nothing that corresponds to labour, much less to labour time.

On this score, Deleuze appeals to the nineteenth-century neoclassical theory of marginalism, which was originally invented to account for the equilibrium of prices within the capitalist regime. If Marx held to the classical theory in which the value of commodities is derived from the quantity of labour required to produce them, marginalists like Stanley Jevons argued that value should instead be analysed in terms of the utility of the 'last' or 'marginal' object (Clarke 1982: 147–50). Business owners know that, beyond a certain limit, the structure of their business will have to change: there are thresholds beyond which an 'assemblage' (*agencement*) cannot maintain its current consistency. For example, how many cows can a dairy farmer purchase without making any changes to his business, such as adding acreage or procuring more equipment? The last cow he could currently buy is the 'marginal object', since if he purchases more, he will have to fundamentally alter the size and structure of his business. More importantly, it is his *anticipation* of the last or marginal cow that determines the price he is willing to pay for the cows he currently needs. If his business can only sustain twenty additional cows, he will not buy fifty, even if their price is substantially discounted. In marginalism, it is the evaluation of the *idea* of the last or 'marginal' object that determines the value of the entire series of real terms.

Although Deleuze finds marginalism weak as a general economic theory, he finds a new field of application for a modified marginalism in non-capitalist formations (ATP 437). In primitive societies, he argues, the object of collective evaluation is not labour time, but rather the idea of the last object or marginal object that governs the series of exchanges, and *agriculture is incapable of entering into these serial schemas*. We can thus conceptualises a difference between the 'limit' and the 'threshold': in a collective evaluation, what is anticipated is the *limit* (the penultimate exchange, which allows one to remain in the same assemblage) but what is warded off is the *threshold* (which would force one to change assemblage). 'It is the evaluation of the last as limit that constitutes an anticipation and simultaneously wards off the last as threshold or ultimate (a new *agencement*)' (ATP 439). The threshold marks the point where stockpiling would begin, and the temporal succession of territories would be replaced by the spatial coexistence and exploitation of different territories: the apparatus of capture.

V

Though the state was not formed by an evolution but appeared in a single stroke, Deleuze and Guattari nonetheless point to an inevitable and internal 'becoming' or mutation of the state-form. The principle of this mutation comes from the same process of overcoding and capture that defines the archaic state, but functions as its supplementary double: the archaic state cannot overcode and capture without at the same time freeing up a large quantity of decoded flows that escape from it. It cannot create large-scale public works without a flow of independent *labour* escaping from its hierarchised bureaucracy of functionaries, notably in the mines and in metallurgy. It cannot create coinage without flows of *money* escaping, and nourishing or giving birth to other powers (notably in commerce and banking). It cannot create a system of public property without a flow of *private* appropriation growing up beside it, and then starting to slip through its fingers. Finally, it is with the rise of private property that *classes* appear, since the dominant classes are no longer part of the state apparatus, but become distinct determinations that make use of a now-transformed apparatus.

This is Deleuze and Guattari's sixth thesis: in a multitude of forms, *the apparatus of overcoding inevitably gives rise to decoded flows that escape the apparatus of capture* – flows of money, flows of labour, flows of property, flows of population (ATP 449; Deleuze and Guattari 1983: 223). If the first great movement of deterritorialisation appears in the overcoding performed by the despotic state, the second movement appears in the decoding of the flows that are set in motion by the despotic state's own apparatus of capture. This is the 'paranoid' vector that is inherent in the state-form (Deleuze and Guattari 1983: 193): the state is at once capture and the impossibility of complete capture, since the state can only overcode by decoding (abstraction). The state cannot presuppose itself without *also* presupposing what escapes its form of interiority, namely, *decoded flows*, which are the figure of the 'outside' (*dehors*) of the state, the inverse of its Idea. Just as the state creates what it captures, it creates what *escapes* its apparatus of capture: it is the state's form of interiority (capture) that at the same time creates the state's absolute outside (decoded flows).

It is this situation that initially gives rise to a diverse variety of state-forms – 'evolved empires, autonomous cities, feudal systems, monarchies' (ATP 459) – all of which will have as their aim the *recoding*, by means of regular or exceptional topical operations, of the products of these decoded flows. For example, the ancient Mediterranean world (Pelagians, Phoenicians, Greeks, Carthaginians) created an urban fabric that was distinct from the archaic imperial states. Both states and cities are social formations that 'deterritorialise' their surrounding rural territories, but cities accomplish this deterritorialisation in a very different manner than states. The state is a phenomenon of *intraconsistency* that captures territories by relating them to a superior arithmetic unity (the despot), by subordinating them to a *transcendent* or mythic order imposed upon them from above. Cities, by contrast, are phenomena of *transconsistency* that bring about an *immanent* deterritorialisation that adapts the surrounding territories to a geometrical extension in which the city itself is merely a relay-point in a vast network of commercial and maritime circuits. The power of the city does not lie above but in the middle; it exists only as a function of circulation, and is a correlate of the road. As such, the city is a singular point through which commerce enters and exits; it is an *instrument of polarisation* rather than an apparatus of capture: 'it effects a polarisation of matter – inert, living or human' (ATP 432). Whatever the flow involved it must be deterritorialised to enter the network, to submit to the polarisation, to follow the circuit of urban and road recoding.

Nonetheless, it was the decoding power of the state-form – and not the city-form – that would ultimately lead to the rise of capitalism. If the state appears fully formed on the horizon of history, capitalism appears only after a long succession of contingent events and encounters. *Anti-Oedipus* provides an analysis of the formation of capitalism, which is similarly defined by a process of decoding and recoding, and it addresses the question posed by historians such as Braudel (Braudel 1973: 308) and Balazs (Balazs 1964: 34–54): Why was capitalism born in Europe rather than, say, in Rome or thirteenth-century China, when all the conditions for it were present but not effectuated (Deleuze and Guattari 1983: 197, 224). What *A Thousand Plateaus* adds to this is an analysis of the new status the state assumes within capitalism as a *model of realisation* (a term that does not appear in *Anti-Oedipus*). Although it is the state that produces capitalism, capitalism in turn transforms and subsumes the state (Holland 2013: 131–5). As Marx showed, capitalism appears when the *generalised* decoding of flows set loose by the state reaches a threshold of consistency that allows two of these unqualified flows – abstract capital and naked labour

– to conjugate in a differential relation. These flows are 'unqualified' or unspecified because, in and of themselves, they have no content: labour can produce a myriad of commodities or services that capital can purchase, but the nature of these products is not qualified in advance (a commodity is a qualified product of a quantity of labour). If the ancient despotic state operated with an abstract semiotics (writing, geometry, money) that was capable of overcoding existing codes, capitalism required for its functioning a new form of abstraction – a new 'regime of signs' – capable of dealing with unqualified flows that have no specifiable content. Deleuze and Guattari's seventh thesis is that it is only *axiomatics* that can play such a role.

VI

But by what right can capitalism be compared with a mathematical notion as precise as axiomatics? In his seminars, Deleuze distinguishes between logical formalisation and axiomatics, which are related but not identical (Deleuze 1980b). The difference is that a logical formalisation is a system of formal relations between *specified* or specifiable elements, whereas an axiomatic is a system of functional relations between *non-specified* elements. Though they have ancient roots, both procedures were given a rigorous status at roughly the same time by Russell (formalisation) and Hilbert (axiomatics). Russell, in response to the self-referential paradoxes generated by set theory (e.g. the barber paradox), had proposed his famous theory of *types*, which is a formalisation based on the principle that *a set cannot contain itself as an element*. The theory establishes a hierarchy of types, and holds that objects of a given type must be constructed exclusively of objects of a preceding type, lower in the hierarchy. Although antiquity was aware of similar paradoxes, such as the liar paradox, it had made no attempt to provide a formalised remedy such as Russell's. Yet it is not anachronistic to think of Deleuze and Guattari's analysis of the state in terms of logical formalism, as if this formalism was already present socially without being formalised theoretically. The claim that the archaic state overcodes agricultural communities means that the 'apparatus of capture' is of *a different type* than the 'agricultural communities'. We find here a logical confirmation of the preceding analyses: the state *cannot* be an agricultural community; rather, the state is a *model to be realised*, a model that transcends the agricultural communities and creates its own ground.

Axiomatisation differs from logical formalisation and has a distinct historical trajectory. In the late nineteenth century, both mathematics and capitalism confronted a *crisis in the foundations*. In mathematics, the lack of 'clear and rigorous' foundations, particularly for the calculus, led Hilbert to propose a programme to ground mathematics in a finite set of axioms – a project that the Bourbaki group in France, starting in 1935, pursued in a series of works entitled *Éléments de mathématique*. At the same time, capitalism was provoking a parallel crisis in the socio-economic realm: its generalised decoding of fluxes had led to a collapse of the foundation that had once been provided by the state. The monetary mass of capital is a continuous or intensive quantity that increases and decreases without being controlled or mastered by any agency. In both capitalism and mathematics, when the foundation collapsed, it was axiomatisation that took over: the foundation was now provided by a set of axioms. The axioms of capital are '*operative statements* that constitute the semiological form of Capital and that enter as component parts into assemblages of production, circulation, and consumption' (ATP 461) – such as legislative, regulative or financial statements: banking legislation, public spending, wage regulation, property laws, human rights statutes and so on. These axioms deal not only with flows of capital (finance), but also with flows of commodities (markets), flows of population (migrants, unions, employment), and flows of matter-energy (oil, gas, electricity). Deleuze even suggests that ultimately 'the true axiomatic is social and not scientific' (Deleuze 1972).

The status of the state has changed accordingly. Modern nation-states are still actualisations of the *Urstaat*, with its Idea of a completely coded flux, but one could say that the concept of a 'model' has altered: the state is no longer a transcendent *model to be realised*, but an immanent *model of realisation* for the axiomatic of capitalism. In model theory, models are the heterogeneous structures or domains in which an axiomatic is realised. Within capitalism, there is a genuine heterogeneity of state-forms – democratic, socialist, communist, totalitarian, despotic – but each of these forms is *isomorphic* in relation to a single global capitalist market (ATP 464). Nation-states differ primarily in the way that they master the flows (ATP 262), either through a multiplication of directing axioms (social democracies) or a subtraction or withdrawal of axioms (totalitarianism). Axiomatics is sometimes seen as a kind of 'automation' of thought, but in reality it should be seen as a specific mode of experimentation, since no one can say in advance what axioms should be chosen, or whether an axiomatic will be consistent. From the viewpoint of its axiomatics, the history of politics can be seen as a history of constant and often decisive errors (ATP 461). The 'Apparatus of Capture' plateau concludes with a detailed analysis of the contemporary nature of the capitalist axiomatic – including analyses of what *exceeds* the axiomatic, such as the power of the continuum (the war machine) and non-denumerable multiplicities (minorities) (ATP 460–73).

VII

How, finally, are we to understand the claim that social change takes place within a *field of coexistence*? Deleuze and Guattari give their response to this question in their final thesis, which recapitulates the others and constitutes the principle of their critique of social evolution: '*All history does is to translate a coexistence of becomings into a succession*' (ATP 430; cf. Lundy 2012). This thesis allows us to distinguish three levels of Deleuze and Guattari's sociopolitical philosophy, which begins with *types*, then evaluates their *powers*, and finally maps out their *becomings*. At the first level, *Anti-Oedipus* initially presents us with a typology of social formations, and these 'types' can be understood in a Bergsonian manner. In *Matter and Memory*, Bergson created his well-known concepts of 'pure memory' and 'pure perception': although perception and memory are always mixed together in experience (de facto), these concepts allowed him to distinguish (de jure) the differences in nature between the two lines or 'tendencies' of pure memory and pure perception. The same is true for Deleuze and Guattari's typology of social formations. Although each type *in fact* coexists with the others within a single field of coexistence – in our contemporary situation, states, war machines and archaic territorialities all coexist within the capitalist axiomatic – each concept is a tool that allows one to demarcate distinctions or differences in kind within the social multiplicity (Bogue 2004: 172–3).

At a second level, however, *A Thousand Plateaus* characterises each of these types in terms of a specific 'machinic process': primitive societies are characterised by mechanisms of anticipation/prevention; states are characterised by apparatuses of capture; nomadic war machines, by the occupation of smooth space; cities, by instruments of polarisation; ecumenical organisations, by the encompassment of heterogeneous formations; capitalism, by decoding/axiomatisation. This is no longer a question of types; rather, each of these processes is a *power* (*puissance*) that indicates a certain *capacity* or *capability* of a social formation. Primitive societies *anticipate* and *ward off*, archaic states *capture*: this is what they 'can do', what they are capable of. In a Spinozistic manner, each of these powers or processes must be grasped *positively* as a determinate quantity of reality (see Sibertin-Blanc 2013: 41–6). The problem with evolutionary schemas is that they tend to view social formations through the prism of the state-form, which leads to the litany of 'societies without' – 'without a state', 'without history', 'without writing.' But this focus on the state-form winds up assigning privation and lack to other formations, severing them from the forms of power that each of them affirms positively. The second level takes us from Bergson to Spinoza: beneath the categorial typology of social formations, one finds an ethological map of their constitutive powers, 'a logic of coessential positivities and coexisting affirmations' (Deleuze 1988: 95).

But the third level is uniquely Deleuzo-Guattarian. Far from being governed by a single form of power, every social formation, both in fact and in principle, is composed of a *plurality* of processes that are in 'perpetual interaction' with each other (ATP 430), and each process can function at a 'power' other than its own. Anticipation-prevention mechanisms, for instance, 'are at work not only in primitive societies, but are transferred into Cities that ward off the state-form, into the state that wards off capitalism, and into capitalism itself, which wards off and repels its own limits' (ATP 437). Similarly, the state is able to capture, not only land, activity and exchange, but also the anticipation-prevention mechanisms themselves, as well as the war machine and instruments of polarisation. And the powers 'become' something other when they enter into relations with each other: the power of the war machine changes nature when it is 'appropriated' by the state, just as the state's apparatus of capture changes nature when it is subordinated to the worldwide capitalist market. This is the sense of the term 'becoming': it is what takes place *between* two multiplicities, changing their nature. What appears in evolutionary theories as a chronological succession is, for Deleuze and Guattari, a phenomenon of transfer or transport between becomings. In each case, one must ask: What is a social formation capable of? What can it tolerate or support? What are the processes that exceed its capacities for reproduction, and put it in question? When does it pass its limit and enter into a new threshold of consistency? How does it *become*? Thus, we have to say that the term 'field of coexistence' does not refer to an external and de facto coexistence of social formations in a historical space-time, but rather to an intrinsic and de jure coexistence of powers and processes in a non-historical space-time, a continuum in which divergent temporalities coexist. This is what Deleuze calls the 'plane of immanence', a field where all the powers of the social machine coexist virtually, in constant becoming, enveloped and implicated in each other in 'a topological space and a stratigraphic time' (Lapoujade 2014: 218).

Chapter 14

The Smooth and the Striated

Henry Somers-Hall

In the fourteenth plateau of *A Thousand Plateaus*, Deleuze and Guattari develop a dichotomy between two kinds of space – the smooth and the striated. What I want to focus on in this chapter is the status of these two conceptions of space. As Deleuze and Guattari note, these two forms of space are only discovered in a mixed form, yet are capable of being analysed de jure through their separation. In this sense, the plateau on the smooth and striated can be seen as something like a transcendental deduction of their ontology of spaces. I will explore what Deleuze and Guattari mean when they say that they want to construct a theo-noology of smooth and striated spaces. I want to look at the ethical implications of this distinction, before looking at some alternative approaches to the issue of space. It should be noted that the question of the striation of space is one that is shared by Bergson, Heidegger, Merleau-Ponty and Sartre among others. The novelty of Deleuze and Guattari's account is in their formulation of the notion of smooth space as a response. I will begin by looking at the notion of striated space itself, and in particular will explore the degree to which we should see it as a structure or as a method, and the interrelation between these two characterisations.

Space and illusion

To begin with, therefore, I want to talk a little about the distinction itself. Deleuze and Guattari introduce the distinction between smooth and striated spaces as an account of the nature of the world. The examples given in *A Thousand Plateaus* suggest that smooth and striated spaces are real constituents of the structure of the world. I will return to the connection between smooth and striated spaces and Spinoza later, but for now, I want to note that when dealing with the related category of the plane of immanence in his work on Spinoza, Deleuze writes that 'this plane of immanence or consistency is a plan, but not in the sense of a mental design, a project, a program; it is a plan in the geometric sense: a section, and intersection, a diagram' (Deleuze 1988: 122). As such, it appears to be the case that there is an objectivity to the notion of space that we use. A section is a structure that takes its characteristic from what it is a section of, even if it is unable to capture the entire nature of it. While this points to smooth and striated spaces being structures that organise the world, Deleuze and Guattari also write that 'the differences [between smooth and striated spaces] are not objective: it is possible to live striated on the deserts, steppes, or seas; it is possible to live smooth even in the cities, to be an urban nomad' (ATP 482). The implication here, therefore, is that smooth and striated spaces are not objective structures, but rather something like ethical choices about how we choose to organise our experience of the world. How do we reconcile these seemingly contrary accounts of the nature of smooth and striated space? We do so, I believe, by recognising that there is a dissymmetry between the terms smooth and striated. To jump ahead somewhat, Deleuze and Guattari will claim that smooth and striated spaces are both tendencies we encounter in the world, rather than states or structures. We fall into a transcendental illusion when we reify these tendencies into states.[1] The asymmetry between smooth and striated spaces emerges when we recognise that smoothness and striation are tendencies of smooth space itself.[2]

Deleuze and Guattari set out their approach to the smooth and the striated by claiming that they are attempting to develop a 'theo-noological model' (ATP 482) of smooth and striated spaces. They gloss this as follows: 'what distinguishes the two kinds of voyages is neither a measurable quantity of movement, nor something that would only be in the mind, but the mode of spatialisation, the manner of being in space, of being for space' (ATP 482). We can find a more illuminating account of the notion of noology in the plateau on the war machine. Here, they write that 'Noology, which is distinct from ideology, is precisely the study of images of thought, and their historicity' (ATP 376). I want to return to what exactly noology studies, but for the moment we can note that an image of thought is a conceptual apparatus that is antithetical to thinking about the world adequately for Deleuze and Guattari. While noology could be seen as some kind of a hermeneutics of suspicion of images of thought which analyses the methodological presuppositions of philosophies, it is more likely to be Deleuze and Guattari's term for the traditional approach to philosophy. As they note, on their reading, thinking itself is without image, and so falls outside the purview of noology:

> Thought is like the Vampire; it has no image, either to constitute a model of or to copy. In the smooth space of Zen, the arrow does not go from one point to another but is taken up at any point, to be sent to any other point, and tends to permute with the archer and the target. (ATP 377)

We can also note that noology's relationship with those thinkers who archetypally operate without images is one of 'confrontation'. As such, it appears that noology is not used by Deleuze and Guattari to designate a field of study in a conventional sense, but rather a general approach endemic in the history of philosophy. As such, noology refers to an approach Deleuze and Guattari wish to avoid. The term, theo-noology, which combines the notion of an image of thought with the concept of a supreme being, is therefore something like Heidegger's conception of ontotheology. I want to turn to this notion of theo-noology next before turning to what a smooth space might be.

Theo-noology and striated space

We can see the central question of smooth and striated spaces as being one of how we organise our understanding of the world. Seeing the world in terms of striated space is therefore to see it in terms of a set of categories. Deleuze and Guattari make a number of claims about these categories, but we can begin by noting that striated space involves 'formed and perceived things' and 'properties' (ATP 479). Striated space is therefore in essence what in *Difference and Repetition* would be called the space of representation. It is the space of made things that will be opposed to a conception of space as process. The question at the heart of the smooth and the striated is one of where the order that we find in the world around us comes from. For the philosopher of striated space, the key categories of order are measure and the subject-property structure.

Now, it is worth noting that what is at issue here is not the structure of the world, but rather a philosophical method whereby a certain structure is used to investigate the world. Counting is a method for dividing up the world, even if this method in turn presupposes a metaphysics. The application of striated space is thus tied to method:

> A 'method' is the striated space of the *cogitatio universalis* and draws a path that must be followed from one point to another. But the form of exteriority situates thought in a smooth space that it must occupy without counting, and for which there is no possible method, no conceivable reproduction, but only relays, intermezzos, resurgences. (ATP 377)

The mode of organisation adopted by the model of striated space involves the demarcation of a space. Just as the imposition of a set of coordinates allows us to specify positions within a landscape, striated space organises the world through a set of distinctions of logical space. In this respect, I want to turn to one of Deleuze's key examples: the distinction between felt making and weaving. Felt is a textile that, according to Deleuze and Guattari, is nomadic in origin. It is constructed by rolling fibres together so that they intertwine in a complex pattern, despite the surface of the felt feeling smooth. Thus, felt is a textile that emerges from the interrelation of a field of heterogeneous elements. Deleuze and Guattari write that it is 'in principle infinite, open, and unlimited in every direction; it has neither top nor bottom nor centre; it does not assign fixed and mobile elements but rather distributes a continuous variation' (ATP 475–6). Weaving, on the contrary, involves the construction of an ordered, delimited structure, involving the interrelation of two elements (the warp and weft). As Deleuze and Guattari note, weaving is for Plato the paradigm case of a royal science, and the model he introduces in order to clarify the nature of the statesman. In this first section, I want to look at Plato, along with another figure for whom weaving provides a paradigmatic case of method: Descartes. I want to go through a number of aspects of how Plato uses this example. The first thing to note is that Plato uses the example of weaving to illustrate his own method of determining the nature of the world. This is the method of division.

The Eleatic visitor gives the following compressed definition of the nature of weaving:

> Well then: all the things we make and acquire are either for the sake of our doing something, or they prevent something's happening to us. Of preventives, some are charms, whether divine or human, warding things off, others forms of defence. Of forms of defence some are ways of arming for war, others forms of protection. Of forms of protection some are screens, others means of warding off cold and hot weather. Of the latter type of protectives some are shelters, others coverings; of coverings one sort consists of things spread under, a different sort of things put round. Of things put round, some are cut out in one piece, while a different sort are compound; of the compound some are perforated, others bound together without perforation; of the unperforated some are made of the 'sinews' of things growing from the earth, others of hair. Of those made of hair, some are stuck together by means of water and earth, others are bound together with themselves. It is to these preventives and coverings manufactured from materials that are being bound together with themselves that we give the name 'clothes'; as for the expertise that especially has charge of clothes – just as before we gave the name of 'statesmanship' to the sort of expertise that especially had charge of the state, so too now shall we call this sort 'the art of clothes-making', from the thing itself? And shall we say that weaving too, in so far as it represented

the largest part of the manufacture of clothes, does not differ at all, except in name, from this art of clothes-making, just as in that other case we said that the art of kingship did not differ from that of statesmanship? (Plato 1997b: 279c–280b)

We can see here that the visitor's account of weaving operates by the progressive reduction of the logical space of what something could be. We begin with a very general term, and then by a progressive specification of this term, we arrive at a definition of the object in question, in this case, the art of weaving. There are some restrictions on the way in which we divide the whole into different parts. In the *Phaedrus*, Socrates states that we should 'cut up each kind according to its species along its natural joints, and not try to splinter any part, as a bad butcher might do' (Plato 1997a: 265e).

The key to the definition, and indeed the key to all sciences for Plato, is the activity of measuring. '[I]t is indeed the case, in a certain way, that all the products of the various sorts of expertise share in measurement' (Plato 1997b: 284e). This in fact has two forms. Either we 'measure the number, lengths, depths, breadths and speeds of things in relation to what is opposed to them' or we 'measure in relation to what is in due measure, what is fitting, the right moment, what is as it ought to be – everything that removes itself from the extremes to the middle' (Plato 1997b: 284e). The first of these cases might equate to something like the science of geometry, while the second is more like the comparison of objects of the world of appearance with the eternal forms. In both cases, we have a comparison of something, the ideal or the standard of measure, with its physical instantiation. Weaving, as an integral part of clothes making, clearly involves measure, in the way that the elements that determine the structure of the material must be related to one another in an orderly and homogeneous way – the textile must follow the structure of the pattern. Similarly, the statesman needs to act in a manner that is appropriate in all cases – to do what is in due measure, to allow the state to reconcile its conflicting tendencies. We can note that weaving for Plato is itself a model that we can use to understand statesmanship. Plato argues that weaving provides a model for statesmanship, as statesmanship involves the weaving together of courage and moderation, just as the weaver combines the warp and the weft of the cloth.

This notion of weaving, and also striated space, as method is also taken up by Descartes, who clarifies its relation to counting. Descartes' method of doubt is intended to remove all presuppositions from his enquiry, and thus allow an absolutely certain method of approaching philosophical problems. As his *Rules for the Direction of the Mind* shows, however, this method still relies on the method of striation we find in Plato. In this regard, it is an important aside to note that Descartes, in the *Rules*, describes weaving and counting as the perfect preparation for philosophical investigation:

> [W]e must not take up the more difficult and arduous tasks immediately, but must first tackle the simplest and least exalted arts, and especially those in which order prevails – such as weaving or carpet making, or the more feminine arts of embroidery, in which threads are interwoven in an infinitely varied pattern. Number-games and any games involving arithmetic, and the like, belong here. It is surprising how much all these activities exercise our minds, provided of course we discover them for ourselves, and not from others. For, since nothing in these activities remains hidden and they are totally adapted to cognitive capacities, they present us in the most distinct way with innumerable instances of order, yet all regular. Human discernment consists entirely in the proper observance of such order. (Descartes 1985b: Rule 10)

The question which is central to this analysis is, what does the nature of dialectic, or weaving, have to do with the nature of space? In order to answer this question, we need to take a brief diversion into Bergson's account of counting. Bergson notes that in order to count a group, we cannot see them simply as a set of heterogeneous elements. If we are counting elements that are different from one another, then as he puts it, 'we can make an enumeration of them, but not a total' (Bergson 1910: 76). Counting thus implies that the elements that we count are identical, or at least that we treat them as identical for the purposes of counting. Nonetheless, counting also relies on the separateness of elements, and it is here that the notion of space is introduced:

> And yet they must be somehow distinct from one another, since otherwise they would merge into a single unit. Let us assume that the sheep in the flock are identical; they differ at least by the position which they occupy in space, otherwise they would not form a flock. But now let us even set aside the fifty sheep themselves and retain only the idea of them. Either we include them all in the same image, and it follows as a necessary consequence that we place them side by side in an ideal space, or else we repeat fifty times in succession the image of a single one, and in that case it does seem, indeed, that the series lies in duration rather than in space. But we shall soon find out that it cannot be so. For if we picture to ourselves each of the sheep in the flock in succession and separately, we shall never have to do with more than a single sheep. In order that the number should go on increasing in proportion as we advance, we must retain the successive images and set them alongside each of the new units which we picture to ourselves: now, it is in space that such a juxtaposition takes place and not in pure duration. In fact, it will be easily granted that counting material objects means thinking all these objects together, thereby leaving them in space. (Bergson 1910: 77)

Counting therefore implies a homogeneous space within which to situate the entities which are counted. It implies the distinction between the one and the many, and hence the notion that organisation is something that is separable from the elements to be organised. In fact, Descartes makes an even stronger claim, equating the dimensions of spatiality directly with measure. As he puts it in the *Regulae*:

> By 'dimension' we mean simply a mode or aspect in respect of which some subject is considered to be measurable. (Descartes 1985b: Rule 14)

Counting, and with it, measure, presuppose a certain form of organisation of the world, therefore. We can see the consequence of this model in Descartes' conception of the actual space of the world. Having developed a striated method of enquiry, he understands the world as a metric field of homogeneous extensions, which has only one property (impenetrability) that exceeds those found in Euclidean geometry:

> God himself has taught us that he has arranged all things in number, weight and measure. The knowledge of these truths is so natural to our souls that we cannot but judge them infallible when we conceive them distinctly, nor doubt that if God had created many worlds, they would be as true in each of them as in this one. (Descartes 1985c: 97)

Noology is therefore the study of philosophical method, from the point of view of those who operate within a field of striated space. Theo-noology presumably adds the further element to this image of thought by grounding it in a moment of transcendence such as a sphere of eternal natures (as we find in the myth of the demiurge in the *Timaeus*), or God as a guarantor of clear and distinct ideas (as in the *Meditations*).

I don't want to go into the criticisms of striated space here, as they are by now quite well rehearsed in the literature, but I will mention their general trend. Essentially, following Bergson, they argue that striated space is favoured because it allows certain forms of practical and political control to be developed. Thus, Platonism ultimately is adopted because it allows the ordering of the city-state – a claim developed by Derrida in his essay on the *pharmakon* (Derrida 1981: 61–172). The mathematicisation of matter allows us to manipulate it precisely, but does so on the basis of a falsification. Zeno's paradox shows the impossibility of understanding movement within a striated space.[3] Similarly, in terms of organic life, Bergson argues vigorously that the discrete nature of elements in a striated space is incompatible with life, which is necessarily open (the reproduction of life requires that an organism's boundaries with the world are not absolute, for instance, and the transversal sharing of DNA in bacteria and higher animals fits badly with the arborescent model of division that

Plato introduces).[4] Deleuze and Guattari posit a transcendental illusion by which we tend to view all bodies in the world as comprehensible under the form of measure.[5] Once we accept an account of the world as measure, the non-metric understanding of the world is an abstraction from the quantifiable world. For Deleuze and Guattari, on the contrary, metric space is a distortion of a more primordial understanding of the world as a field of pure intensity or process.

Smooth space and phenomenology

Resistance to a geometrical conception of method and of space is not a novel development on the part of Deleuze and Guattari. We can see, for instance, in Hegel's rejection of the understanding in favour of reason a move against the mathematicisation of dialectic. Similarly, Bergson's criticisms of counting, or Heidegger's account of enframing, both involve a rejection of the paradigm of striated space. In each of these cases, the account of what one must oppose to striated space differs, however. In order to be clear about what Deleuze and Guattari are proposing to replace striated space with, I want to introduce another philosopher who criticises striated space as a point of contrast – Maurice Merleau-Ponty.

Merleau-Ponty claims that the conception of the world based on a homogenous structure of space is unable to account for the presence of meaning in the world. We do not see a homogeneous world and add meaning to it, as a further layer of organisation. Rather, the space that we encounter in perception is already meaningful, and is already carved up according to possible actions of the body. As such, we live in a world that is constituted as a set of opportunities for action. Rather than perceiving simply objective structures in the world (things), plus a significance, we see the world as containing significance directly. The flame of a candle that has burnt a child appears to that child as directly repellent, just as the alarm clock calls out to be dealt with, for instance. Merleau-Ponty explains this reliance of space on our motor activities and intentions clearly with the example of the blind man:

> The blind man's cane has ceased to be an object for him, it is no longer perceived for itself; rather, the cane's furthest point is transformed into a sensitive zone, it increases the scope and the radius of the act of touching, and has become analogous to a gaze. In the exploration of objects, the length of the cane does not explicitly intervene as a middle term: the blind man knows its length by the position of objects, rather than the position of objects through the cane's length ... Places in space are not defined as objective positions in relation to the objective position of our body, but rather they inscribe

> around us the variable reach of our intentions and our gestures. (Merleau-Ponty 2012: 144)

Thus here metric space emerges secondarily to a space of sense and action that we find in lived experience. Metric space is an extrapolation of, in this case, the blind man's haptic relationship to the world.

What is the basis for Merleau-Ponty's criticism of striated space? Essentially, Merleau-Ponty takes issue with the central feature of the model of homogeneous space. As I said earlier, homogeneous space has the fundamental property of measurability, in that we can compare the objects within it by their superposition upon one another. A consequence of this is that an object within a Euclidean space is invariant to transformation by displacement, or in other words, that the space of Euclidean geometry functions as a homogeneous medium where position does not affect the constitution of objects within it. This allows us, for instance, to analyse clear and distinct ideas without having to take into account their relationships to other ideas. It also makes possible counting, as counting relies on a juxtaposition of elements whose properties are not affected by their relations to one another. Merleau-Ponty therefore formulates his own account of striated space as follows:

> The notion of a geometrical space indifferent to what it contains, or the notion of a pure movement that does not by itself alter the properties of the object, provided phenomena with the inert milieu of existence where each event could be linked to the physical conditions responsible for the intervening changes and where each event thus contributed to this determination of being that appeared to be the task of science. By developing the concept of the 'thing' in this way, scientific knowledge was unaware that its work was based upon a presupposition . . . The natural object remained for us an ideal unity and, according to Lachelier's famous phrase, an intertwining of general properties. (Merleau-Ponty 2012: 55)

Merleau-Ponty's claim is that such an account of the indifference of space to the objects found within it contradicts the basic structure of the perceived world. In fact, every object we perceive is perceived against a background, and this background provides the context which determines the object. In other words, the context of perception cannot be separated from our analysis of an object, and hence the space of perception cannot be seen as homogeneous in relation to the objects it contains, as context determines the actual nature of things. Measure relies on the fact that we could in principle superimpose one object on to another to compare their sizes, and hence on the idea that displacement does not affect the properties of an object. Once we realise that the background is an essential determinant in the perception of the object, we have to renounce the notion of a striated space. As Merleau-Ponty puts it,

When Gestalt theory tells us that a figure against a background is most basic sensible given we can have, this is not a contingent characteristic of factual perception that would, in an ideal analysis, leave us free to introduce the notion of impression. Rather, this is the very definition of the perceptual phenomenon, or that without which a phenomenon cannot be called perception. The perceptual 'something' is always in the middle of some other thing, it always belongs to a 'field'. (Merleau-Ponty 2012: 4)

Smooth space

Is Merleau-Ponty's rejection of striated space therefore an endorsement of a philosophy of smooth space? To begin to answer this question, we can turn to the figure who first developed the distinction between smooth and striated space: Pierre Boulez. As a composer, Boulez is interested primarily in the structure of music. His claim is that, traditionally, sound has been 'striated' by regular measure to allow us to produce music. Standard intervals allow the organisation of sound. Modern music, for Boulez, needs to renounce this structure, and instead operate in terms of a smooth space. Boulez defines it as follows:

> Temperament – the choice of measure – will be an invaluable aid in estimating an interval; in short, it will '*striate*' the surface, the musical space, and will provide our perception – even if it is far from totally conscious – with useful points of reference; in the opposite cases, where partition can be effected at will, the ear will lose all landmarks and all absolute cognisance of intervals; this is comparable to the eye's inability to estimate distances on a perfectly smooth surface. (Boulez 1975: 85)

Now, we can note that this definition of smooth space is one that goes against Merleau-Ponty's claim that all spaces must be composed of heterogeneous elements. For Merleau-Ponty, the basic element of perception is complex – it is a relation between figure and background. Boulez's conception of smooth space here contains no figure, however, and so, on Merleau-Ponty's reading, would be wholly indeterminate. As the Gestalt psychologist Kurt Koffka, who was one of Merleau-Ponty's primary references, notes, we cannot view a homogeneous field without the emergence of visual artefacts which once again split that field into a figure and a background, even if these artefacts are hallucinations (Koffka 1935: 116–17). As such, the smooth space of Boulez cannot be equated with something like the perceptual space of phenomenology.

Deleuze and Guattari's response to Merleau-Ponty's position here would, I think, be the same as that which they make to Alois Riegl's aesthetics. Riegl argues that rather than primitive art being inferior to later realist art, it instead operates according to a different *kunstwollen*, or artistic will. As such, he defines two different kinds of art – optic art and haptic art. Optic art tries to capture the world as it appears, and hence presents the world in terms of a field of depth. While it exists in the ancient world, it finds its philosophical basis in the Christian world, with the appreciation for the imperfections of nature that coincided with the belief that Christ had been made flesh, and hence that the weak and imperfect had moral and aesthetic value. Riegl claims that rather than being an inferior form of art, primitive art, such as that of the Egyptians, in fact operates according to a different motivation. Rather than attempting to enter into a sympathetic relationship with the world, it rejects the subjective appearance of things in favour of its objective structure. Frightened by the imperfections of the world of appearance, it aims at a world outside of this space. In this sense, it rejects the geometry of striated space. Instead, we have the archetypal case of the Egyptian figure pressed flat against the material ground (or even presented against an elevated ground). Instead of relations of depth, we have relations against a plane. As Riegl puts it, 'foreshortenings and shadows (as betrayers of depth) are avoided just as scrupulously as expressions of mental states (as betrayers of the mental life of the soul' (Riegl, quoted in Iversen 1993: 78). Here we have a similar rejection of the kind of geometric representation exemplified by Renaissance painting, which relied heavily on the techniques of metric space to present its vision of the world. Once again, however, what replaces striated space is not itself smooth space. The art of the Egyptian Imperium is in fact a hybrid form of smooth and striated space. As Deleuze and Guattari put it,

> [W]e will not define the haptic by the immobile background, by the plane and the contour, because these have to do with an already mixed state in which the haptic serves to striate, and uses its smooth components only in order to convert them to another kind of space. The haptic function and close vision presuppose the smooth, which has no background, plane, or contour, but rather changes in direction and local linkages between parts. (ATP 496)

At issue, I think, in the case of both Riegl's notion of haptic space and Merleau-Ponty's notion of the Gestalt, is that while both of these models transform our understanding of what form is in a way that takes them away from the traditional model of striated space, both still retain the centrality of the notion of form. Merleau-Ponty moves to a more sophisticated notion of form than found in Descartes, but while the notion of form is maintained, we are unable to fully explore what Deleuze and Guattari take to be central to smooth space – the notion of space as process or intensity. Any introduction of an object into such a space, no matter how subtle, risks crystallising and fixing smooth space into a striated structure.

So what is the structure of smooth space? To return to the example of felt, it has two levels of organisation. On the one hand, it presents a smooth surface – the plane without distances of Boulez. On the other, it is constituted of elements that form heterogeneous connections, folding together in seemingly arbitrary ways. Now, understanding this relationship between the two aspects of smooth space is not as straightforward as it appears. It is counterintuitive to call a space 'smooth' that is constituted from a number of elements that are heterogeneous. It would appear to be the case that if the elements constituting a space were distinct from one another, then the space itself must be discontinuous rather than smooth. This objection emerges from one of the central assumptions of much metaphysical thinking. If we return once more to Descartes' account of philosophy, we can see that if we accept that philosophy deals with clear and distinct ideas, then there is no way of conceiving of a smooth space. Descartes gives the following definition of clear and distinct ideas:

> A perception which can serve as the basis for a certain and indubitable judgement needs to be not merely clear but also distinct. I call a perception 'clear' when it is present and accessible to the attentive mind – just as we say that we see something clearly when it is present to the eye's gaze and stimulates it with a sufficient degree of strength and accessibility. I call a perception 'distinct' if, as well as being clear, it is so separated from all other perceptions that it contains within itself only what is clear. (Descartes 1985a: §45)

For Descartes, having an idea that is clear and distinct means having an idea that is separated/separable from other ideas. As Descartes shows in the *Meditations* in the case of the mind and the body, if we can show that we can formulate clear and distinct ideas of these two categories, then God guarantees that our ideas guarantee their ontological distinction. As such, the criterion of distinctness precludes the possibility of reconciling the unity of smooth space with the heterogeneity of the elements that compose it. If the elements that make up a smooth space are heterogeneous, then they are distinct, and hence the space is discontinuous rather than smooth. So how are we to conceive of smooth space? To get a clear sense of it, we need to return to one of Deleuze's earliest books, his study of Spinoza, the bulk of which was written in the 1950s. Here, Deleuze takes Spinoza to be criticising Descartes for adopting an essentially psychologistic criterion by which we identify the essence of something. 'Clarity and distinctness by themselves give us only an indeterminate knowledge; they fall short of a cause from which all the thing's properties would together follow, leading us only to recognise an object, the presence of an object, from the effect it has on us' (Deleuze 1990a: 153–4). On this reading, then, the Cartesian project of mapping the world in terms of clear and distinct ideas, the method of striated spaces, only touches the surface of the world and not the causes of the impressions we have of it.

To begin to work out the consequences of this rejection of clear and distinct ideas for smooth space, we can note a similarity between this notion and Deleuze's characterisation of Spinoza's concept of a body. In describing a body, Deleuze gives the following account:

> How does Spinoza define a body? A body, of whatever kind, is defined by Spinoza in two simultaneous ways. In the first place, a body, however small it may be, is composed of an infinite number of particles; it is the relations of motion and rest, of speeds and slownesses between particles, that define a body, the individuality of a body. Secondly, a body affects other bodies, or is affected by other bodies; it is this capacity for affecting and being affected that also defines a body in its individuality. (Deleuze 1988: 123)

Here once again, we have two characteristics – a degree of affectivity, and a series of relations of speeds and slownesses between an infinity of particles. These map on to the smooth space and its constituent heterogeneous relations.

Let us go through these two aspects of smooth space in turn, beginning with its smooth homogeneity. We can start by noting that Boulez's account of smooth space as a purely homogeneous field matches well with the description of intensive space developed by the Scholastic philosopher Duns Scotus, a key influence on Deleuze. As Deleuze puts it:

> As long as the wall is white, no shape is distinguished from or in it . . . Let us return to Scotus: whiteness, he says, has various intensities; these are not added to whiteness as one thing to another thing, like shapes added to the wall on which it is drawn; its degrees of intensity are intrinsic determinations, intrinsic modes, of a whiteness that remains univocally the same under whichever modality it is considered. (Deleuze 1990a: 196)

Smooth space is like Scotus's field of intensive whiteness, therefore.[6] In this case, differences are intrinsic to the structure of the space, just as varying degrees of intensity of light are all a part of the same light. As such, it has an organisational structure without the formal boundaries that we discover in either classical or Gestalt models of difference. The determinations we find in smooth space are not, therefore, like the bodies that we find in the space of Euclidean geometry – essentially comprehensible without having to consider their positions and relations. Rather, as with a field of varying illumination, we have determinations which merge with one another at the edges. Deleuze presents this notion of determination in a slightly different context in *Difference and Repetition*:

> Ideas are complexes of coexistence. In a certain sense all Ideas coexist, but they do so at points, on the edges, and under glimmerings which never have

the uniformity of a natural light. On each occasion, obscurities and zones of shadow correspond to their distinction. Ideas are distinguished from one another, but not at all in the same manner as forms and the terms in which these are incarnated. (Deleuze 1994: 186–7)

Thus, for Spinoza, and for Deleuze, determination doesn't rely on a clear and distinct idea of the object. Just as a pattern of light can contain variations within it without ceasing to be one light, smooth space is determined by quantitative differences in intensity across a plane. Determinations are not extrinsic to space, essentially features of bodies within it, but are an intrinsic feature of the space itself. As such, space itself is no longer an inert medium where the displacement of a point across it results in no change in quality.

In this regard, there is a sharp difference between the space of Descartes and that of Spinoza. For Descartes, the position of a body in space is irrelevant to its essence (in the sense in which we can understand a body as being really distinct from other bodies, and thus comprehensible without reference to them). In this sense, in order to understand the interrelations of bodies in a striated space, we need to recognise that the space the bodies inhabit, and which allows them to communicate with one another, is something over and above the bodies themselves. Thus, to represent the bodies requires the addition of the homogeneous space to allow them to communicate. This is the origin of Deleuze and Guattari's claim that striated spaces require a 'supplementary dimension to that to which it gives rise (n +1)' (ATP 265). For a smooth space, while there are distinctions within the plane, these are modes of the plane itself, rather than objects contained within it. While the order of a smooth space is distinguishable, therefore, this distinguishability does not entail that we have a real distinction between determinations and the space they occupy, but rather a purely modal distinction. That is, these determinations are differences *within* the same smooth space, rather than differences between ontologically distinct entities. We can tie this into the claim made by Deleuze that, for Descartes, 'distinctness, taken as a norm of ideas, prejudges the status of things represented by ideas' (Deleuze 1990a: 324).

A consequence of this is that a smooth space is not a container for bodies at all, but is rather a conception of space that contains within itself integrally lines of force and variations in intensity. In this respect, Deleuze and Guattari's citation of Carpenter, Varley and Flaherty's text on Eskimo culture is important in showing the possibility of understanding space in a non-metric sense. They write:

Of course, what appeared to me as a monotonous land was, to the Aivilik, varied, filled with meaningful reference points. When I travel by car I can, with relative ease, pass through a complex and chaotic city, Detroit, for example, by simply following a handful of highway markers. I begin with the assumption that the streets are laid out in a grid and the knowledge that certain signs mark my route. Apparently the Aivilik have similar, though natural, reference points. By and large, these are not actual objects or points, but relationships between, say, contour, type of snow, wind, salt air, ice crack. I can best explain this with an illustration: two hunters casually followed a trail which I simply could not see, even when I bent close to scrutinise it; they did not kneel to examine it, but stood back, examining it at a distance. (Carpenter, Varley and Flaherty 1959)

Deleuze and Guattari introduce this example to show that rather than an extensive space of objects, the Eskimo orient themselves according to variations in the structure of the space around them. They operate according to a different conception of what it is to inhabit a space. Such a space is determined by the relations of elements, which draws us on to the second aspect of a smooth space.

In *A Thousand Plateaus*, smooth space is described as being composed of 'local operations involving changes of direction.' (ATP 478) While the fibres that make up the surface of felt have a form, what is important about them is the way they relate together with one another. The elements that make up smooth space are 'not atoms' (Deleuze 1990a: 204), as atoms would similarly have form. Rather, they are like the simple bodies of Spinoza's *Ethics*. Deleuze gives the following description of these bodies in *Expressionism in Philosophy*:

> The attribute of Extension has an extensive modal quality that actually divides into an infinity of simple bodies. These simple bodies are extrinsic parts which are only distinguished from one another, and which are only related to one another, through movement and rest. Movement and rest are precisely the form of extrinsic determination and external relation between simple bodies. Simple bodies are determined from outside to movement or rest *ad infinitum*, and are distinguished by the movement and rest to which they are determined. (Deleuze 1990a: 205)

How are we to interpret this claim that smooth space is understood through the interrelation of elements? If we say that felt is constituted through the heterogeneous connections of elements, do we not therefore assume that at the level of composition, there are real distinctions between its elements? The answer is that while we may be able to analyse felt into a relation between parts, the distinction between these parts is only ever modal, and is not a real distinction. We find no formal structures, therefore, either at the level of the composition, nor the structure of smooth space.

For Descartes, two kinds of distinctions coincide with one another: real and numerical distinctions. When we look at two different objects in the world and make a distinction between them, then insofar as they differ in shape and relative position, we can declare that they are two really distinct substances, even though they differ only in terms of degrees of extension and extensive position. In other words, for Descartes, two bodies that differ purely in numerical terms can be said to be really distinct. We should note that this conception of smooth space is one that departs radically from the formal nature of striated space. A striated space relies on the notion of measurable form to determine the limits of an object ('like a shape on a wall', Deleuze 1990a: 196), because the determinations are not imposed upon space, whereas in a smooth space, determinations instead form a part of its nature. While there may be modal or numerical distinctions, these distinctions do not coincide with real distinctions between substances or determinations in spaces.

Conclusion

Smooth space can therefore be seen as a way to understand matter as structured without having to bring in the notion of forms or substance. Rather than the organisation of inert material across a homogeneous plane, smooth space is constituted through an active and heterogeneous field of elements that themselves are unformed. Such an approach rejects the moment of transcendence that we discover in the idea of a striated space. As Deleuze and Guattari put it, 'whereas in the striated, forms organise a matter, in the smooth, materials signal forces and serve as symptoms for them.' (ATP 479) Thus, we sense the relations of movement and rest through the intensities of the smooth space, much as the Eskimo navigate their terrain according to the direction of the wind, rather than visible landmarks.

At the beginning of this chapter I claimed that Deleuze and Guattari see the choice between smooth and striated spaces as an ethical choice. I want to return to this theme by asking how we apprehend smooth spaces. As Merleau-Ponty noted, the simplest mode of perception is a figure against a background. As such, smooth spaces require striation in order to find expression:

> If it is true that itinerant geometry and the nomadic number of smooth spaces are a constant inspiration to royal science and striated space, conversely, the metrics of striated spaces (*metron*) is indispensable for the translation of the strange data of a smooth multiplicity ... [Translating] is an operation that undoubtedly consists in subjugating, overcoding, *metricising* smooth space, in neutralising it, but also in giving it a milieu of propagation,

extension, refraction, renewal, and impulse without which it would perhaps die of its own accord: like a mask without which it could neither breathe nor find a general form of expression. (ATP 486)

Smooth space is therefore like Nietzsche's Dionysian, which requires expression through Apollo, and in this respect the reference to Riegl in this plateau is apposite. Riegl, as a good post-Kantian, sees the development of haptic space as an attempt to return to the thing in itself. From this position, we can see why we have an ethical choice here. It is a question of how we conceive the ground of the striation we encounter. For Deleuze and Guattari, to privilege striated space is to fall prey to a transcendental illusion. It is to conflate the condition of presentation of smooth space with space itself. We might consider, however, whether Deleuze and Guattari don't fall prey to a transcendental illusion of their own, in that they push a genuine structure of perception (the heterogeneity of space) beyond the point where form breaks down.

Notes

1. Deleuze explicitly introduces the notion of transcendental illusion in relation to the logic of multiplicities in *Difference and Repetition*. For more on transcendental illusion, particularly in early Deleuze, see Somers-Hall 2009.
2. In this respect, the logic of the smooth and the striated recalls one of Deleuze's earliest philosophical analyses – his reading of Bergson in his early essay on Bergson's conception of difference. Here, Deleuze notes that while matter and duration exhibit two tendencies which differ in kind for Bergson, this differing in kind is one that takes place *within duration itself.* Deleuze puts the point as follows: 'Duration differs from matter, but it does so because it is first that which differs in itself and from itself, with the result that the matter from which it differs is still essentially of duration. As long as we remain within dualism, the thing is where two movements meet: duration, which by itself has no degrees, encounters matter as a contrary movement, as a certain obstacle, a certain impurity that mixes it up, that interrupts its impulse [*elan*], that gives it such and such a degree here, another one over there. But more profoundly, duration is in itself susceptible to degrees because it is that which differs with itself, so that every thing is entirely defined in duration, including matter itself' (Deleuze 2004a: 27). This same logic is still at play in Deleuze and Guattari's characterisation of smooth and striated space, with the smooth as that which differs from itself, and therefore provides the principle of the striated.
3. This criticism is raised by Bergson at several points in his writings. An indicative point would be Bergson 1910: 112–17, where he points out that the same assumptions that lead to the Eleatic paradoxes around motion are necessary conditions for the formulation of modern mechanics.
4. Once again, the notion that life must be conceived of as open can be traced back to Bergson, in this case to *Creative Evolution*. See Ansell Pearson 1999: 168–70 for an account of how this move away from the closed organism to what Deleuze and Guattari call 'machinic heterogenesis' is developed. See also Somers-Hall 2013b for an analysis of Deleuze and Guattari's criticism of the classical account of the organism.

5. Deleuze discusses this in detail in chapter 5 of Deleuze 1994, where he introduces the concept of a 'transcendental physical illusion' (228).
6. For more on the intensive in Deleuze, see Clisby 2015; Mader 2014; Somers-Hall 2013a: 30–5, 174–80.

Chapter 15

Concrete Rules and Abstract Machines: Form and Function in *A Thousand Plateaus*

Ray Brassier

Introduction

What relation between the abstract and the concrete is at issue here? How do 'rules' relate to 'machines'? To answer this question, we first need to distinguish Deleuze and Guattari's 'machinic materialism' from more familiar types of materialism, whether atomistic (Epicurus, Lucretius), mechanicist (Hobbes, d'Holbach), historical (Marx, Althusser), or physicalist (Quine, Lewis). Classical metaphysical materialism, whether atomistic or mechanicist, combines a theoretical proposition about the ultimate nature of reality with a series of practical injunctions about how best to live in accordance with that reality. Historical materialism rejects metaphysics but still attempts to derive a political programme from its account of socio-historical reality. As for physicalism, it is a theoretical proposition that eschews the prescriptive altogether, deferring to physics for its account of ultimate reality. But the materialism laid claim to in *A Thousand Plateaus* is unlike any of the above. It does not pretend to accurately represent an objectively existing 'material reality' (whether natural or social), just as it does not propose practical imperatives derived from universal laws (whether natural or social). It seeks to conjugate an 'abstract matter', conceived independently of representational form, with a concrete ethics, wherein action is selected independently of universal law. Here the abstract is no longer the province of the universal (invariance, form, unity) and the concrete is no longer the realm of the particular (the variable, the material, the many). The abstract is *enveloped* in the concrete such that practice is the condition of its *development*. It is this development which is rule-governed, but in a sense quite independent of the familiar juxtaposition of invariant rule to variable circumstance. Rules are no longer abstract invariants that need to be applied to concrete or variable circumstances. 'Abstract' now means unformed and ultimately, as we shall see, destratified (we will try to understand what this term means below). But the unformed is endowed with positive traits of its own, traits which, from the viewpoint of the representation of 'material reality', are initially confounding. Thus abstract matter is described as constituting a 'plane of consistency' characterised by 'continuums of intensities', 'particles-signs' and 'deterritorialised flows'. Moreover, Deleuze and Guattari insist that this plane of consistency (which they also call 'multiplicity') must be made, since it is not given: '*it is not enough to say* "Long live the multiple!", difficult as it is to raise that cry ... The multiple *must be made* ...' (ATP 6, translation modified, my emphasis). Consistency (or multiplicity) is made by *mapping* what is unrepresented in both thinking and doing. This mapping plays a key role in developing the abstract. To understand how concrete rules develop abstract matter, we have to understand both why *A Thousand Plateaus* retains a distinction between saying and doing and why mapping is a practice that fuses saying with doing. Thus the other sense that 'concrete' has here is practical: mapping the positive traits characteristic of the unformed is a practical matter; one that is constrained by certain rules. What sort of rules? Since abstract matter cannot be represented, the rules or practical injunctions governing its development cannot be read off some pre-existing 'reality'. These rules will be concrete precisely to the extent that they effectuate the abstract. Practice and theory *realise* one another: theoretical concepts are effectuated in practice; practical imperatives are formulated in theory.

Thus, for all its idiosyncratic novelty, *A Thousand Plateaus* conforms to a classical model of philosophising, wherein ontology, understood as the theory of what there is, is one with ethics, understood as a practice or 'art of living'. This is not to say it is a traditional or conservative work: rather, it is an attempt at the contemporary reactivation of the classical task of philosophising, but one where contemporaneity is marked by the rejection of representation.[1] This rejection entails a radicalisation of philosophical pragmatics (indeed, it construes philosophy as a generalised pragmatics) wherein neither the agents nor the functions of practices can be taken for granted. The referent of the communal 'we', constantly invoked by traditional pragmatists (James, Dewey) and their contemporary successors (Rorty, Brandom), is a starting point whose epistemic authority and socio-historical coordinates will be gradually disassembled and replaced by another 'we': that of a minoritarian 'people to come'. By the same token, the habitual functions and goals established around this existing 'we' need to be suspended; normal functioning and established finalities are to be disrupted. This means that for machinic pragmatics, the efficacy of performance can no longer be subordinated to pre-established standards of competence. So long as practice is subordinated to representation, it can only more or less adequately trace a pre-existing reality, according to extant criteria of success or failure. But machinic pragmatics is not geared towards representation; it is an experimental practice oriented towards bringing something new into existence; something that does not pre-exist its process of production. It decouples performance from competence. It does not engage in a utilitarian tracing of the real; it generates a constructive mapping (and as we shall see, a diagramming) of the real: 'What distinguishes the map from the tracing is that it is entirely oriented toward an experimentation in contact with the real. The map does not reproduce an unconscious closed in upon itself; it constructs the unconscious . . . The map has to do with performance, whereas the tracing always involves an alleged "competence"' (ATP 13). Competence is reproductive, but performance is productive. This contrast between tracing and mapping follows from the more fundamental difference between saying and doing proclaimed in the opening pages of *A Thousand Plateaus* (cited above).

Three interrelated questions arise here. First, why does the overcoming of arborescent dichotomy still require a contrast between saying and doing, or representation and production, contemplation and practice? What is the status of this contrast? Secondly, what does performance freed from the constraint of competence actually *do*? Is performance to be understood as an act, an activity, an action, a production or a practice? These are all related yet distinct ways of conceptualising *doing*. Is mapping a variety of *doing* that is not normatively governed and achievement-oriented? Can one perform a mapping without any regard for competence? Competence need not be teleological: not all norm-governed doing is goal-oriented; nevertheless, an immanent standard is still a *standard*. Finally, if making the multiple is not susceptible to norms of competence, what is it that *makes the difference* between success and failure in constructing the plane of consistency? We will return to these questions below when we consider the way in which machinic pragmatism is supposed to operate a selective construction of the real (the plane of consistency).

Stratification

The disruption of utilitarian order, of the fixed goals, standards and practices through which reality is reproduced, cannot be immediately achieved. Since (as Deleuze repeatedly insists) we always start in the middle, we start stratified, organised, subjectified. Thus the practical challenge is to understand how we can de-stratify, dis-organise, and de-subjectify without lapsing into religious self-abnegation: 'to reach, not the point where one no longer says I, but the point where it is no longer of any importance whether one says I' (ATP 3). But why would this point of apparent indifference between owning or abnegating one's subjectivity be worth reaching? If such a point is worth reaching, it cannot be indifferent to this difference. Something must be retained: something of the subject, something of the sign, something of the organism:

> That which races or dances upon the plane of consistency thus carries with it the *aura* of its stratum, *an undulation, a memory or tension*. The plane of consistency retains just enough of the strata to extract from them variables that operate in the plane of consistency as its own functions. (ATP 70–1, my emphasis)

What will be retained on the plane of consistency is the *torsion* of destratified intensities, particles, signs and flows. Yet because the point of torsion is indiscernible from the vantage of anyone invested in the importance of distinction between self and not-self, personal and impersonal, its approach requires *caution*, which is of course one of the book's famous watchwords.[2] Caution is required for the composition of the plane of consistency. This is the relevance of the concrete rules for its composition. Thus to understand how concrete rules are articulated with abstract machines we have to understand how the composition of consistency according to rules requires *deformalising* stratified functions and subjecting them to the torsion of absolute movement: 'A movement is absolute when, whatever its quantity and speed, it relates "a" body considered as multiple to a smooth space that it occupies in the manner of a vortex' (ATP 509). Absolute movement (or deterritorialisation) is attained through the *deformalisation* of stratified function. Deformalisation ensures the continuity of intensities, the emission of particle-signs, and the conjunction of deterritorialised flows on the plane of consistency. Thus abstract matter is de- or un-formed, which means destratified. Stratification is the source of all formalisation; conversely, deformalisation is the operator of destratification. But what is stratification?

The theory of stratification is among the most impressive, but also most perplexing, achievements of *A Thousand Plateaus*. I think it is absolutely central to its entire conceptual construction; without it, nothing works. But its pivotal role is often overlooked. The theory of stratification is a theory of the self-organisation of matter. It is unabashedly metaphysical; indeed, it is perhaps the most ingenious and ambitious metaphysical hypothesis proposed by any twentieth-century materialists. Attempts to assimilate *A Thousand Plateaus* to the parameters of contemporary critical theory have encouraged the tendency to limit the scope of stratification to the experiential realm. But stratification cannot be confined to the phenomenological or epistemological registers. It is not a function of representation; representation is a function of stratification. Thus the theory of stratification is not just an extension of Deleuze's critique of the epistemology and metaphysics of representation in *Difference and Repetition*. It lays out the ontological conditions under which representation becomes possible. Already in *Difference and Repetition*, it was clear that representation is not an extrinsic grid which we superimpose upon reality. Reality generates its own representation. But representation remains a kind of transcendental illusion; a cavern within which an inverted image of the real holds sway, one that prevents us from penetrating to the imperceptible conditions of perception (the virtual). The theory of stratification lays out the real processes through which this cavern, this inversion and this image are successively generated *on the same level* as the real (rather than above or beneath it). It levels the superposition of planes through which *Difference and Repetition* maintained the virtual (the imperceptible) in a position of transcendence vis-à-vis the actual (the perceptible). Stratification explains the genesis of representability as a facet of the auto-production of the real as such, rather than as a consequence of the transcendent hiatus between virtual and actual.[3]

Stratification is the double-articulation of content and expression. This double-articulation is the condition of all order, structure and regularity. But stratification is complex. Both the articulation of content and that of expression are bifurcated. At the elementary physical level, content is articulated by splitting material flows into successively coordinated molecular units. Molecular substance is formally coordinated: this is the substance and form of content. Expression is articulated by establishing 'functional, compact, stable structures' (ATP 41), and constructing molar compounds on to which these structures are superimposed. Molar compounds are formally structured: this is the substance and form of expression. Stratified content is formed matter; stratified expression is structured function. Both articulations are segmented and the bi-univocal relations between segments of content (formed matters) and segments of expression (structured functions) are the source of every real structure, whether physical, biological or sociopolitical. Thus material reality comprises three fundamental types of strata: physico-chemical, biological and anthropomorphic (or *allomorphic*, because the anthropomorphic strata have the power to colonise the others). Only the first gives molar expression to molecular content: biological and allomorphic contents are not necessarily molecular, nor are their expressions necessarily molar. But what is common to every stratum is the coordination of *structured function* (expression) and *formed matter* (content). Matter is assigned a determinate function on the basis of its formation (whether physical, organic or sociocultural); function is assigned a determinable form on the basis of its substance (whether molecular, cellular or semiotic). This is the crux of all stratification as immanent principle of the self-organisation of matter.

Yet stratification is also a process of division. Strata 'shatter the continuums of intensity, introducing breaks between different strata and within each stratum' (ATP 143). This division is real, not ideal (it is not dialectical). Strata split and segment, but they also conjoin and connect. Thus Deleuze and Guattari insist on the *real* (as opposed to formal) distinction between content and expression. It is a difference in being, not just a difference in thought. Stratification is a real synthesis establishing a common root for expressive form and expressed content. Thus there is an isomorphism of content and expression: 'their independence does not preclude isomorphism, in other words, the existence of the same kind of constant relations on both sides' (ATP 108). This isomorphism makes of stratification an instance of 'divine judgment', which is to say, ontological as opposed to cognitive (or transcendental) synthesis: 'Indeed, the significance of the doctrine of synthetic judgment is to have demonstrated that there is an a priori link (isomorphism) between Sentence and Figure, form of expression and form of content' (ATP 108). Where Kant's doctrine of synthetic judgement traced the isomorphy of intelligible form and sensible content back to the activity of the transcendental subject, stratification anchors the isomorphy of expressive form and expressed content in the functioning of the abstract machine, the ultimate source of stratic synthesis. Concrete assemblages presuppose the articulation of structured function and formed matter. But they do so insofar as each envelops an abstract machine.

Abstract envelopment

What is an abstract machine? Here are two definitions: 'The abstract machine exists *enveloped* in each stratum, whose Ecumenon or unity of composition it defines, and *developed* on the plane of consistency, whose destratification it *performs* (the Planomenon)' (ATP 73, my emphasis). 'We define the abstract machine as the aspect or moment at which *nothing but functions and matters remain*' (ATP 141, my emphasis). The abstract machine is Janus-faced: on one side, it accounts for the unity of composition (i.e. synthesis) proper to strata, insofar as these allocate structured functions to formed matters. This is to say that it performs a stratificatory function. But on the other side, it decouples structure and substance, form and content, deforming both expressive function and expressed matter. This is its destratificatory role. Stratification and destratification are two aspects of a single, indivisible machinic process, straddled by every abstract machine.

In its destratifying role, the abstract machine draws the plane of consistency by articulating a non-formal function with a formless matter. What it retains of stratic expression is the tensor, the a-signifying sign which indexes a continuum of intensive variation. What it retains of stratic content are heterogeneous intensities, or more precisely, different degrees of different intensive qualities: degrees of temperature, speed, conductivity, resistance, dilation, etc. These are the expressive traits of unformed matter. Thus the non-formal function is composed of tensors expressing different degrees of different qualities of intensity. It does not coordinate constants and variables, measuring continuous degrees of difference, but conjugates different kinds of differences in degrees. This is why it composes a continuum of variation, where variation is no longer subordinated to a fixed, homogeneous domain of variables. Instead, it distributes discontinuous differences in the kinds of degree (different degrees of heterogeneous qualities). Bonta and Protevi (2004: 48) give the following examples of non-formal functions: the channelling of differences in temperature by a heat engine and the imposition of conduct by a discipline. To diagram a complex phenomenon, whether epidemic, market or swarm, is to draw its non-formal function.

Thus abstract no longer means universal, ideal, or eternal; it is a function of variation: 'there is no reason to tie the abstract to the universal or the constant, or to efface the singularity of abstract machines insofar as they are constructed around variables and variations' (ATP 92–3). Tensors quantify continuous variation, not through unities of measure but through multiplicities of measurement. Quantity is no longer subordinated to invariant units of measure (number as unity); it indexes the qualitative particularity of heterogeneous intensities such as speed, temperature, conductivity, etc. (number as multiplicity). Consequently, magnitude varies according to the variation of the qualities it measures:

> Number is no longer a universal concept measuring elements according to their emplacement in a given dimension, but has itself become a multiplicity that varies according to the dimensions considered (the primacy of the domain over a complex of numbers attached to that domain). We do not have units of measure, only multiplicities or varieties of measurement. (ATP 8)

This is to say that there is no fixed unit of measure for the differences in dimension of a multiplicity, only a variety of measurements; a non-metric multiplicity numbering the qualitative heterogeneity of dimensions without referring to a common element or numerical base.

Tensor signs are indices of this qualitative heterogeneity or continuous variation of intensities. Thus the tensor sign expresses the diagrammatic function of deformalised expression. This deformalisation of expression is a prerequisite for the quantification of writing proclaimed at the beginning of *A Thousand Plateaus*: 'quantify writing. There is no difference between what a book talks about and how it is made' (ATP 4). To quantify writing is to conjugate expression and construction, structured function and deformalisation, stratification and destratification. This is the function of the diagram. Thus non-formal functioning is *diagrammatic*:

> A diagram has neither substance nor form, neither content nor expression ... Whereas expression and content have distinct forms, are really distinct from each other, function has only 'traits', of content and of expression, between which it establishes a connection: it is no longer even possible to tell whether it is a particle or a sign. A matter-content having only degrees of intensity, resistance, conductivity, heating, stretching, speed, or tardiness; and a function-expression having only 'tensors', as in a system of mathematical, or musical, writing. *Writing now functions on the same level as the real, and the real materially writes.* The diagram retains the most deterritorialised content and the most deterritorialised expression, in order to conjugate them. (ATP 141, my emphasis)

The diagramming of informal functions and formless matters not only conjugates signs and particles on the plane of consistency; it expresses the auto-construction of the real, the machinic unconscious.

Thus the alternative to stratic synthesis is not analysis – the formal disintrication of the abstract and the concrete as invariant form and variable content – but another kind of synthesis; which is to say, an alternative intrication of the abstract and the concrete. This synthesis is not cognitive but practical: it is the diagramming of the junction between non-formal functions and unformed matters. Tensors perform a diagrammatic function: they are the operators of torsion through which deformalisation composes intensities, sign-particles and flows on the plane of consistency. Diagrammatic composition is the identification of these points of torsion. But this composition requires concrete rules: 'There are rules, rules of "plan(n)ing", of diagramming ... The abstract machine is not random; the continuities, emissions and combinations, and conjunctions do not occur in just any fashion' (ATP 70–1). Thus it is the rules of *planification* ('planing') that ensure consistency, not decoding, deterritorialisation or destratification as such. These rules extract deformalised functions from strata: 'the plane of consistency is occupied, drawn by the abstract Machine . . .' (ATP 70).

Concrete development

It is concrete rules that effectuate the abstract. They develop the abstract machines enveloped in the strata. But this development hinges upon the distinction between stratification and assemblage (*agencement*). Because stratification is the precondition for every machinic assemblage, and assemblages are at once territorial and deterritorialising, assemblage is the practical condition for the development of the abstract. *Agencer* is a verb: to assemble. It is because concrete assemblages already envelop abstract machines that they can develop them: *planification* or planing is the concrete development of the enveloped abstract. It cuts across physical, biological and anthropomorphic strata to compose unformed matters, anorganic life and non-human becomings. Thus rules of destratification = rules of *planing* = development of the enveloped.

Nevertheless, the distinction between Sentence and Figure, expression and content, saying and doing, remains necessary precisely insofar as it is not only a real consequence of stratic synthesis but also a condition of development or planing. Consequently, destratification is not the abolition of the difference between saying and doing, or competence and performance; it is their informal re-articulation, one which retains an expression that has been decoupled from organic function, just as it retains a content that has been released from its organising form. Development renders performance indissociable from competence.

But how then are we to understand *selection*? How does performance operate a selection between greater or lesser degrees of connectivity (or dimensions) on the plane of consistency? How can it discriminate between greater or lesser degrees of development? How are we to measure the extent of construction? Here again the answer is: through concrete rules.

Concrete rules orient us in the composition of consistency; they provide an immanent measurement for the degree of continuous variation: 'Constant is not opposed to variable; it is a treatment of the variable opposed to the other kind of treatment, or continuous variation. So-called obligatory rules correspond to the first kind of treatment, whereas optional rules [*règles facultatives*] concern the construction of a continuum of variation' (ATP 103). Thus concrete rules are optional, which is to say that they are neither universal imperatives nor context-sensitive directives. While the former presuppose the stratified distribution of constants and variables, through the constancy of principles and variety of circumstances, the latter presuppose an empiricist pragmatism that merely relativises principles to the constancy of organic or psychological self-interest. But optional rules cannot simply be contrasted with necessary or categorical imperatives as if they were merely contingent or hypothetical imperatives. They are not hypothetical imperatives because they cannot be formulated with regard to any pre-established practical goal or utilitarian objective. Their form cannot be: 'If you want X, do Y', where X is relatively constant with regard to the variable Y, because the functional coordination of Y as means to end X remains entirely beholden to the stratification of function, whether physical, organic or subjective. Nor are optional rules merely 'contingent', since contingency is merely the stratic obverse of necessity. Concrete rules are 'optional' to the extent that they are constituted by their own selection, 'as in a game in which each move changes the rules' (ATP 100). This is why concrete rules are formulated in the shape of questions, the answers to which transform the assemblage within which they have been formulated. They are rules of assemblage that operate a selection according to the ways in which the assemblage under construction conjoins saying and doing, function and matter.

Thus concrete rules of assemblage are distributed along two axes of questioning. The first axis asks: Which content? (i.e. which regime of signs?) Which expression? (i.e. which system of bodies?): *'In each case, it is necessary to ascertain both what is said and what is done'* (ATP 504, my emphasis). The second asks: What are the cutting edges of deterritorialisation? What abstract machines do they effectuate?

> The concrete rules of assemblage thus operate along these two axes: On the one hand, what is the territoriality of the assemblage, what is the regime of signs and the pragmatic system? On the other hand, what are the cutting edges of deterritorialisation, and what abstract machines do they effectuate? (ATP 505)

The answers to the first set of questions specify the assemblage's type of signification and its degrees of territoriality: its expression and its content, or what it says and what it does. The answers to the second set of questions specify the assemblage's type of abstract machine and its degree of deterritorialisation: its non-formal function and its unformed matters. In answering this second set of questions, we identify the point of indiscernibility between saying and doing. Thus, for instance, itinerant metallurgy is the content of which nomadism is the expression; the mode of signification proper to the nomad war machine is numerical, or counter-signifying, while its territoriality consists in smoothing space. Numbering number is the tensor of nomadic distribution, which occupies space without categorising it. Counting without measuring is constructive deformation; hence the war machine's high index of deterritorialisation, both social and cognitive.

Practical mediation

Consequently, in answering both sets of questions, we determine the concrete rules and perform the diagramming function. Specifying our signifying regime and measuring our degree of territorialisation is the condition for diagramming the interaction of function and matter beyond the strata. Thus diagramming is akin to engineering: it is a cognitive operation carried out with a view to effectuating certain practical imperatives under specific material constraints. It lets us see to what extent a line of flight is liberatory *for us* insofar as we find ourselves in between strata and metastrata: 'In effect, consistency, proceeding by consolidation, *acts necessarily in the middle,* by the middle, and stands opposed to all planes of principle or finality' (ATP 507, my emphasis). Acting in the middle, diagramming deformalises stratified signs and substances to achieve consistency.

This is why Deleuze and Guattari repeatedly insist that the distinction between territorial and deterritorial, smooth and striated, strata and body without organs, is not the difference between good and bad, let alone a matter of good versus evil.[4] Deterritorialisation is not a theological imperative. There is no transcendence vis-à-vis the strata; consistency is not oriented towards an end-point or final state where territories, codes and signs have been definitively eliminated and the strata abolished. Since we are always in the middle – in between the organic, subjectified, signifying and the inorganic, a-subjective, a-signifying – the consolidation of consistency can only proceed from a certain stratified vantage point, whence different possibilities of action become assessable. The resort to the notion of 'possibility' is certainly awkward here given Deleuze and Guattari's Bergsonism, which entails rejecting possibility as an artefact of representation. But it is difficult to avoid, just as it is difficult to unyoke the term 'practice' from the notion of 'action', which seems to invite an appeal to a disavowed notion of subjective agency. Yet *agencement* is not without agency. The concept of machinic assemblage decouples agency from subjectivation and reallocates it to pre-individual collectivities. Assemblage is a-subjective agency. The need for concrete rules of assemblage is a consequence of the fact that our power of assemblage, our capacity for assembling, for connecting and consolidating consistency, is constrained both by our degree of territorialisation and our type of signifying regime. Territories, signs and codes are conditions of consistency. But they are *enabling* conditions. This is why '*alloplastic* [i.e. anthropic] *strata . . . are particularly propitious for the assemblages*' (ATP 514, my emphasis).

Thus *A Thousand Plateaus* does not wholly revoke the privileging of the human standpoint. It does not simply jettison philosophical humanism and the problematic of the subject (as elaborated from Descartes to Kant, Hegel and Heidegger) the better to plunge directly into the inhuman maelstrom. Its methodological sophistication, which is to say its account of diagramming as the real materially writing itself, precludes appeals to the 'intuition' or 'lived experience' of the real. Deleuze and Guattari understand that we cannot simply jump out of the strata on to the plane of consistency (whether we ought to accept the metaphysics of stratification is another matter, which we will return to below). We cannot simply nullify everything that distinguishes the human from the non-human by philosophical fiat. This is where Deleuze and Guattari's careful cartography of the layers of stratification exposes the uninterrogated phenomenological biases of certain strands of posthumanist metaphysics. Machinic pragmatics starts from a stratified vantage point that is unavoidably anthropocentric; yet it is precisely the preservation of a certain strategic anthropocentrism that prevents it from lapsing into anthropomorphism and projecting human properties on to non-human reality. Such projection is characteristic of every metaphysics that believes it can simply disregard Kant's access problem – what are the conditions under which human beings can think and know about non-human reality? Rather than ignore the constraint of human subjectivation in a way that only reinforces it and transplants human characteristics into the non-human, Deleuze and Guattari propose to use our stratified condition – our organic, subjectified, signifying state – as a leverage point for the development of consistency.

The problem of selection

The development or consolidation of consistency is inherently selective. As we know, it is concrete rules that operate the selection and ensure the consolidation. Two questions immediately arise pertaining to selection: 'What is being selected?' and 'How is it being selected?' The answer to the first question is: Whatever increases the degree of connectivity and the dimensions of consistency. The answer to the second is: Through the concrete rules that allow us to discriminate between increases or decreases in degrees of connectivity and dimensions of consistency. But now it becomes apparent that the answer to the first question is already the answer to the second. The selected 'what?' is also the selecting 'how?' This is to say that it is the plane itself that is the operator of selection:

> The plane *sections* multiplicities of variable dimensions . . . The plane is like a row [*enfilade*] of doors. And the concrete rules for the construction of the plane obtain to the extent that they exercise a selective role. *It is the plane, in other words, the mode of connection, that provides the means of eliminating the empty and cancerous bodies that rival the body without organs, of rejecting the homogeneous surfaces that overlay smooth space, and neutralising the lines of death and destruction that divert the line of flight. What is retained and preserved, therefore created, what consists, is only that which increases the number of connections at each level of division or composition*, thus in descending as well as ascending order (that which cannot be divided without changing in

nature, or enter into a larger composition without requiring a new criterion of comparison . . .) (ATP 508, my emphasis)

An *enfilade* is a series of communicating rooms each connected to the other by a single adjoining door, so that one cannot enter a room or move from one to the next by means of an external corridor. The corridor is the supplementary dimension of transcendent overcoding with regard to the series of interconnected rooms. To characterise the plane of consistency as an '*enfilade* of doors' is to say that there is no extrinsic dimension (corridor) by means of which its intrinsic dimensions (rooms) could be related to one another. What connects each room is its door or threshold. The threshold or limit of a multiplicity or assemblage is accessible only from within it. Each threshold is a mode of connection from room to room, multiplicity to multiplicity. But the mode of connection is the plane itself. It is the plane that connects the dimensions through which it is composed. This means that the criteria of selection (concrete rules) are discernible only from the vantage of an assemblage (dimension) already composing the plane. Recall that the selection is operated by diagramming content and expression, what is said and what is done within an assemblage, but in such a way that this diagramming determines a non-formal function and a formless matter that have become indiscernible, performing a saying that is also a doing. This is diagramming as the consummation of machinic pragmatics: to achieve a thinking-doing that develops the real while the real envelops it in turn. Selection becomes creation as participation in the auto-construction of the real. Thus it is the plane (i.e. the mode of connection) that selects itself through the concrete rules of assemblage: connection (consolidation) is the selection of connection. This is a-subjective agency insofar as every selection operated by concrete rules within an assemblage is also the self-selection or auto-consolidation of the plane itself.

There is a troubling circularity here, although it is one deliberately engineered by Deleuze and Guattari. Consistency is consolidated by increasing its number of connections and thereby its dimensions. The consolidating selection is effected through concrete rules, which are in turn determined by us, for who else can answer the questions that determine the rules? Since the plane does not pre-exist its practical construction, *we decide* what increases or decreases connectivity on the plane; yet the plane also decides through us. But this seems to introduce a fatal reversibility into the relation between concrete assemblage (the stratified) and abstract machine (the destratified). The real's auto-selection through us is just as much our selection of the real. Our decisive role in the composition of consistency, which is supposed to be the concrete development of the enveloped (the destratified), requires re-enveloping the abstract within the concrete (the stratified). The absoluteness of relativity (connection) becomes indistinguishable from the relativity of absoluteness (the body without organs as disconnection). But then are we not absolutely relativising the absolute? And if we are, doesn't machinic pragmatics risk lapsing into its less glamorous, more prosaic majoritarian cousins, either pragmatic individualism or liberal pragmatism?

The qualities of power

This reversibility or relativisation is symptomatic of a more fundamental difficulty: How do we determine the measure of consistency? One cannot construct without increasing, even if this increase is not measured in units. So how do we select what to increase given that it cannot be measured in fixed units? What are we constructing, given that we must proceed by subtracting unity, so that the extent of our constructive activity cannot be gauged in terms of constancy, regularity or order? How do we measure the dimensions of a consistency devoid of constancy? Two successive passages seem particularly relevant here. The first occurs on the book's penultimate page:

> [T]here is a whole process of selection of assemblages according to their ability [*aptitude*] to draw a plane of consistency with an increasing number of connections. Schizoanalysis is not only a qualitative analysis of abstract machines in relation to the assemblages, *but also a quantitative analysis of the assemblages in relation to a presumably pure abstract machine*. (ATP 513, my emphasis)

In this passage, Deleuze and Guattari seem to affirm the possibility of attaining a quantitative measure of an assemblage's capacity for increasing degrees of connectivity and dimensions of consistency. If this capacity can be assigned a quantitative measure, then selection operates on the basis of this measure: assemblages are selected or deselected according to the magnitude of their 'ampliative' capacity (i.e. increasing degrees of connectivity and dimensions of consistency). Capacity would presumably be cashed out here in terms of a Spinozist notion of power: the power to affect and be affected. Assuming a rough equivalence between modes and assemblages, every assemblage would be characterised by a degree of reality (consistency) corresponding to its power of affecting and being affected. As Deleuze writes of Spinoza: 'A thing has all the more reality or perfection insofar as it can be affected in a great number of ways: *quantity of reality always finds its reason in a power that is identical to essence*' (Deleuze

1968b: 83–4, my translation). Power is identical to essence as actuality, not potentiality: essence is existence as act. Thus essence is the power of acting, of affecting and being affected, whose increase converts passivity into activity: 'The power of acting is the only real, positive, and affirmative form of a power of being affected' (Deleuze 1968b: 204, my translation). The reality of affectivity derives from the power of activity: the greater the power of acting, the greater the power of affecting and being affected. But what determines this increase in power? For Deleuze's Nietzsche, the power of acting is a function of the quantity and quality of forces composing a body. Crucially, however, quality is that aspect of quantity 'that cannot be equalised out in the difference between quantities' (Deleuze 1983: 43–4). Thus quality is the intensity of force. Differences in the quantity of force are generated by different qualities of force, i.e. different intensities (speed, heat, resistance, conductivity, etc.) What Deleuze calls 'the absolute genesis' of the qualities of force is attributed to the will to power (Deleuze 1983: 51). Power is the being of force, its reality or actuality. But because power is will to power, self-intensification, it is the quality proper to the will to power that determines the qualities of forces. The qualitative difference proper to power is affirmative or negative; the qualitative difference proper to forces is active or reactive. Thus differences in the power of acting, in the capacity to affect and be affected, follow from the fundamental difference in the quality proper to power, which is either affirmative or negative. But if what is selected is difference in power, and the only quantity proper to power is determined by its quality as either affirmative or negative, then it is the quality of power that determines its quantity in terms of its capacity to affect and be affected. In other words, it is the affirmative will to power that selects between the affirmative and negative qualities of power. Assemblages that increase connectivity and consistency are those that select between increases and decreases in connectivity and consistency. The selection of assemblages reiterates the deliberate circularity in Deleuze's account of the selection of will to power.

The trouble, however, is that this difference in the quality of power is already actual. If differences in the capacity to act ultimately reduce to differences in the qualities of forces, as either active or reactive, then the difference in power on the basis of which selection is supposed to discriminate between assemblages has already been determined: it is already a difference in actuality (since the differences in modal power already correspond to differences in their attributive expression). This is to say that difference in power is already a difference in being. Flattening essence on to existence as power of acting effectively levels the distinction between making a difference in being (selecting) and accepting a difference in being as given, since the *essential* differences in degree of activity, which is to say differences in the quality of power, have already been made (i.e. selected). Thus the distinction between affirmative and negative types of will to power threatens to slip into an essential difference between types of potency. Yet the distinction between types of power was supposed to be a function of selection: making *is* (supposed to be) selecting.

The relative absolute

Ultimately then, the quantitative difference in power on the basis of which selection is supposed to operate requires a qualitative difference whose reason or ground is ontological, which is to say already actual or in effect. Thus the operative criterion for selecting between degrees of actuality, or powers of acting, turns out to be rooted in the quality, not quantities, of power: affirmativeness. If selection is the affirmation of affirmation (as in Deleuze's account of the dice-throw), then an assemblage's self-affirmation is effectively indistinguishable from that of the plane of consistency. Given this ambiguity, one might ask: Can we distinguish between personal self-affirmation and the impersonal self-affirmation of the machinic unconscious?

In the second of the two passages mentioned above (which occurs on the last page of the book), Deleuze and Guattari openly acknowledge the difficulty of measuring an assemblage's degree of proximity or distance vis-à-vis the 'pure' abstract machine:

> On the alloplastic [anthropic] strata, which are particularly propitious for the assemblages, there arise abstract machines that compensate for deterritorialisations with reterritorialisations, and especially for decodings with overcodings or overcoding equivalents. We have seen in particular that *if abstract machines open assemblages they also close them.* An order-word machine overcodes language, a faciality machine overcodes the body and even the head, a machine of enslavement overcodes or axiomatises the earth: these are in no way illusions, but real machinic effects. *We can no longer place the assemblages on a quantitative scale measuring how close or far they are from the abstract machine of the plane of consistency.* (ATP 514, translation modified, my emphasis)

Thus while conceding the difficulty of measuring degrees of connectivity and consistency, Deleuze and Guattari attribute this difficulty to the imperialism of the anthropic strata – in other words, to the anthropomorphisation of the earth. Yet the overcoding, enslavement and axiomatisation they allude to here may be symptoms of their own underlying equivocation between personal and impersonal self-affirmation; an ambiguity reiterating the reversibility between voluntarism and determinism, concrete and abstract, relative and absolute, which we have already noted. The 'pure' abstract machine is consistency as point of indiscernibility between saying and doing, the absolute development of the enveloped. But the alloplastic strata generate abstract machines that re-envelop what has been developed on the physical and biological strata: every sign becomes signifying, every haecceity is subjectified, every smooth space is striated. This systematic re-envelopment renders it difficult if not impossible to measure an assemblage's degree of development vis-à-vis *the* abstract machine or plane of consistency. A fatal indiscernibility is inaugurated such that it becomes impossible to say whether the absolute is in the relative (the abstract in the concrete), or the relative in the absolute (the concrete in the abstract).

This predicament points to a still deeper problem. In order to stave off this indiscernibility, it must be possible to measure degrees of deterritorialisation relative to an absolute movement – the full body of the earth, the deterritorialised, the cosmic egg, etc.[5] This is the absolute in terms of which we measure degrees of deterritorialisation and types of assemblage. Thus, the absolute

> expresses nothing transcendent or undifferentiated. It does not even express a quantity that would exceed all given (relative) quantities. It expresses only a type of movement qualitatively different from relative movement. A movement is absolute when, whatever its quantity and speed, it relates "a" body considered as multiple to a smooth space that it occupies in the manner of a vortex. (ATP 509)

Absolute movement – the torque of a vortex – is *qualitatively* different from relative movement as well as the measure of relative movement. But the retention of this absolute movement seems to violate the prohibition on transcendence precisely insofar as relativity is defined negatively as a diminution, a limitation or relativisation of absolute movement. How can we measure the relativisation of movement negatively as a diminution of absolute movement unless we can specify the positivity of absolute movement independently of its limitation? Vortical torque may have the absoluteness of an intensive quality, but why should this particular quality of movement be the defining characteristic of the absolute? Its qualitative absoluteness remains relative to that of every other quality of movement. (Despite their Spinozism, Deleuze and Guattari reject the thesis that determination is negation.) Thus the distinction between relative and absolute remains relative because there is no immanent access to the absolute that would bypass the strata (which is to say, the absolute's self-limitation).

The question remains: why does absolute movement relativise itself? If the absolute is a quality of movement, rather than a quantity, what accounts for this difference in quality from the viewpoint of that which is already relative? The problem is that Deleuze and Guattari maintain a traditional qualitative conception of the absolute while insisting that this quality is neither negatively defined (as infinite vis-à-vis other finite qualities) nor wholly inaccessible and transcendent vis-à-vis the relative and immanent. They want to be able to specify absoluteness as a determinate quality of movement. But the differences in the qualities of intensity – intensive matter's expressive traits – cannot be absolutised without absolutising the relations between bodies within which they manifest themselves. The notion of absolute intensity is limitative vis-à-vis the continuums of intensities, but Deleuze and Guattari want to invert the relation between absolute and relative to define relative intensity limitatively in regard to absolute intensity. Thus they have to give a positive account of limitation on the basis of a negative account of the unlimited, or the absolute, since the latter is precisely that whose positive characteristics are defined negatively in relation to its own limitation: *de*-territorialised flows, *a*-signifying particles, *non*-formal functions, form*less* matters. The body without organs does not lack anything, but what it does not lack can only be defined in terms of that which falls short of it, that which is not full, that which is limited with regard to it, i.e. the stratified. Thus destratification presupposes stratification; but stratification only makes sense with regard to a concept of the destratified whose positive characteristics are drawn exclusively from the strata.

Conclusion

The consistency of machinic pragmatics stands or falls with the theory of stratification. The latter is in many ways a magnificent construction, drawing creatively on an impressive array of scientific work (most notably that of François Jacob, Jacques Monod, René Thom and Ilya Prigogine).[6] Yet it remains wholly speculative for all that. Its dazzling ingenuity should not blind us to the very obvious questions it continues to raise: *How do they know? Why should we believe that reality is really like that?* Dismissing these questions as Kantian hang-ups is a facile rhetorical manoeuvre, unworthy of the seriousness of the book's philosophical ambition. Without stratification, the consistency of *A Thousand Plateaus* unravels: it is the single thread tying together its fantastically intricate lines of thought. Yet it is the thread that cannot be *verifiably* tethered to anything outside the book.

Thus, for all its paeans to the primacy of exteriority, *A Thousand Plateaus* is ultimately a self-enclosed, self-sufficient construction; but one rooted in a gesture of negation that it cannot avow or integrate within itself. What it rejects is representation, together with its 'arborescent' dichotomies between inside and outside, subjectivity and objectivity, truth and falsity. It tries to purify this rejection of negation by construing rejection as selection and negation as a quality of power. Thus the rejection of representation (together with all its dichotomies, oppositions and negations) is not supposed to be a denial but a mere effect or consequence of the book's selection of affirmation over negation. Rather than seeking to justify itself, this is a book that insists on affirming its own power, which is precisely the power of affirmation. But as we saw, the attempt to reduce negation to affirmation and denial to selection rests upon the affirmation of a difference between affirmative and negative power which turns out to be all but essential. Differences in the quality of power (affirmative or negative) turn out to be fundamental differences in being. By the same token, making the difference between affirmation and negation turns out to be indiscernible from accepting it as something that is already given; which is to say, representing it. This indistinction testifies to a fundamental inconsistency, which might also be called a contradiction, between what the book *says* and what it *does*. Despite its extraordinary ingenuity, *A Thousand Plateaus* cannot give a wholly positive account of the limit between the relative and the absolute, the finite and the infinite. This is to say that its systematic disavowal of dialectics, negativity, interiority and transcendence leads it to hypostatise the difference between negative and positive, inside and outside, immanence and transcendence, into a brute given, an ultimately transcendent datum: stratification. Everything in the book relies on giving a positive sense to the *de-* in destratification, or delimitation, but this positive sense is merely the inversion of the limitation of absolute movement that it cannot but presuppose as its starting point: stratification. Thus the book absolutises limitation in a forlorn attempt *not* to define the absolute limitatively. Circumventing negation and mediation, which is to say the constraints of justification, it seeks to install itself immediately (or immanently) *in between* the relative and the absolute, but in doing so ends up absolutising in-between-ness. But can this absolute in-betweenness be so confidently contrasted with the utilitarian compromise which is the fabric of the everyday?

Notes

1. Thus Deleuze's insistence that *A Thousand Plateaus* is a work of '[p]hilosophy, nothing but philosophy . . .' (Deleuze 1980a: 99).
2. 'Every undertaking of destratification (for example, going beyond the organism, plunging into a becoming) must therefore observe concrete rules of extreme caution' (ATP 503). See also ATP 171–83.
3. See especially ATP 281–4. Miguel de Beistegui has convincingly argued that Deleuze

and Guattari contrast the plane of transcendence, or development, which maintains a classical hierarchical distinction between (transcendental) condition and (empirical) conditioned, albeit in the form of unconscious virtuality and conscious actuality, to the plane of immanence, or consistency, where the difference between stratificatory and destratificatory processes is unfolded on a single level, such that the principle of perceptibility cannot but be perceived together with that which it renders perceptible. See Beistegui 2010: 47–76.

4. E.g. 'There is a rupture in the rhizome whenever segmentary lines explode into a line of flight, but the line of flight is part of the rhizome. These lines always tie back to one another. That is why one can never posit a dualism or a dichotomy, even in the rudimentary form of the good and the bad' (ATP 9).

5. '[W]hat is primary is an absolute deterritorialisation, an absolute line of flight, however complex or multiple – that of the plane of consistency or body without organs (the Earth, the absolutely deterritorialised). This absolute deterritorialisation becomes relative only after stratification occurs on that plane or body: It is the strata that are always residue, not the opposite' (ATP 56).

6. Nevertheless, the parochialism of this list should give us pause: all French, all writing in the 1970s. Can a theory so ambitious afford so narrow an evidential base? The other chief inspiration is, of course, the Danish linguist Louis Hjelmslev, originator of the distinction between content and expression.

Bibliography

References to *A Thousand Plateaus* use the abbreviation ATP in the text and refer to this edition: Gilles Deleuze and Félix Guattari (1987), *A Thousand Plateaus*, trans. Brian Massumi, Minneapolis: University of Minnesota Press. Quotations have been transposed into British English.

Abraham, Nicholas, and Maria Torok (1986), *The Wolf-Man's Magic Word: A Cryptonymy*, trans. Nicholas Rand, Minneapolis: University of Minnesota Press.
Adkins, Brent (2015), *Deleuze and Guattari's* A Thousand Plateaus: *A Critical Introduction and Guide*, Edinburgh: Edinburgh University Press.
Adkins, Brent, and Paul Hinlicky (2013), *Rethinking Philosophy and Theology with Deleuze: A New Cartography*, London: Bloomsbury.
Ahmed, Sara (2010), *The Promise of Happiness*, Durham, NC: Duke University Press.
Alliez, Eric (2004 [1993]), *The Signature of the World, Or, What is Deleuze and Guattari's Philosophy?*, trans. E. R. Albert and A. Toscano, London: Continuum.
Alliez, Eric (2011), 'Rhizome (With No Return). From Structure to Rhizome: Transdisciplinarity in French Thought', *Radical Philosophy* 167: 36–42.
Alter, Robert (ed. and trans.) (2004), *The Five Books of Moses: A Translation with Commentary*, New York: W. W. Norton.
Anderson, Perry (1979), *Lineages of the Absolutist State*, London: Verso.
Anon. (2006 [1937]), *The Secret History of the Mongols*, 2 vols, trans. Igor De Rachewiltz, Leiden: Brill.
Ansell Pearson, Keith (1999), *Germinal Life: The Difference and Repetition of Deleuze*, London: Routledge.
Antonioli, M. (2003), *Géophilosophie de Deleuze et Guattari*, Paris: L'Harmattan.
Ayasse, Manfred et al. (2003), 'Pollinator Attractor in a Sexually Deceptive Orchid by Means of Unconventional Chemicals', *Proceedings of the Royal Society B: Biological Sciences* 270: 517–22.
Bachelard, Gaston (1943), *L'Air et les songes*, Paris: Corti.
Bachelard, Gaston (1948), *La Terre et les rêveries du repos*, Paris: Corti.
Badiou, Alain (2000 [1997]), *Deleuze: The Clamor of Being*, trans. Louise Burchill, Minneapolis: University of Minnesota Press.
Balazs, Etienne (1964), 'The Birth of Capitalism in China', in *Chinese Civilization and Bureaucracy*, trans. H. G. Wright, New Haven, CT: Yale University Press.

Barthes, Roland (1967 [1964]), *Elements of Semiology*, trans. Annette Lavers and Colin Smith, New York: Hill and Wang.
Beasley-Murray, Jon (2010), *Posthegemony: Political Theory and Latin America*, Minneapolis: University of Minnesota Press.
Beckett, Samuel (1965), *Proust and Three Dialogues with George Duthuit*, London: John Calder.
Beistegui, Miguel (2010), *Immanence: Deleuze and Philosophy*, Edinburgh: Edinburgh University Press.
Bell, Jeffrey A. (2009), *Deleuze's Hume*, Edinburgh: Edinburgh University Press.
Bell, Jeffrey A. (2016), *Deleuze and Guattari's What is Philosophy?*, Edinburgh: Edinburgh University Press.
Bergson, Henri (1910 [1889]), *Time and Free Will*, trans. F. L. Pogson, London: Allen and Unwin.
Bersani, Leo (1990), *The Culture of Redemption*, Cambridge, MA: Harvard University Press.
Best, S., and D. Kellner (1991), *Postmodern Theory: Critical Interrogations*, New York: Guildford Press.
Bogue, Ronald (2004), 'Apology for Nomadology', *Interventions* 6.2: 169–79.
Bogue, Ronald (2012), 'Nature, Law and Chaosmopolitanism', in Rosi Braidotti and Patricia Pisters (eds), *Revisiting Normativity with Deleuze*, London: Bloomsbury.
Bonta, Mark, and John Protevi (2004), *Deleuze and Geophilosophy: A Guide and Glossary*, Edinburgh: Edinburgh University Press.
Boulez, Pierre (1975 [1971]), *On Music Today*, trans. Susan Bradshaw and Richard Rodney Bennett, London: Faber and Faber.
Braidotti, Rosi (2013a), 'Nomadic Ethics', *Deleuze Studies* 7.3: 342–59.
Braidotti, Rosi (2013b), *The Posthuman*, New York: Wiley.
Braudel, Fernand (1973 [1967]), *Capitalism and Material Life, 1400–1800*, trans. Miriam Kochan, New York: Harper & Row.
Braudel, Fernand (1992 [1967]), *Civilization and Capitalism, 15th–18th Century*, Vol. I: *The Structure of Everyday Life*, trans. Siân Reynolds, Berkeley: University of California Press.
Burk, Drew S. (2013), 'Living Network Ecologies: A Triptych on the Universe of Fernand Deligny', *Ecology of Networks*, posted 23 April, http://sites.fhi.duke.edu/ecologyofnetworks/2013/04/23/living-network-ecologies-a-triptych-on-the-universe-of-fernand-deligny/ (accessed 27 June 2017).
Butler Samuel (1872), *Erewhon: or, Over the Range*, London: Trübner and Ballantyne.
Canetti, Elias (1978 [1960]), *Crowds and Power*, trans. Carol Stewart, New York: Seabury Press.
Canguilhem, Georges (1994), *A Vital Rationalist: Selected Writings from Georges Canguilhem*, ed. François Delaporte, trans. Arthur Goldhammer, New York: Zone Books.
Carneiro, Robert L. (2003), *Evolutionism in Cultural Anthropology: A Critical History*, Cambridge, MA: Westview.
Carpenter, Edmund, Frederick Varley and Robert Flaherty (1959), *Eskimo*, Toronto: University of Toronto Press.
Chemero, Anthony (2009), *Radical Embodied Cognitive Science*, Cambridge, MA: MIT Press.
Childe, V. Gordon (1951 [1936]), *Man Makes Himself*, New York: New American Library.
Childe, V. Gordon (2009 [1958]), *The Prehistory of European Society*, Nottingham: Spokesman.
Chomsky, Noam (1957), *Syntactic Structures*, Berlin: Mouton de Gruyter.
Chomsky, Noam (1965), *Aspects of the Theory of Syntax*, Cambridge, MA: MIT Press.
Christiansen, Ellen Juhl (1995), *The Covenant in Judaism and Paul: A Study of Ritual Boundaries as Identity Markers*, Leiden: Brill.
Clarke, Stanley (1982), *Marx, Marginalism, and Modern Sociology*, London: Macmillan.

Clastres, Pierre (1989 [1974]), *Society Against the State: Essays in Political Anthropology*, trans. Robert Hurley with Abe Stein, New York: Zone Books.
Clastres, Pierre (1994), 'Primitive Economy', in *The Archaeology of Violence*, trans. Jeanine Herman, New York: Semiotext(e).
Clausewitz, C. von. (1982 [1832]), *On War*, Harmondsworth: Penguin.
Clisby, Dale (2015), 'Deleuze's Secret Dualism? Competing Accounts of the Relationship between the Virtual and the Actual', *Parrhesia* 24: 127–49.
Colebrook, Claire (1999), 'A Grammar of Becoming: Strategy, Subjectivism, and Style', in Elizabeth Grosz (ed.), *Becomings: Explorations in Time, Memory, and Futures*, New York: Cornell University Press, 117–40.
Culler, Jonathan (2001 [1981]), *The Pursuit of Signs: Semiotics, Literature, Deconstruction*, Ithaca: Cornell University Press.
Culler, Jonathan (2002 [1975]), *Structuralist Poetics: Structuralism, Linguistics, and the Study of Literature*, London: Routledge.
Damasio, Antonio (1994), *Descartes' Error*, New York: Avon.
Damasio, Antonio (1999), *The Feeling of What Happens*, New York: Harcourt.
Day, Richard (2005), *Gramsci is Dead*, Ann Arbor, MI: Pluto Press.
DeLanda, Manuel (1992), 'Nonorganic Life', in Jonathan Crary and Sanford Kwinter (eds), *Incorporations*, New York: Zone Books, 128–67.
DeLanda, Manuel (1997), *A Thousand Years of Nonlinear History*, New York: Zone Books.
DeLanda, Manuel (2002), *Intensive Science and Virtual Philosophy*, London: Continuum.
DeLanda, Manuel (2006), *A New Philosophy of Society*, New York: Continuum.
Deleuze, Gilles (1968a), *Différence et Répétition*, Paris: PUF.
Deleuze, Gilles (1968b), *Spinoza et le problème de l'expression*, Paris: Minuit.
Deleuze, Gilles (1969), *Logique du sens*, Paris: Minuit.
Deleuze, Gilles (1972), 'Seminar of 22 February. On *Anti-Oedipus* and *A Thousand Plateaus*', http://www.webdeleuze.com/ (accessed 27 June 2017).
Deleuze, Gilles (1978), 'Lecture on Spinoza: *Cours Vincennes* 24 January 1978', https://www.webdeleuze.com/textes/14 (accessed 27 June 2017).
Deleuze, Gilles (1979a), 'Seminar of 6 November. On State Apparatuses and War-Machines', http://www2.univ-paris8.fr/deleuze/ (accessed 27 June 2017).
Deleuze, Gilles (1979b), 'Seminar of 20 November. On State Apparatuses and War-Machines', http://www2.univ-paris8.fr/deleuze/ (accessed 27 June 2017).
Deleuze, Gilles (1979c), 'Seminar of 27 November. On State Apparatuses and War-Machines', http://www2.univ-paris8.fr/deleuze/ (accessed 27 June 2017).
Deleuze, Gilles (1980a), 'Interview with Catherine Clement', *L'Arc* 49 (rev. edn, 1980): 99.
Deleuze, Gilles (1980b), 'Seminar of 26 February. On State Apparatuses and War-Machines', http://www2.univ-paris8.fr/deleuze/ (accessed 27 June 2017).
Deleuze, Gilles (1981), 'Seminar of 10 March. On Spinoza', http://www2.univ-paris8.fr/deleuze/ (accessed 27 June 2017).
Deleuze, Gilles (1983 [1962]), *Nietzsche and Philosophy*, trans. H. Tomlinson, London: Athlone.
Deleuze, Gilles (1984 [1963]), *Kant's Critical Philosophy*, trans. H. Tomlison and B. Habberjam, London: Athlone.
Deleuze, Gilles (1988 [1970]), *Spinoza, Practical Philosophy*, trans. R. Hurley, San Francisco: City Lights.
Deleuze, Gilles (1989 [1985]), *Cinema 2: The Time Image*, trans. H. Tomlinson and R. Galeta, London: Athlone.
Deleuze, Gilles (1990a [1968]), *Expressionism in Philosophy: Spinoza*, trans. Martin Joughin, New York: Zone Books.
Deleuze, Gilles (1990b [1969]), *The Logic of Sense*, trans. M. Lester, New York: Columbia University Press.

Deleuze, Gilles (1991a), *Bergsonism*, trans. H. Tomlinson and B. Habberjam, New York: Zone Books.
Deleuze, Gilles (1991b), *Empiricism and Subjectivity: An Essay on Hume's Theory of Human Nature*, trans. Constantin V. Boundas, New York: Columbia University Press.
Deleuze, Gilles (1993), *The Fold: Leibniz and the Baroque*, trans. T. Conley, Minneapolis: University of Minnesota Press.
Deleuze, Gilles (1994 [1968]), *Difference and Repetition*, trans. Paul Patton, New York: Columbia University Press.
Deleuze, Gilles (1995a [1990]), *Negotiations 1972–1990*, trans. Martin Joughin, New York: Columbia University Press.
Deleuze, Gilles (1995b), 'Le "je me souviens" de Gilles Deleuze', *Le Nouvel Observateur* 1619, 16–22 November, 50–1.
Deleuze, Gilles (2003 [1981]), *Francis Bacon. The Logic of Sensation*, trans. D. W. Smith, London: Continuum.
Deleuze, Gilles (2004a [2002]), *Desert Islands and Other Texts 1953–1974*, ed. David Lapoujade, trans. Michael Taormina, New York: Semiotext(e).
Deleuze, Gilles (2004b [1964, 1970, 1976]), *Proust and Signs*, trans. Richard Howard, Minneapolis: University of Minnesota Press.
Deleuze, Gilles (2006 [2003]), *Two Regimes of Madness: Texts and Interviews, 1975–1995*, ed. David Lapoujade, trans. Ames Hodges and Michael Taormina, New York: Semiotext(e).
Deleuze, Gilles (2012), 'Gilles Deleuze: From A to Z', interview with C. Parnet, ed. P-A. Boutang, trans. C. J. Stivale, Los Angeles: Semiotext(e).
Deleuze, Gilles (2015), *Lettres et autres textes*, Paris: Minuit.
Deleuze, Gilles, and Félix Guattari (1976), *Rhizome*, Paris: Minuit.
Deleuze, Gilles, and Félix Guattari (1983 [1972]), *Anti-Oedipus*, trans. R. Hurley et al., Minneapolis: University of Minneapolis Press.
Deleuze, Gilles, and Félix Guattari (1986 [1975]), *Kafka: Toward a Minor Literature*, trans. Dana Polan, Minneapolis: University of Minnesota Press.
Deleuze, Gilles, and Félix Guattari (1994 [1991]), *What is Philosophy?*, trans. Hugh Tomlinson and Graham Burchell, New York: Columbia University Press.
Deleuze, Gilles, and Claire Parnet (1987 [1977]), *Dialogues*, trans. Hugh Tomlinson and Barbara Habberjam, New York: Columbia University Press.
Deligny, Fernand (1975), 'Cahiers de l'immuable', *Voix et voir, Recherches* 1.18.
Deligny, Fernand (2013), *Cartes et lignes d'erre: Traces du réseau de Fernand Deligny, 1969–1979*, ed. Sandra Alvarez de Toledo, Paris: L'Arachnéen.
Deligny, Fernand (2015 [2008]), *The Arachnean and Other Texts*, trans. Drew S. Burk and Catherine Porter, Minneapolis: Univocal.
Derrida, Jacques (1981 [1972]), *Dissemination*, trans. Barbara Johnson, Chicago: University of Chicago Press.
Derrida, Jacques (1982 [1972]), *Margins of Philosophy*, trans. Alan Bass, Chicago: University of Chicago Press.
Derrida, Jacques (2002) 'Force of Law: The "Mystical" Foundation of Authority', in Gil Anidjar (ed.), *Acts of Religion*, London: Routledge, 230–98.
Descartes, René (1984 [1701]), 'The Search for Truth by Means of the Natural Light', trans. Dugald Murdoch and Robert Stoothoff, in John Cottingham, Robert Stoothoff and Dugald Murdoch (eds), *The Philosophical Writings of Descartes, Vol. II*, Cambridge: Cambridge University Press, 400–20.
Descartes, René (1985a [1644]), 'Principles of Philosophy', trans. Dugald Murdoch, in John Cottingham, Robert Stoothoff and Dugald Murdoch (eds), *The Philosophical Writings of Descartes, Vol. I*, Cambridge: Cambridge University Press, 177–292.
Descartes, René (1985b [1628]), 'Rules for the Direction of the Mind', trans. Dugald Murdoch, in John Cottingham, Robert Stoothoff and Dugald Murdoch (eds), *The*

Philosophical Writings of Descartes, Vol. I, Cambridge: Cambridge University Press, 7–78.

Descartes, René (1985c [1633]), 'The World', trans. Dugald Murdoch, in John Cottingham, Robert Stoothoff and Dugald Murdoch (eds), *The Philosophical Writings of Descartes, Vol. I*, Cambridge: Cambridge University Press, 81–98.

Devaux, Émile (1933), *Trois problèmes: l'espèce, l'instinct, l'homme*, Paris: Le François.

Dosse, François (2010 [2007]), *Gilles Deleuze and Félix Guattari: Intersecting Lives*, trans. Deborah Glassman, New York: Columbia University Press.

Dosse, François (2012), 'Deleuze and Structuralism', in Daniel W. Smith and Henry Somers-Hall (eds), *The Cambridge Companion to Deleuze*, Cambridge: Cambridge University Press, 126–50.

Duffy, Simon (2013), *Deleuze and the History of Mathematics: In Defense of the 'New'*, London: Bloomsbury.

Dumézil, Georges (1988 [1940]), *Mitra-Varuna: An Essay on Two Indo-European Representations of Sovereignty*, trans. Derek Coltman, New York: Zone Books.

Eliot, T. S. (1972 [1954]), *Selected Poems*, London: Faber.

Emperaire, J. (1955), *Les nomades de la mer*, Paris: Gallimard.

Engels, Friedrich (1972 [1884]), *The Origin of the Family, Private Property, and the State*, New York: International Publishers.

Evans-Pritchard, E. E. (1940), *The Nuer: A Description of the Modes of Livelihood and Political Institutions of a Nilotic People*, Oxford: Clarendon.

Fink, B. (1997), *A Clinical Introduction to Lacanian Psychoanalysis: Theory and Technique*, Cambridge, MA: Harvard University Press.

Foucault, Michel (1977 [1975]), *Discipline and Punish*, trans. Alan Sheridan, New York: Vintage.

Foucault, Michel (1984 [1972]), 'Preface', to G. Deleuze and F. Guattari, *Anti-Oedipus: Capitalism and Schizophrenia*, trans. R. Hurley, M. Seem and H. R. Lane, London: Athlone.

Foucault, Michel (1989a [1969]), *The Archaeology of Knowledge*, trans. A. M. Sheridan Smith, London: Routledge.

Foucault, Michel (1989b [1961]), *Madness and Civilization: A History of Insanity in the Age of Reason*, trans. R. Howard, London: Routledge.

Foucault, Michel (2003 [1997]), *'Society Must Be Defended': Lectures at the Collège de France 1975–1976*, ed. Mauro Bertani and Alessandro Fontana, trans. David Macey, New York: Picador.

Foucault, Michel (2013 [2011]), *Lectures on the Will to Power, Lectures at the Collège de France, 1970–1971*, ed. Daniel Defert, trans. Graham Burchill, New York: Palgrave.

Freeman, Walter J. (2000a), *How Brains Make Up Their Minds*, New York: Columbia University Press.

Freeman, Walter J. (2000b), 'Emotion is Essential to All Intentional Behaviors', in Marc Lewis and Isabela Granic (eds), *Emotion, Development and Self-Organization: Dynamic Systems Approaches to Emotional Development*, New York: Cambridge University Press.

Freud, Sigmund (1962a [1918]), 'From the History of an Infantile Neurosis', in *The Standard Edition of the Complete Psychological Works of Sigmund Freud*, Vol. XVII, trans. James Strachey, London: Hogarth Press.

Freud, Sigmund (1962b [1909]), 'Little Hans', in *The Standard Edition of the Complete Psychological Works of Sigmund Freud*, Volume X, trans. James Strachey, London: Hogarth Press.

Freud, Sigmund (1962c [1915]), 'The Unconscious', in *The Standard Edition of the Complete Psychological Works of Sigmund Freud*, Volume XIV, trans. James Strachey, London: Hogarth Press.

Freud, Sigmund (1975 [1920]), *Beyond the Pleasure Principle*, trans. J. Strachey, New York: W. W. Norton.

Gardiner, Muriel (1971), *The Wolf-Man*, New York: Basic Books.

Genosko, Gary (1994), *Baudrillard and Signs: Signification Ablaze*, New York: Routledge.
Genosko, Gary (1998), 'Guattari's Schizoanalytic Semiotics: Mixing Hjelmslev and Peirce', in Eleanor Kaufman and Kevin Jon Heller (eds), *Deleuze and Guattari: New Mappings in Politics, Philosophy, and Culture*, Minneapolis: University of Minnesota Press, 175–90.
Godelier, Maurice (1978), 'The Concept of the "Asiatic Mode of Production" and Marxist Models of Social Evolution', in David Seddon (ed.), *Relations of Production: Marxist Approaches to Economic Anthropology*, London: Frank Cass.
Graeber, David (2011), *Debt: The First 5,000 Years*, New York and London: Melville House.
Graves, Will (2007), *Wolves in Russia: Anxiety through the Ages*, Calgary: Detselig Enterprises.
Grousset, R. (1970 [1939]), *The Empire of the Steppes*, trans. N. Walford, New Brunswick, NJ: Rutgers University Press.
Guattari, Félix (1995 [1992]), *Chaosmosis: An Ethico-Aesthetic Paradigm*, trans. P. Bains and J. Pefanis, Sydney: Power Publications.
Guattari, Félix (2011 [1979]), *The Machinic Unconscious*, trans. Taylor Adkins, New York: Semiotext(e).
Guattari, Félix (2013 [1989]), *Schizoanalytic Cartographies*, trans. A. Goffey, London: Bloomsbury.
Guattari, Félix (2014 [1989]), *The Three Ecologies*, trans. Ian Pindar and Paul Sutton, London: Bloomsbury.
Guattari, Félix (2015), *Psychoanalysis and Transversality*, trans. A. Hodges, Los Angeles: Semiotext(e).
Gueroult, Martial (1934), *Dynamique et metaphysique leibniziennes*, Paris: Les Belles Lettres.
Hadot, P. (1995 [1981]), *Philosophy as a Way of Life*, ed. M. Chase, trans. A. I. Davidson, Oxford: Blackwell.
Hansen, Mark (2000), 'Becoming as Creative Involution? Contextualizing Deleuze and Guattari's Biophilosophy', *Postmodern Culture* 11.1.
Heidegger, Martin (1993 [1949]), 'Letter on Humanism', in *Basic Writings*, trans. David Farrell Krell, New York: Harper Collins.
Hjelmslev, Louis (1961 [1943]), *Prolegomena to a Theory of Language*, trans. Francis J. Whitfield, Madison: University of Wisconsin Press.
Hjelmslev, Louis (1970 [1963]), *Language*, trans. Francis J. Whitfield, Madison: University of Wisconsin Press.
Holland, Eugene W. (2003a), 'Representation and Misrepresentation in Postcolonial Literature and Theory', *Research in African Literatures* 34.1: 159–72.
Holland, Eugene W. (2003b), 'To the Editor', *Research in African Literatures* 34.4: 187–90.
Holland, Eugene W. (2008a), 'Jazz Improvisation: Music of the People-to-Come', in S. O'Sullivan and S. Zepke (eds), *Deleuze, Guattari and the Production of the New*, London: Continuum, 196–205.
Holland, Eugene W. (2008b), 'Schizoanalysis, Nomadology, Fascism', in Nick Thoburn and Ian Buchanan (eds), *Deleuze and Politics*, Edinburgh: Edinburgh University Press, 74–97.
Holland, Eugene W. (2011), *Nomad Citizenship*, Minneapolis: University of Minnesota Press.
Holland, Eugene W. (2013), *Deleuze and Guattari's* A Thousand Plateaus, London: Bloomsbury.
Hubac, Pierre (1948), *Les nomades*, Paris: La renaissance du Livre.
Hume, David (1978 [1739–40]), *Treatise of Human Nature*, Oxford: Clarendon.
Iversen, Margaret (1993), *Alois Riegl: Art and History*, Cambridge, MA: MIT Press.

Jacob, François (1973), *The Logic of Life: A History of Heredity*, trans. Betty E. Spillman, New York: Pantheon.
Jacob, François (1974), 'Le modèle linguistique en biologie', *Critique* 30.322: 197–205.
Jacobs, Jane (1970), *The Economy of Cities*, New York: Vintage.
James, Henry (1919), *In the Cage*, London: Martin Secker.
Juarrero, Alicia (1999), *Dynamics in Action: Intentional Behavior as a Complex System*, Cambridge, MA: MIT Press.
Kant, Immanuel (1929 [1781]), *Critique of Pure Reason*, trans. Norman Kemp Smith, New York: St. Martin's.
Kant, Immanuel (1987 [1790]), *Critique of Judgment*, trans. Werner S. Pluhar, Indianapolis: Hackett Publishing.
Keller, Evelyn Fox (2000), *The Century of the Gene*, Cambridge, MA: Harvard University Press.
Koffka, Kurt (1935), *Principles of Gestalt Psychology*, London: Routledge.
Kripke, Saul (1982), *Wittgenstein on Rules and Private Language*, Cambridge, MA: Harvard University Press.
Lacan, Jacques (1981 [1973]), *The Four Fundamental Concepts of Psycho-Analysis*, trans. A. Sheridan, ed. Jacques-Alain Miller, New York: W. W. Norton.
Lacan, Jacques (1993 [1956]), *The Seminar of Jacques Lacan, Book III: The Psychoses*, trans. R. Grigg, ed. J.-A. Miller, New York: W. W. Norton.
Lacan, Jacques (2006 [1966]), *Écrits: The First Complete Edition in English*, trans. B. Fink, in collaboration with H. Fink and R. Grigg, New York: W. W. Norton.
Lacan, Jacques (unpublished typescript), *The Seminar of Jacques Lacan Book X: Anxiety 1962–1963*, trans. Cormac Gallagher, http://www.lacaninireland.com (accessed 27 June 2017).
Lampert, Jay (2011), *Deleuze and Guattari's Philosophy of History*, London: Bloomsbury.
Land, Nick (2013), 'Making it with Death: Remarks on Thanatos and Desiring Production', in Ray Brassier and Robin Mackay (eds), *Fanged Noumena: Collected Writings 1987–2007*, Falmouth: Urbanomic, 261–88.
Lapoujade, David (2014), *Deleuze, les mouvements aberrants*, Paris: Minuit.
Leroi-Gourhan, André (1993 [1964]), *Gesture and Speech*, trans. Anna Bostock Berger, Cambridge, MA: MIT Press.
Leving, Yuri (ed.) (2012), *Anatomy of a Short Story: Nabokov's Puzzles, Codes, 'Signs and Symbols'*, New York: Continuum.
Litaker, Justin (2014), 'Capitalism and Social Agency', PhD dissertation, West Lafayette, Purdue University.
Lull, Vicente, and Rafael Mico (2011), *Archaeology of the Origin of the State: The Theories*, Oxford: Oxford University Press.
Lundy, Craig (2012), *History and Becoming: Deleuze's Philosophy of Creativity*, Edinburgh: Edinburgh University Press.
Lundy, Craig (2013), 'Who Are Our Nomads Today? Deleuze's Political Ontology and the Revolutionary Problematic', *Deleuze Studies* 7.2: 231–49.
Mader, Mary Beth (2014), 'Whence Intensity? Deleuze and the Revival of a Concept', in Alain Beaulieu, Edward Kazarian and Julia Sushytska (eds), *Gilles Deleuze and Metaphysics*, Lanham, MD: Rowman and Littlefield, 225–48.
Maggiori, Robert (2000), *Libération*, 4 May.
Margulis, Lynn (1998), *Symbiotic Planet*, New York: Basic Books.
Marx, Karl (1965 [1857]), *Pre-Capitalist Economic Formations*, trans. Jack Cohen, New York: International Publishers.
Marx, Karl (1981 [1894]), *Capital: Volume 3*, trans. David Fernbach, Harmondsworth: Penguin.
Massumi, Brian (1992), *A User's Guide to Capitalism and Schizophrenia: Deviations from Deleuze and Guattari*, Cambridge, MA: MIT Press.

Massumi, Brian (2002), *A Shock to Thought: Expression after Deleuze and Guattari*, London: Routledge.
May, Todd (2000), 'Philosophy as Spiritual Exercise in Foucault and Deleuze', *Angelaki: Journal of the Theoretical Humanities* 5.2: 223–9.
Mauss, Marcel (1954 [1925]), *The Gift: Forms and Functions of Exchange in Archaic Societies*, trans. Ian Cunnison, London: Cohen and West.
Merleau-Ponty, Maurice (2012 [1945]), *Phenomenology of Perception*, trans. Donald A. Landes, London: Routledge.
Meunier, J. (1977), *Les gamins de Bogotà*, Paris: Lattès.
Miller, C. L. (1993), 'The Postidentitarian Predicament in the Footnotes of *A Thousand Plateaus*: Nomadology, Anthropology, and Authority', *Diacritics* 23.3: 6–35. Reprinted as 'Beyond Identity: The Postidentitarian Predicament in *A Thousand Plateaus*', in *Nationalists and Nomads: Essays on Francophone African Literature and Culture*, Chicago: University of Chicago Press, 1998, 171–244.
Miller, C. L. (2003), '"We Shouldn't Judge Deleuze and Guattari": A Response to Eugene Holland', *Research in African Literatures* 34.3: 129–41.
Miller, J. Hillis (1995), 'The Other's Other: Jealousy and Art in Proust', *Qui Parle* 9.1: 119–40.
Milner, Jean-Claude (2013), 'Forme et structure ou le conte des faux jumeaux', *Les temps modernes* 676: 120–43.
Mithen, Steven (1999), *The Prehistory of the Mind: The Cognitive Origins of Art, Religion, and Science*, London: Thames & Hudson.
Monod, Jacques (1971 [1970]), *Chance and Necessity: An Essay on the Natural Philosophy of Modern Biology*, trans. Austryn Wainhouse, New York: Vintage.
Morgan, Lewis Henry (1877), *Ancient Society; Or: Researches in the Lines of Human Progress from Savagery through Barbarism to Civilization*, London: Macmillan.
Nabokov, Vladimir (1997), *The Stories of Vladimir Nabokov*, New York: Vintage International.
Negarestani, R. (2008), *Cyclonopedia: Complicity with Anonymous Materials*, Melbourne: re.press.
New York Times (1917), 'Russian Wolves', http://query.nytimes.com/mem/archive-free/pdf?res=9E0DE3DD103BE03ABC4151DFB166838C609EDE (accessed 27 June 2017).
Nietzsche, Friedrich (1994 [1887]), *On the Genealogy of Morality*, ed. Keith Ansell-Pearson, trans. Carol Diethe, Cambridge: Cambridge University Press.
Nietzsche, Friedrich (2001 [1886]), *Beyond Good and Evil*, ed. Rolf-Peter Horstmann, trans. Judith Norman, Cambridge: Cambridge University Press.
O'Sullivan, S. (2006), *Art Encounters Deleuze and Guattari: Thought Beyond Representation*, London: Palgrave.
O'Sullivan, S. (2012), *On the Production of Subjectivity: Five Diagrams of the Finite–Infinite Relation*, Basingstoke: Palgrave.
O'Sullivan, S. (2018), 'Deleuze against Control: Fictioning and Myth-Science', *Theory Culture Society* 33(7–8): 205–20.
O'Sullivan, S., and S. Zepke (eds) (2008), *Deleuze, Guattari and the Production of the New*, London: Continuum.
Pacotte, Julien (1936), *Le réseau arborescent, schème primordial de la pensée*, Paris: Hermann.
Patton, Paul (2000), *Deleuze and the Political*, London: Routledge,
Patton, Paul (2001), 'Nietzsche and Hobbes', *International Studies in Philosophy* 33.3: 99–116.
Patton, Paul (2010), *Deleuzian Concepts: Philosophy, Colonization, Politics*, Stanford: Stanford University Press.
Patton, Paul (2013), 'From Resistance to Government: Foucault's Lectures 1976–1979', in C. Falzon, T. O'Leary and J. Sawicki (eds), *A Companion to Foucault*, Oxford: Blackwell, 172–88.

Perloff, Marjorie (2003), *The Futurist Moment*, Chicago: University of Chicago Press.
Plato (1997a), 'The Phaedrus', trans. Alexander Nehemas and Paul Woodruff, in John M. Cooper (ed.), *Plato: Complete Works*, Indianapolis: Hackett Publishing, 506–56.
Plato (1997b), 'The Statesman', trans. C. J. Rowe, in John M. Cooper (ed.), *Plato: Complete Works*, Indianapolis: Hackett Publishing, 294–358.
Plekhanov, Georgi V. (1992 [1908]), *The Fundamental Problems of Marxism*, New York: International Publishers.
Plotnitsky, A. (2005), 'Manifolds: On the Concept of Space in Reimann and Deleuze', in S. Duffy (ed.), *Virtual Mathematics*, Manchester: Clinamen Press, 187–208.
Poulantzas, Nicos (1974), *Fascism and Dictatorship*, London: NLB.
Protevi, John (2000), 'A Problem of Pure Matter: Fascist Nihilism in *A Thousand Plateaus*', in K. Ansell-Pearson and D. Morgan (eds), *Nihilism Now! Monsters of Energy*, London: Macmillan, 167–88.
Protevi, John (2001), 'The Organism as the Judgement of God: Aristotle, Kant and Deleuze on Nature (That is, on Biology, Theology and Politics)', in Mary Bryden (ed.), *Deleuze and Religion*, London: Routledge, pp. 30–41.
Protevi, John (2009), *Political Affect: Connecting the Social and the Somatic*, Minneapolis: University of Minneapolis Press.
Protevi, John (2012), 'Deleuze and Life', in Daniel W. Smith and Henry Somers-Hall (eds), *The Cambridge Companion to Deleuze*, Cambridge: Cambridge University Press, 239–64.
Protevi, John (2013), *Life, War, Earth*, Minneapolis: University of Minnesota Press.
Proust, Marcel (1981 [1913–27]), *Remembrance of Things Past*, 3 vols, trans. C. K. Scott Moncrieff and Terence Kilmartin, New York: Random House.
Rae, Gavin (2014), *Ontology in Heidegger and Deleuze*, New York: Palgrave Macmillan.
Reid, J. (2003), 'Deleuze's War Machine: Nomadism Against the State', *Millennium: Journal of International Studies* 32.1: 57–85.
Robert, P. (1993), *Le nouveau petit Robert: Dictionnaire alphabétique et analogique de la langue française*, Paris: Le Robert.
Sahlins, Marshall (1961), 'The Segmentary Lineage', *American Anthropologist* 63: 322–45.
Sahlins, Marshall (1972), *Stone Age Economics*, Chicago and New York: Aldine Atherton.
Sauvagnargues, Anne (2013), 'Ritournelles de temps', *Chimères* 79: 44–59.
Schacht, Hjalmar (1967), *The Magic of Money*, London: Oldbourne Books.
Schivelbusch, Wolfgang (2006), *Three New Deals: Reflections on Roosevelt's America, Mussolini's Italy, and Hitler's Germany, 1933–1939*, New York: Henry Holt.
Sedgwick, Eve (1990), *Epistemology of the Closet*, Berkeley: University of California Press.
Serres, Michel (1993), *Les origines de la géométrie*, Paris: Flammarion.
Serres, Michel (2001 [1977]), *The Birth of Physics*, trans. Jack Hawkes, Manchester: Clinamen Press.
Sibertin-Blanc, Guillaume (2007), 'L'analyse des agencements et le groupe de lutte comme expérimentateur collectif', *Savoirs, Textes, Langage*, 7 February, http://stl.recherche.univ-lille3.fr/seminaires/philosophie/macherey/macherey20062007/sibertin07022007.html (accessed 27 June 2017).
Sibertin-Blanc, Guillaume (2009), 'La malédiction du justicier, le bouc et le prophète: éléments pour une théorie des modalités théologico-politiques de subjectivation', *META: Research in Hermeneutics, Phenomenology, and Practical Philosophy* 1.2: 320–47.
Sibertin-Blanc, Guillaume (2010a), 'Cartographie et territoires. La spatialité géographique comme analyseur des formes de subjectivité selon Gilles Deleuze', *L'Espace géographique* 39.3: 225–38.
Sibertin-Blanc, Guillaume (2010b), *Deleuze et l'Anti-Oedipe: La production du désir*, Paris: PUF.
Sibertin-Blanc, Guillaume (2013), *Politique et État chez Deleuze et Guattari*, Paris: PUF.

Simondon, G. (2005), *L'individuation à la lumière des notions de forme et d'information*, Grenoble: Millon.
Simpson, J. A., and E. S. C. Weiner (eds) (1989), *The Oxford English Dictionary*, 2nd edn, 20 vols, Oxford: Clarendon.
Smith, Ali (2008), *Girl Meets Boy*, Edinburgh: Canongate.
Smith, Daniel (2012), *Essays on Deleuze*, Edinburgh: Edinburgh University Press.
Smith, Michael E., Jason A. Ur and Gary Feinman (2014), 'Jane Jacobs' "Cities First" Model and Archaeological Reality', *International Journal of Urban and Regional Research* 38.4: 1525–35.
Somers-Hall, Henry (2009), 'Transcendental Illusion and Antinomy in Kant and Deleuze', in E. Willatt and M. Lee (eds), *Thinking between Deleuze and Kant*, London: Continuum, 128–50.
Somers-Hall, Henry (2012), *Hegel, Deleuze, and the Critique of Representation*, Albany: SUNY Press.
Somers-Hall, Henry (2013a), *Deleuze's Difference and Repetition: An Edinburgh Philosophical Guide*, Edinburgh: Edinburgh University Press.
Somers-Hall, Henry (2013b), 'The Logic of the Rhizome in the Work of Hegel and Deleuze', in Karen Houle and Jim Vernon (eds), *Hegel and Deleuze: Together Again for the First Time*, Evanston, IL: Northwestern University Press, 54–75.
Spinoza, Benedict de (2001 [1670]), *Theological-Political Treatise*, trans. Samuel Shirley, Indianapolis: Hackett Publishing.
Stalin, Joseph (1940 [1938]), *Dialectical and Historical Materialism*, New York: International Publishers.
Taylor, Frederick (2013), *The Downfall of Money: German Hyperinflation and the Destruction of the Middle Class*, New York: Bloomsbury.
Terada, Rei (2001), *Feeling in Theory: Emotion after the 'Death of the Subject'*, Cambridge, MA: Harvard University Press.
Thesiger, W. (1959), *Arabian Sands*, London: Longmans Green (2008 reissue in Penguin Classics).
Theweleit, Klaus (1987–89), *Male Fantasies*, Minneapolis: University of Minnesota Press.
Thompson, Evan, and Francisco J. Varela (2001), 'Radical Embodiment: Neural Dynamics and Consciousness', *Trends in Cognitive Sciences* 5.10: 418–25.
Tokei, Ferenc (1958), 'Les conditions de la propriété foncière dans la Chine de l'époque Tcheou', *Acta Antiqua* 6: 245–300.
Tokei, Ferenc (1979 [1966]), *Essays on the Asiatic Mode of Production*, trans. William Goth, Budapest: Akademiai Kiado.
Toynbee, A. (1947), *A Study of History*, Oxford: Oxford University Press.
Ulman, G. L. (1978), *The Science of Society: Toward and Understanding of the Life and Work of Karl August Wittfogel*, The Hague: Mouton de Gruyter.
Varela, Francisco J. (1995), 'Resonant Cell Assemblies: A New Approach to Cognitive Functions and Neuronal Synchrony', *Biological Research* 28: 81–95.
Varela, Francisco J., F. J. Lachaux, J.-P. Rodriguez and J. Martinerie (2001), 'The Brainweb: Phase Synchronization and Large-Scale Integration', *Nature Reviews: Neuroscience* 2: 229–39.
Virilio, P. (1976), *L'insécurité du territoire*, Paris: Stock.
Virilio, P. (1990 [1978]), *Popular Defense and Ecological Struggles*, trans. Mark Polizzotti, New York: Semiotext(e).
Virilio, P. (2006 [1977]), *Speed and Politics*, trans. Mark Polizzotti, New York: Semiotext(e).
Vladimirtsov, Boris Iakovlevich (1948), *Le régime social des Mongols: Le féodalisme nomade*, Paris: Maisonneuve.
West-Eberhard, Mary Jane (2003), *Developmental Plasticity and Evolution*, New York: Oxford University Press.
Widder, Nathan (2001), 'The Rights of Simulacra: Deleuze and the Univocity of Being', *Continental Philosophy Review* 34: 347–453.

Widder, Nathan (2004), 'Foucault and Power Revisited', *European Journal of Political Theory* 3.4: 411–32.
Widder, Nathan (2012), *Political Theory after Deleuze*, London: Continuum.
Will, Edouard (1955), 'Refléctions et hypothèses sur les origines du monnayage', *Revue numismatique* 17: 3–24.
Williams, James (2008), *Gilles Deleuze's Logic of Sense: A Critical Introduction and Guide*, Edinburgh: Edinburgh University Press.
Wittfogel, Karl A. (1957), *Oriental Despotism: A Comparative Study of Total Power*, New Haven, CT: Yale University Press.
Wittgenstein, Ludwig (1986 [1953]), *Philosophical Investigations*, trans. G. E. M. Anscombe, Oxford: Blackwell.
Woolf, Virginia (1978 [1928]), *Orlando*, St Albans: Granada.
Wunderlich, Dieter (1972), 'Pragmatique, situation d'énonciation et Deixis', *Langages* 7.26: 34–58.
Zorn, Rachel (2012), 'L'Amiral Cherche une Maison à Louer', in Caroline Bergvall, Laynie Browne, Teresa Carmody and Vanessa Place (eds), *Conceptual Writing by Women*, Los Angeles: Les Figues.
Zourabichvili, F. (2012 [1994]), *Deleuze: A Philosophy of the Event: The Vocabulary of Deleuze*, trans. K. Aarons, Edinburgh: Edinburgh University Press.

Index

abstract machine, 52–5, 60, 102–3, 156–7, 165–6, 181, 260–79
accelerationism, 183
affect, 173, 176–7, 254, 273–4
Ahmed, Sara, 148–9
Althusser, Louis, 92–3
Apparatus of Capture, 216, 223–41
Aristotle, 15
Artaud, Antonin, 60
assemblage, 17, 33–9, 42–5, 54, 62, 75–80, 85, 100–3, 214, 268–9, 274
axiomatics, 238–40

Bachelard, Gaston, 13
Badiou, Alain, 1–3, 5, 31
Barthes, Roland, 48
becoming-animal, 174–5, 184
becoming-imperceptible, 182–7
becoming-music, 187
becoming-women, 184
Bergson, Henri, 3–4, 29–30, 172–3, 240–1, 247–8
black hole *see* white wall
body without organs, 52–3, 99–114, 277
Boulez, Pierre, 251, 254
Braudel, Fernand, 229–30
Brunswick, Ruth Mack, 33
Butler, Samuel, 11

Canguilhem, Georges, 61–2
capitalism, 28, 44, 128–30, 160–2, 216–17, 235–41
chaos, 175–6, 193–202
Childe, V. Gordon, 228
Chomsky, Noam, 14, 19, 25, 77–80

Clastres, Pierre, 216, 228–9
Clausewitz, Pierre, 220–1
collective assemblage of enunciation, 38–9, 43–5, 67–9, 71–80
concept, 2–4, 11, 191–2
content-expression distinction, 34–9, 43–5, 48–50, 56–60, 76–81, 103, 140–5, 264–5
control society, 161–2
counting, 247–8
cow, 9

Damascio, Antonio, 109–10
decoding, 52–3, 156, 236–7
Deleuze, Gilles
  Bergsonism, 29–30
  Difference and Repetition, 2–5, 11–13, 15–16, 20, 73–4, 80–1, 91, 165, 197, 202, 208
  Empiricism and Subjectivity, 69
Deleuze, Gilles and Félix Guattari
  Anti-Oedipus, 24, 28–9, 47, 100–1, 104–5, 165, 216, 223–4
  Kafka: Toward a Minor Literature, 17–18
  What is Philosophy?, 70–1, 174–6, 192–3
Deligny, Ferdinand, 24, 142–4
Derrida, Jacques, 8n
Descartes, René, 14–15, 246–8, 253, 255
desire, 17–18, 93–4, 99–102, 119–20, 128–30, 157
destratification *see* stratification
diagram, 176–82, 267

dialectics, 29–31
drug, 185, 187

Eliot, T. S., 135–6
Engels, Friedrich, 230
essence, 2–4, 273–4
ethics, 61, 63, 177, 202–4, 261

faciality, 115–33, 155
fascism, 108–9, 167–70
felt, 245, 256
flow, 53–4, 104–5, 107, 159–61, 232–9
Foucault, Michel, 44, 59, 116, 123–7, 158, 177, 221
Fox Keller, Evelyn, 112
Freud, Sigmund, 23–4, 29–30, 32–4, 36–9, 44–5

geometry, 30, 248, 250, 254
God, 60–1, 92–5, 103–5, 128–30, 152–3
    Lobster, 61, 103–4

habit, 70–1, 81, 200
Hamlet, 142
Hansen, Mark, 110–11
Hegel, Georg Wilhelm, 7
Heidegger, Martin, 39–40
Hjelmslev, Louis, 35, 48–50, 84–5, 140–3
Holland, Eugene W., 212–13
Hume, David, 69–72

idea, 233–4
image of thought, 4–5, 174–5, 197, 208, 219, 243–9
incorporeal transformation, 37, 66–80, 164–5
intensity, 4, 32, 41–2, 53, 105–6, 254–5

Jacob, François, 55–6
Jacobs, Jane, 229–30
James, Henry, 145–7

Kafka, Franz, 17–18, 167
Kant, Immanuel, 6, 15–16

labour, 44, 225–6
Lacan, Jacques, 19, 119–23, 190
Laruelle, François, 176n
learning, 12, 72–5, 78–9, 91
Leroi-Gourhan, André, 57–8

line, 134–51
    of flight, 18, 95–6, 137, 150, 155–6, 158, 169
    rigid, 158
Lovecraft, H. P., 178, 180

major-minor distinction, 80–2, 160
map, 7–9, 17, 22–4, 143, 261
marginalism, 235–6
Martinet, André, 48
Marx, Karl, 33–4, 223–4, 232–3
Mauss, Marcel, 228–9
May '68, 163–7
Merleau-Ponty, Maurice, 249–52
microfascism, 167–8
micropolitics, 154, 158–63, 165–70
milieu, 50–2, 195–6
Miller, Christopher, 212–13
Milner, Jean-Claude, 84
molar, 40–1, 56–7, 105–6, 264
molecular *see* molar
multiplicity, 20–1, 29–34, 40, 43, 271

Nabokov, Vladimir, 87
Nietzsche, Friedrich, 90–1, 128–30, 179, 220
nomad, 206–8, 245
nomadology, 206–22
noology *see* image of thought

objet a, 220
Occupy movement, 163–7
Oedipus, 28–9, 39, 43
order words, 7–13
organism, 100–13
O'Sullivan, Simon, 8n
other, 119–22
overcoding, 49
Ovid, 147, 150

paranoia, 87–90
Patton, Paul, 61
phenomenology, 249–51
plane of consistency, 20–1, 52–5, 261–3
plane of immanence, 174
plateau, 5–6, 7–8, 9
Plato, 6, 15, 245–6
porphyry, 13, 14
posthumanism, 144–5
power, 159, 273–4
    central, 159
    power-over and power-with, 162
pragmatics, 77
probe-head, 185

Proust, Marcel, 22, 88–90
psychoanalysis, 16, 28, 33–4, 38–42

refrain *see* ritornello
regime of signs, 84–98, 227
rent, 224–5
representation, 263–4
Research Excellence Framework, 18
rhizome, 7–8, 12, 17–26
rhythm, 193–4
Riegl, Alois, 251–2
ritornello, 190–205
root-book, 5–7, 13–15
Russell, Bertrand, 238

Saussure, Ferdinand, 48, 140, 142
Schivelbusch, Wolfgang, 168
Science Fiction, 11–12
Scotus, Duns, 254
segmentarity, 152–63, 167–8
sign, 84–6
signifiance, 115–18, 130–1
signifier, 86–7, 116–20
singularity, 53
Smith, Ali, 147–51
society
   primitive, 154
   state, 155
space, 199–200
   smooth/striated, 209–11, 242–59
Spinoza, 173, 175, 177, 181, 240–1, 254–7
state, 154, 203, 207, 215–18, 223–41
strata, 50–2
   alloplastic, 55–60

inorganic, 51, 55–60
linguistic, 36–9
stratification, 47, 62–3, 106–9, 115–16, 262–5
structuralism, 83–4, 86–7, 91–2
subject, 119–22
system, 2–3

Tarde, Gabriel, 166–7
territory, 192
time, 199–200
tree, 13–15, 18–19

univocity, 32
Urstaat, 232–4

Varela, Francisco, 112–13
violence, 227–8
Virilio, Paul, 217
virtual, 53–4, 105–7

war, 217–21
war machine, 203, 206–22
wasp and the orchid, 21–2
weaving, 245–7
Weimar Republic, 65–9
white wall, 53–4, 117–19
Wittfogel, Karl, 233
Wittgenstein, Ludwig, 39–40, 67–8, 75–6
Woolf, Virginia, 136–7, 178

zone of indiscernibility, 159, 162
Zorn, Rachel, 137
Zourabichvili, François, 200–1

EU representative:
Easy Access System Europe
Mustamäe tee 50, 10621 Tallinn, Estonia
Gpsr.requests@easproject.com

www.ingramcontent.com/pod-product-compliance
Lightning Source LLC
Chambersburg PA
CBHW052057300426
44117CB00013B/2171